RESEARCH METHODS FOR SOCIAL SCIENCE

We work with leading authors to develop the strongest educational materials in Social Sciences, bringing cutting-edge thinking and best learning practice to a global market.

Under a range of well-known imprints, including Prentice Hall, we craft high quality print and electronic publications which help readers to understand and apply their content, whether studying or at work.

To find out more about the complete range of our publishing, please visit us on the World Wide Web at: www.pearsoned.co.uk

Research Methods for Social Science

A Practical Introduction

RONALD A. McQUEEN
AND CHRISTINA KNUSSEN

An imprint of **Pearson Education**

Harlow, England · London · New York · Reading, Massachusetts · San Francisco
Toronto · Don Mills, Ontario · Sydney · Tokyo · Singapore · Hong Kong · Seoul
Taipei · Cape Town · Madrid · Mexico City · Amsterdam · Munich · Paris · Milan

Pearson Education Limited
Edinburgh Gate
Harlow
Essex CM20 2JE
England

and Associated Companies throughout the world

Visit us on the World Wide Web at:
www.pearsoned.co.uk

ISBN-10: 0-13-040456-X
ISBN-13: 978-0-13-040456-5

British Library Cataloguing-in-Publication Data
A catalogue record for this bookF is available from the British Library

Library of Congress Cataloging-in-Publication Data

McQueen, R. A.
  Research methods for social science : a practical introduction / Ronald A. McQueen and Christina Knussen.
    p. cm.
  Includes bibliographical references.
  ISBN 0-13-040456-X
  1. Social sciences—Methodology. 2. Social sciences—Research—Methodology. I. Knussen, Christina. II. Title.

H61 .M4174 2002
001.4'2—dc21

2001058750

10   9   8   7   6   5   4   3   2
11   10   09   08   07   06   05

Typeset by 35 in 9.5/11pt Times

Contents

How to explore this book

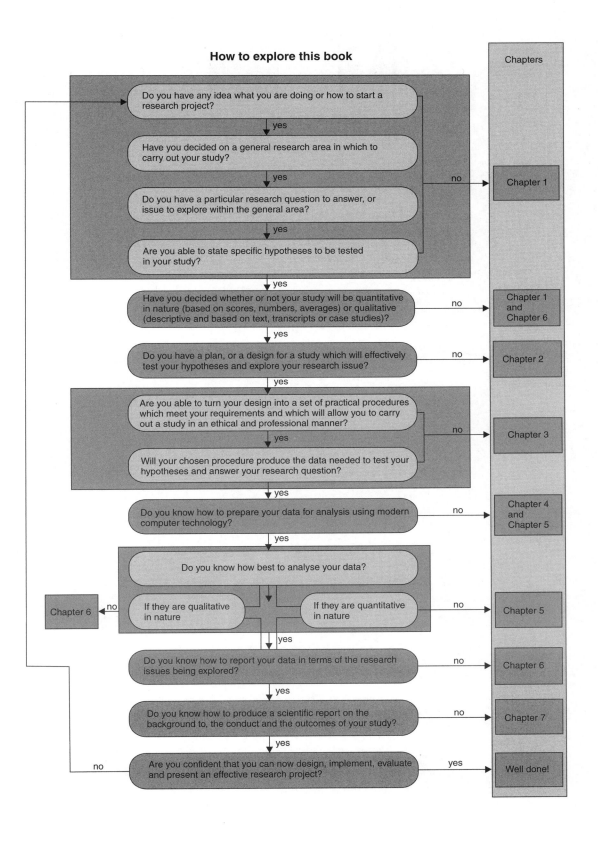

	Chapters

Do you have any idea what you are doing or how to start a research project?

↓ yes

Have you decided on a general research area in which to carry out your study?

↓ yes

Do you have a particular research question to answer, or issue to explore within the general area?

↓ yes

Are you able to state specific hypotheses to be tested in your study?

no → **Chapter 1**

↓ yes

Have you decided whether or not your study will be quantitative in nature (based on scores, numbers, averages) or qualitative (descriptive and based on text, transcripts or case studies)?

no → **Chapter 1 and Chapter 6**

↓ yes

Do you have a plan, or a design for a study which will effectively test your hypotheses and explore your research issue?

no → **Chapter 2**

↓ yes

Are you able to turn your design into a set of practical procedures which meet your requirements and which will allow you to carry out a study in an ethical and professional manner?

↓ yes

Will your chosen procedure produce the data needed to test your hypotheses and answer your research question?

no → **Chapter 3**

↓ yes

Do you know how to prepare your data for analysis using modern computer technology?

no → **Chapter 4 and Chapter 5**

↓ yes

Do you know how best to analyse your data?

Chapter 6 ← no — If they are qualitative in nature | If they are quantitative in nature — no → **Chapter 5**

↓ yes

Do you know how to report your data in terms of the research issues being explored?

no → **Chapter 6**

↓ yes

Do you know how to produce a scientific report on the background to, the conduct and the outcomes of your study?

no → **Chapter 7**

↓ yes

Are you confident that you can now design, implement, evaluate and present an effective research project?

no ←   yes → **Well done!**

Preface

For many undergraduate students, the prospect of planning and carrying out a research project fills them with a certain unease, if not dread – a prospect made worse by the fact that most current social science degrees now contain a compulsory component, in which research methods play a central role. Which means *they have to do it!*

Part of the difficulty for students is a conceptual one. Many people are simply unsure as to the precise nature, scope and role of research methods. For those with a grasp of the topic though, there is often little relief, due to the almost certain likelihood that somewhere along the line statistics will rear its ugly head. Nor is opting for a more qualitatively-based approach an 'easy way out', as many students believe, since qualitative research places just as many demands on the researcher as its quantitative counter-part, only of a different kind. Add the general fear of numbers to the insecurity about research methods overall, and we have a surefire recipe for student angst.

While no one would ever try to make the claim that understanding research and the analytical procedures that serve it is easy, there is no reason why the subject should be either intimidating or inaccessible. Regrettably though, this is often the case since a great deal of what is currently written on social research – and much of this is of an extremely high quality – is more suitable for teachers, academics and researchers, people who usually have considerable experience and a keen interest in the material. Often, however, this same material can prove too much for many students who lack experience, are mathematically weak, or for whom the topic of methodology is a requirement rather than an interest.

With these points in mind, and with the intention of offering a practical guide to designing, carrying through and, indeed, surviving a research project, the following textbook has been written. It is a book for students, based on many years of teaching methods, and incorporating the experience of having supervised countless research projects at introductory, honours and postgraduate level. It has been written with an understanding of, and sensitivity to, the concerns and misgivings of the majority of undergraduates, and in the hope that the study of research methods, and all that goes with it, will become not only an accessible activity, but a rewarding one also.

The aims of this book

The purpose of writing this book is to provide not only an introduction, but also a practical guide to the planning, implementation and presentation of research. While the entry level and style of the material make it accessible to any student of the social sciences, irrespective of their degree level, the text is directed primarily at undergraduate students embarking, perhaps for the first time, on the treacherous course of designing and carrying out a major piece of research.

Structurally, the book follows the accepted procedure for the conduct of any study – while recognising the unique nature of qualitative research – from the initial selection of a topic to the preparation of a final report. For the novice, this structure will in itself serve as a guide, leading from the conceptual processes involved in the development of ideas through all the intermediate stages of design, methodology and analysis, and offering real practical help whenever possible. For the more advanced student, each chapter can be regarded as a free-standing unit, offering in-depth treatment of a single topic, itself broken down into smaller, relatively independent sections. For example, for the student already involved in the design of a questionnaire, there is a section on ethical considerations; for students at an earlier stage, there are sections covering decisions on whether or not to use closed- or open-ended items. For those at the very beginnings of a study there is help on the distinction between qualitative and quantitative approaches; for those at the planning stage of their study there is guidance on independent-group and repeated measures – and other notorious design complexities; and for students at the end of the data gathering stage, an introduction to analytical techniques is offered. As a conclusion, the final chapter is concerned with presentation issues, both in written and oral formats, with a section on procedures for referencing, which should come as a boon not just to student researchers, but to their supervisors also.

Fundamental to the entire book, however, is a sympathetic understanding of the student's approach to research methods. Several years of dealing with dismayed (and sometimes sobbing) undergraduates have gone into the design of this text and an appreciation of the real difficulties experienced by many students is expressed at the beginning of each chapter, where a selection of typical cries for help is presented. It is our hope that, as far as it is possible, these cries for help will not go unanswered.

The structure of this book

This text is divided into a number of discrete chapters, presented in the conventional sequence of activities that comprise a research project, such that even a student lacking a background in research methods, and without so much as an idea where to begin, can progress from the most basic of decisions to the competent handling of data.

Each chapter deals with a specific topic and, although reference is occasionally made to other sections, each can be viewed as a stand-alone unit. In addition to topic headings, an outline of the contents is offered prior to the main body of the text, and there is a review summary at the end. There is an Explanation of terms highlighted in **bold** within the text at the end of each chapter.

At the beginning of each new chapter, there is a series of comments, typical of the average student's perception of an issue, and reflecting commonly expressed queries:

How do I start?
Where do I get numbers from?
What's the difference between a variable and a condition?
What questions should I ask?
Am I looking at differences or relationships?
Should I be writing any of this down?

Far from an attempt at flippancy, the inclusion of such – albeit often humorous – statements is an attempt to say that *we understand*, and that we will do our best to resolve these issues in the text.

Where a statistical content is relevant, examples have utilised SPSS (version 10, applicable to both PC and Macintosh users) for both analysis and presentation. In all such cases, full explanations of procedures used, commands, and hints, have been offered. After all, the book is designed to provide a complete introduction, offering everything the student needs to get started.

What it will not do is provide mathematical proofs or detailed calculations involving formulae, and there are a number of reasons for taking this approach:

- This is not a statistics textbook, rather it is a general introduction to the much broader field of research methods. The inclusion of complex calculations would detract from, and might possibly impede, the attainment of its purpose.
- There are currently many dedicated statistical texts available to students and it would be impossible here to more than scratch the surface of what is done so competently elsewhere. Consequently, there are hardly any numbers in this book, although where appropriate, reference is made to a variety of accessible statistical sources, and these should be consulted for a deeper understanding of the material that is offered here only in introductory form. Indeed, it is hoped that many readers, wishing to explore the concepts presented here more fully, will actively pursue their interests in this way, since it is often only through the processes of computation that particular procedures can be fully understood.
- With developments in software and the wide availability of computers, both at home and within colleges and universities, it is rare nowadays for any student to attempt manual calculations of, for instance, *t*-tests, ANOVAs or correlations. (Fear not – these terms will be fully explained elsewhere.) It is far more important that students understand the concepts of any analysis they undertake, recognising not just what a particular statistical test is doing, but also how and when to use it.
- The actual experience of most undergraduates at the moment – and this is likely to be the future pattern – involves the interpretation of statistical outputs far more than actual calculations. To this end, we have concentrated on discussing various designs, the respective outputs available in SPSS, and how to make sense of them.

How this book can be used

There are various ways in which this book can be used, depending on the student's particular needs, background and experience in designing and carrying out a piece of research.

For those new to research methodology, or to those just about to embark on their first research exercise or project, and who haven't a clue where to begin, the various chapters are laid out in the logical sequence of activities, ideas and procedures that form the structure of all studies. Newcomers need merely start at the beginning, at Chapter 1, where routes and suggestions are offered in terms of exploring theories, coming up with ideas and using the literature.

An important feature here is the flowchart at the beginning of each chapter, explanatory diagrams that allow the reader to navigate quickly through the various parts of the book, leading them directly to those sections and illustrations that are of most relevance to individual projects.

As with all the major elements of the text, each chapter is subdivided into sections, dealing with discrete issues, and one option might be to dip in to particular topics, concentrating on those specific sections that are of interest. Within each chapter various illustrative boxes provide examples of the most common types of study available to undergraduates, highlighting and expanding upon issues introduced within the text and offering various alternative – and often humorous – slants on the research process.

An alternative approach to using this book is to selectively review those chapters or sections that meet particular needs as they arise. This approach will probably be of most use to the more advanced student who already has a research topic to explore, but who doesn't know how best to design their study; who might have chosen a sample, but could use some guidance on how best to word questionnaire items; or who might even have gathered all their data and now needs help in choosing the best analytical test.

For those in this position, the various sections are clearly labelled, both within the text and as an overview to each chapter, and are sufficiently free-standing to answer most questions.

It remains only to wish you luck with your individual research projects; we hope that you enjoy the book.

Ronald A. McQueen
and
Christina Knussen

Note: this book is supported by an accompanying website (http://www.booksites.net/mcqueen) at which the data sets used for illustration (e.g. M&K data set 1) can be viewed in full.

Acknowledgements

Many individuals and organisations have contributed to this book by way of advice, guidance, encouragement or permissions. We would like to thank the following:

Alan Tuohy for his expertise on all matters statistical
Paul Flowers for his research advice
Marian Miller, our indefatigable librarian
David Bell and Cathie Wright for their forbearance
Debra Hiom, Karen Ford and Lesly Huxley
Chi Tang
Billy Budd

And all our undergraduates whose worries and concerns were responsible for our interest in writing this book in the first place.

The authors wish to give special thanks to SPSS Inc. for providing permission to reproduce screenshots and output generated from SPSS software. SPSS is a registered trademark, © SPSS Inc. It should be noted that any errors in the presentation of statistical output are the responsibility of the authors and not SPSS.

SPSS can be contacted at:

SPSS Inc.,
444 North Michigan Avenue,
Chicago, IL 60611

Publisher's acknowledgements

We are grateful to the following for permission to reproduce copyright material:

Box 1.7 is reproduced by kind permission of the authors, and of the British Psychological Society [BPS].

The BPS can be contacted at:

British Psychological Society,
St Andrew's House,
48 Princess Road East,
Leicester LE1 7DR

In addition, the publishers would like to thank SOSIG and Age Concern Enterprises for providing permission to reproduce screenshots for Boxes 1.8 and 1.9 respectively.

SOSIG can be contacted at:

Institute for Research and Learning Technology,
8-10 Berkeley Square,
Bristol BS8 1HH
Tel: +44 (0) 117 928 7117
Email: sosig-help@bristol.ac.uk

Age Concern Enterprises can be contacted at:

Walkden House,
10 Melton Street,
London NW1 2EB
Tel: 020 8765 7845
Fax: 020 8765 7880

The publishers wish to give special thanks to SPSS Inc. for providing permission to reproduce screenshots and output generated from SPSS software. SPSS is a registered trademark, © SPSS Inc. It should be noted that any errors in the presentation of statistical output are the responsibility of the authors and not SPSS.

SPSS can be contacted at:

SPSS Inc.,
444 North Michigan Avenue,
Chicago, IL 60611

Introducing research methods

Cries for help

- *I have to do this research project but don't know where to start.*
- *I have this idea, but don't know how to turn it into a study.*
- *I'm scared of numbers.*
- *I'm interested in what people really think – how can I possibly research that?*

In Chapter 1, we introduce the concept of scientific research, discuss why it is important and examine the various approaches that can be taken. Specific guidelines are offered on commencing a research project, exploring the background to a topic, conducting information searches and making initial decisions on the type of study to be carried out. For novice student researchers, and especially for those about to begin their first research project, this chapter represents the starting point of the process.

The accompanying flowchart can be used to guide you to sections of particular interest. Alternatively, if the entire process of conducting a research project is new to you, you might prefer to work through each section in order.

1.1   Social science research: the background

Research in what have become known as the **social sciences** goes back a long way – as long, in fact, as people have been interested in society and those who live in it. Not surprisingly then the aims of this type of research, the philosophies behind it and the various practices and procedures used to carry it out – its methodologies – have varied and developed considerably over the years.

In its early days, attempts to explain the human condition, to identify causes or make predictions, were inextricably tied up with metaphysics and theology. The fates not only of individuals, but also of entire cultures and societies, were seen to be determined by the movements of the planets, or made accessible through the interpretation of religious writings. At one time, the most learned and respected individuals in society were astrologers and members of the clergy; even practitioners of what are sometimes called the 'black arts' were viewed as having a valuable insight into human affairs and all could make a healthy living predicting the next onset of rain, the outcome of a battle or the likely prospects of a particular suitor.

This faith in the power of external forces over our lives and the pursuit of mystical explanations has

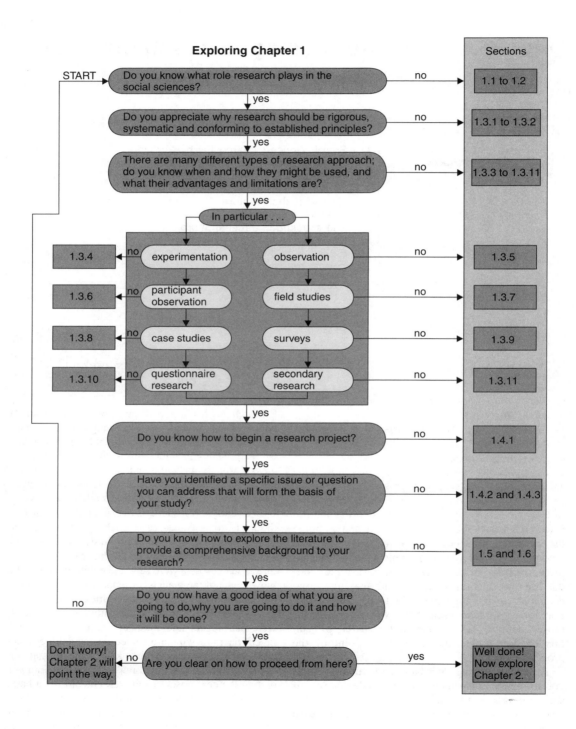

Exploring Chapter 1

Sections

START

Do you know what role research plays in the social sciences? — no → 1.1 to 1.2

↓ yes

Do you appreciate why research should be rigorous, systematic and conforming to established principles? — no → 1.3.1 to 1.3.2

↓ yes

There are many different types of research approach; do you know when and how they might be used, and what their advantages and limitations are? — no → 1.3.3 to 1.3.11

↓ yes

In particular . . .

1.3.4 ← no	experimentation	observation	no → 1.3.5
1.3.6 ← no	participant observation	field studies	no → 1.3.7
1.3.8 ← no	case studies	surveys	no → 1.3.9
1.3.10 ← no	questionnaire research	secondary research	no → 1.3.11

↓ yes

Do you know how to begin a research project? — no → 1.4.1

↓ yes

Have you identified a specific issue or question you can address that will form the basis of your study? — no → 1.4.2 and 1.4.3

↓ yes

Do you know how to explore the literature to provide a comprehensive background to your research? — no → 1.5 and 1.6

↓ yes

Do you now have a good idea of what you are going to do, why you are going to do it and how it will be done?

↓ yes

no ← Are you clear on how to proceed from here? — yes → Well done! Now explore Chapter 2.

Don't worry! Chapter 2 will point the way.

formed part of the human belief system for centuries – even today, many individuals are avid readers of their daily horoscope with some basing quite major decisions on their own particular astrological reading. At the time of writing there exists a large section of the community astonished by the fact that the world did not end on 14 July 1999, as predicted by the sixteenth-century philosopher, Nostradamus. Many people fully expected their lives to change dramatically at this time while others – the authors included – merely took the day off. (Well, you never know!)

This emphasis on mystical forces, while dominating much of human enquiry through the ages, was not universal however: as early as the fifth century BC a more rational, controlled form of research was being practised in many fields, one relying more on observation and experimentation than on the supernatural. Hippocrates stands out as a pioneer of this new, scientific approach, an approach which continued to gain ground over successive generations until, in the nineteenth century, the conventional reliance on mysticism was soundly laid to rest with the emergence of a new positive philosophy, and the methodology that went with it. Known as **positivism**, the approach proposed a fresh way of studying the world, and in particular the social world, emphasising only that which was directly (or positively) observable. Moreover, the techniques for this different form of objective research were to borrow much from the physical sciences, evolving into a new, scientific method which came to dominate social research. With this new emphasis on observation, objectivity and experimentation the social scientist was born; sociology emerged as a distinct discipline while psychology experienced one of the most dramatic expansions in its history – the dominance of the introspective, almost philosophical approach of the Freudians gave way to an experimental psychology which, with its reliance on quantifiable research, forms so much a part of the field today.

While the scientific method still dominates social research, today there are many variants, offshoots and, of course, critics, all of which are merely part of a natural process of evolution. More than any other discipline, social science continues to develop and change, in keeping with the object of its study. Society is not a static thing – it is subject to many influences, both from without and from within; it exhibits trends, fashions and shifting concerns; it is only reasonable that a discipline that purports to study society and its people shows the same kind of dynamism. The sections that follow look more closely at the various types of social research and their relevance to the contemporary student of the social

sciences, while the further reading section at the end of the chapter provides an opportunity for further exploration of the history of social research.

1.2 Social science research: aims

The major aim of studying social issues in any context is to increase our understanding about the forces that drive our world. This is merely a reflection of other forms of scientific endeavour and is an expression of a general human curiosity about the world we live in. But there is more to social science than mere understanding: like all other sciences, an evolution of understanding is part of the promotion of change, or intervention, for the attainment of some form of improvement in our environment. Fusion research for instance looks beyond an explanation of matter at atomic levels towards the possibility of a cheap energy source in the future; medical research has as its ultimate aim longevity and the elimination of disease. Both of these examples, however, are in some respects overgeneralised, if not trite, since we know quite well that atomic research has always brought with it political and military agendas, while medical research has been, variously, theoretical, political, social and economic in its goals. Similarly, while we can argue that, at a general level, social research aims to apply an understanding of society to an overall improvement in the human condition, we are also aware that social research can be used to liberate, to inform (social policy) and as an instrument of government. It is a fact of life then that research can serve a number of masters and this is as true of social research as of any other discipline.

There is an additional problem here and it is an ethical one: as with all forms of investigation, it is possible to abuse the findings of social research, to use them not for betterment, but for exploitation and manipulation. We have already made reference to the way in which nuclear research has become a major force in the armaments industry. Similarly, the type of social engineering fostered by many members of the medical profession in Nazi Germany reflects a clear set of social and political values, and no matter how unacceptable these might be today, they nonetheless drove an entire philosophy of human endeavour. But one might wonder whether it is any less exploitative for advertisers to use an understanding of social strata to persuade people to buy products they do not need, or for planners to use information on the voting characteristics of a population as a guide to the routeing of rail and motor-way links. These are issues to which we will return later in the section on Ethics (Chapter 3, section 3.7).

1.3   Research and scientific method

1.3.1   The nature of research

All scientists have their own particular view of the purpose of research, but essentially, research is carried out in order to describe, understand and explain, and predict, with each of these reflecting a progressively sophisticated function. At its simplest level, research on any subject aims to describe a phenomenon or a process that has previously been inaccessible or only vaguely understood. By way of example, a medical sociologist investigating patterns of hypertension within the country might have noted that distinct clusterings of high blood pressure occur in different regions. Closer inspection might reveal higher incidences of hypertension in those regions hosting large numbers of particular ethnic minorities. In order to explain this, the researcher would embark upon a **study** aimed at understanding the mechanisms of hypertension and identifying contributory factors. If, for the purpose of argument, it was observed that blood pressure problems were present only in some minorities, that it was not related to social class, gender or equivalised income and that the condition did not extend to second generation offspring, then our researcher is close to understanding the nature of the issue. It may well be that elevated blood pressure is a function of 'imported' diet and lifestyle, combined with the problems faced by certain minorities in integrating into a novel culture. This would explain why the problem was only present in some minorities and not others, and why it had all but disappeared by the second generation. If our researcher's understanding is valid and the explanation true, then he can take the next step – prediction. In the face of a continuing influx of displaced

peoples it might now be possible to predict the type and extent of demands that will be placed on local health provision. All of which, in turn, will have implications for various aspects of policy and funding. All of these activities – describing, explaining and predicting – represent important functions of research and are the goals of many researchers. But how are these goals achieved?

1.3.2   Scientific method

In order to understand any social phenomenon, there are a number of things we can do. We can take an armchair, introspective approach and simply think about the world, applying our own past experience and self-knowledge to the problem. Indeed, much of what we believe to be true in life is based on this very approach. Intuition, feelings or beliefs about the way things are contribute to a large part of how we perceive the world and – as a rough and ready, rule of thumb guide to life – it's not a bad approach: the superstitious belief that walking under a ladder will bring us bad luck will at least prevent the pot of paint falling on top of us – or even the painter; the fear of flying many of us experience will prevent us becoming victims of an air disaster and our almost reflexive sense of danger in the presence of multi-legged creepy crawlies might prevent a fatal bite from the Australian funnel web spider. However, reliance on such a scheme for negotiating life is by no means foolproof and can, in some cases, lead to a complete misconception of 'the way things are'. The gambler who, on observing a run of 10 reds on the roulette wheel, places his entire savings on black (because it *must* be black's turn) is likely to leave the casino wearing only his underpants because his intuitive view of the probability of events is flawed. Like many people, he has assumed that consecutive runs of the wheel are connected and that the laws of chance must eventually balance out. Similarly, the parent who, on observing two sunny weekends in a row, plans an

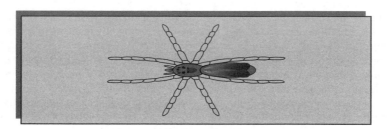

Figure 1.1.

outdoor children's party for the third, is inviting disaster. (The authors, showing a marked disregard for the northern European climate, can attest to this.)

Closer scrutiny of the flying example will also show the limitations of the intuitive approach since, in comparison to road travel, flying remains one of the safest modes of transport. And as for our poor arachnophobic, unless he lives in Australia, that particular denizen is unlikely to be a problem, while most of the other species of wrigglers and scuttlers actually serve a useful function in the world.

The point of all of the above is that the usual way we approach the world is flawed, subjective and judgemental. It may get us by, on a day to day basis, but it's not an approach designed to accurately describe, explain or predict. To be able to do this, we need a more rigorous, systematic and scientific approach to life. Which is precisely what a great deal of research methods in the social sciences is all about.

Science really only takes off where intuition stops; many of our ideas about gambling, flying, spiders and the rest may well be true, but until they can be proved they remain at the level of heuristics, old wives' tales, unsupported beliefs or even superstition. Science takes the next step and attempts to find this proof, using a variety of methods which have evolved over many years and which are designed to answer the question: 'How do you know?' (How do you know walking under a ladder will result in negative consequences? How do you know that people in higher social classes will experience higher levels of life satisfaction than people in lower social classes? How do you know women are intellectually superior to men?)

While not always the case (see section 6.2.2, 'Grounded theory'), the usual starting point of scientific research is **theory**, and theory is simply a general set of beliefs about the way the universe, or a part of it, operates – often, in fact, those very intuitions, rule of thumb heuristics and general beliefs discussed above. Theories can be vague, ill-defined and personal (I have this theory about why the dog does that…!) or they can be concise, well structured and supported by a large body of evidence (as in social learning theories). Either way, theories provide the descriptive and explanatory functions of research introduced at the beginning of this chapter. The major difference between theory and intuition, however, is that while intuition is usually based on belief, feelings or even faith, theory is a much more systematic thing. Any researcher attempting to develop a theory is constantly asking the questions: Does this describe…? Does this theory explain…? How do you know that?

Consequently, a theory demands more thought and more enquiry than any heuristic. A theory will be based on observations, experience and the experiences of others; it will represent a balance of perceptions and information; and it will be held up as presenting a better view of the world than possible alternatives. However, by far the most important aspect of a theory is that if it is correct, if it provides an accurate description of the world, then it will predict events that have not yet occurred.

Having said this, however, we have already intimated that there will be cases in which scientific enquiry will not begin with theory: consider the situation in which we have no experience, where we don't have any sets of observations on which to base predictions, in which we have no guesses. The early anthropologists encountered this very problem as they attempted to understand cultures that were in many respects alien to them. Likewise, many modern researchers will from time to time find themselves in situations with which they are totally unfamiliar, in which the experience required to generate a theory is absent. The exploration of street gang culture might be a good example here, or the problems encountered by AIDS sufferers; for most of us these scenarios represent completely different worlds from our own, worlds that we are poorly equipped, at an experiential level, to understand. In this type of situation the starting point for scientific enquiry is not theory, but rather the lengthy processes of gaining experience, of involvement and of observation on which theory is based. Much more will be made of this in Chapter 6, Qualitative research.

1.3.3 Hypotheses

Theories are usually general views or propositions about the world, representing the best descriptions and explanations we can come up with. We may have arrived at them through observing people and noting trends, through thinking about our own behaviour, or through discussions with others who share our interest in similar social issues. However, such theories will never develop beyond the level of being just one of many possible explanations, unless we can produce evidence to suggest that our theory is actually better than all the rest.

This is where the predictability issue comes in. If a particular theory represents an accurate description and explanation of events, it ought to predict what will occur in specific instances. Consider a theory of learning: if we believed that learning occurred simply by associating one event with another (a general theory) then we should be able to make a prediction, or an **hypothesis**, about what would happen in a particular learning situation. Assume we were able to find a dog noted for its uncontrollable drooling at the sight of food. If our theory of learning held true, then presenting some other stimulus (say, the sound of a bell) every time the animal was offered food would eventually lead to an association between the two events (food and the bell). Ultimately the dog would salivate to the sound of the bell only. If an experiment along these lines were tried, and the prediction borne out, then we would have evidence in support of our more general view of behaviour. The more our predictions come true and the more hypotheses we can accept, the stronger our theory becomes. If our hypotheses are rejected, or our predictions produce contradictory results, then our theory weakens.

One important point to note here is that while it's all very well to propose hypotheses based on a general theory, unless the predictions that form a part of these hypotheses can be tested, then the theory will never develop. Many theories concerning national or global economics will never develop simply because no one (in their right mind, at any rate) would attempt to put them into practice, due to the potentially catastrophic consequences of getting it wrong. Alternatively, the theory that man evolved, not naturally from early mammals, but as a result of alien intervention and genetic engineering is all very well, yet unless we can come up with a way to test this view, the theory will remain forever at the level of idle speculation. The hypothesis that examining the DNA of Jurassic rodents would show up this tampering is simply untestable. (See section 1.4.3 for further discussion on hypotheses.)

1.3.4 Experimentation

So far, the scientific process has been presented as a systematic development from general theories to more specific hypotheses. The next step is to consider how best to test these hypotheses. There are several options available to the researcher – surveys can be carried out, questionnaires compiled, observations made; the choice will depend on a number of elements, such as the type and number of subjects being used, the context in which the research is being carried out, ethical issues and practical problems. However, the approach most often associated with

rigorous research, and the one that characterised the early days of social research in particular, is that of experimentation, and this will be our starting point.

The very term, **experiment**, beloved of psychologists possibly more than any other social researcher, implies control; an experimenter controls all aspects of the environment in which a study is carried out (as far as this is possible). She determines the nature of the subjects taking part in her study; she decides on all tasks and activities that will form part of the experiment and she controls the sequence in which events are experienced. But why would such a high level of control be required?

At the risk of sounding obvious, every social event is extremely complex. Any single action, be it at an individual, group or community level, can be linked to and influenced by a multitude of factors, all of which are tangled up in such a way that it is often impossible to identify cause and effect relationships. A researcher studying decision making would find the mix of possible influences daunting. Motivation would obviously play a part – we often choose things that will satisfy needs within us (a need to be loved, a need to be successful, etc.); learning too is important, since much of what we do is habitual in nature; and then there is perception, with different people seeing issues and problems in different ways. Gender too will be an issue, since males and females will have been shaped by their upbringing to have different values, while personality factors may lead inward-looking introverts rarely to select the same options as the more outgoing extrovert.

Just think of your own decision to study the social sciences – all of the above factors would have played some part in your decision, as would attitudes towards the course, aspirations, availability of appropriate modules or degree structures and what your friends did. Even where you lived would play a part since geographic location will be related to opportunity structure, the nature of prerequisite education and other social determinants of choice. Clearly, if asked why you chose to do this subject, once you started to really think about it you would be surprised at the number and variety of contributory factors. This is why the researcher, wishing to study such a complex process, may well choose to do so under laboratory conditions: here he can determine the type of decision to be made, control the environment in which the process occurs and restrict the many sources of variation among his subjects. Only then does it become possible to isolate and manipulate specific factors and record their impact on behaviour.

Or at least, this is the widely held view among certain types of researchers.

Occasionally some phenomena are deemed too complex to be adequately studied even under the most rigorous of experimental conditions and in those instances, some researchers have resorted to using different, and much less complex, species. Ethologists studying primate behaviour, for instance, might more readily identify conditions underlying different social hierarchies than if the object of study was a human society. And within the field of psychology, a great deal of what we now understand about learned behaviour has developed from studies on rats, pigeons and, in Pavlov's case, dogs – the rationale being that although the end product may represent a universal phenomenon, in lesser species learning is easier to isolate and manipulate.

While experimentation is often seen as the backbone of any science, within the social sciences it is not without its critics. True, the method reduces the number of confounding, interrelated and sometimes downright nuisance factors that might interfere with an object of a study, yet in achieving this it is possible to argue that the essential nature of what we are studying has been lost. While there are undoubtedly some aspects of the individual that can only be studied under controlled laboratory conditions – functions of the brain, memory, the senses, to mention but a few – much of what we do as part of our day to day lives is a product of many interacting, interfering and contradictory factors, a function of the society in which we live. A laboratory experiment may well be able to tease out pure, uncontaminated cause and effect relationships, but often at a cost: consider that most experimental subjects are not 'real' people but (with apologies to our readership) college or university undergraduates. This group is not typical of the population at large – students are bright, motivated, young and, generally speaking, happy to volunteer to participate in an endless cycle of mindless studies dreamed up by their professors and peers. Add this bias to experimental tasks created for their simplicity and ease of measurement, and all in a clinical environment free from outside contaminants, and you have, quite simply, artificiality. In some cases experimentation can refine behaviour to such a point where all relevance to real life has been lost and it becomes impossible, or at least pointless, to try and generalise from experimental findings to the real world. A big enough problem when dealing with humans, but what do you do when your subjects are rats?

This issue is known, not surprisingly, as the **generalisation problem**, describing the sometimes problematic process of applying observations from one situation to another in which conditions might be quite different and for which the original findings might no longer be relevant. However, it also reflects a conflict between two methodological positions, or philosophies: that between reductive analytic approaches and the holistic perspective.

The classic, traditional method for studying just about anything can be described as conforming to a reductive analytic model. This is a straightforward scientific approach whereby a given issue is reduced to its various components and the element of particular interest is then analysed. The examples of experimentation above reflect this view. In the early days of medical investigation, if you wanted to know how the brain worked, you got hold of a brain (discarding the rest of the body) and commenced an examination. This is largely why people still talk about the brain as 'grey matter' – dead brains, lacking a continuous blood supply, are grey. They are also, of course, dead, making it difficult to apply any research findings to the fully functioning, living (and pink) organ. Similarly, nuclear research into the properties of electrons would have reduced atomic particles to their constituent parts, isolated the element of interest, and subjected it to analysis.

As an approach to investigation the reductive analytic method has merit. By removing a key component from its environment or context, you remove the possibility of contamination by other things. A social example might concern research into families, their members and relationships. We might for instance be interested in the specific role of motherhood – what makes a mother? What personal qualities does a person need to successfully adopt the motherhood role? In this scenario family groups would be reduced to their constituent components (mother, father, children, household), the mother isolated and then analysed in terms of her nature and key characteristics (see Figure 1.2).

The feeling here would have been that the mother's role continually interacts with other components of the family situation, and elements like children, role expectations, partner characteristics and so on will invariably reflect on how the mother behaves. It could be argued that these other factors would fudge, obscure or contaminate the very mothering characteristics that were the focus of interest. As we have observed, however, these very 'contaminating' factors are what provide the essence of this role in real life; we are, after all, social beings and the activity of attempting to reduce an essentially social and

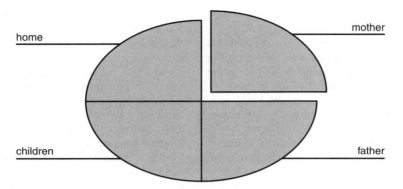

Figure 1.2   The reductive analytic approach.

interacting process to its components serves only to dilute and obscure that process. For this reason many early studies failed to properly describe and explain the actual interactions involved. In much the same way as leadership can only be understood by looking at how leaders behave within the context of an organisation, with its attendant elements of subordinates, task and culture, so a true picture of the mother's role could not emerge until mothers were viewed within the context of specific family interactions.

This alternative, holistic view argued that any process which, in its normal functioning, interacts with other processes, can only really be understood when viewed in its context – the whole situation has to be considered, and not just its parts. Taking this particular view largely (though not completely) precludes the experimental approach. If we wish to study behaviour in its natural context, using real people, doing real things, then we have to adopt a different strategy, one in which the researcher does not manipulate and does not control. In this scenario the researcher becomes an observer, rather than an experimenter.

1.3.5   Observation

Observations can vary in nature from the kinds of casual observations from which we notice, in an unplanned way, certain salient things about our environment, through the kinds of naturalistic or **ethographic** observations in which animals are studied in their natural habitats, simply to see what they do, to a systematic form of observation in which the researcher has a predetermined scheme relating to particular types of event and structured methods for recording information.

Box 1.1   Some observations on observation

1   'I noticed a funny thing at the bank today.' *The casual observer*

2   'During a period of 20 interactions, the number of eye contacts between bank tellers and customers increased by 40% when interactions were opposite sexed, compared to an average of only five contacts per minute for same-sexed people.' *The systematic observer*

This approach to the study of behaviour is truly holistic, in a way in which experimentation can never be. People observed in their 'natural habitat' tend to produce more typical behaviours, a major implication of which is that findings of observational research can usually be generalised quite validly to other, similar, situations. Experimentation, as we pointed out, can produce findings that, because of the artificiality of the experimental set-up (subjects, task, context), can be difficult to generalise to real life. Quite simply, the further our research setting is from real life, the greater the likelihood that findings will be atypical.

However, before we go overboard in our praise of this method, it has to be recognised that, just as with experimentation, the very factors that make an **observation study** so valuable a research tool also represent its major drawbacks. Observing behaviour in natural surroundings, without manipulation or attempts to control other factors, means that what we see will be a product of many interactions. Consequently, identifying cause and effect relationships will sometimes be impossible, because many contributory causes will be tangled up with one another. To further complicate the issue, it is not strictly true to claim that an observation approach allows people to behave naturally; often, when we become aware that we are being watched, our behaviour changes. Consider the common experience of passing a high street shop window and suddenly seeing yourself on a television monitor: almost without thinking, the stomach is sucked in, the shoulders pressed back and our normal slouching shamble replaced by a graceful stride. (Or so the authors find.) Or think of the student whose performance on a statistical problem improves dramatically when the tutor peers over her shoulder. Or her hapless neighbour, who falls to pieces in the same situation. There are many examples of this phenomenon, known variously as a 'mere presence effect', a 'social facilitation/inhibition effect', an 'observer' or 'experimenter' effect, and, in some situations, a 'Hawthorne effect', a name taken from an early series of industrial studies in which the impact of observers on work behaviour was noted. Whatever term is used to describe the effect, they all serve to demonstrate the same thing – the known presence of an observer invariably affects the behaviour of the person being observed in one way or another.

There is one final point to be made here, and it is an important one. Observation is, by its very nature, a human, judgemental activity in which we note when a behaviour occurs, and classify such behaviour, usually according to some kind of scheme. In planned, social research we often have a clearly defined set of behaviours in which we are interested, plus a logical plan for recording and coding what we see (see Box 1.1). However, because we are human, and since most of our everyday observations are coloured by a variety of factors – social, political, sexual, cognitive, motivational and so on – it is actually quite difficult to guarantee that what we apparently observe is actually what is happening. Consider the observation of a glance from one individual to another. If we are attempting to describe what has happened, how do we decide if the glance was casual, intimate, hostile, curious, friendly, aggressive, questioning, contemptuous, or whatever; or even if the 'glance' itself actually took place? We rely on experience, we seek other cues – e.g. was the glance accompanied by a smile? a frown? a raised eyebrow? We might even make a guess. In short, most forms of observation involve judgement of one kind or another and, as all social science undergraduates quickly learn, human judgement is not something that can be wholly trusted. Remember the

---

Box 1.2   Truth is in the eye of the beholder

This was a triumph of skill over strength, of confidence over complacency in which the opposing team were outmatched, outplayed and outperformed. There is no doubt that the best team won.
(Fan of the winning team)

This was an example of the worst excesses of football today, in which the winning team hacked its way to victory on the back of foul play and a blatantly partisan attitude from the referee. We were robbed!
(Fan of the losing team)

---

axiom of the researcher introduced in the previous section: 'How do you know?'

It is important to point out, however, that many of the problems with observation methods can be dealt with – some through rigorous advance planning, and some through sophisticated statistical techniques that can effectively control for the influence of intervening factors, in an after-the-fact manner. Chapter 2, which deals with how studies are designed, will explore these matters more fully, while the next section on participant observation further develops the 'How do we know?' issue.

1.3.6   Participant observation

One of the problems of being human (many would argue *the* problem) is that when it comes to observing anything – ourselves, other people, our society, other cultures – we do not do this as completely objective and honest recorders of what is actually there. We are not like that – we are not machines, we are not blank slates on which the reality of our surroundings is written in a passive manner. Rather we interact with our world, we are active in our judgement of what goes on around us and our perception of events is based on our experience, our background and culture, and on who we are. In other words, we are subjective creatures, and our perceptions are therefore also subjective.

This tendency for people not to see the world as it is has been long understood and researchers in the field of visual imagery have used this understanding to illustrate such perceptual effects through various forms of visual illusion. The figure in Box 1.3 contains physical information that does not change no matter who looks at it. Yet it will often happen that two

Box 1.3   Now you see it...

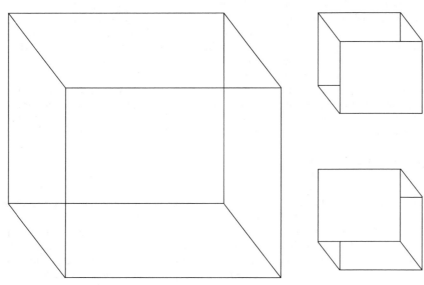

The large, three-dimensional cube above is a reversible image. The information contained in the lines and angles is constant and is therefore the same for us all. Yet not everyone 'sees' the same cube and the two smaller images show the two alternative views of the same object. The point, and one beloved by illusionists and circus performers everywhere, is that we do not perceive the world objectively. This is as true of the social world as of the physical.

different people will see completely different figures – and this despite the fact that this particular image is now widely known. Nor is this effect restricted to the physical environment – the human tendency to perceive the world in anything but objective terms applies to the social world also, as Box 1.2 illustrates.

It is because of this human characteristic (there is no point in calling it a failing since this is simply how we are) that the recurring question 'How do you know?' is so irritatingly pointed. Whenever we report something, how do we know we are reporting what actually happened, as opposed to an interpretation of what occurred based on the fact that we are male, as opposed to female; black as opposed to white; old as opposed to young; wealthy as opposed to impoverished, and so on.

One way round this is to apply the rigours of science that we have introduced in the preceding sections. Aware that we do possess limitations researchers have often resorted to experimentation and dispassionate observation in an attempt to control for our subjective tendencies, and a great deal of what is often regarded

as 'science' adheres to these processes. For some, however, even these rigorous approaches are not sufficient. It could be argued (and it often is) that no matter how carefully and objectively a researcher sets up an experimental study, it will be impossible for him to remain totally uninvolved or unaffected by the mix of social, cultural and personal influences that have made him what he is.

An alternative approach, and it is worth pointing out that this involves not just a procedural alternative but also a philosophical one, is exemplified in the particular methodology of **participant observation**.

On the face of it this approach is the very antithesis of conventional scientific research in that it questions a number of the fundamental principles of scientific methodology:

- don't get involved;
- begin research from the standpoint of theory;
- be objective.

In anthropological research the unique problems set by attempting to study cultures of which we had no experience and very little understanding precluded a dispassionate approach. After all, how could you understand something with which you had no experience by staying as far away from it as possible? Similarly, how could you develop theories about a society about which you had no understanding? The only solution, or at least so the early anthropologists thought, was to get involved.

Participant observation required that the researcher became involved with, indeed became a part of, the society she was studying. Only by developing a history of experience within a particular society would it be possible to propose theories about its structure and functioning.

On the face of it, this approach runs counter to the principles of objective science, but in reality it was only a shrewd understanding of the issues surrounding the question 'How do you know?' that forced the anthropologist to accept that allowing himself to be absorbed by the society he was studying was the only way in which it could be studied. Moreover, more than any other approach to research, participant observation can be regarded as truly holistic, a form of holism in which even the researcher has become a part of the whole.

Outside of the anthropological setting, the approach has become more generally known as **ethnography**, a form of in-depth, holistic analysis of the structure and processes of culture. The approach came to wider prominence in the 1980s with the rise of what became known as feminist research, the aim of which was to investigate the changing role of women and their experiences in modern society. In particular, the approach underlined the point about bias in perceiving the world, whether such bias be determined by culture, experience or gender.

If all of this seems astonishingly complicated, then it is. For most undergraduates, the rules and procedures for experimentation, or conventional observational research are well within reach. For ethnographic research, however, the rules often seem vague, the procedures complex and the timescales lengthy. For this reason, few undergraduates could realistically attempt – nor would they be encouraged to attempt – an ethnographic study which required some form of participatory research, especially given the one-, or at the most, two-semester timescale available for methodology projects. However, because the approach is now an accepted component in the repertoire of the modern-day researcher, and because there may well be instances in which undergraduate projects might benefit from an ethnographic perspective, further discussion is offered in Chapter 3, Carrying out your study and in particular, Chapter 6, Qualitative research. In addition, for those students especially interested in the area, the concluding section of this chapter offers some useful texts for further reading.

1.3.7 Field studies

It should be becoming clear that typical methods of exploring the social world are not without their problems. An experiment usually has all the advantages of controlling for interfering factors, at the expense of realism, whereas observation studies show the reverse – lots of realism, but no controls. There is, however, another approach which, potentially, possesses the advantages of both, while minimising the disadvantages – field research.

A **field study** involves subjects behaving in their natural surroundings, but with the researcher given the opportunity of actively manipulating aspects of the environment and noting the outcome. This can be in a covert manner, in which confederates are used and unobtrusive observations taken, as in studies on pedestrians violating the red man 'Don't Walk' signs at street crossings in response to the behaviour of models from an apparently different social class, or it can resemble a conventional, controlled experiment in which a group of production workers operate under a new type of supervisory regime and their output is compared with that of an identical group, working under a standard management scheme. This kind of unobtrusive approach offers the researcher an alternative to experimentation and observation which goes some way towards handling the difficulties with those methods. Field research though is not without its own set of drawbacks:

- One of the guiding principles of all social research is that people participate willingly, and only with their informed consent – i.e. they are aware of what is being done and, given that awareness, have agreed to participate. Furthermore, it is an accepted standard now that people have the right to withdraw from any research, without prejudice and at their own volition. There is also an expectation that the individual's rights on confidentiality and anonymity will be secured. However, in the kind of unobtrusive observation study which is common to certain kinds of social research, participants are usually unaware that their environment has been manipulated, nor do they know that their responses are being recorded, or even videoed. Consequently they are not willing participants in the study, they have not had an opportunity to give informed consent and, arguably, their rights to anonymity and confidentiality have been violated. This is an important ethical issue, which will be more fully explored in Chapter 6 (section 6.3.2).

- Where the research is more overt in nature, involving for example manipulation within a hospital, school or factory, various forms of experimenter effect will come into play, possibly interfering with the aim of the study.

- Any research involving changes or manipulations within an institution runs the risk of interfering with and undermining normal organisational processes, practices and procedures. Consequently, unless a study can guarantee minimal disruption, or unless there is a strong rationale for the study, it is unlikely that such research would be permitted. Most organisations now support their own ethics committees, whose purpose is to safeguard their employees, patients and relevant individuals. Such committees nowadays are unlikely to approve research which is disruptive or unethical. It is also worth pointing out that – while this will rarely be an issue for undergraduates – such committees will also pass judgement on more practical elements of a study, such as whether or not a large enough sample has been used, or important extraneous factors have been considered.

1.3.8 Case studies

Most of the above discussions on the methods available to the social researcher involve working with large numbers of people. This is based on the view that the more people for whom a prediction holds true, or across whom observations are consistent, then the more likely we are to accept an hypothesis and provide evidence for a theory. However, there are certain situations in which it might not be possible to conduct research in the conventional way. We may only have access to a few subjects, or the event we are interested in may be so unusual that there only ever are one or two subjects to study – consider trying to investigate coping behaviour of mothers with sextuplets, or the memory problems of people suffering accidental brain damage, and you'll get the idea. In situations like these, a **case study** approach is often the only option available to the researcher – an attempt to gather information on an individual from as many sources as possible.

Case study data are usually highly descriptive, and may take the form of interview notes, observations and video material; they can comprise personal introspections, narrative and psychometric measurements – in fact, anything at all that can offer an insight into an individual might be used. The approach rarely involves experimentation in the usual sense of the word, but may involve observation of events over a period of time as a result of a particular form of, say, drug treatment, policy change or other form of intervention. Not surprisingly, the case study approach has been closely associated with medical research, but it needn't be exclusively so, since any instance of novelty or limited subject numbers will lend itself to this technique – studies on the experiences of astronauts, of people who have encountered near-death phenomena or, indeed, of the mother with the large family, would naturally suggest this type of in-depth approach.

The beginnings of an investigation, or the exploration of a new area might also benefit from the extremely detailed analysis of just one single subject. Modern psychoanalysis is built on the personal introspections of the early theorists like Freud and the detailed case notes on individual patients; likewise the development of space technology, from the design of space suits to the interior colour schemes of crew quarters, derived from the experiences of only a handful of pioneering astronauts. As a way of initially exploring issues, of gathering rich, descriptive data and providing the first steps in hypotheses generation, the case study approach is ideal, and is often used as the basis for subsequent, larger scale research.

As with all previous methods of research, the case study is not without its own problems. All the disadvantages of observer biases discussed earlier will also come to bear on the single subject case – an observer may well attend selectively to the information presented to him, may overvalue some events at the expense of others and may even be guilty of a form of motivated perception, if the aim of the study is to promote a favoured belief or theory. The subject herself, if relying on memory or introspection to provide descriptions of experiences and emotions, may fall victim to the many factors that influence our recall for past events. Not to mention the tendency, present in us all, to modify our view of the world and our role in it, to play down anything that might show us in a poor light, or to modify our behaviour in terms of what we believe to be the researcher's expectations – a particular problem with the case study approach since the intensive nature of the relationship between the participants allows the subject to study the researcher even as she herself is being studied.

There is a final problem here, already encountered during our brief discussion on experimentation: the generalisation problem. There are many ways to explain why it is sometimes difficult to expand findings from a study involving a sample to the population as a whole. We have already encountered some of these, and they include problems like the artificiality of an experimental situation, or the inability to control for interfering factors in an observation study. In the case study though, there is the added problem that there is only one (or only very few) subject(s), and it would be very difficult to make an argument for generalising observations on an individual to society as a whole. However, this is not necessarily an issue, since the purpose of many case studies is not to find out something about people in general, but about this individual in particular. And where a broader perspective is the aim, a case study could be used to provide a first, tentative hypothesis about human behaviour, which would be the starting point of a larger piece of research.

From the above review it should be clear that the conduct of a case study is a highly specialised thing. It requires much skill, probably a good deal of experience on the part of the researcher, infinite patience, a willingness to become involved and a lot of time. In undergraduate research, while the willingness and patience may well be there and, arguably, the experience and skill could be acquired, the limiting factor will be time. Case studies are lengthy procedures and, like participant observation, may well be out of the reach of most undergraduates. However, if the time should be available, there is no better way to become acquainted with, not just the subject of the investigation, but with oneself also, than the case study.

1.3.9 Surveys

A method of data collection which, in comparison with the other techniques available, is perhaps the most typical of research approaches in social research is the survey. Either as a kind of structured interview or in its more common printed, self-report format, surveys aim to generate primarily descriptive information. Consequently, the other stated functions of social research, those of explanation and prediction, tend to be somewhat less accessible by this method (but not unattainable). Nevertheless, the survey remains a primary instrument of research. From the

massive government census that attempts to describe the state of the nation in 10-yearly snapshots, through the ubiquitous market research interviews occurring on every street corner, to the frenetic political polling that takes place in the lead-up to every election, surveys provide huge quantities of descriptive information. For those researchers, however, whose main concerns are with cause and effect, with hypotheses and theory, the quality of survey information is often viewed as too limited (e.g. the proportion of the population who intend to vote Conservative at the next election; what percentage of income is spent on leisure pursuits; how many households own a microwave, etc.), although there are statistical techniques that allow certain inferences to be made with such data. The main contribution of the survey to social research is not so much in the type of data it generates, but in the rigours of its approach to data gathering. Sampling techniques, methods for dealing with bias in our subjects, ways of ensuring that a sample accurately reflects the population as a whole, all owe much of their evolution to the simple survey, and provide an important foundation for developments in the next and last methodology to be discussed – questionnaire research.

1.3.10 Questionnaire-based research

Although some might take issue with describing a research approach in terms of the main data gathering instrument to be used, the popularity of questionnaire-based studies in general, and the extent to which questionnaires often form an essential component in other methodologies such as experimentation and observation, (particularly within the undergraduate population), make it worthy of special consideration here.

A great deal of contemporary research is carried out using questionnaires, as we have already intimated in the previous section on surveys, which is where questionnaires are most frequently found. In this context they are essentially descriptive tools, generating information on what people do (proportion of the population who voted Labour; the frequency of GP visits in different geographic regions, etc.), and on their views, thoughts or beliefs about certain issues (level of support for the government's policy on welfare; the extent to which respondents agree with the introduction of mandatory occupational pension schemes, and so on). Even in the controlled and rigorous environment of experimentation, data can often be collected by means of a questionnaire, which in this context can be a sophisticated test instrument containing items on attitudes, perceptions, judgements and strength of emotion. Furthermore, when combined with other, established instruments, such as stress measures, attitude scales, measures of self-esteem or any of a large number of tests that have been developed over the years – many of which are in themselves a form of questionnaire – we have at our disposal an extremely powerful technique for not just describing, but also explaining, and predicting. Well-constructed questionnaire-based research – be it an experiment, an observation study or a survey – can demonstrate relationships, explore differences and test hypotheses; in some respects it acts as an amalgam of observational and experimental approaches, with responses to questions serving as observations across a wide range of individuals. Moreover, if the right kind of information is sought, real cause and effect relationships can be examined, allowing for similar kinds of controls to be exercised as those used in classical experimentation – always remembering of course that what is being measured is not what people actually do, but what they *say* they do, a proviso that must always be borne in mind when interpreting questionnaire data.

An added advantage of the questionnaire, however, is that it is a potentially quick, cheap and straightforward method of obtaining information. Large numbers of questionnaires can be administered simultaneously and, if items are correctly constructed, data can be readily collated using various kinds of scoring keys devised by the researcher, as opposed to the need for lengthy interpretation. Moreover, since little is usually required in the way of facilities (laboratory space, computers, instrumentation, technical support) questionnaires are among the most readily implemented of research procedures, and it is for this reason that they remain a favourite of undergraduate students everywhere. There is, however, a danger in assuming that because questionnaire-based studies appear easy, cheap and straightforward to implement, they are in some

way better than other approaches; some researchers would even go as far as to claim that, because of the nature of this method, it is almost impossible to obtain useful information of any sort (remember, questionnaires invite people to make judgements, state views and recall events, among other things, inviting the possibility of bias in all its forms). Other potential problems can arise as a result of the process of handing out questionnaires. As with any survey, unless the sample filling in our forms truly represents the group or population we are interested in, any findings will be unrepresentative.

And finally, returning to the earlier comment about the apparent simplicity of the questionnaire, it is useful to remember that, in this kind of research, you get what you ask for – no more no less. The skill of asking the right questions and in the right way is an exacting one, and will be discussed in greater detail in Section 3.4.1 on questionnaire design.

1.3.11   Secondary research

Research in which the individual or group responsible for the design of a study actively participate in its implementation is known as primary research, and information gleaned in this way is termed **primary data**. However, there are many instances in which the data required to answer a research question will have been already collected by others. Whenever we use data of this kind our research is termed secondary research and the data **secondary data**.

Most research relies to some extent on secondary data. Whenever we review the findings of previous research as part of a literature review, or consult government statistics, or even read a chapter in a textbook, we are using information that we ourselves played no part in gathering. However, it is possible, and indeed quite acceptable, to rely on secondary data as *the* data for a study. An investigator exploring changing trends in national earnings might find that the information she needs is already available in government census statistics, obviating the need to carry out a lengthy study of her own. Similarly, research into health and education issues can be well served by using General Household statistics (data collected at regular intervals and made available to social researchers through the office of National Statistics). In cases like this the researcher is able to explore and analyse existing data to meet the requirements of her own research. Not surprisingly perhaps, using secondary data for one's research has distinct advantages:

Box 1.4   A simple sample example

Unbelievably, 95% of our sample, representing the population at large, strongly agreed with the statement that the police in this country would benefit from increased powers of arrest, detention and personal exemption from prosecution.

(*Questionnaires administered to a random sample of 200 subjects, outside New Scotland Yard, London*)

- Secondary data can be obtained quickly – the entire process of developing questionnaires or test instruments and carrying out lengthy research procedures is unnecessary.
- Secondary data can be obtained cheaply – though not always freely, since many organisations charge for access to their information – dispensing with the need to actively collect data which will in itself have clear funding implications for the research.
- The scope of secondary data will often exceed what the individual might achieve on their own. Consider the national census: how many researchers could even dream of surveying every individual of voting age in the entire country?

Clearly secondary data are of great potential value to the social science researcher. However (isn't there always a however?), there are a number of disadvantages to secondary data which must also be understood:

- Secondary data have usually been collected, in their original format, to meet a particular research purpose. Consequently, the way in which measures have been taken, or the range of responses, might not meet the needs of the current research.
- Secondary data are often available only as summary data. It is not always clear what original categories and responses might have been before the original researchers recoded variables, deleted certain data or summarised information.
- Secondary data are rarely current. Most major government surveys, for instance, are carried out only every few years. Research based on the most recent national census, at the very worst, could be as much as nine years out of date.

Despite these drawbacks secondary data research remains popular in the social sciences. Moreover, the approach is a favourite among tutors and supervisors as a training ground for their own students. Analysis of secondary data will be considered in Chapters 4 and 5.

1.4 Beginning a research project

1.4.1 Choosing a research area

This is where it starts: as an undergraduate student of a social science you are now preparing to design and implement a study – either on your own or as part of a group – and the first question to be dealt with is: Where do I begin?

The starting point is normally the selection of a **research area**. Should the study be on the general topic of social policy? Should it be on educational issues? Or occupational? Clinical or what? How do you choose?

The simple answer is probably to begin with a general area which is of personal interest. One particular module in your course of study may appeal to you more than others and you might decide to conduct a study in this field, or there might be a contemporary issue that suggests a study to you: at the time of writing, current media topics are bullying in schools, attitudes towards the police and the impact of falling stock market values on pension schemes. Government policy on a number of issues – welfare, fuel prices, crime – is also much in the public mind, and any one of these issues would represent an interesting and fruitful research area; indeed, scanning the newspapers remains a consistent source of research topics for the student of contemporary society, always providing that their natural desire to tackle the great issues of life can be tempered by practical considerations. Personal observation is another potential source of research – you may have noted something about the way human interactions change inside a lift, or how people sometimes appear happier on sunny days than on rainy ones. Or perhaps a particular textbook has stimulated an interest in an issue (even reading this passage might have drawn you to the idea of looking at bullying in schools), or a recent article in a scientific journal might point to a new area of research. Even your poor, overworked tutors can be a useful source of mental stimulation. Most university staff have their own pet research fields, and all of us are suckers for even a modest display of interest from students – it is only too easy to wheedle research ideas from academics who will be more than pleased to talk about what concerns them.

There is a special situation which, for some, offers a potential short-cut to research ideas, and it involves access to special participant groups; many students, for matters of conscience, or for financial reasons, find themselves involved with subject groups outside the normal student population – some work part time in offices, some do weekends for burger chains, while others offer up their spare time to help out in nursery groups or as volunteer carers. In such instances, access to particular groups might in itself offer a rich source of ideas – in addition to solving the perennial problem of finding people willing to participate in your study. Where such opportunities are available, they should be considered as extremely useful sources

---

> **Box 1.5   Where the ideas come from**
>
> Contemporary issues – press, media, societal, health
> Personal observations/theories
> Academic interests
> Journal articles
> Staff expertise
> Access to subject groups

of inspiration, providing the ethical implications of doing so are understood; the step from convenience to exploitation is a short one.

Most students will readily settle on an area of interest from any one, or a combination of the sources outlined above, but for anyone who still has difficulty choosing a topic, the simplest solution is to try a few of the approaches mentioned and generate a list of possible topics. The next stage is to take each topic in turn and decide whether or not there is a specific aspect of this issue which is of interest – this becomes the Research Question.

1.4.2   The research question

The research question acts as a kind of anchor for a study. It identifies the area in which the research is being carried out, it clearly defines the aim of the research and, very often, it also indicates any sub-issues that might be involved in the study. In many instances it will also dictate the nature of the study – be it observational, case-based, experimental, etc.

For these reasons, considerable thought should go into formulating the research question; get it right and it acts as a continuous reminder of what a particular study is all about and provides a guide through all the subsequent stages of design, implementation and data analysis. Get it wrong and you will flounder. A common problem with undergraduate projects arises when students approach the data analysis part of a study with no clear idea of what kind of analysis they should be doing, and why. Some of this can be attributable to a generalised fear of statistics within the student population, but much of it will also be due to having lost sight of the research question, or having a question which is too vague and fails to provide sufficient direction. And really, we cannot emphasise this point enough. So often supervisors are confronted by students who, having completed most of the work involved in a project, verge on the near-hysterical

because, *'I don't know what I'm doing anymore'*. Needless to say, the typical response will be along the lines of, 'What were your hypotheses? What were the original aims of your study?'

Generally speaking, the research question provides a statement of the overall aims of a piece of research and indicates, in broad terms, what you are trying to do. This is different from the previous exercise of selecting a topic area in which to carry out your research, a distinction which, unfortunately, is a continuous source of annoyance to undergraduates everywhere. Choosing a topic is, as it appears, merely the selection of which field you wish to work in: community, educational, economic, or whatever. Constructing a research question, however, requires that you select a quite specific issue from within this topic area. For instance, you might be interested in the general, medical issue of recovery time following major heart surgery, having noted that such recovery is an extremely variable thing. This interest might subsequently resolve into the research question of 'What factors contribute to variation in post-operative recovery times?', thus providing a starting point for the subsequent study, and a reminder of what it was all about. Such a research question identifies the area in which you will be working and also provides the important statement of what you are trying to do. However, the research question at this stage is still a relatively general thing. It requires refinement or qualification, so the next stage in the process is to turn our rather general question into something more specific – what precisely is it about post-operative recovery that we wish to investigate?

1.4.3   Proposing a testable hypothesis

The research question gives us our starting point, but before we can begin our study, we need to home in on something more specific – we need to refine our research question. Developing our medical example from the previous section, we now need to qualify the issue of those factors that might contribute to variation in recovery times. To assist this refinement, we may review previous research in the area, consult colleagues or refer to personal observations, coming up with a number of more specific questions, such as: Is age related to recovery time, or general health, or social class? And are there other factors involved? Do women recover more speedily from surgery than men? Do post-operative counselling schemes reduce

---

Box 1.6 From the general to the specific

The general topic
1 I'm interested in physical and psychological responses to traumatic surgical procedures (or what happens to people after operations).

The research question
2 What factors contribute to variation in post-operative recovery times?

The hypothesis
3 The mean recovery time (days) for patients in social grouping III undergoing a surgical procedure will be significantly longer than the mean recovery time (days) for social grouping I patients undergoing identical procedures.

---

recovery times? Does the kind of operation have an impact? Is the personality of the patient important? Or the particular hospital in which the operation is carried out? All of these are logical extensions of the original question, the difference being that they now offer something specific that can be tested – they offer the basis for a research hypothesis. (See Box 1.6.)

1.4.4 Deciding on a type of study

We have already indicated that there are a number of ways to address a research issue – we can conduct surveys, we can set up an observation study, we can design a laboratory experiment, and so on. The choice of which approach to take will involve a number of factors: Do we want to study behaviour as it occurs in its natural habitat, without any kind of external interference or manipulation? Or do we want to control certain factors and study behaviour in a more rigid environment? In most cases, the research area and the research question will point to a particular type of study; in others, practical or ethical issues will play a part. For an undergraduate study, a particular department might not have the technical staff or equipment to support certain projects, whereas others might be rich in audio-visual suites and observation chambers. For some studies ample numbers of subjects might be available, making a questionnaire-based **project** attractive, while for others, access to likely participants may be so limited as to necessitate a case study approach. Whichever method is chosen, however, they all require the same adherence to the principles governing all social research – the study should be

systematic, professionally conducted and with due respect for the rights of the individual.

1.5 Reviewing the literature

A fundamental part of any study is a thorough knowledge of the area in which the research is to be carried out and a familiarity with other research on the same, or related topics. Without this information we would never know that our brilliant, ingenious project had actually been published two years previously, or that the paper on which we are basing our own work had been subsequently refuted by the original authors. Moreover, the essential, reasoned justification for our work would be impossible unless we were able to provide a balanced review of previous research in the area. And to be able to do this we must read, and read widely.

In some cases this might involve tracking down back copies of newspapers. Some research is based on contemporary issues, with relevant material available through library sources, either as hard copy (i.e. originals), on microfilm or, where facilities permit, on a computerised system. Unfortunately, many students – and even highly qualified researchers – often ignore the rich reservoir of material available through the popular media. After all, television and newspapers provide an expression of society's concerns and obsessions and anyone hoping to explore a contemporary social issue, like attitudes towards AIDS, the police or the provision of care in the community, could do worse than review a few back copies of their local and national newspaper.

Textbooks, providing they are recent publications, also provide a useful source of background information, although it is in the nature of textbooks that the material covered is, of necessity, general in nature. However, they can offer useful reviews of topics of interest, in addition to providing sources of more specific reading in their reference sections, including details of key articles on which much contemporary research will have been based. It is worth remembering though that textbooks provide secondary data – they present, summarise and often interpret original or primary work and it is not always the case that such interpretations fully reflect the intentions of original authors.

For many students in the social sciences, however, journals will provide their main source of background and reference material, and in a burgeoning area like ours, the sheer number and variety of journals is both intimidating and satisfying. Journals are regular publications (sometimes monthly, quarterly or annually) closely attached to particular scientific domains and comprising a collection of articles, reports and research papers reflecting current work in particular fields. The studies described and the reports presented offer information on current research that is about as up to date as it is possible to get. Moreover, before any material is accepted for inclusion in a journal, it is subjected to a process of peer review, in which other researchers and academics have the opportunity to comment (often anonymously), evaluate and offer suggestions for improvement. Consequently, for anyone wishing to explore a particular issue in any detail, journals will represent a key source of primary information. Typical contents of a journal issue might be an editorial, commenting on any particular trends or themes represented in the particular issue, a number of research reports on a variety of topics within the discipline, and possibly a book review or two.

For established researchers, keeping track of relevant research in their own area is usually quite straightforward. By and large they will subscribe to a relatively small range of journals, reflecting personal interest and

providing a locus for their own publications. For the undergraduate, however, perhaps embarking on their first major study, the wealth of sources and information available to them can be quite overwhelming. A cursory glance through any library catalogue of academic publications will turn up several hundred references to social research, presenting a hopeless task for the uninitiated. Fortunately, information management (librarianship, for the novice) has evolved to the point that even the greenest of undergraduates can negotiate the wealth of information available to them to find what they want. Most research material is regularly catalogued and entered into what are termed 'Abstracts' (sociological, political, psychological, educational, etc.) or indexes. Indexes provide listings of research in particular fields, usually offering information on subject, author, date and journal of publication – just the type of information we need in the early stages of reviewing a topic. Abstracts, on the other hand, provide a listing of the abstracts, or summaries of various pieces of research, and they provide a brief but concise review of what a study was about and what the findings were. In many instances this is as far as the researcher will want to go. If done properly (see Chapter 7 on writing up research), an abstract will describe in

---

Box 1.7 A typical abstract

Increasingly some journals are requiring abstracts to be presented in a structured format which, should this become the norm, would make life easier for undergraduates who always seem to have difficulty with this part of a report. Below is a typical structured abstract showing both the format and the amount of detail expected here.

Title Chronic fatigue syndrome: symptoms, appraisal and ways of coping.

Objectives The aim of the study was to investigate the contributions of measures of appraisal and ways of coping (relative scoring) to two clusters of symptoms of chronic fatigue syndrome (CFS; fatigue and emotional disturbance), using multiple regression analysis.

Design A cross-sectional design was employed within a framework provided by the Lazarus & Folkman model of stress.

Methods Participants ($N = 81$) were drawn from CFS support groups. Self-report questionnaires were used, including measures of symptoms (Ray, Weir, Phillips & Cullen, 1992). Ways of coping with CFS (Ray, Weir, Stewart, Miller & Hyde, 1993), and appraisal of the illness (Browne *et al.*, 1988).

Results When symptoms of emotional disturbance were controlled, those experiencing more symptoms of fatigue were more likely to perceive CFS to be stressful, were less likely to feel that they could do anything about the illness, and were relatively more likely to cope through seeking information. Those experiencing more symptoms of emotional disturbance were less likely to have an optimistic outlook and were less likely to attempt to cope by accommodating to the illness, irrespective of symptoms of fatigue.

Conclusions The results confirmed the utility of the Lazarus & Folkman model of stress within this domain. The use of relative coping scores clarified the potential importance of accommodating to the illness. Overall, the results underlined the need to further develop measures and methodologies in this area.

Christina Knussen and Deborah Lee (1988)

(This abstract is reproduced here with the kind permission of the authors, and of the British Psychological Society (BPS)).

The BPS can be contacted at:

British Psychological Society,
St Andrew's House,
48 Princess Road East,
Leicester LE1 7DR)

concise terms the research issue addressed by a study, the research design implemented, key procedural elements and a summary of the findings. Enough, usually, to inform a judgement about whether or not this research is of relevance to the current topic. Box 1.7 offers a typical example.

For the computer literate, however, most university libraries now offer electronic search facilities that serve similar if not superior functions, while the Internet is a vast resource for the researcher. Research sites are proliferating at such a rate, however, that any guidance we offer here is likely to be out of date by the time you read it. Having said this though, at the time of going to press, a typical resource – and an excellent one at that – may be found at the SOSIG site (the Social Science Information Gateway). Access is normally via a networked personal computer or a library information system. By entering a few key terms a full listing of relevant abstracts can be displayed on screen, although care should be exercised in the selection of search terms – an unwary user who

simply requests a search for any journal article with the word 'attitudes' in the title would spend weeks sifting through the mountain of returns. Selecting 'attitudes and Alzheimer's' on the other hand would generate a relatively small and much more specific selection of articles. Box 1.8 shows the home page of the SOSIG website.

As Box 1.8 shows, SOSIG offers access to several sites of social interest. A search can be focused on a particular discipline, such as Women's Studies, or can be of a more general nature, relying on key words, as we have done in our example. Designating a search for items on 'care of the elderly' searched all of the sites, and produced the information shown in Box 1.9.

Other common sources of electronically stored information are MEDLINE, which offers an index of international articles from medical and biomedical journals, ASSIA (Applied Social Science Index and Abstracts), which is concerned primarily with health and social services publications and BIDS (Bath Information and Data Services). This latter service is

---

Box 1.8   Electronic searching

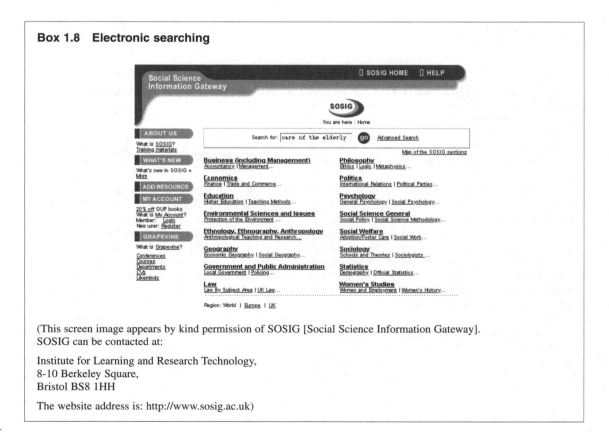

(This screen image appears by kind permission of SOSIG [Social Science Information Gateway]. SOSIG can be contacted at:

Institute for Learning and Research Technology,
8-10 Berkeley Square,
Bristol BS8 1HH

The website address is: http://www.sosig.ac.uk)

Box 1.9

Results for: care AND of AND the AND elderly
1 - 10 from 31 matches   1 2 3 4 Next

Debate of the Age (The)
Alternative Title: Millennium Debate of the Age
Description: This web site features The Debate of the Age, a resource sponsored by Age
Concern England to mark the millennium. Age Concern is using the millennium as a time to look at
the changing demographic patterns confonting the UK. The site includes a collection of facts and
statistics illustrating the growing elderly population, shrinking work force, different patterns in
marriage, child-bearing and lone parenthood, all of which will bring change over the next twenty
years. The debate is fuelled by the Millennium Papers. These were prepared in the Autumn of
1999 by five study groups whose interim reports, produced in 1998, provided the source
material for the Debate of the Age. The Millennium Papers addressed the five key themes of the
Debate of the Age and are entitled: The Future of Health and Care of Older People; Paying for
Age in the 21st Century; Future Work and Lifestyles; The Future of the Built Environment; and
Values and Attitudes in an Ageing Society. In addition to the full text of the papers (in .pdf
format) full text of reports on the debate are also available. + Full Record
Keywords: millennium, elderly, United Kingdom, population, statistics, retirement, life
expectancy, older people, ageing, health care, social policy, demographics, income, pensions,
UK, old age, care of the elderly
http://www.ageconcern.org.uk/

(This extract appears by kind permission of Age Concern.
Age Concern can be contacted at:

Age Concern Enterprises,
Walkden House,
10 Melton Street,
London NWI 2EB)

---

now available through most academic libraries and provides access to a vast data store owned by the Institute for Scientific Information and through which access can be obtained to more than 7,500 journals worldwide. The search process is similar to that used for SOSIG-based materials, reflecting a trend that is likely to continue.

In the event that our study is based on one specific piece of published research – perhaps the aim is to develop an idea, or explore a novel aspect of previous work – then our starting point would be the Science or the Social Science Citation Index. This particular index focuses on individual studies, and identifies any subsequent research that has cited the original. It is a useful method for following particular trends in a research area and is also now available through the BIDS data service.

For those keen to review research in progress, but not necessarily published, the Internet now offers direct links to individuals in university departments all over the country; while still at an embryonic level, information pages are appearing every day, outlining interests, publications and ongoing work. It is conceivable that, within a relatively short time, surfing the net will provide the most direct route to current social research.

1.6 Evaluating research

Much of the foregoing has emphasised the need to read widely around a topic before embarking on the design of a specific study. However, simply consuming journals and textbooks in an effort to amass information is, in itself, not enough. When we read and consider the work of others, we need to do so critically, adopting a questioning, and sometimes downright suspicious perspective. The importance of this stance is obvious when one considers that, for the purposes of research, we are not merely trying to find out more about an issue, we are also looking for flaws in a theory, limitations in the way a study has been carried out, or possible sources of development. After all, it could well be that the very limitations of an early study provide us with the impetus for our own work, yet we would never have identified those limitations had our approach not been critical.

Asking questions while reviewing the work of others is a skill most undergraduates are expected to acquire as they progress through a degree course – the trick is in knowing what questions to ask. In the field of social research, this process is possibly more straightforward than in other areas, due to the manner in which research is carried out. Earlier sections of this chapter emphasised the logical, systematic and scientific nature of research, and because the study of human society now tends to follow an established structure, our questioning can follow similar systematic guidelines.

The first object of doubt in consideration of any study will be the literature review and background information cited in support of the research. We would want to know if the review seemed broad enough to provide thorough and balanced coverage of an issue:

1 Are there any aspects of the research issue that, in your view, seem to have been overlooked, or not fully considered?
2 Does the review provide a sound basis for the research question being explored?
3 Do hypotheses follow logically from what has gone before?

If, at any time while reading a rationale for research, we find ourselves saying 'Yes, but what about...?' this could indicate a weakness or limitation. Combine this with our earlier consideration of doubt, contained in the question 'How do you know?' and we have at our disposal our own, private secret weapon.

If a review is broad in coverage, the research issue clearly stated and rationally justified, and the hypotheses logical extensions of what has gone before, the next area of concern is the design of the study. When we read this section, we are evaluating the plan drawn up by the researcher to examine the hypotheses. What we should be asking ourselves is:

1 Does this seem like a good way of exploring the issue?
2 Will all the considerations raised as being relevant to the research question be covered with this particular approach?
3 Does it seem practical to research an issue in this way?
4 Are there any ethical problems with this approach?
5 Is there a better way to do this?

Once again, if we find ourselves saying, 'Yes, but what about...?' then there may be some problem with the design.

If a researcher's plan or intentions for a study seem acceptable, the next thing we want to know is, how successfully was the plan executed? Some studies, for instance, require many subjects, yet obtaining volunteers in large numbers is not always possible. Our judgement here would have to be whether or not failure to obtain sufficient subjects, or subjects of the right type, detracts from the study in any way. Generally speaking, close scrutiny of research procedure might highlight difficulties experienced by the researcher, or deviations from the original design which might lead us to question whether or not the research issue has actually been addressed.

When it comes to considering the results of a research study, many undergraduates find themselves bemused, if not intimidated, by the information presented to them. In part, this is due to the relative statistical unsophistication common among undergraduate students and, while this is a facility that will develop as the individual matures, there are always some research designs that rely on complex analytical procedures inaccessible to most students. There is also the possibility that a researcher, due to his own statistical limitations or (and this is thankfully rare), in an attempt to deliberately mislead, may present results that are ambiguous or incomplete. Either way, it is sometimes difficult for the student to make a judgement on the validity of research findings from consideration of the results. However, there are some guidelines that can be applied:

1 Are the results clearly presented – do tables and figures offer a clear indication of what happened?
2 Is it made clear that the hypotheses have been supported or refuted?
3 Do the results appear to address the issues raised during the literature review?
4 Do the analyses seem appropriate?
5 Do the data suggest some other form of analysis that has been overlooked?

Posing these questions will at least go some way towards evaluating the quality of research, yet this section of a published study will always be problematic since rarely will actual data be available to the reader. In most cases, if the reader wishes to look at actual scores or measurements, or even the precise calculations and computer outputs on which analyses are based, she must contact the researcher in question with a special request to look more closely at the data. Most undergraduates, reviewing literature for their own research, will be unlikely to gain access to primary data in this way.

The discussion section of a published study is often the most interesting, for it is here that the authors can explore their results in greater detail, consider the way in which they conducted themselves and, generally speaking, review the whole issue on which the study was based. The kind of questioning we should be considering here might take the following form:

1 Have the authors effectively considered and explained the results, making it clear what the outcome of the study was?
2 Did any unexpected findings emerge and were the authors able to explain these in light of the research question originally posed?
3 Were the authors able to relate the findings to the research question?
4 If the study failed to support the hypotheses, are the authors' explanations convincing?
5 Have the authors recognised and discussed any limitations in their work?
6 If the authors have speculated about their research findings, does this speculation seem justified?
7 Overall, does the study add anything to our understanding of the original issue?

All of the above examples merely represent typical questions the student might ask of a piece of social research. The list is not exhaustive, and not all of these issues will be relevant to every study. The point though is that we should get into the habit of approaching published material from a critical point of view, an approach that will not only offer us an improved understanding of other people's work, but also might make us more professional in our own. After all, anything that we ourselves might someday publish will be viewed from precisely this critical perspective and we could find ourselves faced with that most lethal of all questions: 'How do you know?'

1.7   The structure of a research project

By now, if you have read the preceding sections you will have a good idea of how a research project is carried out. This final section presents an outline of the main steps.

1 Selection of a field in which to carry out a study.
2 Carrying out a literature review on the topic.
3 Statement of a research question (what the study is trying to do).

4 Providing a rationale for the research question.
5 Refining the rationale into a number of specific and testable hypotheses.
6 Designing and planning an appropriate way of testing the hypotheses.
7 Implementing the plan and gathering data (carrying out the study).
8 Analysing data and presenting the results of the study.
9 Discussing the data, reappraising the research question in the light of findings, and considering the entire rationale, conduct and theoretical basis for the study.

1.8   Review

This chapter has attempted to provide an overview of social research, explaining the reasons why such research is carried out, and providing a general guide to the various processes and limitations of the many different approaches that can be taken to the study of social behaviour. The chapters that follow take a more detailed look at the design and conduct of research.

1.9   Explanation of terms

case study an intensive and detailed study of a very small number of subjects – and sometimes only one – usually over a period of time. The case study can encompass a number of both qualitative and quantitative methods.
ethnography the in-depth, holistic analysis of the structure and processes of culture.
ethography the study of the behaviour patterns of animal species within their natural habitats.
experiment a procedure for gathering data that involves an experimenter manipulating key aspects of a study, such as the way in which subjects are assigned to groups, the experiences they encounter and the way in which measures are taken.
field study a procedure for gathering data in which the researcher operates within a natural, as opposed to an artificial or laboratory, setting.
generalisation problem a common difficulty in research in which the findings of a study might

not be typical of, or generalisable to, the world at large.

hypothesis a specific prediction about some aspect of the universe, based on the more general beliefs that comprise a theory, e.g. 'there will be a significant difference in the mean income of a group of male and female managers tested over a comparable range of job level'.

observation study a procedure for gathering data in which the researcher does not manipulate key elements of a study, but instead observes behaviour as it occurs naturally.

participant observation observation of a group or society of which the observer has become a part. Significant here is involvement and experience with the object of study.

positivism a term describing the new 'positive' approach to the study of society proposed by Auguste Comte in the nineteenth century. The approach emphasised objectivity and has formed the basis of much social research up to the present.

primary data data actively collected by, and therefore under the control of, a researcher as part of the implementation of a study.

project an undertaking (for the purposes of this textbook) whereby a study is devised and carried out as part of a formal undergraduate course. Such an undertaking is usually assessable.

research a process of investigating, scrutinising or studying an issue, usually conducted according to a set of predetermined guidelines and procedures.

research area the general area of interest in which the research is carried out, e.g. welfare, organisational, educational.

research question a general issue within an area of interest that provides the basis for a study: e.g. are there sex differences in certain elements of political opinion? Sometimes referred to as the research issue.

scientific method a set of established procedures for the conduct of research, common to all disciplines.

secondary data data collected and organised by others, but forming the basis for new, or current research.

social science a term applied to any of a number of disciplines concerned with some aspect of society and the activities of its members, and unified by a common set of methodological practices, procedures, standards and ethics.

study a planned investigation of a specified topic or issue involving a systematic process of reading, exploration, experimentation and research.

theory a general set of beliefs about some aspect of the universe that may or may not be supported by evidence, e.g. 'women are superior to men in all respects'.

1.10   Further reading

Karlsen, S., Primatesta, P. and McMunn, A. *Health survey for England – the health of minority ethnic groups '99*, http://www.officialdocuments.co.uk/doh/survey99/hse99-07.htm#7.5

Knussen, C. and Lee, D. (1998) Chronic fatigue syndrome: symptoms, appraisal and ways of coping. *British Journal of Health Psychology*, **3**: 111–121.

May, T. (1997) *Social Research: Issues, Methods and Process*, 2nd edition. Buckingham: OUP.

Punch, K.F. (1999) *Introduction to Social Research: Quantitative and Qualitative Approaches*. London: Sage.

Robson, C. (1993) *Real World Research: A Resource for Social Scientists and Practitioner-researchers*. Oxford: Blackwell.

Stewart, D.W and Kamins, M.A. (1993) *Secondary Research: Information Sources and Methods*, 2nd edition. Thousand Oaks, CA: Sage.

Useful websites

ASSIA (Applied Social Science Index and Abstracts). At: http://www.shef.ac.uk/library/libdocs/hsl-ngh1.-html

BIDS (Bath Information and Data Services). At: http://www.bids.ac.uk

MEDLINE. At: http://www.nlm.nih.gov/medlineplus/

SOSIG (Social Science Information Gateway). At: http://www.sosig.ac.uk/

JISC (Joint Information Systems Committee) A Resource Guide for the Social Sciences. At: http://www.jisc.ac.uk/

CHAPTER 2

Planning a study – the design

Cries for help

- *Would an interview be better than a survey?*
- *How do I tell an independent variable from a dependent one?*
- *Can I do this without numbers?*
- *How many subjects should I get?*
- *Would a qualitative study be better (easier, quicker) than a quantitative one?*

Once a topic for exploration or research has been decided upon the temptation to 'get out there' and start interviewing, observing or measuring is almost irresistible. Unfortunately, no matter how laudable such commitment among one's students might be, it has to be said that haste and untempered enthusiasm at this stage are more likely to lead to frustration and failure – not to mention poor grades – than the hoped-for satisfaction of a piece of work well done. The wise student will take a step back from their pet project here and allow themselves the time to think things through, and for a number of very good reasons: it is rarely the case that there is only one way to explore an issue but it is true that some ways will be better than others. Some thought at this point in a research project could well identify possible flaws with one particular approach not present in another, and also avoid the often-seen comment in the conclusion section of many undergraduate reports along the lines of: 'This study might have been carried out more effectively using interviews to explore participants' opinions, rather than the survey method which overlooked a number of key issues.' A second reason for emphasising the importance of this planning stage is that no study is perfect. Things go wrong. **Murphy's Law** (or Sod's Law, as it is sometimes called) states that if something can go wrong, it will go wrong, and this is as true of research as of any other aspect of human activity. A more reasonable way to consider this of course is that, with something as complex as society and the people within it, there will always be a multitude of interacting factors, effects, influences, accidents and coincidences, all of which conspire to undermine our observations, explorations and experiments with unpredictability. Or, to put it another way, if something can go wrong, then it probably will – unless we have allowed for it. And the only way we can allow for it is if we have taken the time to think our study through. Which is what this planning stage is all about.

This chapter examines the different ways in which a study can be planned, identifying some of the most common research approaches available to the student and illustrating the many things that can go wrong. It covers the essential characteristics of good research design, explains the terminology and offers examples of the various options with discussion on the advantages and disadvantages of each. For students who have already identified a research issue to investigate, and who have

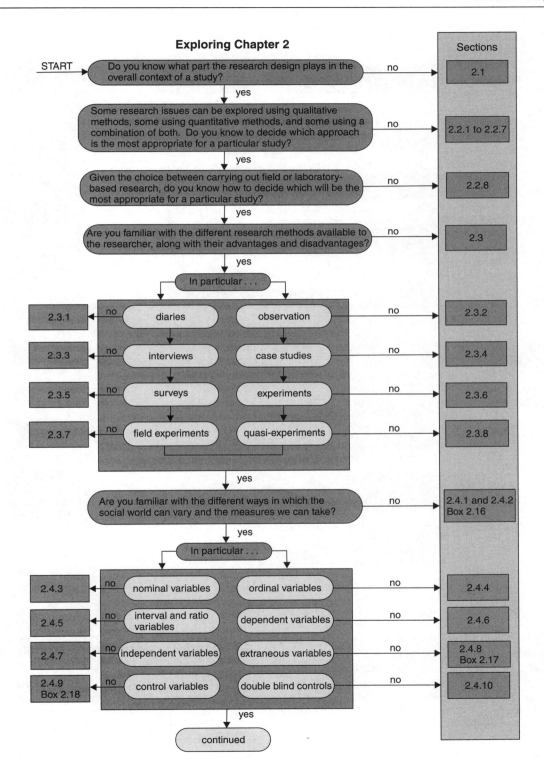

Exploring Chapter 2

START → Do you know what part the research design plays in the overall context of a study? — no → Sections: 2.1

yes

Some research issues can be explored using qualitative methods, some using quantitative methods, and some using a combination of both. Do you know to decide which approach is the most appropriate for a particular study? — no → 2.2.1 to 2.2.7

yes

Given the choice between carrying out field or laboratory-based research, do you know how to decide which will be the most appropriate for a particular study? — no → 2.2.8

yes

Are you familiar with the different research methods available to the researcher, along with their advantages and disadvantages? — no → 2.3

yes

In particular . . .

2.3.1 ← no — diaries   observation — no → 2.3.2
2.3.3 ← no — interviews   case studies — no → 2.3.4
2.3.5 ← no — surveys   experiments — no → 2.3.6
2.3.7 ← no — field experiments quasi-experiments — no → 2.3.8

yes

Are you familiar with the different ways in which the social world can vary and the measures we can take? — no → 2.4.1 and 2.4.2 Box 2.16

yes

In particular . . .

2.4.3 ← no — nominal variables   ordinal variables — no → 2.4.4
2.4.5 ← no — interval and ratio variables   dependent variables — no → 2.4.6
2.4.7 ← no — independent variables   extraneous variables — no → 2.4.8 Box 2.17
2.4.9 Box 2.18 ← no — control variables   double blind controls — no → 2.4.10

yes

continued

Exploring Chapter 2 *continued*

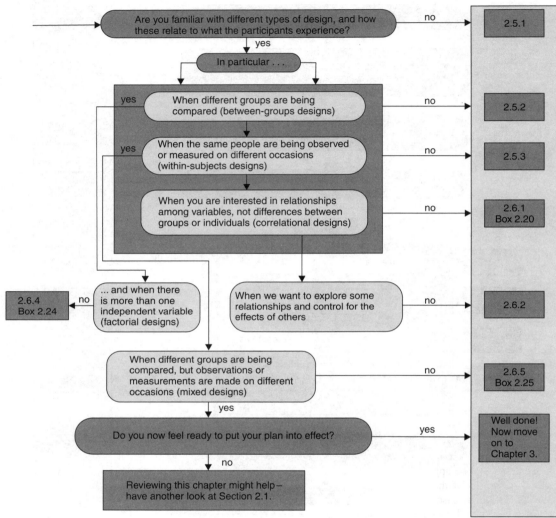

gone as far as proposing hypotheses to test, this section represents the next stage in the research process – how to plan a systematic, scientific and ethical study that will effectively explore the research issue under investigation or test the specific hypotheses proposed.

If you have specific questions on planning a study, please consult the flowchart above. Alternatively, beginning with Section 2.1, the entire process is explained in a logical sequence.

2.1   The purpose of a research plan

There are two main reasons for establishing a detailed plan for a research study. The first concerns purely practical issues, such as which sections of the population we are going to sample; should the study be qualitative or quantitative in nature; would it be more effective using questionnaires to obtain our data, or would interviews be a richer source of information. Moreover, as outlined in the introduction to this chapter, it provides us with the ideal opportunity to consider what might just go wrong with our study, and to prepare various strategies for dealing with problems.

The second purpose of this planning stage is to produce a detailed, formal statement of how the study is to be carried out, identifying variables, key procedures and strategies. This becomes the **research design** and represents one of the central parts of a study on which an undergraduate's work will be judged. Section 2.3 considers this formal element in more detail while the next section explores the practical issues.

2.2 Research plans and practicalities

2.2.1 Qualitative or quantitative?

A common question asked by students of social sciences is whether or not their study should be qualitative or quantitative in nature, and it is also one of the most difficult to answer. One of the reasons for this is that, although they are generally viewed as quite distinctive approaches to research, they can also be regarded as merely different ends of the same dimension, an informational continuum that runs from the numerical and purely quantitative to the highly descriptive and linguistic, with various levels in between:

Qualitative   Quantitative

Another problem in trying to take an 'either–or' stance is that there are many instances in which both approaches would be appropriate and others in which some combination of the two would be suitable. Yet again, there will be cases in which only one of these methodologies will do; there are many issues involved. Before we consider these, however, it is worth highlighting the differences between the two approaches, or, alternatively, depending on your point of view, between the two ends of this single continuum of research methodology.

Quantitative research reflects the philosophy that everything in the social world can be described according to some kind of numerical system – a person's sex can be represented by the number 1 (for male, for example) or 2 (for female); views on government policy on welfare can be expressed as a number on a scale (e.g. 1 indicating total disagreement with policy and 7 representing total support) and all forms of behaviour can be similarly quantified. All of us have encountered rating scales and numerical measures at one time or another and this is where the term 'quantitative' comes from. The underlying belief is that only by adopting such a rigorous approach and by reducing all aspects of our universe to a common numerical system can true precision be achieved; just as with school algebra, it is only when we identify a common denominator that we can carry out comparisons, project trends and identify differences among individuals, groups and communities. Furthermore, expressing the social world in numerical terms opens the way to an impressive range of statistical analytical techniques which allow researchers to describe and draw inferences according to certain conventions that most other researchers, students, scientists and policy makers are familiar with. By way of example, a quantitative approach would allow us to compare male and female samples on average income over the course of a working life, and decide whether or not any differences are statistically significant, as opposed to merely different but not meaningfully so. Such an approach could allow us to explore patterns of discriminatory behaviour among police forces over a 10-year period, and identify whether or not variation is random, or part of, for instance, a racist trend, and so on. In short, the quantitative approach is concerned with averages, variation, differences and relationships, and it represents one of the major research approaches within the social sciences, both historically and currently. Chapters 4 and 5 are primarily devoted to the quantitative approach and the statistical analysis of quantitative data.

Qualitative research is, on the face of it, quite distinct from its quantitative counterpart, and has its roots in anthropology, interpretivism and psychoanalysis. It is both a philosophy and a procedural approach; it is sometimes seen as a reaction against numerically-based experimentalism and it comprises a set of principles in its own right. It also forms part of a huge, and sometimes acrimonious, debate among researchers and academics over the issue of quantitative precision versus descriptive richness, a debate which has forced some protagonists to view the two approaches as mutually exclusive rather than as different elements of a single, unitary process.

Qualitative studies are not primarily, or at least initially, concerned with numbers – they don't measure on scales, they don't look for averages and they don't aim for statistical precision. However, what they do share with quantitative approaches is the fundamental principle behind all social research in that they are attempting to explore and describe, explain and predict. It's just that they go about it in a different way, as the following example illustrates.

Imagine going to a darts match with the aim of exploring the behaviour of the fans. Now a quantitative researcher might begin with a theory about audience behaviours, plus a set of hypotheses about what the fans will do under varying circumstances (their player is winning, losing, or the match is abandoned). This could be tested using a structured questionnaire given out before and after a match, scores compiled, averages calculated and conclusions drawn from statistical analysis. But supposing you don't begin with the advantage of a well thought-out theory, let alone any hypotheses – suppose you don't actually have any idea how fans behave at darts tournaments, other than what appears as sensationalist stories in tabloid newspapers, and there is no literature to provide anything more than the vaguest of clues. Or you might feel that numerical data provide information on the measurable aspects of behaviour only, and very little information about the complexities of life as a darts follower. Questionnaires and surveys are useless here, since such approaches require that you have a pretty good idea what you want to find out right from the start, so you know what questions to ask. In this case you might decide simply to observe what goes on around you, taking notes, recording conversations, or even video-

ing behaviour. Or perhaps you might feel that the detached approach isolates you too much from what is actually happening and you decide that the best way to understand is to become one of the fans yourself – to travel with others to and from tournaments, to meet socially and to experience games yourself as part of the crowd. With this approach your data are quite different and quite special – they comprise notes, diaries, transcriptions of interviews; there will be recordings of how people feel and what they think, as opposed to merely what they do. There will even be information on how you, the researcher, feel about what's going on. This is qualitative information and Box 2.1 offers an illustration, while Chapter 6 provides a more detailed discussion of this approach.

Box 2.1 illustrates some of the ways in which qualitative and quantitative approaches to research can differ and allows us now to consider the circumstances under which the student might use one as opposed to the other. It is worth noting, however, that all the following discussions are generalisations and, on their own, would not necessarily determine the nature of a particular study. It is the balancing of all these issues against one another that will finally determine the nature of a research project. Figure 2.1 presents an 'at a glance' decision chart that summarises the following discussions.

Box 2.1   Getting to the point

Often the same scenario, when looked at from different points of view, can be described in very different ways.

The quantitative researcher writing on the behaviour of darts supporters might offer the following:

The mean number of hostile displays (as measured by a hostility scale developed by the researcher) across 15 games was 21.6 for the home supporters and 13.93 for the visitors during the same period. An independent t-test for the hypothesis that there will be no difference in hostile displays for home or visiting fans produced the following:

$$t \text{ (equal variances)} = 6.88; df = 28; p < 0.05 \text{ (two-tailed)}$$

The null hypothesis is rejected. There is a statistically significant difference between the hostile behaviours displayed by the home and visiting fans. Further inspection of the means...

(Note: if all of these numbers represent a mystery to you, all will be explained in Chapters 4 and 5.)

The qualitative researcher on the other hand might produce something like this:

My first impression was that the overtly aggressive behaviour of the fans – comprising mainly taunts and jeers about the dubious parentage and sexual deviancy of the opposing supporters – was misleading. During the course of the first two matches the feeling that came from the supporters around me was one of good-natured enjoyment. Talking to the group I came to know after one match it appeared that these fans actually liked some of the opposing supporters: 'You need to come when the guys from the Green Man are playing – their fans are great. We know the same songs, like, and we take it in turns with the verses.' By the end of the first quarter of the tournament I was beginning to develop a theory about the behaviour of...

For a more detailed discussion of this type of research, the article by Lofland & Lofland (1995) in the further reading section at the end of this chapter is ideal.

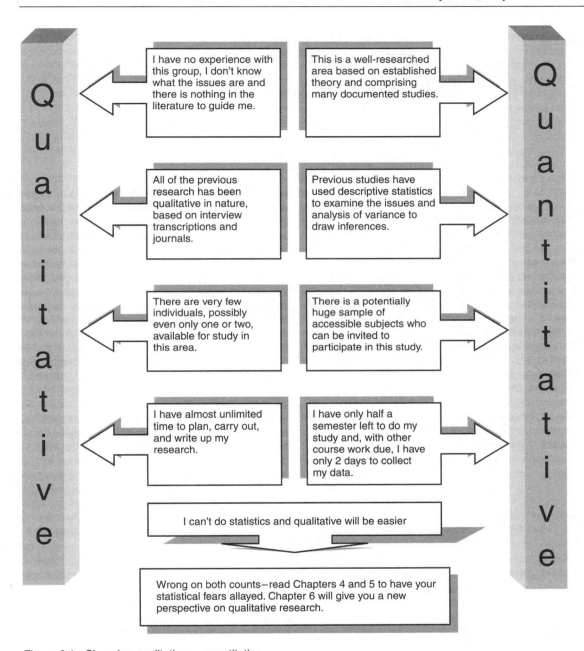

Figure 2.1   Choosing qualitative or quantitative.

2.2.2 Is the study based on a well-defined theory?

A lot of undergraduate research (and postgraduate, for that matter) follows the work of previous research and attempts to build upon established theory, either by developing or broadening our knowledge of social issues, or in terms of questioning existing views and positions. Consequently for many issues there already exists a body of knowledge explaining and describing

---

Box 2.2

I am considering a project to study the latent aggres-siveness of Wimbledon tennis audiences but I have no idea where to begin; I don't even understand the game.

vs

The National Householder Survey of 1997 identified males in occupational category 5 as having the greatest average income. Will a replication in the new millen-nium produce different results?

Box 2.3

I would like to design a study to investigate the experi-ences of all those who have walked on the moon. How can I do this?

vs

My study aims to explore the attitudes of the entire stu-dent population of the university.

---

what happens in different situations, along with asso-ciated hypotheses which predict future outcomes.

When our own research is attempting to extend exist-ing theory or to test or modify hypotheses then we are beginning our work from the standpoint of already having a pretty good idea about what is going on in a particular situation and what we are expecting to find. In a case like this, in which the research is likely to be fairly well structured and where we are testing spe-cific hypotheses, it is likely that our approach will be quantitative in nature: we will be trying to demonstrate differences in measured or observed events under different circumstances, or over time, and we will prob-ably be relying on statistics for proof of these effects. This is classic quantitative territory, in which compari-sons with, or developments from, existing theory and research are made on the basis of statistical analyses.

In cases in which the area of interest is novel, how-ever, for which there is no, or at least a limited, estab-lished body of research and theory, or in which we have no experience, then it is likely that we will take a qualitative approach. Theories and hypotheses about the situation we are exploring may well emerge as a result of our observations and experiences, but the initial approach here is qualitative. A look at the exam-ples in Figure 2.1 should give you the idea while Chapter 6 takes a more detailed look at this issue.

2.2.3 Are the numbers of subjects likely to be very small?

As a general – though not universal – guide, quantita-tive research has, as a preference, large sample sizes. This is largely a function of the statistical analyses that comprise an important element of this approach, since the value or 'power' of many statistics increases with the numbers of individuals being measured. Indeed, some analyses require certain minimum numbers of

observations to be viable, an issue covered in more depth in Chapter 3, Section 3.2. In practical terms, what this means is that, if your study will allow access to only small numbers of individuals (say, for instance, you are interested in studying the unique difficulties experienced by multiple birth mothers), then there may be very few women in this category, making the mass assessment procedures common to quantitative research impractical. A situation like this may lend itself more to a qualitative approach involving observa-tion, interviews, journals and diaries. It must be pointed out though that size is not everything – there will be occasions in which an area of research presents large numbers of subjects but in which qualitative methods are still preferred. A study on football hooliganism is a good example, if this particular area is outside our experience, as were the early anthropological studies of entire cultures whose structures and processes were completely novel; another look at the example in Figure 2.1 will illustrate this. Conversely, there are cer-tain areas in psychology in which repeated measures are taken from a very small sample – as in the areas of perception, memory and cognition – which are tradi-tionally explored quantitatively (although the power of such small-scale studies might be questioned). An example might be of a small group of experimental subjects tested over a large number of trials on their ability to detect differences in pitch between a standard and a comparison sound tone, a common procedure in certain areas of psychological interest. Having said this though, it remains generally true that quantitative stud-ies rely on large samples and the statistical techniques that go with them.

2.2.4 Are there time constraints on your study?

Again, although it is not a universal rule, qualitative research is generally longer term in nature than quan-titative. The processes involved make it so.

Box 2.4

In a study of employee satisfaction we have only two days in which to gather all our data. Production in the factory cannot be interrupted for longer...

vs

Your five year mission is to boldly go and explore...

Repeated observations of how a section of the community responds to new conditions or changes in public policy, the need to be accepted as part of a group if participation will be a component of the research, or the simple logistical problems of preparing for and carrying out successive interviews, all require time. Data collected for quantitative research, which often aims to take a large number of simultaneous measures from a sample, via some standardised procedure, such as a questionnaire, can be considered very quickly. An attitudinal survey can be administered to many subjects at a single administration and the data gathered in the time it takes to fill in and collect the questionnaires; an experiment comparing the output of two factory groups working under different environmental conditions can produce measures on all the participants in the time it takes to carry out the experiment. Even the analysis stage of a study is linked to this time factor: quantitative data, by their very nature (scores on rating scales; frequency of different classes of voting behaviours; time taken to commute set distances using public transport and so on) are readily analysed via a number of established and well-structured procedures. The advent of modern statistical computer packages makes this task even easier so that quite complex analyses can be carried out in a matter of minutes (see Chapters 4 and 5 for examples of statistical analyses and the special contribution of computer software). The analysis of qualitative information is somewhat different. Consider that a qualitative research project will have generated not numbers or scores, but text, in all likelihood – transcriptions of interviews and conversations, journals and diaries, commentaries made by the researcher herself and assorted notes containing various observations, thoughts, ideas and speculations. Moreover, given that much of this text might in turn have been prepared from original recordings, both video and audio, then the scale of the task involved in qualitative analysis becomes clear. This is not something that can be done in an afternoon. Reviewing the text of conversations and

interviews, searching for trends, recurring issues, looking for what hasn't been said as much as for what has, is a long-term activity, even with the aid of modern text analysis software (see Chapter 6, Section 6.2.3).

All of this means that if there are time constraints on your study it may not be possible to design and carry out a qualitative piece of research, or at least not one of an ambitious nature. This has real implications for many undergraduate projects, especially those of a single semester duration – usually 12 to 15 weeks at the most. Which is why, at the outset of a study, at this planning stage it is important to consider the time scale available for the project. The best-conceived qualitative study in the world will come to nothing – and realise poor grades – if there is not enough time to complete the planned series of interviews or observations, or to make sense of the hundreds of pages of textual material the study produced.

2.2.5 Is there a qualitative or quantitative tradition in the area of your study?

As we have intimated earlier, a lot of undergraduate research will be based on previous work. You might, for instance, be reviewing whether or not the career prospects for women have really changed under a new government; you might be exploring changes in the incidence of drug use under a new needle replacement policy; or you might be re-evaluating the social behaviour of pre-school children in the light of a newly discovered sex-linked social gene. In many of these cases the previous research will reflect a distinctive philosophy, type of design and set of procedures. Some of the previous research in your area of interest will have been typically qualitative, some quantitative and yet more an amalgam of both approaches. In many instances, therefore, in following on from previous research you would be likely to adopt the same or similar approach to that of the original. In this way

Box 2.5

In the original study on which the change in government policy was based, focus groups identified the issues of...

vs

The average rate of decline in the South American newt population can be expressed in terms of the following mean and standard deviations...

you can draw direct comparisons and talk sensibly about trends and developments in ways impossible if you were to use a completely different methodology. Indeed, a common piece of advice given by supervisors is that their students look at how previous research has been carried out in the area, to give them an idea of how to plan their own work. As usual, however, a word of caution is necessary here and we must remind ourselves to be wary of sweeping statements – there will be instances in which adopting the same approach as previous research will be counter-productive. Sometimes, adopting a different methodology will throw up findings and perspectives on a situation that would have been missed if the traditional approach were adhered to. It is often worth asking yourself the question: would we get the same results if we carried out the study differently? See Box 2.6 for an example.

2.2.6   Is there a qualitative or quantitative philosophy among the staff and supervisors in your department?

It remains to be said on this issue that departments, and individuals within those departments, will have their own preferences for a particular methodological approach. Some will have been brought up in the quan-

---

Box 2.7

My professor is one of the leading exponents of qualitative research in the country…

vs

'I'm a multiple regression man myself,' said the supervisor to his project group.

---

titative tradition, and will possess the wide range of statistical skills required by that tradition, whereas others will have a qualitative background. Consequently it is likely that, depending on where you do your research, and who supervises it, you will be expected, or at least encouraged, to adopt a particular approach. This is not to say that such institutional pressures will be totally inflexible in their expectations and guidance, since all good supervisors will ultimately encourage you to take the approach that best suits the topic and the circumstances. But it is worth remembering that, among the factors that will determine whether or not your study will be qualitative or quantitative, you will have to take into account the preferences and predispositions of your supervisors.

2.2.7   Does it have to be one or the other?

It is not always the case that a particular study need be wholly qualitative or quantitative. Certainly, as we have suggested at the beginning of this discussion, there are cases in which only one of these approaches will work, but there will also be many situations in which either will do, with the final choice of methodology based on some combination of the various points mentioned above. There are also cases in which a combination of the two approaches is appropriate. Consider the example outlined in Box 2.6. Here we have a scenario in which the initial quantitative procedure failed because the researchers had not fully understood the issues or the concerns of the people involved. Far better to have begun this study with a qualitative exploration of the behaviour and worries of the group, using interviews, discussions, diaries, etc., and from here developed both a theory and hypotheses about their experiences. If it were appropriate, the study could then progress to a larger scale, quantitative stage with the development of a questionnaire based on the initial findings of the qualitative exploration. Much advanced research is of this nature, in which

---

Box 2.6   It depends on how you do it

In a study designed to investigate the adequacy of a discretionary allowance paid to pensioners in a particular region, a questionnaire was constructed in which respondents were asked to respond to various items on lifestyle, spending behaviour and leisure. The results of the survey indicated that, without exception, all those surveyed experienced considerable levels of financial hardship and it was concluded that the discretionary allowance was inadequate for this group.

A follow-up project to identify areas of greatest hardship used a different approach. Open-ended interviews and small group discussions replaced the earlier structured questionnaire and it emerged that for all but the section of the sample suffering from chronic illness, the discretionary allowance was adequate and helpful. The concerns of the whole group were that responding in any other way to the questionnaire might lead to the loss of the discretionary allowance.

Sometimes the conclusions of a study are very much a function of the methods used.

the distinctions between qualitative and quantitative begin to blur, but it will be observed that we are not describing minor studies here, either in terms of cost or time constraints; it would be most unlikely for the undergraduate to attempt something quite so ambitious.

Figure 2.1 presents a summary of the case for qualitative or quantitative research, as far as undergraduates are concerned. The final choice of research methodology will depend, not on any single scenario, but on a balance of all of the examples offered. And even here there may be issues, not yet discussed, that might have a role to play in the final decision.

2.2.8 Field or laboratory-based research

Aside from the qualitative–quantitative issues discussed in the previous sections an important consideration for researchers is whether or not their work should be carried out 'in the field' or in the laboratory. This is an important distinction, and one that subsumes a number of issues we have already encountered; the decision whether or not to embark upon a field study will depend on:

- *The nature of the research topic.* Often the field/laboratory decision is made for the researcher, as when an anthropologist wishes to observe a novel culture. There are obvious practical problems in moving an entire social community into a laboratory and, in any event, the whole point of this type of research is to explore the group in its natural setting. Similarly, studies on how various sections of the community respond to changes in social, medical or economic policy; how attitudes change with successive governments; and how people's lifestyles are affected by, for example, broad national swings from public to private enterprise cultures, could not be investigated in a laboratory. The nature of all of these examples requires that the research be located within the community itself. On the other hand, the industrial sociologist interested in the satisfaction of employees working under different management styles, or the social psychologist studying the effects of group pressure on the expression of attitudes, may prefer the laboratory setting, in which the single element of interest can be studied in isolation and free from the (interfering) influence of other factors.
- *Historical or traditional approaches to the study of this particular topic.* As noted in the previous

sections on qualitative and quantitative research, there are areas that are traditionally either field or laboratory oriented. The points made above about social change and anthropology apply equally well to the tradition argument – this is the way this type of research is carried out. The same is true for most kinds of attitudinal research and surveys, by their very nature, take place in the real world. Alternatively, researchers working in the areas of perception, learning and memory, and psychologists studying elements of human cognition, will be working in what has historically been a laboratory-based discipline. For the undergraduate faced with the problem of carrying out a field study or not, again one useful solution is to consider how previous research in the area has been conducted.

- *The novelty of the issues or of the context in which issues are to be explored.* This point has been considered earlier during our review of qualitative research in which we argued that in situations outside our experience or for which there is no history of previous research, our initial explorations are likely to be qualitative. They are also likely to take place in the field, involving observations and/or participation, the keeping of journals and interviews – attempts to develop possibly a first understanding of events in a particular social context. It is only once we have a well-developed theory and testable hypotheses (possibly following on from the previous exploratory stage) that we might consider a more detailed, laboratory study of particular aspects in which we can instigate various controls, interventions and manipulations.
- *The decision whether or not the research is to be qualitative or quantitative, and the factors contributing to that decision.* Many students of the social sciences believe intuitively that field research is qualitative whereas laboratory research is quantitative. This is true only up to a point: certainly methods involving the keeping of diaries, of observing behaviour or carrying out unstructured interviews are clearly qualitative and recognised as central to the field tradition. However, surveys, structured observational studies based on predetermined categorisations, structured interviews and questionnaire-based studies, while equally field oriented, are further towards the quantitative end of the research continuum. By contrast, experimentation, the traditional laboratory methodology, emphasises measurement, but there is also much scope, even in controlled settings, for qualitative measurements. See Box 2.8 for an illustration.

Box 2.8   Imagine the scenario...

- In an experimental study designed to measure the effects of group pressure on the expression of attitudes, subjects first complete an attitude questionnaire in isolation and responses are measured as mean (average) scores across a number of issues.
- In a second stage, subjects are asked to express similar attitudes publicly in a group setting. Again, attitudes are measured as mean scores.
- Quantitative analysis would compare the two sets of scores in terms of differences in the individual and group averages, variation around these averages, amount of shift from one condition to another and the direction of change, if any.
- Qualitative analysis might comprise covert observations of individuals in the group setting, followed by an unstructured interview to explore more fully what the experimental subjects were thinking and feeling when subjected to the group pressures.

This example illustrates that, contrary to popular belief, laboratory-based research need not be solely quantitative.

- *The facilities available to us.* On a practical note it must be said that laboratory research can place high demands on departmental facilities and technical support. Not all departments have fully equipped video suites with one-way mirrors and state-of-the-art editing facilities, nor can every institution stretch to the wide range of sensors, emitters and IT equipment required of some experimental designs. Even the allocation of an empty classroom might not be possible due to timetabling pressures. Where practical constraints exist the researcher has to face the issue of whether or not their own particular research is possible. And if not, the design might need to be changed; it would not be the first time that a supervisor has uttered the words: 'It's a great idea, but you can't do it.'

To summarise, if our aim is to explore events as they occur naturally, then we conduct field research – we use real people, moving through a real social environment and doing real things. Our approach can be either qualitative or quantitative. If our aim is to explore phenomena that do not occur naturally, or that are hidden or obscured in the natural social world, then we would opt for a laboratory study. Again the approach can be both qualitative or quantitative here, although since most laboratory research tends to be experimental, the emphasis is more often on the quantitative. Ultimately the decision about carrying out field or laboratory studies has to be made by the researcher, on the basis of the following questions:

- Can this study be done in the field, and if so, what would be the advantages, drawbacks and practical problems of doing so?
- Can this study be done in the laboratory, and if so, what would be the advantages, drawbacks and practical problems of doing so?

So far we have considered the issues of whether or not our research should take place within a qualitative or quantitative context, and whether or not it should be field or laboratory based. It is now appropriate to review the specific types of research design and methods available to us within these contexts. We will start by introducing some of the common approaches.

2.3   Methods

There are many techniques available to the researcher that allow her to explore, describe, draw inferences, examine issues and so on. These research methods, as they are termed, vary considerably in terms of relative advantages and disadvantages in differing contexts, in terms of complexity, in terms of the type of data they generate, and in terms of underlying philosophies. Many of these were introduced in Chapter 1 and the sections that follow discuss these further, and offer additional methods not previously considered, with more extensive discussion of both the theoretical and practical issues found in Chapter 6, for qualitative methodologies, and Chapter 3, for the more quantitative approaches.

2.3.1   Diaries

As the name suggests, a diary is a record, maintained by the research subject or subjects, covering a range of previously identified activities or events. It is not therefore a diary in the conventional sense of keeping a note of birthdays and anniversaries, nor is it the more intense and often random record of hopes, fears and aspirations expressed in the journals of committed diarists. Rather, research diaries are records of events, activities, thoughts and feelings recorded according to some predetermined plan agreed between the researcher and diary-keeper. They can be unstructured, allowing the diarist to keep a record of events as they see fit, following only the most general of instructions about what is to be recorded, or they can be highly structured devices, much like self-report questionnaires which impose a quite rigid structure on the record-keeping activities of the individual. At one level, basing research on records kept by others might seem an easy option to the lazy student researcher, but of course this is never the case – maintaining a diary that will meet various research criteria and provide the right amount and quality of information to explore some issue effectively, requires a great deal of preparation on the part of the researcher, especially if records are to be of the structured variety. The diarist has to know what precisely is to be recorded, when such records are to be made (e.g. as events occur, at specific points, or as summaries at the end of the day), and how they are to be made. Naturally, this is impossible unless the researcher fully understands these procedures and is able to provide a clear structure to the diarist's activities. And there are other issues – motivation is an important one, since maintaining a regular diary can be irksome and time-consuming. The capabilities of diarists themselves will also have to be taken into account, since individuals vary in their level of linguistic sophistication and abilities in self-expression. Clearly, diaries won't be suitable for all situations, or for all people, but where they can be used they offer a potentially rich source of qualitative information. Moreover, they provide descriptions of events as experienced and witnessed by the participants themselves and without the sometimes distancing effects of observations, with all their potential for bias and misperception. For students considering using diary methods as part of their research the further reading section at the end of this chapter offers some useful references.

2.3.2 Observation

As with the diary method, observation studies appear, at least on the surface, quite straightforward: they involve no manipulation by the researcher, no interference or intervention; the observer simply 'observes' events in the natural social world. For this reason the approach is sometimes termed 'naturalistic observation' and makes an important contribution to ethnographic (naturalistic) research, as discussed in Chapter 1 and also in later chapters of this book. However, as with the diary method, the term 'simply' is inappropriate.

Observation studies can be applied equally well to both qualitative and quantitative research, although the nature of the observation and the amount of pre- and post-observation work required of the researcher will differ for each approach. In qualitative research, where observations are being used perhaps to provide an initial exploration of the social world, to 'discover' something about a group or society or as a first tentative step in generating an hypothesis, the observations are unstructured. Understandably so, since structure implies certain expectations on the part of the researcher which tend to run counter to the openness to experience required of qualitative studies. However, this is difficult – knowing what to record, when and how, requires training and experience. Undergraduates following a social methods course may well have sufficient instruction and contact with appropriate guides and examples to attempt an unstructured observational study, but without this kind of background it must be said that this type of research is not for the unwary, the unprepared, or those short of time. The writing up of field notes in addition to the records taken during the course of observations, plus the complexities of analysing these types of data place real constraints on the individual, as discussed previously in Section 2.2.4. Further, it is implicit in the term 'observation' that the researcher has to be there, and it may well be that in order to record effectively a process of change, interaction or long-term relationships, the researcher has to be there for a lengthy period of time. The exception is when video equipment is used, but the observer still has to watch the recordings, and using this approach raises its own set of issues, both practical and ethical. Chapter 3, which concerns itself with the processes of actually carrying out research, addresses these issues more fully.

Structured observations differ in a number of ways from the above approach. Found primarily in quantitative research, they are used to explore issues that may already have been identified and understood, and to test hypotheses. Consequently they require a great deal of preparatory work since it has to be determined in advance precisely what information is being sought – what is to be measured, how it is to be classified or categorised and when observations are to be made. In some cases the study may be so structured that a coding sheet or checklist can be used, with the observer noting or ticking off particular events as they occur. The production of such coding sheets though is almost an art and will require considerable effort on the part of the researcher, including some form of pilot research and even, perhaps, a pre-study involving unstructured observations to initially identify the kinds of things that can be measured. However, once all these preparations have been made, the researcher is able to enter the observation situation knowing what he is looking for and knowing how he is going to report it, a slightly easier task than that falling to the unstructured observer, who may well, at least during the initial stages, have very little idea of what is going to occur, and for whom the difficult work, that of analysing a mountain of filed notes, video and text, is still to come. Examples of different types of coding sheets can be found in Robson (1993), cited in the further reading section at the end of this chapter.

2.3.3   Interviews

There are many types of interview but perhaps the most important distinction, for research purposes, is that between structured and unstructured. The unstructured interview is an important tool for the qualitative researcher and as with naturalistic observation there is no predetermined set of expectations on the part of the researcher. Questioning is open-ended, encouraging free expression on the part of the interviewee and this kind of interview offers a rich source of descriptive information. In the purely unstructured interview there is rarely any attempt to categorise narratives. If this were the point of the exercise then this would come later, at the analysis stage, since this is a common approach in ethnographic studies and the aim is to learn about and describe something about the social world. However, as with unstructured observations, these kinds of interviews are difficult for the inexperienced undergraduate – there are important issues about the conduct of such interviews and encouraging people to express themselves; there are practical problems concerning the recording of narrative; and there are the difficulties inherent in the analysis of such rich, descriptive material. Having said this though, the unstructured interview remains a central and popular research instrument in its own right, and it can also be used to great effect in conjunction with other methods of data gathering – an extremely powerful combination can involve diaries maintained by research subjects, followed up by unstructured (or semi-structured) interviews, to further probe, explore and clarify. See Chapter 6 for a fuller review of this, and related approaches.

Structured interviews, as the term suggests, impose a definite structure on the conduct of an interview, the type of questioning, methods of recording and analysis of information. The approach here is often more quantitative in nature and clear objectives will have

been identified in advance of the first interviews (e.g. we want this information from interviewees; we want to find out about particular types of beliefs or experience; we want to test a particular hypothesis). Indeed, as with structured observation, structured interviews can be conducted using checklists and coding sheets, acquiring all the characteristics of a verbally administered questionnaire. Analysis here is potentially straightforward since these types of data are susceptible to conventional statistical tests, but the preparation stage, in which issues are identified, questions selected and pilot tested and modes of record-keeping decided upon, is demanding.

2.3.4   Case studies

As already stated in Chapter 1, the **case study** is not in itself a research method, rather it is an approach to social research that embodies a number of methods. As the term implies, this type of research concentrates usually on a single case – an individual, an event, or perhaps an organisation. The research is intensive, with the aim being to discover something about the unique nature of the case and every weapon in the researcher's arsenal will be needed. Whether it is the study of a single individual, a family group or an organisation undergoing some kind of upheaval, the researcher might use diaries, observations, interviews, questionnaires, in fact anything that might offer an insight into a case. We have already discussed case studies in Chapter 1 and it might be worth the reader reviewing our comments on the issues of generalisation and bias. For the undergraduate considering this approach the most obvious application is in the situation where the interest is not necessarily in society in general, or in all people, but in one particular person, or one particular family, or section of society, or one particular organisation. It remains to be pointed out that all of the reservations associated with the various methods already considered – and those that follow – will be relevant in the case study approach.

2.3.5   Surveys

As we have already intimated (Chapter 1, Section 1.3.9), the survey serves as the most widely used quantitative method in social science research. Surveys are used to offer a kind of snapshot of a section of society at a particular point in time with the intention being to generalise from that group to the population as a whole.

Clearly this is a very different approach from that of the case study discussed above, in which the aim is to learn something primarily about the case being studied without (usually) making inferences about the wider context in which the case is located. Surveys attempt to discover things about the wider society by studying small samples from that society. Usually surveys take the form of a questionnaire, administered either randomly or to pre-selected individuals (see Chapter 3 for further discussion on the processes of conducting a survey), and these questionnaires can be self-report (i.e. the respondent answers questions on her own) or administered via interview, as is typical of many market research surveys.

A researcher would consider using a survey approach if a number of elements were present: first she would need to have a good idea of what she was looking for before developing a questionnaire. This is almost self-evident because questionnaires are highly structured instruments with quite specific items (questions). Moreover, the types of response that can be made in surveys are usually predetermined (by the researcher) and might be limited to a simple Yes–No response, or to a choice among a number of limited response categories, requiring that the researcher fully understands the nature and scope of the issues, behaviours, opinions or attitudes being explored. (See Chapter 3 for a more detailed consideration of questionnaire design.) This kind of structured approach then is designed to explore well-defined issues and, sometimes, specific hypotheses, although some critics would argue that the kinds of data generated in surveys limit analysis to the descriptive level and would not provide enough information to make inferences and test hypotheses. Sections 2.4.2 to 2.4.5 on levels of measurement explore this issue more fully.

A second requirement for the survey design is a reasonably large sample. Given that a common way of expressing the findings from survey research is in the form of the frequency of response to certain categories (e.g. the number of women who supported an issue as opposed to the number of men), if only four or five people were surveyed any results would be pretty meaningless. So access to reasonable numbers is a requirement here.

A great deal of the work in survey research is 'front end', in that, while the administration phase is usually speedy and straightforward, this only comes after lengthy preparation and planning: the social issues have to be well understood, possibly even derived from an original exploratory study; decisions have to be made on the type and number of items contained in

questionnaires; decisions must be made on how individuals are to be allowed to respond; decisions must be made on whom, and how many are to be surveyed. Moreover, as this is quantitative research, a particular orientation to the data is required and the researcher will need to be familiar with a variety of statistical techniques to make sense out of survey responses. The expression and analysis of survey data is considered in some detail in Chapter 4.

2.3.6 Experimentation

We have previously examined the role of experimentation in the social sciences (Chapter 1) and made the point that, while it is no longer the central component of all social research, it remains one of the major methods. The key characteristics are manipulation, measurement and control, and the aim is the demonstration of cause and effect relationships. Not surprisingly then, experiments are located squarely in the quantitative researcher's camp and, with its emphasis on control, it is often assumed that the experiment is a laboratory-based methodology (see Section 2.2.8). The psychologist attempting to condition a rat to press a button in a Skinner Box is a common image of experimentation: the rat's behaviour is manipulated by the experimenter's use of reward; the experiment takes place in a controlled environment, in which any other factors are prevented from influencing the rat's behaviour; precise measurements are taken on the frequency with which desired behaviour is exhibited, and under what reward conditions. The aim is to demonstrate that lever-pressing (the effect) can be manipulated by associating the behaviour with some reward or stimulus (the cause).

This type of procedure is readily translated into research with people and psychologists in particular have relied heavily on the experimental approach to investigate such diverse topics as human cognition, learning and memory, child development and even social behaviour; the appeal has always been that with the ability to control outside influences genuine cause and effect relationships can be identified. Box 2.9 in section 2.3.8 provides an example whereby in the true experiment the possibility of a subject's age, or sex, or political belief affecting their perceptions of being a victim of crime can be controlled by careful matching of the groups.

Many social science students, and particularly those specialising in psychology, will want to carry out an experiment in preference to the other types of study. Electing to do a laboratory-based experiment will depend though on a number of factors:

Figure 2.2.

- When the study is based on a well-developed theory and there are specific hypotheses.
- If there are likely to be extraneous variables that might obscure the effect being investigated.
- If the effect being explored is very subtle and unlikely to be visible under non-controlled situations.
- When the issues under investigation are traditionally approached experimentally.

In addition to these factors, there will be other issues to consider, many of which have been covered previously in our discussion of laboratory versus field research (Section 2.2.8) and before a decision on planning this kind of study is taken, it would be useful for the reader to review this material. Another important issue concerns the artificiality of traditional experimentation and the generalisation problem that goes with it – specifically, if a social situation becomes so rigid that most naturally occurring elements are removed, how likely is it that our findings will truly reflect real life? Again this has been considered elsewhere and you might wish to have another look at our discussion of the generalisation problem in Chapter 1. Finally it must be pointed out that laboratory-based experiments are often demanding of facilities – whether it be physiological test equipment, video suites or even a couple of classrooms. Unless a department can stretch to this kind of support it is unlikely that the conventional experimental approach is for you.

2.3.7 Field experiments

A way out of the problem of artificiality, and a method often preferred by social researchers, is to carry out experimentally-based field research. As the term suggests, this involves the conduct of a controlled experiment in a real social setting, using real people doing real things (as opposed to performing some repetitive laboratory task). However, manipulation remains a key element here and invariably some aspect of the environment will be changed, controls introduced and precise measures taken. An education authority selecting a single school to trial various changes to the length of the teaching day is carrying out a field experiment; a medical authority comparing the effects of a new cancer treatment against a placebo group is carrying out a field experiment; an industrial sociologist measuring changes in productivity levels for a group working under various levels of illumination and incentive plans is carrying out a field experiment. In this kind of research all the key features of true experimentation are present, except the research takes place in the field. Consequently this method has provided a major contribution to our understanding of social issues and represents a continuing favourite for funded research. However, it should be obvious from these comments that field experimentation is rarely within the grasp of the average undergraduate – it is the domain of organisations, education and health authorities and university departments. They are costly exercises, in both money and time, they are potentially intrusive and there are important ethical issues involved in manipulating people in the real world. Moreover, and of particular interest to undergraduates contemplating experimental field research, the processes whereby research is funded and supported make it rare for field experimentation to be approved for anyone below the status of a research department, or without a track record of published work in the area.

However, all is not lost, for there are many situations in which the experimental method can be applied when all the requirements of experimentation cannot be fully met, as the next section explains.

2.3.8   Quasi-experimentation

We have pointed out in previous sections that while there is a broad range of methods available for research, not all of these methods will be suitable for the undergraduate. The previous example, that of experimentally-based field research, is a case in point. Few students will have the authority, contacts or background to successfully approach a school, hospital, social community or organisation with the hope of making changes or intervening in some way. This is especially true if such interventions might affect individual health, welfare or productivity. However, if it is not necessary to adhere strictly to the tenets of true experimentation, then it becomes possible to carry out what is in effect an approximation to an experiment, both in the laboratory and in the field. See Box 2.9.

Recall that one of the central characteristics of the experiment is that subjects are assigned to groups or conditions by the experimenter, or as a result of experimental manipulation (either randomly or in a manner which will control for other factors), and it is this that often causes the greatest difficulty for the student researcher, especially in the field. However, when one considers that there exist in society many naturally occurring groups, subdivisions, types and categories, then it is possible to conduct research that has many of the hallmarks of an experiment without the need to manipulate participants into different experimental conditions. For instance, if we are interested in the role

---

Box 2.9   Is this truly an experiment?

A true experiment
A sample of undergraduates is subdivided into two groups by a researcher, such that each group comprises a similar distribution of males and females, ages and expressed political belief. One group is presented with a communication discussing increasing crime rates in modern society while the other is presented with a stock market review for the previous 12 months. On completion of the presentations all participants complete a 'victim of crime' questionnaire, in which they rate their likelihood of being involved in a variety of crimes during the coming year.

A quasi-experiment
A random sample is drawn from the population and a 'victim of crime' questionnaire administered. Profile data are also collected on respondents' age, sex and, in particular, newspaper readership. On return, individuals' perceived likelihood of being involved in a crime over the coming year are compared for those in the tabloid readership group and those in the broadsheet group.

On the face of it, the above examples are similar – they both measure attitudes, they both compare two groups in terms of the quality of information available to participants and they would both test similar hypotheses. However, only the first can be called a true experiment.

In a true experiment groups that are being compared are artificially created or manipulated by the researcher. Possible extraneous variables that might affect the outcome of the study are controlled as part of the experimental design. In the quasi-experiment, naturally occurring groupings tend to be used (e.g. males vs females; young vs old), controls are often impossible as part of the design and extraneous variables have to be dealt with later, during the analysis stage.

---

of women in the workplace we might devise a 'job satisfaction', or 'perception of promotion prospects' questionnaire and administer this to a group of male managers and a group of female managers of our acquaintance. We might go further and compare our own findings to those from similar studies carried out in previous decades, or add other refinements. The point is though that this is essentially an experimental design – two groups are being compared on some issue, measurements will be taken and some form of statistical analysis carried out to determine the significance or otherwise of any differences between the groups. The deviation from true experimentation is twofold. First, the participants in our study have not been randomly assigned to each of the **treatment** groups (how could they be?); the groups existed already and, by their nature, could not be manipulated. Second, it is not possible to control for other factors – we might argue that differences in the person–job relationship might have more to do with the ages of the individuals rather than their sex; or the type of job they are doing, or the level, or the fact that the people in our study are working for different types of organisation. Consequently, should we detect a difference between the perceptions of male and female managers, any one factor, or some combination of these other factors, might be responsible. This, however, is the price that must be paid in quasi-experimental studies but, given that the approach opens up so many avenues of research, particularly for undergraduate projects, it is a price most of us are willing to pay. Furthermore, given that the opportunity exists to obtain additional data from participants (their ages, for instance), it is indeed possible to control for the influence of extraneous variables after the study has been carried out, using various statistical procedures. Some of these are discussed in Chapter 5.

2.4   The nature of research design

The following sections consider the specifics of research design with a detailed discussion of all the elements the student must deal with in the planning of any study. While more directly relevant to quantitative designs, much of what follows will be of use to anyone struggling with the complexities of both the issues and the language of research in general. Students adopting a qualitative approach, however, should refer in the first instance to Chapter 6.

2.4.1   The principles and language of design

Remember that the whole point of a design is to plan a study that will effectively explore an issue, answer a question or test an hypothesis (unless the research is qualitative, in which case the aims might be quite different – see Chapter 6). To do this successfully we need to be able to identify a number of things. We need to know what we are going to measure, we need to know who we are going to measure and we need to know what can go wrong. Most importantly we need to know these things before we start our study – or at

---

Box 2.10   Research designs, and how to look like an idiot

'no useful findings can be reported due to subjects' apparent inability to follow even the simplest of experimental instructions'

'the survey was abandoned following the return of only two postal questionnaires from a possible sample of 300'

'the favourable response of the sample to proposed increased national funding of social research had to be disregarded on discovery that, inadvertently, all subjects were delegates at the annual BSA conference'

Humorous as these examples are, they do illustrate the types of frustrating outcomes typical of poorly designed research. More attention to advanced planning would have prevented each of these gaffs.

---

least, try and anticipate them. A vague and badly worked out set of football game tactics will end in a shambles and inevitable defeat. A sound game plan on the other hand, with everyone knowing exactly what they are supposed to be doing, stands a much better chance of succeeding. Things can still go wrong of course – we are dealing with people after all, and Murphy's Law is pervasive, showing little mercy for research plans; even the best thought-out designs can end in disaster, but at least this will be less often than in the case of no design at all. The next section begins our consideration of the key components of a good research plan, and introduces the sometimes complex language of design, while Box 2.10 suggests some possible consequences of poor advance planning.

2.4.2   Variables and levels of measurement

If you have no background in research whatsoever, and if this represents your first encounter with the subject, then it is possible that even the notion of a variable may be obscure. Put simply, a variable is the most general of all terms to describe absolutely anything in the universe that can change (or vary). The rainfall in Scotland is a variable; age is a variable; different social groups to which we belong are variables, as are scores on an attitudinal or opinion questionnaire. More significantly, anything that can vary can also be subjected to analysis, whether qualitative or quantitative, an important point when it comes to assessing the outcome of a study.

In a great deal of research the aim is usually to demonstrate that one thing causes or influences another thing, or that something is related to something else. For instance, we might want to show that the rituals whereby leaders achieve political power vary from community to community; that practice produces an improvement in the performance of some experimental task; that belonging to one group as opposed to another determines longevity or proneness to particular health problems; that people's mood varies depending on which day of the week it is, and so on. All of these things are variables – aspects of our world that can vary, or change – and they represent the tools of the researcher; being able to prove that one variable changes due to the influence of some other factor is, by and large, the whole point of the research process.

The observant reader might have noticed something odd in the above explanation, concerning the nature of the variables used as examples. Undoubtedly factors like group membership, days of the week and performance are all variables – they can change. But each of these factors is clearly different from the others in some significant way: the time taken to perform a task, or the number of errors made is somehow different from whether or not it is a Monday or a Tuesday. And both of these in turn are also different from the variable that identifies whether or not subjects belonged to the male group as opposed to the female group, or whether you live within a socialist or fascist state. They are all certainly variables, but each is a different kind of variable. Understanding these differences is a relatively straightforward matter and requires merely that we look more closely at the composition of a variable, considering its components, the relationship between them and the way in which they can be measured. The next three sections demonstrate this process.

2.4.3 Levels of measurement: nominal or category variables

Most aspects of our universe can be measured in more than one way, with the choice of particular method a function both of the nature of what is being measured and of the researcher's judgement and preference. Measuring a subject's age, for instance, can be a precise thing, in which age is expressed in years, months and weeks, reflecting the true character of this particular variable. Alternatively, age can be expressed in terms of a particular category into which it falls (16 to 25, 26 to 35, etc.) or merely as an order of relative magnitude (old, middle-aged, young). Each of these

measurement systems varies descriptively, in terms of precision, and also in terms of what can be done with the information. The existence of different measurement systems though can be problematic, and a common source of anxiety among undergraduates is how best to measure the various components of a study. However, historically, this problem has not been confined to undergraduate students.

In 1941 the experimentalist S. S. Stevens presented a classification of measurement scales before the International Congress for the Unity of Science, a classification that emerged from a number of years of intensive research within the scientific community in general, and in the field of psychophysics in particular. Debate over the most effective systems for measuring aspects of signal detection (sound, loudness, pitch, etc.) ultimately led Stevens to propose four different measurement scales, varying in level of precision. The scales were **nominal, ordinal, interval** and **ratio** and they represent the classifications that are now in common usage throughout the social sciences today. The classification though is arguably incomplete, ranging as it does from the purely quantitative to the 'almost' qualitative, and this can be explained by the fact that Stevens and his colleagues were embedded in the empirical tradition with its emphasis on numerical measurement. As is explained below, nominal scales merely apply a numerical notation to information that differs qualitatively, yet there exists a further point along our continuum in which the purely qualitative can be found, as Box 2.11 illustrates.

At the extreme qualitative end of this scale, data take the form of verbal or written descriptions of events, perceptions, thoughts and feelings. Certainly these descriptions can themselves be coded in various ways into categories, making the information slightly less qualitative as it moves towards the quantitative end of the scale, and in some studies this is precisely

---

Box 2.11 A new dimension of levels of measurement

Qualitative   Quantitative

⟵――――――――――――――――――――――⟶

text   nominal   ordinal   interval & ratio

The original dimension of measurement scales proposed by the early empiricists can today be extended to include purely qualitative data of the kinds generated in many types of observational, case study and diary-based research.

what happens. However, there exist sets of procedures that are uniquely qualitative and these are considered in some detail in Chapter 6, which emphasises qualitative research. It should be pointed out that presenting measurement and scaling in this way is purely a matter of convenience. It is useful to think of information as existing on a single continuum but, as we have pointed out earlier, certain purists would be appalled at the prospect of qualitative and quantitative being viewed other than as completely different and separate approaches, and this is true of researchers in both camps. We, however, feel that the distinctions are not quite so clear cut and have expressed this view at various points throughout the text, even though we have tended to treat the two approaches separately. The rest of this chapter will concentrate on the quantitative levels of the measurement scale.

Much of what occurs in our universe can be explained in terms of the group or category to which particular events belong, and this represents one of the simplest ways in which things can vary. The gender variable in the previous section, for example, is a category variable, insofar as the components, or elements, that make up the variable are categories. In this instance, there are only two categories, but we can readily identify other category variables that contain more components – the astrological sign system comprises 12 categories, whereas a typology of political affiliation may be made up of three major parties and a handful of lesser parties.

An important consideration here concerns the relationships between the various components of category variables, relationships that are purely qualitative as opposed to quantitative. This means that being in one particular category simply makes you different (in a qualitative sense) from other categories; there is no implication of such differences being quantifiable in any way and the categories exist in name only, with the names simply supplying descriptive characteristics of each category. Hence the frequently used term *nominal* variable. Returning to the sex variable, the terms male and female describe the characteristics of subjects in each category, but make no suggestion of any intermediate, quantifiable steps between the two. They are merely different. Moreover, to suggest that the male category is in some way better than the female category would be totally inappropriate (not to mention a danger to the health of one of the authors) for this kind of variable.

In terms of research, nominal variables are used most frequently as grouping variables, allowing subjects to be observed or compared on the basis of belonging to one group or another. A quasi-experimental approach comparing males with females on some measurable aspect of opinion is a common design element, while other studies might involve such variables as occupational class, ethnic group, regional location or even the random assignment to experimental groups A, B or C.

One of the most common sources of nominal variables is in survey and market research, in which the

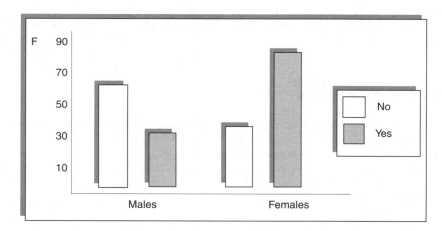

Figure 2.3 Frequency of response (F) to the questionnaire item *Do you support a referendum on the introduction of a single European currency?* for a sample of males and females.

information being sought from subjects is in terms of which particular response category they would choose for a given variable. A market researcher might, for example, be interested in people's preferences for breakfast cereal, or a political researcher might be trying to measure attitudes towards a referendum issue (possibly using a questionnaire item such as: 'Do you support a referendum on the introduction of a single European currency?'). Here, the nominal variable of food preference might have four categories – corn flakes, bran, muesli and kippers, while the attitudinal issue of support for a referendum might only have two – Yes and No (Figure 2.3).

Using the language of research design, all such variables are category or nominal variables, although the more accurate terminology would be nominally-scaled category variables, since the components that comprise them are measured on a nominal scale.

2.4.4 Ordinally-scaled variables

The previous section described the basic structure of category variables, i.e. in which the various components of a variable merely represent differences among categories. Such differences are purely nominal (in name alone) and imply nothing quantitative about the relationships among them; rather categories define groupings that differ from one another in a qualitative way. As such, they are often frowned upon by more numerically-oriented researchers, which is both unfair and unjustified since, as has already been intimated, category variables and nominal scaling provide the foundations of a great deal of survey and questionnaire research. Moreover, the use of category variables does not preclude the possibility of quantitative relationships among the components of a variable, as the following will illustrate.

Previously, the grouping of events into categories (subjects, responses on a survey item, etc.) has been expressed merely in terms of qualitative differences among them. It is, however, possible, in the categorisation of variable components, to imply a quantitative relationship. Hence, subjects in Group A might differ from subjects in Group B, not just by being different, but in terms of the direction these differences take. If, instead of subdividing a variable into nominal categories (Groups A, B, C), we use the categories of Best, Next Best and Worst, we have altered the variable from a nominal one to an ordinal one, in that the components can be presented in some kind of numerical order. It can still be classed as a category variable, but now there is a quantitative element in the relationship among the components. It is important to be aware, however, that the relationships among the elements of an ordinal variable can only take the form *greater than* or *less than*. There is no implication of how much greater or less and, while being able to place categories in some sort of order is a useful development in the measurability of our universe, it only goes a little way towards numerical sophistication (Figure 2.4).

There are, however, a number of statistical procedures available for the analysis of data that are in an ordinal format and, consequently, some researchers prefer to work more with ordinal than nominal variables. The use of ordinal categories, however, is not simply a matter of individual preference – sound practical or statistical reasons will always determine the nature of the variables to be used in a study.

Typically, ordinally-scaled variables are found in cases where subjects are assigned categories or groups on the basis of some kind of ranking or order effect (High Income; Moderate Income; Low Income; or a researcher's estimate of Most Extrovert; Moderately Extrovert; Introvert), or in which responses and behaviour are themselves ranked. Asking subjects to rank

3rd   2nd   1st

Figure 2.4 In a race between a sports car, a hare and a Patagonian tortoise, the sports car came first, the rabbit second and the tortoise third. This is an example of an ordinal scale. What this type of measurement will not show is by *how much* the sports car outpaced the hare, or how far behind the hare the tortoise came.

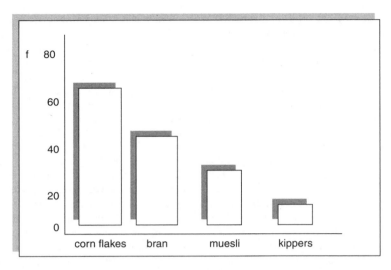

Figure 2.5 Ordinally-scaled data: subjects' responses to an item on breakfast choice, ordered in terms of most to least preferred (note: this is a bargraph).

Box 2.12

How likely are you to take a foreign holiday in the next 12 months?

highly unlikely	unlikely	likely	highly likely
1	2	3	4

---

breakfast cereals in order of preference, as opposed to merely selecting their favourite one (as in the previous, nominal example) will produce ordinally-scaled data. Similarly, when a study requires subjects to respond to a questionnaire item that offers a range of options, these options can often take the form of ordered categories. A typical item on research surveys might take the form shown in Box 2.12.

In this instance the response categories are not only different from one another, but provide a specific order of response. An individual choosing one of the categories is placing himself on an imaginary probability continuum, and can therefore be described as more likely than some or less likely than others to produce the stated activity. What cannot be ascertained of course is just how much more likely one category is than another. It is the classic school grade problem most of us have experienced at some time – if all we know is that Carol was first in arithmetic and Jonathan

second, we actually have very little information on the relationship between the two pupils, other than the order in which they performed on the test. Lacking would be any information on the magnitude of this relationship, which would considerably enrich our understanding of what actually occurred. Consider how much more useful it would be to know that Carol's mark was 85, and Jonathan's 84, or even that Carol scored 85 and Jonathan only 40. In both examples we have a far greater understanding of the relationship between the two pupils than if all we knew was that one scored better than the other. This is the problem with all ordinal variables.

2.4.5 Interval and ratio-scaled variables

This final type of variable incorporates the most sophisticated form of scale, and is often the most preferred by numerically-oriented social scientists, and certainly statisticians, due to the type and amount of information provided. Here, the components of the variable are not discrete categories, nor are they categories that are ordered according to some ranking system. In fact, the elements that comprise this type of variable are not really categories at all, but rather a range of values that differ from one another in some systematic way. By way of example, if performance on some experimental task were to be measured under conditions of varying temperature, then both variables in this study would be interval-scaled. Temperature is represented by a range of values, but more importantly, the difference (interval) between one temperature and another is the same as the difference between any other two temperatures (i.e. the interval between 14° and 15° represents the same change as the difference between 26° and 27°).

Likewise, if performance on the task can be measured by speed of response, or number of errors, these variables comprise a range of values, each of which differs by the same amount from the next. The difference between interval and ratio measures concerns the existence of a true zero point – interval scales may well have an arbitrary zero point, as does temperature, but this is not the same as a true zero, or starting point for the scale. (The temperature scale ranges from plus to minus.) A variable like age on the other hand, or response rate, has a true zero point that reflects the beginning of the scale; all of these examples are interval, but only the latter two cases are ratio. Figure 2.6 in Box 2.13 illustrates the measurement of an interval-

scaled variable, and note how this is depicted in a different manner from the previous nominal and ordinal examples (as in Figures 2.3 and 2.5).

The advantage the interval- (and ratio-)scaled variable has over other forms of measurement lies in its susceptibility to statistical analysis. Most quantitative research relies on statistical procedures to support hypotheses, validate theories and answer research questions, and while both nominal and ordinal variables have their own procedures, many researchers feel that only when data are available in at least interval format can useful analysis begin. (Note, this is not a position with which the authors agree but we nonetheless recognise the levels of sophistication possible with interval-scaled variables.) The calculation of averages, measures of spread and other valuable statistics are only possible with interval-scaled variables, allowing an impressive range of analytical techniques to be used.

2.4.6 Dependent variables (DV)

The starting point for designing many studies is to identify what it is we are trying to measure. To some

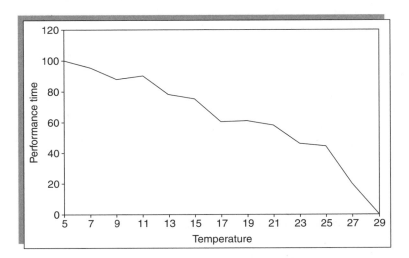

Figure 2.6.

Figure 2.6, termed a line chart, shows how the average speed of a group of cyclists covering a measured distance declines as ambient temperature increases. Both performance and temperature are continuous variables, with performance measured on a ratio scale (with a true zero point) and temperature measured on an interval scale.

Box 2.13 Interval- and ratio-scaled data

this might seem an odd thing to say – surely it will be obvious what the study is about, and what measures are to be taken, but it wouldn't be the first time that an undergraduate student has asked in hushed and somewhat embarrassed tone, what it is they are supposed to be looking at. Moreover, if the study is exploratory, the identification of issues may well be the aim of the research, rather than the starting point. Having said this though, a common way to deal with this problem of insecurity about what is to be measured is to return to the research question posed at the outset. For example, the issue of whether or not females are more prone to addiction suggests immediately that we are trying to measure some aspect of alcohol intake, drug use, or some other form of over-indulgence (chocolate, sex, shopping). If we believe that some economics tuition methods are superior to others, then we are most likely interested in measuring some aspect of academic performance, and so on. Looking at the hypotheses we - proposed following from the literature review will tell us even more explicitly what the study is trying to achieve (and if it doesn't, then our hypotheses are flawed). In the social gene example for instance (Section 2.2.5), an hypothesis might be that social behaviour in pre-school children will vary according to gender. This allows us to be more specific about what we are measuring – some aspect of behaviour, as measured by an appropriate observational instrument, using young children as subjects. These aspects of behaviour we are trying to measure are the dependent variables; they represent the outcome of the study and they provide the quantitative material that allows us to answer the research question. They are termed dependent because they are believed to be caused by (dependent upon) other factors – some naturally occurring and some the result of the researcher's manipulation. In the case of the social gene idea, the proposition is that social behaviour is dependent upon (caused by) a sex-linked gene; in the tuition example, we are trying to demonstrate that pass grades are dependent upon particular tuition methods. Remember, when in doubt, always return to the research issue and hypotheses – what questions are you asking and what are you predicting? It is a relatively short step towards identifying what *outcomes* could be measured in answer to these questions, and it is this step that identifies the dependent variables. (In fact, occasionally the dependent variable is also termed the **outcome variable**, another piece of jargon that might actually help if the point is still not clear.)

Sometimes, the outcome of a study can be measured in more than one way, allowing for the possibility of two or more dependent variables. Consider the example of a study in which performance on some experimental task is to be the dependent variable (dependent on some factor such as training, experience, attention or some other eventuality). In such cases a straightforward and readily available measure is usually taken as an indication of performance, such as the time, in seconds, taken to carry out the task. However, other measures will also be possible – the number of errors made during performance of the task, for instance. One might expect that one measure would serve to reinforce the other, which would in itself be a useful finding – the more experienced a subject is, the shorter is the time to complete the task, and the fewer errors made. An alternative outcome, however, might be that while the time taken to perform a task remains constant, irrespective of experience, the number of errors produced would decline. An experienced cyclist, for instance, might take the same time to cycle from point A to point B as would a novice, but he would run over fewer migrating newts. Had this study been carried out using only the one dependent variable, the relationship between experience and performance would not have been demonstrated. Using more than one dependent variable, however, demonstrates that a relationship does exist, although it is not always apparent. Box 2.14 illustrates the point.

On a final note, it will be observed that both these variables (speed and errors) are interval-scaled variables. It is of course possible for dependent variables to comprise any of the variable types outlined in Section 2.4.3 on levels of measurement.

2.4.7   Independent variables

The previous section identified the dependent variable as an essential component in any study, that aspect of the social world that changes, and whose change can be measured as a consequence of the influence of some other factor. That other factor, the aspect of the environment that is (assumed to be) responsible for changes in a dependent variable, is termed the independent variable.

It is called independent because any changes to or variations within this variable are not dependent upon, or influenced by, any other factor in the study. Manipulation of this variable is under the control of the researcher. It is she who assigns subjects to groups and who selects how comparisons are to be made. Consequently, this variable can be regarded as relatively independent of any other factor (except of course the judgement of the researcher who makes the initial decision on which variables to include in a study).

Box 2.14 Two dependent variables

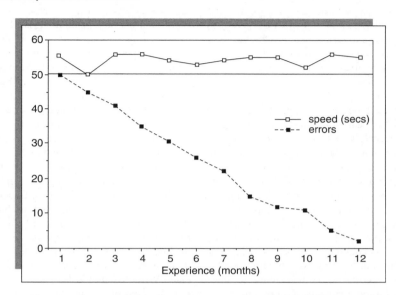

Figure 2.7 Two different effects (outcome/dependent measures) of the same independent or causal variable.

Figure 2.7 demonstrates the sometimes paradoxical finding of an independent variable giving rise to two very different outcomes. If we were to measure industrial output we might find that experience has little effect on the number of machine units produced: it takes experienced workers the same length of time to produce a unit as novices. However, were we to look at a different measure, such as the number of errors made, we might well observe a decline with experience. Alternatively, reverting to our occasional cycling example, experience might have little effect on the speed with which a given distance is covered, but might well be related to a decline in error rate, to the relief of migrating newts.

The relationship between these two kinds of variable is assumed to be a cause and effect one, with change in an independent variable producing some kind of corresponding change in the dependent one. In fact, the general aim of most research is to demonstrate that such a relationship actually exists. Are attitudes towards rises in interest rates affected by occupational category? i.e. are changes in attitudes (dependent variable) determined by occupational group (independent variable)? Do reaction time scores decline as the measured amounts of alcohol ingested by experimental subjects increases? i.e. are changes in reaction times (dependent variable) caused by changes in alcohol consumption (independent variable)? Are scholastic grades (dependent variable) a function of the sex of the individual (independent variable)? These are all examples of attempts to point to relationships between the two different kinds of variable, a process that underlies a great deal of social research.

We have already seen that a study need not involve just one dependent variable, and the same is true of independent variables. Certainly, a common design for a research project – especially at undergraduate level – attempts to relate one independent variable to one dependent one. This makes for simplicity, both in the conduct of a study and subsequently at the analysis stage, where statistical procedures for this kind of research design are relatively straightforward. However, as we are continually reminded by experience, people are complex and it is rare that any event in our world would be influenced by only one factor. The notion of multicausality implies that for any event there will be a variety of causes.

The implications for research are that a number of independent variables are likely to be at work in the determination of some dependent, or outcome variable, and it is here that an important decision must be made by the researcher: do we concentrate on one single factor that we believe is the key causal variable, and in so doing somehow eliminate or minimise the impact of all the other factors? Or do we attempt to include all the important variables and examine their combined effects on the dependent variable?

The solution to this dilemma is never easy and provides one of the trickiest challenges for the researcher, not to mention the impact on the overall quality of the research itself. Get it wrong and opt for the single independent variable design and you risk ignoring or minimising key causal factors. Alternatively, combining several independent variables might serve only to dilute the effects of a single, key factor.

Ultimately these risks have to be borne by the individual, but they can be minimised; knowing the research area in detail and building on a thorough literature review of the particular issues being explored in a study, will allow a pretty good guess as to the likely relationships between independent and dependent variables. After all, the process whereby hypotheses are proposed requires the researcher to have made a number of judgements about cause and effect from the early stages, helping to at least reduce the chances of choosing the wrong option.

The issues involved in minimising the effects of other factors are discussed in the next section, but for the moment we will take a closer look at the case of more than one independent variable.

Returning to our earlier example in which we examined performance on some organisational task, let us assume that the literature implied that, not only would experience be a factor, but that there might be sex differences also. It would of course be possible to carry out two separate studies, one in which output was measured as a function of the subjects' experience, and a second in which males and females were compared. This though would be clumsy and time consuming. More important, by treating both factors separately we are ignoring the implication that they might act in combination to influence performance, and we might miss any interaction that exists between the two. Box 2.15 illustrates the point, demonstrating that, while increasing experience does result in a decline in quality errors for female subjects, males demonstrate a dramatic increase in faults with experience. Why this should be the authors have no idea – this is merely an unfortunate example proposed for illustration purposes. Pity about the newts, all the same.

Box 2.15   Interacting independent variables

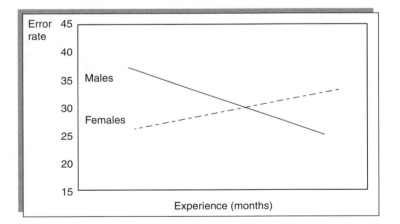

Figure 2.8.

Variation in the number of production faults recorded for male and female assembly-line workers. A similar pattern might be observed among cyclists of varying experience whereby error rate might refer to the number of migrating newts accidently run over.

There is one final point worth mentioning before we leave our consideration of independent variables. Recall that Section 2.4.3 on levels of measurement identified a number of different types of variable, differentiated in terms of their structure and composition (nominal, ordinal and interval). Just as it is possible to have dependent variables measured on each of the scales, so we can have nominal, ordinal and interval-scaled independent variables. In the newt-squishing example we have become stuck with, there are two types of independent variable at work: sex, which is a nominally-scaled variable, comprising the two categories of male and female, and experience, which is an interval-scaled variable. Independent variables can take any of the forms, and can be studied in any combination. As a further complication, most independent variables can also be dependent variables. Consider a study trying to demonstrate that stress-proneness (as measured by some form of questionnaire) might be caused, or at least influenced, by geographical area, with the driving, competitive urban dweller suffering more continual pressure than his more laid-back, rural counterpart. Here, stress-proneness is the dependent variable. In another study, however, a researcher might be interested in the relationship between stress-proneness and alcohol abuse. In this instance, stress-proneness has become an independent variable.

In short, there is a case for arguing that there are no independent or dependent variables in the universe, only variables. It is how we perceive and use them that makes the difference. Box 2.16 illustrates this.

2.4.8 Extraneous variables

While it is the aim of most studies to demonstrate a relationship between an independent and a dependent variable, there will be instances in which this anticipated relationship will fail to materialise. One obvious reason for this is that there is no relationship between the variables and that our study was based on an inappropriate premise. (Consider an investigation trying to equate the hours of exercise taken by individuals in a week to their performance in an examination. We would be very surprised to find any relationship between the two variables.) Another possible explanation, however, is that there is a relationship between the variables under investigation, but a relationship that has been obscured, or interfered with by some other, unanticipated factor – an **extraneous variable**.

Extraneous variables are so called because they lie outside the planned structure of a study – either ignored, on the assumption that their influence on some dependent variable will be minimal, unanticipated by the researcher, or acting as a nuisance factor that interferes with the planned scope of a study. They are, in effect, all the other independent variables that comprise the multicausal nature of human activity and their effects have to be anticipated as far as possible.

The previous section raised the problem in terms of what can be done with all these variables through the use of more than one independent factor; if the researcher believes that change in some outcome is determined by a combination of, or interaction between, two independent variables, then these variables become a part of the research design itself. However, if the aim of a study is to concentrate on the influence of one, key variable on its own – even though it is recognised that other factors will be at work – then all other possible causal factors are seen, not as contributory elements, but as irritations whose effects have to be minimised. By treating these factors, not as independent variables in their own right, but as extraneous elements in a study that have somehow to be eliminated, the impact of the key independent variable (or variables) can be examined.

The issue ultimately resolves into a matter of perception. In any given situation a large number of variables will always be present; whether or not we choose to treat them as independent or extraneous variables, however, depends on how we view the outcomes we are ultimately interested in. If we believe a particular dependent variable changes as a function of several factors, and we want to explore the relative importance of these factors, either in combination, or by way of interactions, then we are treating our causal factors as independent variables. If, on the other hand, we want to determine the precise influence of only one factor on a dependent variable, then all the other influencing factors have to be treated as extraneous variables. To adapt the concluding statement made at the end of the section on independent variables, there are no independent, dependent or extraneous variables in the universe, only variables. It is what we do with them that makes the difference. How extraneous variables are dealt with is considered in the next section. In the meantime, Box 2.17 looks more closely at the 'independent or extraneous' issue.

2.4.9 Controls

The procedure whereby the influence of extraneous variables on some dependent measure is minimised or

Box 2.16   Different types of variable

The following are examples of various hypothetical studies. Independent and dependent variables are identified for each example, as are the variable types in terms of their levels of measurement.

Category (nominal or ordinal) variables   Continuous (interval or ratio) variables

1. Urban and rural dwellers will record differing levels of proneness to stress.

Independent variable   Dependent variable

Nominally-scaled variable with two categories   Interval-scaled variable
(urban or rural)   (scores on a stress questionnaire)

2. General health (as measured by the number of GP visits in a year) will be determined by occupational class.

Independent variable   Dependent variable

Ordinally-scaled variable with five categories   Interval-ratio-scaled variable
(professional; managerial; skilled;   (number of GP visits)
semi-skilled; unskilled)

3. Attitude towards the provision of child-care facilities at work will be a function of whether or not managers are male or female, as measured by the question: 'Do you support the provision of a nursery space within the office area?'

Independent variable   Dependent variable

Nominally-scaled variable with two groups   Nominally-scaled variable with two groups
(male and female)   (Yes and No)

4. The number of newts run over by cyclists will be related to their cycling experience.

Independent variable   Dependent variable

Interval/ratio-scaled variable   Interval-ratio-scaled variable
(months cycling experience)   (number of dead newts)

removed is termed **control**. In a study that attempts to relate some occupational measure such as job level (independent variable) to an index of stress (dependent variable), if the researcher feels that the likely influence of a subject's sex has to be minimised in his study, then we say that the gender effects are controlled for.

There are a number of ways in which extraneous variables can be dealt with although, since the main source of such influences has to do with characteristics of the subjects themselves (age, gender, education, personality, etc.), the commonest way to deal with them is to control the way in which individuals are assigned to

Box 2.17   Independent or extraneous?

Recovery times following major heart surgery are known to vary considerably from one individual to another. The major factors that contribute to this variability have been identified as post-operative exercise; the sex of the patient; the fitness level of the patient prior to surgery; certain 'medical' factors, such as length of time under anaesthetic; certain personality variables, such as Type A versus Type B; and even the particular health authority in which the operation was carried out.

If a researcher were interested in determining the relative impacts of these factors on post-operative recovery times, then all these variables would be treated as independent.

Independent	Extraneous	Dependent
exercise	none	recovery times
personality		
prior fitness		
gender		
medical		
health authority		

If the researcher felt that most of these factors were relevant in determining variability in recovery rates, but regarded the health authority in which the operation was carried out as irrelevant (but still having a possible influence), then all the variables with the exception of the health authority would be treated as independent variables. The authority would be regarded as an extraneous variable whose effects would have to be minimised.

Independent	Extraneous	Dependent
exercise	health authority	recovery times
personality		
prior fitness		
gender		
medical		

A third version of this study might reflect a specific interest in the role of different health authorities on the speed of post-operative recovery. In this scenario, although all the variables would be recognised as being important, the major interest is in the role of the health authority. Consequently all the other factors are viewed as extraneous.

Independent	Extraneous	Dependent
health authority	exercise	recovery times
	personality	
	prior fitness	
	gender	
	medical	

groups. In the above example, relating personality types to stress, if we felt that males were inherently more stress-prone than females anyway, this sex-linked effect could well obscure the personality factor we are interested in. A simple control is to ensure that the sex composition of one group (Type A personality, for example) matched the sex composition of the other (Type B personality). More simply, we ensure there are the same number of males as females in each group. This would serve to minimise the influence of the particular extraneous variable, or at least ensure that its effects were similar in both groups.

This process of matching subject characteristics can be extended to most extraneous factors. Subjects can be matched on the basis of age, education, personality, shoe size and, in fact, almost any variable that might be regarded as extraneous to a research design. Unfortunately, the process of matching tends to prove costly in terms of sample sizes. If the only factor we wanted to match subjects for was, for instance, gender, then there is little problem: there are lots of men and women around. However, if we consider the example cited in Box 2.17, if we tried to find even just two groups of subjects, all of whom were matched on the variables of gender, prior fitness, medical factors, health authority and, more than likely, age and specific type of operation, then it is extremely unlikely that we would have more than a handful of subjects to compare in each exercise condition. This then is the problem with using matching procedures to control for extraneous variables: if we attempt to take into account the multitude of ways in which people differ, we find that there will be very few who actually share the same nature, background and psychological composition, certainly too few for any kind of valid study. In reality, however, most researchers accept the impossibility of eliminating all sources of variability, opting for what they believe will be the main nuisance factors for their particular study. Taking this approach of course allows for the possibility of key influencing factors being overlooked

but then social research can never be perfect and it would not be the first time that an otherwise sound study had been undermined by the influence of an unexpected extraneous variable. Consider the example in Box 2.18, in which a hapless educational researcher is attempting to demonstrate the worth of a new mode of learning.

2.4.10   A special case – the double blind control

There is a particular kind of control that is worth mentioning, not because it is special, or different in

---

Box 2.18   Let's eat

Imagine a study in which it is believed that there is an easy route to learning: eating this textbook (no doubt seasoned with a little salt and garlic, left over from a previous study involving frogs) will lead to an increased understanding of research methods unattainable by any other study method.

In a simple study, two groups are used, one ingesting the textbook and one studying in the usual manner (attending lectures, etc.). At an end of semester test we find that the eating group outperform the other; smugly we claim that we have proved our hypothesis and prepare to sell our new training method to the world, prior to retiring to a South Sea island.

Unfortunately, before we can buy our tickets, a slightly better researcher than ourselves points out a crucial flaw in our findings – all the people in the textbook eating group were female, while all the people in the conventional group were male. It is possible that the females would have outperformed the males in any case and this could be the explanation for their success, not the experimental treatment. In short, our attempt to demonstrate a relationship between study technique and academic performance was interrupted by something we hadn't accounted for – a nuisance, or extraneous variable.

Upset by this discovery we postpone early retirement and decide to repeat the experiment under more rigorous conditions. Again we obtain two groups but this time we ensure there are the same numbers of males and females in each, hence controlling for a possible sex effect. Again the textbook eating group proves superior and, unable to suppress a smile, we present our results to our critic.

Regrettably, this person *is* a better researcher and points out that, although we've taken sex differences into account, it so happens that all the subjects in the eating

condition were introverts, while the other group comprised mainly extroverts and the performance differences could well be attributable to these differences in personality type.

Depressed now, we accept that there was indeed another nuisance variable we forgot about and once again we repeat the experiment. This time we ensure both groups contain similar distributions of males, females, extroverts and introverts. Once more we find a performance difference between the groups and await the comments of our critic with trepidation, if not anticipation.

Congratulating us on our attempts at rigour, our critic does, however, point out that all the subjects in the textbook eating group were born under the star sign of Sagittarius, whereas the other group comprised mainly Scorpios. Incensed, we retire from educational research life and take up writing textbooks instead.

The alternative to matching subjects is simply to assign individuals to groups in a random fashion. Certainly, doing things this way allows for the possibility of some kind of bias to develop (there may be more males in one group than another, or a group may be unusual in the number of older people present), but if subject numbers are kept high enough, the influence of one or two unusual subjects will be minimised.

Ultimately the decision whether or not to match or randomly assign subjects is a matter of judgement. If the researcher is convinced there will be one or two key variables that must be controlled for, then matching will provide the best solution. Where there is no single major extraneous variable that would dramatically affect the outcome of a study, or where subject numbers are likely to be small, randomisation is probably the answer.

some way from other kinds of procedures – after all, there are only variables and it is up to us what we do with them – but because the procedure puts the role of the researcher herself into perspective. From much of the foregoing discussion on variables, it would be easy to get the impression that most of the problems with extraneous effects are to be found in the participants used for a study; their biases, personal characteristics and limitations seem to be continually interfering with the research process and it is the lot of the overworked but brilliant researcher to deal effectively with all these problems. This view, however, is somewhat demeaning of our subjects, and presents ourselves in a positive light that is more in the mind of the researcher than in reality. Of course, we as researchers are just as flawed, possessing the same quirks and foibles as our subjects – we are all people after all – and because of this, the possibility exists that limitations within a study may be due to factors within ourselves just as much as within our subjects. Moreover, since any given study is likely to concern an hypothesis we will have developed ourselves, we are likely to have a keen interest in its outcome.

In recognition of this and to control for a peculiar kind of researcher effect, the double blind control has evolved, a technique that achieved a certain amount of fame in the explosion in drug trials of the 1960s, but that has its place in any situation in which some factor within the experimenter might influence an outcome.

Visualise a study in which a new 'smart' drug is to be tested on human subjects. The drug is believed to improve learning and problem solving ability and subjects have been selected to participate in an appropriate drug trial. Of course, if only one group of subjects were used, and they knew they were taking an intellect-enhancing substance, the expectation associated with this knowledge would in itself produce an improved performance on some task, hence masking a possible real drug effect.

The normal method of dealing with this is to use a second group to whom a placebo has been administered (i.e. a neutral substance), and with none of the subjects knowing who has been given the real drug. Subjects are blind to the experimental manipulation in what is usually termed a **single blind design**. However, the fact that the *experimenter* knows which is the real drug group might lead him inadvertently to inform subjects of the fact (through non-verbal cues), or to allow his expectations to influence the recording of results. To control for this effect, the researcher himself must also be blind to the experimental manipu-

lation. Hence the term **double blind control**, with neither subject nor researcher being aware of the precise manipulation.

2.5 Design elements in research

2.5.1 Research design introduced

In Chapter 1 social research was discussed in terms of describing, explaining and predicting something about the social world we live in. The methods available to us for doing this are many and varied and we have already introduced the major approaches in previous sections. However, whether or not the approach is by survey, questionnaire, observation or interview, most of the methods used in our research will share a number of important elements and adhere to a common language of design. The exception here is qualitative research which, as we have previously stated, possesses certain unique characteristics requiring different treatment. However, for much of the work carried out by undergraduates – whether survey, observation, or whatever – the general approach will be quasi-experimental in nature.

By quasi-experimental we refer not so much to the rigid, laboratory-based work of the cognitive psychologist, but to the more general set of procedures (and this does not of course exclude laboratory research) whereby groups of people are compared, or individuals are observed and measured at different times. In most cases, as far as design elements and technical language are concerned, it does not matter whether we are using surveys, interviews or, indeed, experiments – the components of our research are the same. In this respect it could be argued that most social research is quasi-experimental, in that it follows a common set of rules. And these rules, and the language associated with them, form the basis of the remaining sections of this chapter.

2.5.2 Between-subjects designs (independent groups designs)

The most basic kind of research design involves two groups being compared on some outcome measure. Typically, in the case of a true experiment, one group receives one kind of experimental procedure (a treatment), and the second group a different kind. Often, one of these groups actually experiences no kind of experimental manipulation whatsoever, so as to serve as a comparison with the treatment group. This comparison group is then termed the **control group**, with the group receiving the treatment termed the **experimental group**. The assumption is that if both groups were similar on some measurable characteristic prior to the experiment, yet demonstrated differences after the experiment, then the change must have been due to the experimental treatment.

In a quasi-experiment the same general procedures apply, but in this instance, rather than manipulating individuals into one group or another, the researcher makes use of groups that already exist. For instance, a survey might be interested in the differences between males and females on some opinion measure, or in the lifestyles of different occupational groups. (Note: the distinctions between true and quasi-experiments have been discussed previously but if you are still puzzled, a review of Sections 2.3.6 to 2.3.8 will help.)

In the language of research design, the different groups being compared represent the different categories of an independent variable. They could be the male and female components of a gender variable, they could be the experienced versus inexperienced categories of the skill variable in the cycling example or they could be the non-treatment (control) group and treatment (experimental) groups of our textbook eating study (Box 2.18). Other frequently used terms for the components of an independent variable are **conditions** (the gender variable comprises two conditions – male and female) and **levels** (there were two levels of skill – experienced and inexperienced).

In social research that adopts the quasi-experimental stance, the assumption is that the different groups to which people belong, naturally, will in themselves have an impact on some aspect of their lives. This by and large is often the basis of the hypotheses that are being explored. In true experimentation though, the underlying assumption is that the two (or more) groups are essentially similar at the outset, in terms of something we are interested in observing or measuring, but that this will change following the researcher's manipulations. This is a considerable assumption, considering the many ways in which people differ, and it is highly likely that if any two groups of subjects were drawn at random from the population at large there would be substantial differences on a number of important characteristics among the subjects. This problem is not confined of course to experimentation, since even when existing groups are to be used, it is more than likely that people within those groups will differ in other ways (e.g. we may wish to compare a male group and a

female group, but our participants will differ in more ways than just their sex – intelligence, class, age, education and so on will all vary). Nevertheless, this process of **random** assignment to groups is the commonest way of setting up a study. However, although the problem of individual differences is well understood by most researchers, the general expectation is that, providing group sizes are large enough, individual differences will become at least diluted, if not totally balanced. This does, however, require fairly large samples and in situations where numbers are likely to be small, randomisation might produce unexpected group differences.

These issues have been raised earlier, in the sections looking at extraneous variables and controls (Sections 2.4.8 and 2.4.9), and, just as then, a possible solution to the individual differences problem is **matching**.

When participant numbers are limited, or where one or two extraneous variables are identified as having possible confounding effects on a measured experimental outcome, the process of matching subjects in the two comparison groups can be used. This would have the effect of deliberately balancing the groups on key factors, factors that otherwise would act like independent variables in their own right. Generally speaking, the process of balancing groups is highly desirable, since it should serve to minimise the effects of individual differences. In practical terms, however, random assignment is often preferred because of its simplicity and by far the majority of undergraduate projects adopt this approach. Moreover, matching can become counter-productive, if matches are sought on too many factors – the more potential sources of variation are controlled for, the fewer subjects are available to meet our requirements, until group sizes become so small as to make any kind of experimental comparison unviable.

2.5.3   Within-subjects designs (dependent groups designs; repeated measures designs)

The major alternative to the independent groups design is the within-subjects design. Here, each subject experiences each condition of an independent variable, with measurements of some outcomes taken on each occasion. As in the between-subjects situation, comparisons are still made between the conditions, the difference being that now, the same subjects appear in each group or level. In a memory study, for example, a group of subjects might be required to

Box 2.19   A perfect match

Two sets of identical twins were divided into a control group and an experimental group, with each group containing one half of the sets of twins. By way of manipulation, the experimental group was subjected to a television viewing diet of Australian soaps, exclusively, for the duration of one week, while the control group was free to pursue its normal and varied viewing habits for the same time period. At the end of the experimental trial, both groups were assessed on intellectual functioning, using a standard questionnaire. The results are shown in Figure 2.9.

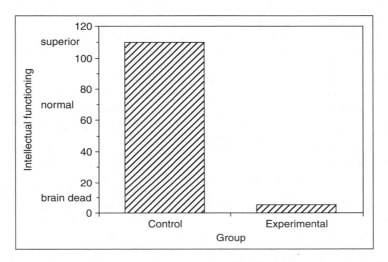

Figure 2.9   Differences in a measure of intellectual functioning as a result of experimental manipulation.

Clearly, because the subjects were drawn from sets of identical twins, there is no possibility of arguing that the observed differences in the outcome variable could be attributed to gender, age effects, initial differences in intellectual functioning, or any other significant variable. The results then can only be explained by the treatment received by the experimental group and not the control group, hence confirming the fears of parents everywhere.

recall lists of common nouns under different conditions of interference. For example, during the interval between initial learning of one particular list and recall, subjects might experience a passive activity, such as watching television. In a repetition, the same subjects learn a different (but similar to the first in terms of difficulty) set of common nouns with a more active, problem solving activity taking place between initial learning and recall. Subjects would then be compared on their recall under each of the conditions. Comparisons are not being made between different sets of subjects, but within the same subjects across different conditions. **Longitudinal** research does the same thing. A group of 7-year-old children could be observed and interviewed at this moment in time, then contacted again in five years, and then five years after that, and so on, providing a useful record of social changes over time.

The major advantage in using this particular design, and one of the reasons many researchers opt for the approach whenever possible, is that it almost entirely eliminates the problems of individual variability which represent the main drawback of between-group designs. Recall that, when different subjects comprise the different categories of an independent variable, any observed differences on a corresponding dependent variable, while possibly due to the experimental factor under investigation, could equally be due to different people being in each group: even if variation in an outcome measure is not directly caused by variation among subjects, such individual differences will often interfere with the direct relationship between independent and dependent variables.

In the memory example above, had we chosen a conventional between-groups design, with one group of subjects in the passive condition and a different group in the active one, any observed differences in recall could readily have been caused by unpredicted or uncontrolled differences between the subjects themselves. If this were considered a danger, we would have had to resort to either randomisation with a large number of subjects, or the complicated process of matching subjects on key characteristics. None of this is necessary when within-subjects designs are used since individual differences have been effectively eliminated.

A further advantage of the within-subjects approach is that subject numbers are much reduced. Even the most basic of between-subjects studies requires a minimum of two groups, whereas a similar study using the within-subjects procedure needs only one. The same individuals are used for each condition, making the approach especially useful in situations where there are only a few available subjects. In undergraduate research, where competition for a limited subject pool is often fierce, the need for smaller subject numbers might be a distinct advantage, although this must be balanced against the fact that subjects may well be exposed to a more lengthy procedure involving repeated measures.

In addition to the above positive arguments for using repeated measures designs, there are some instances in which no other method is feasible – longitudinal research for instance, in which a number of variables expected to change over time are measured, really couldn't be attempted in any other way. The alternative, **cross-sectional** approach which uses different groups of subjects of different ages, while more immediate, will most likely exhibit huge variability due not simply to individual differences, but also to the widely different age groups used. Comparing a group of 20-year-olds with a group of 60-year-olds goes beyond mere age differences, incorporating considerable changes in culture, society and experience which will have a huge impact on almost any imaginable variable. A longitudinal approach, using repeated measures, can follow the changes and developments taking place within the same group over a number of years – today's 17-year-old subject is the same 7-year-old we observed 10 years ago.

Other situations in which the within-subjects design is to be preferred are those in which the relationships between an independent and a dependent variable are believed to be real, consistent but very slight. Under such circumstances a between-groups design with all its attendant sources of subject variability would probably completely obscure such effects.

By and large, many between-groups studies can be redesigned to take advantage of the within-subjects approach, reducing the need for large subject pools and controlling for a good deal of undesirable variability. A major exception is when the independent variable providing the basis for comparison in a study is of the subject profile variety (typical of most quasi-experimental research). These are characteristics like age, gender and occupational class – key descriptive aspects of a person that place them into some mutually exclusive category. With the variable of gender, a given subject can only ever be either male or female, and with the exception of one or two remarkable cases, it is impossible to conceive of a study in which some measure is repeated once subjects have changed from one sex to the other. (Studying certain rare species of frog might allow this!) Consequently, when independent variables take this form the only possible design is between-groups. Within-subjects designs are really only possible when the independent variables take the form of either treatment or temporal differences.

Despite the generally positive regard many researchers have for the within-subjects approach to research, the procedure is not without its own problems. The main drawback is the simple fact that it is the same subjects who experience all the conditions within a variable, allowing for the very real possibility that experience of one treatment will influence measurements on another. The most obvious **repetition effect** is a practice phenomenon. If, in our textbook eating example (Box 2.18), the same subjects were used in a before and after design (i.e. subjects are tested in the no-treatment condition, and then retested after consumption of the book), it is likely that an improvement in test performance might be partially due to the subjects simply getting better at the task. If it is the case that exposure to repeated treatments, irrespective of order, results in a generalised practice effect, there is little the researcher can do, other than resort to a between-groups design, swapping the practice problem for the individual differences problem. As ever, the choice as to which design will be the most appropriate comes down to a matter of judgement on the part of the researcher, and a decision as to which effect will prove the more serious.

Repetition effects that are more difficult to deal with are those that are unpredictable. Experience of one treatment might improve performance in another condition, as in a practice effect, but not in a third; or prior experiences might inhibit performance at a later stage. Furthermore, the order in which treatments are experienced might produce differing effects. The solution to this problem is to manipulate the order in which subjects experience the different conditions, such that while one subject might be presented with treatments in the order A, B, C, another subject would undergo the treatments in the order B, A, C, and so on. This process, known as **counterbalancing**, serves to reduce the influence of any one particular repetition effect by restricting the number of subjects to whom it would apply.

There are various ways in which counterbalancing can be achieved. The most complete and effective method is termed, not surprisingly, complete counterbalancing. Here, every possible order of treatments is presented to subjects repetitively until every subject has experienced all combinations. While this is the most effective method for dealing with a mixture of known and unknown repetition effects – the effect of any one order effect is balanced against every other order – there is an obvious drawback. The more conditions there are in an independent variable, the more combinations of different orders are possible and, as the number of conditions increases, so the counterbalancing procedure becomes rapidly impractical, not to mention exhausting for your subjects.

One way round this is to opt for a partial, or incomplete, counterbalancing procedure in which the number of combination treatments is reduced, while at the same time trying to ensure that repetition effects are minimised. Unlike the complete counterbalancing procedure, each subject encounters each treatment only once, but in a different order from the next subject, and so on. An obvious advantage of this approach is that, in a study involving a number of conditions, there is a good chance that the researcher will still be alive at the end of it (death by old age or following a revolt by subjects is minimised). The disadvantage is that any interaction effects between individual subjects and order of treatment presentation cannot be controlled for. Needless to say, this process is potentially complex and there are several models for producing an effective counterbalancing design, most of which go beyond the introductory nature of this book. Moreover, few undergraduates will have either the time or resources to operate at this level of complexity with possibly the majority of supervisors steering their protégés towards something more economical. However, in the event that your own work *is* more complex than a basic two treatment, or even three condition repeated measures design, we recommend the Shaughnessy and Zechmeister (1994) text, which offers a most acceptable discussion on advanced counterbalancing techniques.

2.6 Developments in research design

2.6.1 Correlational designs

All of the foregoing discussion has emphasised the conventional orientation to experimental or quasi-experimental design, one in which the objective of a study is to explore the relationship between an independent variable and a dependent one. This relationship is usually evaluated in terms of some observed difference in a dependent measure, caused or influenced by one experimental condition or treatment as opposed to another. Moreover, such differences are invariably expressed in terms of an appropriate statistical measure, such as an average, or **mean** – such that we might state that the average number of errors made by novice cyclists was 45, but by experienced cyclists, only 15. (Extensive discussion on statistics appears later in this book.) Alternatively, we might present the results of a repeated measures study as the mean score at Time 1 = 15; the mean score at Time 2 = 45.

A further characteristic of this kind of research design is that the independent variables are usually nominal or category variables. In the between-subjects examples, differences between subjects were in terms of the group or category to which they belonged; the within-subjects examples involved subjects being measured successively over differing treatment or time categories. Returning to Box 2.16, however, you will observe that one kind of independent–dependent relationship involved a causal factor of the continuous, interval-scaled variety. Thus, rather than having a number of discrete categories to act as our predictor, we have instead a series of measures, observations or scores on some kind of scale. Equating irritability scores to variations in temperature would be one such example; the number of rail accidents in a given region as a function of the amount of investment would be another; length of post-operative recovery times as a function of the patient's age, a third.

This type of design, in which both the independent and the outcome variables are interval-scaled, is called a correlational design. In some respects the method can be regarded as an extension of the previous approaches. The range of values on the independent variable could, at a stretch, be regarded as a many category nominal variable; alternatively, some researchers and statisticians would regard the category analysis type of design as a special case of the correlation method. This is not a common interpretation though and correlational approaches are sufficiently different from others to have both their own procedures and statistical analyses.

Correlational designs are concerned with relationships – specifically, a study using the approach is interested in the type of relationship, and the strength of the relationship between two variables. Box 2.20 illustrates this.

Box 2.20   Taking the heat out of correlation

Following growing speculation concerning the relationship between incidents of road rage and variations in temperature, a researcher notes the frequency of reported traffic incidents under this category over a given time interval, and records the temperature at each observation. The data obtained are shown in Table 2.1.

Table 2.1   Showing temperature values and their associated road rage rates.

Observation	Temperature °C	No. of road rage incidents
1	11	1
2	11	3
3	13	4
4	15	4
5	18	6
6	19	8
7	22	11
8	25	15
9	31	13
10	34	20

Table 2.1 indicates the key characteristic of a correlation study: each observation comprises two measures, one on an independent variable, and the other its corresponding dependent value. Here it is noted that, on the first observation, when the temperature is 11°, one incident of road rage occurred. On the second observation, temperature was again 11°, but this time, three incidents are noted. When a temperature of 13° occurred, there were four incidents, and so on.

When this information is plotted on a graph, which is the conventional method of dealing with correlational data, Figure 2.10 is generated. Known as a **scatterplot**, each plot indicates both a measure on the independent variable and its associated dependent value. It is the practice in this type of plot to denote the independent, or causal factor, on the horizontal (x) axis, with the corresponding dependent variable on the vertical (y) axis – even in cases where we are merely assuming some element of causality between the variables.

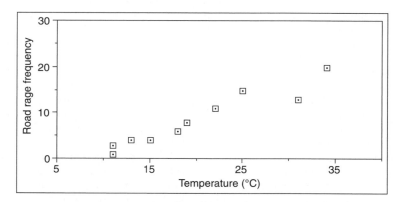

Figure 2.10   The relationship between incidents of road rage and temperature.

Table 2.1 containing the data has already indicated that a relationship exists between the two variables, a relationship depicted visually in Figure 2.10. Clearly, as temperature increases, so does the incidence of road rage.

In Box 2.20, the relationship between the two variables is of a particular kind. As one variable changes, the other variable changes in the same direction (as temperature increases, the number of reported road rage incidents also increases). In such cases we state that a **positive correlation** exists between the two variables. Moreover, in this example, because for each unit increase in temperature there is an almost proportional increase in rage rates, we can claim that there is a strong correlation between the variables. A similar illustration appears in Box 2.21, in which a hypothetical relationship between the amount of time people spend studying and exam marks is shown. Amazingly, there appears to be a strong positive correlation between these two variables, which might come as something of a surprise to many students.

Box 2.21   Amazing facts about exams

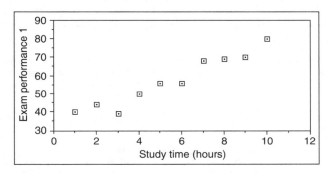

Figure 2.11   The relationship between study time and exam performance.

The first scatterplot, Figure 2.11, demonstrates a strong positive correlation between the two variables: as one variable (study time) increases, so the other (exam performance) also increases. Moreover, as one variable changes, the other changes by a (almost) proportional amount. (Note: if the change were perfectly proportional, the plots would form a straight line.)

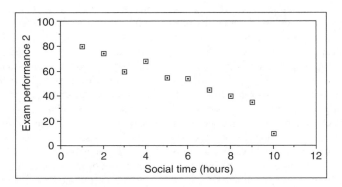

Figure 2.12   The relationship between the amount of socialising behaviour and exam performance.

In Figure 2.12 there is still a strong relationship between the variables, since as one changes, the other changes by a similar amount. In this instance, however, as socialisation time increases, exam performance decreases, indicating that the correlation is a negative one.

continued

Box 2.21 *continued*

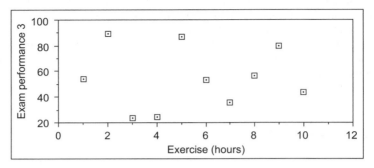

Figure 2.13 The relationship between exercise and exam performance.

In the final correlation example, Figure 2.13, the scatterplot shows a weak, if not non-existent relationship between the two variables. In fact, with such a clearly unrelated pair of variables, without resorting to statistics (which would be pretty pointless in any case), it is impossible even to suggest whether or not such a relationship is positive or negative.

Frequently we come across relationships that clearly demonstrate strong correlations between variables, but in which the direction of the relationship is different from that previously considered. In other words, as one variable changes in one direction, the corresponding variable changes in the other – a **negative correlation**. Box 2.21 offers the example of relating exam performance to the number of hours spent in social behaviour – going to the pub, clubbing, watching movies, spending time with friends, etc. Almost as surprising as the previous finding, it would seem that the more time our hypothetical students spend socialising, the poorer is their exam performance, with those whose entire spare time is spent down the pub doing worst.

Both of these examples demonstrate strong relationships, but there are many instances in which two variables are only weakly related, or not related at all. Figure 2.13 in Box 2.21 demonstrates the point, showing that varying amounts of physical exercise seem to have no bearing whatsoever on examination performance, which is precisely what we would expect.

The **correlation** approach is a popular and powerful research tool but, as with all attempts to study the social world, it is not without its own set of problems.

One of the difficulties encountered when looking at things that are related is the fact that such relationships are not necessarily consistent. Consider the case of exam preparation and the common undergraduate problem of motivation. Most students would agree that without a certain level of motivation, studying is an extremely difficult, if not unlikely activity. Not until examinations or assignments begin to loom and pressure begins to mount do many students find within themselves the ability to sit down with notes and textbook. We might then hypothesise that there will be a relationship of sorts between motivation level and examination performance, since the more motivated students will study more and therefore be better prepared. However, as most students know from bitter experience, this relationship between motivation and performance is not necessarily linear. It is by no means the case that continually increasing motivation levels will produce a consistent improvement in assessment performance. In the case of the poor student who has left her studying to within one week of a final examination (hard to believe, we know), while she may be highly motivated to study, the associated high level of stress (not to mention panic) might in fact interfere with her ability to concentrate. Motivated or not, the last minute studier might ultimately do worse than the moderately motivated student who has been working for much longer. Box 2.22 gives the idea.

There are many instances in which the curvilinear relationship can catch out the unwary researcher, especially when a study involves some developmental or age-related process. However, this would really only be

Box 2.22   **Wanting it is not enough**

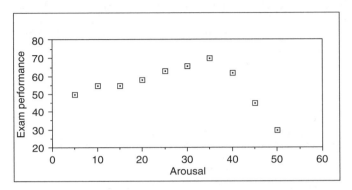

Figure 2.14   The relationship between arousal level and exam performance.

Motivation, as measured by a psychological arousal questionnaire, demonstrates a strong relationship with examination performance. However, this relationship is not linear, but curvilinear. Up to a certain point, increasing levels of psychological arousal relate positively to exam performance. Beyond this point, the direction of the relationship changes and increasing arousal produces a decline in performance.

a problem if purely statistical evidence of a relationship were sought. Relying on a numerical value as a measure of correlation (known as a **correlation coefficient**) would lead us to assume there was an extremely weak relationship between the two variables – the strong positive effect would be effectively cancelled out by the negative. A glance at the pictorial presentation of the relationship though would immediately show that these two variables are in fact closely linked; a salutary lesson indeed to the unwary researcher.

The most significant issue concerning this type of design involves the notion of causality. Normally, when a dependent variable is linked with some independent factor, the implication is that change in the outcome measure is in some way caused, or at least influenced, by the independent variable. This, by and large, is the point of all research and a great deal of this section has already been devoted to the many factors that can undermine attempts to demonstrate such a relationship. With correlational research, the cause and effect relationship is further complicated by the fact that, just because two events occur in juxtaposition, this doesn't mean that one has caused the other. Box 2.23 provides a simple but effective example of this phenomenon.

By way of explanation, let's take a closer look at our temperature and road rage example. (The authors

recognise the bizarre nature of the illustration, but at least there are no newts!) The example so far has demonstrated that as temperatures rise, so the incidence of road rage also rises. By implication, changing temperatures cause variations in rage, but to assume this would be to make a serious mistake, and one that even experienced researchers have made in their time. The essential fact about correlation is that it merely describes observations of events that coincide. This relationship though could just as readily be spurious, coincidental or serendipitous as causal (see Box 2.23). On the face of it, temperature and rage rates do seem to be related, but supposing this is an accidental relationship? We could hypothesise that what is actually happening is somewhat more complex, and that the major player here is sunspot activity, an astronomical event that when on the increase is known to have a number of effects on our climate. Certainly increased global temperatures are associated with solar activity, but what if an additional consequence were an intensification of the warm winds that sweep across Europe, Asia and North America in the summer months. Such winds (sometimes called the faune, mistral and other local names, depending on where you happen to be at the time) have been associated in the popular press with increased depression, irritability and emotional changes in some individuals. If this is indeed the case, then the increase in road rage incidents could well be due to the raised irritability levels that attend these winds. Temperature changes, while related to rage, are merely an associated – but not causal – event.

This is a common problem with correlational research, and is the result of our old adversary, multicausality. As we have pointed out previously, for any event there will be many influencing factors – some important, some minor and some that simply interfere. And correlational research is no less a victim of this phenomenon than any other methodology.

Box 2.23   Is it real or is it not?

There are many things in our universe that are related. Our mistake is often to assume that such relationships are meaningful in some way, when in fact they might be related merely because they do happen to be in the same universe.

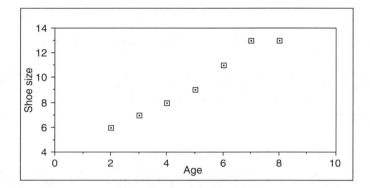

Figure 2.15   The relationship between age and shoe size.

In Figure 2.15 we observe that as young children age, their shoe size increases. Not surprising since, in our early years, the maturation process includes physical growth.

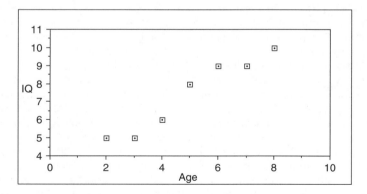

Figure 2.16   The relationship between age and a measure of IQ.

Again, Figure 2.16 shows that there is a relationship between certain aspects of intellectual functioning and age (5-year-olds perform better on some intellectual tasks than 4-year-olds; 4-year-olds do better than 3-year-olds, and so on). Once again, intellectual development is a part of the age-related maturation process.

continued

Box 2.23 *continued*

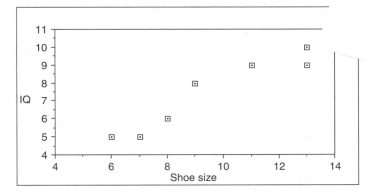

Figure 2.17 The relationship between shoe size and a measure of IQ.

Finally, Figure 2.17 demonstrates the ground-breaking discovery that the bigger your feet, the brighter you are likely to be. The authors firmly believe, however, that this apparent relationship is purely accidental, or spurious. The two events are related only because they occupy the same universe. They appear to be related because they are both surface expressions of a deeper, more fundamental process – the profound and all-encompassing developmental process that occurs with age.

2.6.2 Developments in correlational research

The procedures for controlling for, or incorporating, the effects of other variables in correlational studies are much the same as in the group comparison approach. We can attempt to keep other potential influences constant, we can decide that the influence of other factors is important and therefore incorporate them into our design, or we can control for extraneous variables statistically.

The first option is not always available in correlation research, since we are often dealing with naturally occurring events over which we can exert little or no control (this is why correlation studies are often regarded as quasi-experimental procedures). However, there are some things we can do. In our temperature example for instance, if we had taken temperature readings from different countries across the world, along with corresponding local road rage reports, we might have found that the variation in these traffic incidents was largely based on cultural factors, or other variables of a national or geographic origin. The logical solution here would be to restrict our observations to one particular location. Then, if we still generated the same relationship between

temperature and rage, we would be more certain that the key factor was indeed temperature changes, and not the geographic region in which the observations were made. Of course if, having removed the effects of geographic region, we no longer observe our relationship, then we have made a major error in judgement.

In situations where, rather than trying to eliminate the effects of one or more additional independent variables, we wish to include them in our design, then the second of our options can be applied. In this instance, instead of the usual bivariate (two variable) approach, we adopt what is known as a multi-correlational design. In its implementation this is a straightforward procedure, involving the simultaneous gathering of data on all the variables that are believed to be interrelated. Determining the combined effects of several variables on some outcome though is more complex, requiring sophisticated statistical analysis and familiarity with the procedures of multiple correlation and regression analysis. Complex as these techniques are, a number of statistical computer packages exist that deal with the process in a manner accessible even to undergraduates. However, at this stage it is enough to mention that the procedure exists. Later chapters of the book will look more closely at analytical techniques.

fortunately, opportunities for the experimental trol of confounding variables are often unavailable correlational research – usually because the variables under investigation may be naturally occurring phenomena that don't lend themselves to manipulation. Continuing our road rage example, we may well recognise that sunspot activity is an important variable in determining these rates, but if we wish to somehow minimise its effects so that we can concentrate on the temperature effect, we might find it impossible to do so: solar activity may vary continually, or may be so interrelated with temperatures that restricting observations to one particular level of activity results in only one temperature. In a situation like this, the only recourse is statistical control. If two variables are so inextricably linked that there is no way to experimentally eliminate the effects of one so as to assess the effects of the other, the technique of **partial correlation** can be applied. As with regression though (to which partial correlations are linked), this is a complex procedure and will be dealt with later. For the moment it is useful to realise that, when all else fails, some variables can be manipulated statistically in correlational research, with the effects of one extraneous factor – or even many factors – being controlled for as part of an analysis.

2.6.3 Complex designs

Early on in this chapter, the relationship between cause and effect was considered (Sections 2.4.6 and 2.4.7). The key point made was that society is complex and therefore subject to many influences or, to use the language of research design, any dependent variable is likely to be influenced by a number of independent variables. So far, however, most of our discussion has revolved around the one independent variable case, with other possible causal factors being regarded as nuisance variables to be controlled for and their effects minimised. Sometimes though we are prepared to enter the murky waters of multicausality and accept that more than one factor, or independent variable, might be determining variation in some outcome measure. And once we have taken this step, we have travelled far beyond the relatively straightforward – but nonetheless respectable – world of two group comparisons into a much more complex environment. And to understand a complex environment, we need complex designs.

As far as correlation research is concerned, the issues involved in moving from bivariate to multi-

variate research are discussed in Section 2.6.2. With studies involving group comparisons, however, although the concepts are similar, the procedures differ.

2.6.4 Factorial designs

When we take a multi-factor approach to social research we design studies that have two or more independent variables, each of which can have two or more conditions. Moreover, not only are we looking for differences between every possible combination of conditions, but we are also looking for interactions among them. This type of study is termed a factorial design, and is carried out as follows.

Let's return for a moment to our hypothetical study of newtophobic cyclists. In this example it has been argued (not unreasonably) that performance on the task would be largely a function of level of skill – with performance measured in the number of errors made, or poor newts run over. Previously, while it was accepted that other factors might also have an impact on performance, these additional elements were treated largely as nuisance variables to be eliminated or controlled. However, should we decide that these other factors are important in their own right, and that, far from having their effects minimised, they should themselves be regarded as causal factors, then we have moved to a many independent variable study. In a variant of our newt example, assume that we have identified two main factors likely to cause variability in performance – skill level (novice or expert) and terrain (easy or difficult). A study set up on this basis would be termed a 2×2 (two by two) factorial design. There are two factors, or independent variables in the study, the first of which comprises two conditions, or levels, and the second of which also has two conditions. Had we identified three levels of skill and two levels of terrain, this would give us a 3×2 factorial design. Moreover, if we proposed the existence of a third independent variable, such as gender (male or female), then we would have a $3 \times 2 \times 2$ design.

If all of this sounds unnecessarily complicated, it is because factorial designs don't consider just the isolated, or main effects of variables. If this were all we were interested in there would be nothing to prevent us carrying out a series of isolated studies in which each variable was considered on its own: we would perform one study in which performance

---

Box 2.24   A factorial design with interactions

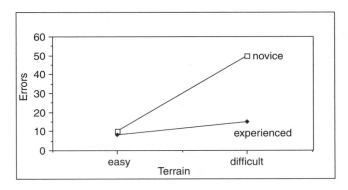

Figure 2.18   Effects of skill level and terrain on performance.

The results of our study on cycling show that while skill level is a key determinant of performance, its effects depend on the second factor, terrain. When the ground is easy, experienced and novice riders produce similar numbers of errors. It is only with difficult terrain that the effects of skill level can be observed.

---

is measured for skilled and novice cyclists, and a second study in which performance is measured for easy and difficult terrains. What we would miss with this approach is the possibility of an interaction – for example, that skill level on its own might not dictate performance, but that its impact depends on the type of terrain. Box 2.24 illustrates how the two factors might interact.

The great advantage of this type of study is that not only can we observe the **main effect** of each independent variable on its own, but also, because every possible combination of conditions is considered, any **interaction effects** can be seen as well. This opportunity to explore interactions is of immense importance since, as we have now ascertained, events in our social world are the outcome of a large number of interacting factors – and to fully appreciate such events we must have access to these interactions. Chapter 5 offers a number of illustrations of factorial designs.

2.6.5   Mixed designs

There are occasions when our research question is not concerned merely with differences between groups of individuals, or changes that might occur over a number of trials, or treatments. Sometimes we are interested in finding out what happens to group differences over

time, or from one situation to another – in particular, we wish to know if there is an interaction between the two events. In other words, we are considering a design that comprises both between- and within-subject elements.

By way of example, we may wish to explore the debate on the value of exercise in reducing hypertension levels. The general feeling amongst many general practitioners is that blood pressure can be controlled by exercise alone and without the need for medication. Less clear is the type of exercise that is most beneficial and we may wish to compare the effects of general fitness or cardiovascular training (running, cycling, etc.) against strength training (weight lifting). On the face of it this is simply a single factor (type of exercise) two group comparison study (fitness versus strength). However, as most medical and sports practitioners would argue, the effects of training vary over time, and we might want to introduce a temporal element into our study. Specifically, we want to test for a cumulative effect of exercise at four different times – a within-subjects element.

What we now have is a **mixed design** in which the effects of the different types of exercise can be evaluated in terms of the different times at which measurements are taken. In statistical terminology this would be termed a two-way mixed factorial study, in which one factor is between-subjects and the other within-subjects. The final box in this chapter, Box 2.25, demonstrates this.

Box 2.25   Mixing it up

In a mixed design, two groups of hypertensive subjects, participating in either a fitness or strength training programme, are measured over four time periods, each separated by one month. As this particular design is exploring the cumulative effects of exercise over time, no counterbalancing is required.

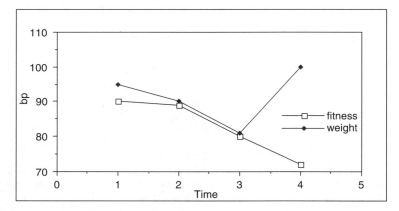

Figure 2.19   Changes in resting (diastolic) blood pressure measured at four different times.

Figure 2.19 indicates that during the first three time periods, blood pressure declines for both training groups (a within-group effect, but no between-group effect). In the fourth time period, although the fitness group experiences a continued decline in blood pressure, the weight group exhibits a dramatic reversal (a between-group effect).

2.7   Review

In this chapter we have explored the basic elements of research design, beginning with a consideration of the types of variables encountered in a study and outlining the various ways in which variables can be related. The classical designs have been discussed in terms of comparing different groups of subjects, or using the same subjects repeatedly, along with the relative merits and disadvantages of each approach, and an introduction has been made to more sophisticated layouts. By the end of this chapter you should be able to plan an effective study, identify independent and dependent elements and devise ways of dealing with extraneous factors. It should also be clear how a particular study fits into the traditional between-subjects, within-subjects or correlational designs. As a final check on how well the various design matters have been explained in this section, the flowchart at the very beginning of Chapter 2 should be reviewed, hopefully with a far greater understanding of design issues than before reading the chapter.

2.8   Explanation of terms

between-subjects design a design in which comparisons on some outcome variable are made between different groups of subjects.

bivariate research involving a relationship between two variables.

case study research involving the detailed analysis of a single unit of interest – this could be an individual, a family group or an organisation – where the focus of the research is the unit itself.

condition a subject profile characteristic or element of an experimental manipulation that distinguishes one group of subjects from another (in between-subjects designs), or one observation period from another (in within-subjects designs).

control any mechanism, device or manipulation whose function is to minimise the effects of some extraneous or confounding influence in a study.

control group a group that receives no treatment in an experiment, usually to provide a basis for comparison with an experimental group on some outcome measure.

correlation a relationship between two variables, assumed to be connected in some meaningful way. Specifically, if one variable changes, the other, correlated variable will also change in some systematic manner.

correlation coefficient a numerical value that indicates the magnitude and nature of a correlation. Expressed as a value between 0 and 1, and either positive or negative.

counterbalancing a method of manipulating the order in which subjects experience experimental treatments in a within-subjects design. The technique eliminates or reduces the effects of repetition, such as practice, boredom, fatigue or experience.

cross-sectional design refers to research in which simultaneous observations are made on different subjects.

double blind control a method of eliminating the effects of 'knowledge of the experiment' on the outcome of an experiment, in which neither the subjects nor the experimenter know the nature of a manipulation. The term 'double' is appropriate since both elements of the experimental situation (subjects and experimenter) are blind to the manipulation. See also 'single blind design'.

experimental group the group that is subjected to some form of treatment in an experiment.

extraneous variable a variable present in an experiment that might interfere with or obscure the relationship between an independent and a dependent variable.

independent groups design as between-subjects design.

interaction effect the varying influence exerted by an independent variable on some outcome measure, as a result of some other factor.

interval scale a system of measurement in which observations are made on a scale comprising equal intervals. (The distance between two adjacent units on this scale is the same as the distance between any other two adjacent units.) Temperature, for example, is usually measured on an interval scale. See also 'nominal', 'ordinal' and 'ratio' scales.

level the commonly used term for a condition in factorial designs.

longitudinal research in which repetitive observations are made on a sample of the same subjects over a lengthy period of time.

main effect the influence exerted by an independent variable on some outcome measure, without the effect of any other linked or related factor.

matching a process whereby subjects in each group in a between-subjects design are matched on a number of key characteristics (between-subjects, matched groups design).

mean a statistic that provides a measure of central tendency and is simply the arithmetic average of a number of observations. The statistic forms the basis of comparison in between-subjects studies.

mixed design an experimental design that incorporates both between- and within-subjects elements.

Murphy's Law a clichéd American colloquialism that claims that if something can go wrong it will. It should serve as a warning to all researchers to plan their work in advance and anticipate problems before they emerge.

negative correlation a relationship in which, as measures on one variable increase, measures on the other decrease.

nominal scale a system of measurement in which observations are placed into categories that differ from one another qualitatively. The variable 'sex' is nominally scaled. See also 'ordinal', 'interval' and 'ratio' scales.

ordinal scale a system of measurement in which observations are placed into categories that differ from one another quantitatively; the differences between categories are in terms of relative magnitude (greater than; less than). See also 'nominal', 'interval' and 'ratio' scales.

outcome variable an alternative term for dependent variable.

partial correlation a statistical technique in which the influence of a third variable is removed from the relationship between two correlated variables.

positive correlation a relationship in which, as measures on one variable increase, measures on the other variable increase also.

randomisation a process whereby subjects are randomly assigned to groups in a study, the purpose being to compare them on some outcome measure. See also 'between-subjects design'.

ratio scale a system of measurement in which observations are made on a scale comprising equal intervals and on which there is a true zero point. Measurement of 'response time' on an experimental task would be on a ratio scale. See also 'nominal', 'ordinal' and 'interval' scales.

repeated measures design a type of experimental design in which a series of observations are repeated on the same subjects within a single experiment or study. See also 'within-subjects design'.

repetition effects the possible influence on an observation of previous trials or treatments in a within-subjects design. Such effects can be of a generalised, practice effect in nature, or more specific and unpredictable.

research design the formal plan of a research study in which all the elements necessary to test an hypothesis are identified and detailed. Such elements include independent and dependent variables, extraneous elements and controls, relevant experimental manipulations and significance levels to be applied. Sometimes abbreviated to merely 'design'.

scatterplot a special type of graphical presentation in which the relationship between two variables is plotted.

single blind design an experimental design in which subjects are unaware of the particular experimental condition they are participating in – control or experimental. The term 'single' is appropriate since only one element of the experimental relationship (the subjects) is blind to the precise nature of the manipulation. See also 'double blind control'.

treatment the experimental manipulation to which subjects are exposed in an experiment.

within-subjects design an experimental design in which the same subjects are tested on some outcome measure at different times, or under different conditions.

2.9   Further reading

de Vaus, D.A. (1996) *Surveys in Social Research*, 4th edition. London: UCL Press.

Dyer, C. (1995) *Beginning Research in Psychology: A Practical Guide to Research Methods and Statistics*. Oxford: Blackwell.

Lofland, J. and Lofland, L.H. (1995) *Analysing Social Settings: A Guide to Quantitative Observation and Analysis*, 3rd edition. Belmont, CA: Wadsworth.

Robson, C. (1993) *Real World Research*: *A Resource for Social Scientists and Practitioner-researchers*. Oxford: Blackwell.

Sarantakos, S. (1998) *Social Research*, 2nd edition. Basingstoke: Macmillan.

Shaughnessy, J.J. and Zechmeister, E.B. (1994) *Research Methods in Psychology*, 3rd edition. New York: McGraw-Hill.

CHAPTER 3

Carrying out your study – the procedure

Chapter summary	**3.1** The role of procedure
	3.2 The stuff of research – who will you use?
	3.3 Secondary research
	3.4 Using questionnaires in research
	3.5 Special techniques for information gathering
	3.6 Using standard instruments in research
	3.7 Conducting ethical research
	3.8 Review
	3.9 Explanation of terms
	3.10 Further reading

Cries for help

- *How many subjects do I need?*
- *Where can I get subjects?*
- *What do I do if no one returns my questionnaire?*
- *What do you mean, is it valid?*

Let's assume you have now designed the perfect study, you've identified the key variables, considered everything that could go wrong and built failsafes into your plan. The next step is to put your plan into practice. This chapter deals with all the procedural details of implementing a design: how to carry out a survey, conduct an observation study, design a questionnaire or perform an experiment. The different kinds of measuring instruments are discussed, along with the related issues of reliability and validity, and consideration is given to secondary sources of measurement. Practical problems, such as obtaining subjects, preventing bias and data collection are also dealt with. And because your design is so detailed and absolutely foolproof, what can possibly go wrong? Read on…

3.1 The role of procedure

In Chapters 1 and 2 we looked at what might be regarded as the intellectual, or thinking, components of a study: carrying out a literature review, identifying research issues, designing the study and so on. Now, though, it is time to get out there and put your design into practice – known technically as the procedural part of a study. For some, this can represent a daunting moment, being the point at which all their ideas must now be put into action with all the attendant possibilities for disaster. Others though find the actual implementing of a study the most satisfying part of the whole exercise – an opportunity to see their plans come together, and the point at which real data or insights begin to emerge, perhaps providing the first evidence in support of a theory, or even the first tentative suggestion that there is a role for theory at all. Either way, the process is not without its own set of pitfalls, and what follows is an attempt to identify the common procedural problems and offer ways of dealing with them.

Exploring Chapter 3

Sections

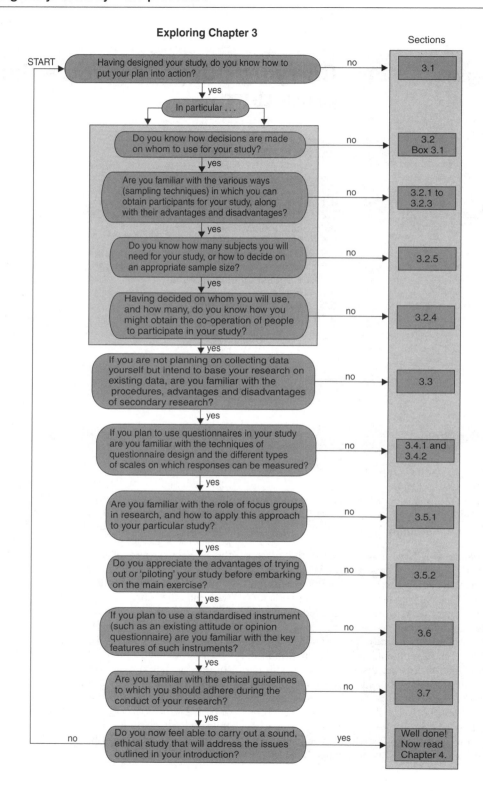

START — Having designed your study, do you know how to put your plan into action? — no → 3.1

yes ↓

In particular . . .

Do you know how decisions are made on whom to use for your study? — no → 3.2 Box 3.1

yes ↓

Are you familiar with the various ways (sampling techniques) in which you can obtain participants for your study, along with their advantages and disadvantages? — no → 3.2.1 to 3.2.3

yes ↓

Do you know how many subjects you will need for your study, or how to decide on an appropriate sample size? — no → 3.2.5

yes ↓

Having decided on whom you will use, and how many, do you know how you might obtain the co-operation of people to participate in your study? — no → 3.2.4

yes ↓

If you are not planning on collecting data yourself but intend to base your research on existing data, are you familiar with the procedures, advantages and disadvantages of secondary research? — no → 3.3

yes ↓

If you plan to use questionnaires in your study are you familiar with the techniques of questionnaire design and the different types of scales on which responses can be measured? — no → 3.4.1 and 3.4.2

yes ↓

Are you familiar with the role of focus groups in research, and how to apply this approach to your particular study? — no → 3.5.1

yes ↓

Do you appreciate the advantages of trying out or 'piloting' your study before embarking on the main exercise? — no → 3.5.2

yes ↓

If you plan to use a standardised instrument (such as an existing attitude or opinion questionnaire) are you familiar with the key features of such instruments? — no → 3.6

yes ↓

Are you familiar with the ethical guidelines to which you should adhere during the conduct of your research? — no → 3.7

yes ↓

no ← Do you now feel able to carry out a sound, ethical study that will address the issues outlined in your introduction? — yes → Well done! Now read Chapter 4.

3.2 The stuff of research – who will you use?

One of the most commonly expressed concerns of undergraduates everywhere relates to subjects: what kind of subjects should they get? How do they get them? How many do they need?

The first question ought to be a straightforward one to answer since in many respects the whole research issue in general, and the research question in particular (see Chapter 1), will probably have identified a number of important population characteristics, especially if the study is along quasi-experimental lines in which the independent variables are themselves subject, or profile variables. If, for example, a study is exploring gender effects on some index of social activity, it is clear that our subjects would have to comprise a mix of males and females. If we are concerned with attitudinal differences among university students taking different degrees, then our subjects would of course be students, differentiated by course of study, and so on.

The design section of a research project (see Chapter 2) will have further refined our subject characteristics, since the purpose of a design is to develop a plan that will answer the research question while at the same time preventing extraneous or confounding factors from interfering with the study. Since many such interfering factors are themselves participant variables, dealing with them is often enough to narrow down our subject requirements even further. By way of illustration, our gender and social activity

example had logically required that subjects be of both sexes. However, in the design of an appropriate study, we may have concluded that, if genetic factors contribute to social activity in females but not in males, such differences will become diluted over time, as boys acquire the skills that girls are potentially born with. Therefore our subjects are not just males and females, but males and females young enough for the effects of hereditary factors to be still visible. In short, we may decide that our subjects should be of pre-school age.

In our student example above, if our review of previous attitudinal research intimates that the predicted differences might require time to evolve, or crystallise, then not only are we looking for students following different career paths, but students in their later or final years.

The key to grasping the significance of the 'Who do I study?' problem lies in an understanding of the relationship between **samples** and **populations**, and an appreciation of how the event we are studying varies within the population. By population, we mean the entire set or subset of entities that comprise the group we are interested in. This could be the population at large, representing humanity in general, or it could be pre-school children or particular social groups; it could be the student population of your own university or college; or it could even be – for a neuropsychologist studying brain functions – other species. Whenever we carry out a piece of research the ultimate aim is to demonstrate that what we discover in the course of our observations, questionnaire or survey is relevant to the wider population. Of course, the

---

Box 3.1 Choosing participants

Research topic	Possible subjects
A study investigating gender differences in criminal activity.	Males/females of varying ages.
A study investigating sex differences in criminal activity, controlling for the effects of social learning.	Male and female children of pre-school age.
A study investigating sex differences in criminal activity within a mobile sample.	Male and female cyclists of varying ages.
A study investigating revenge behaviour of tailed, web-footed amphibians of the salamander family, on perambulating socially aware hominids.	Newts of varying ages.

In most instances the nature of the subjects required for a particular study can be readily identified by the nature of the research topic itself.

ideal way to ensure this relevance would be to test everyone in that population; this way we could say with a certain confidence that 'this is what people do', or 'university undergraduates behave in this way in this situation'. Unfortunately, testing an entire population (currently standing at some 7,000 million people) is just a bit impractical, with even sub-sets of this group being so large as to be out of reach, so research, even the most impressively funded, tends to concentrate on a smaller version of a population – a sample. The hope is, of course, that what we learn about the sample will be true of the wider population, and the trick here is to ensure that the subjects who comprise our sample are really representative of the population we wish to explore, an issue briefly considered in Chapter 1. However, irrespective of the size and scope of the population, the aim in studying a sample will always be representativeness: if our population contains both males and females, our sample must have a similar distribution of sexes; if there are varying ages in the population, our sample must reflect such age differences also. And if the proportion of males to females in the general population is uneven, then our sample too should, ideally, reflect this imbalance.

It is worth noting, however, that the cause of representativeness can be overstated. Case studies for instance are concerned, not with the population as a whole, but the specific object of the case itself – be it an individual, a family group, a school or a hospital. In effect, the membership of the case *is* the population. There are other instances in which slavish adherence to the principles of representativeness can generate unnecessary complications in a study when the object of investigation is not susceptible to particular sources of variation. In certain areas of cognitive psychology (e.g. testing visual acuity or responses to audio signals) and in some medical research it might be safe to assume that measures will not vary as a result of, say, sex and social class, or regional location and culture. In instances like this, while it might not be true to say that any old subjects would do, it is likely that the much-put-upon undergraduate would be an acceptable research subject here. What a researcher learns about vision and hearing, for instance, from a student sample is likely to be true of the population at large, up to a point – for even these relatively universal functions will vary with age and so **generalisations** from an undergraduate sample would have to be made with caution. Likewise, medical research on the effects of a new stress-reducing drug might make few demands on the individual's profile characteristics, since the emphasis is on purely physiological factors. When studying more complex, interacting social variables, however (opinions, motivation, stress, general health, economic disadvantage, voting intentions), when measures are likely to vary among individuals and groups of individuals, the issue of representativeness becomes central.

When research involves dependent variables that are known (or assumed) to co-vary with other factors (general health, for instance, will vary depending on our age, sex, class, etc.), the need for subjects in a sample to truly reflect the important characteristics of the population becomes an important requirement. Otherwise we would find ourselves in the position of claiming that a finding is true of the particular group studied, but not necessarily of anyone else, a problem known variously as **sample bias**, situational bias and situation specificity, all reflecting the possibility that particular groups might be over-represented in a study. While all researchers should be aware of this issue, the problem of sampling is particularly keen when research is based on the survey method. How often have opinion samples, market research surveys and political polls been discounted or proved wrong because the sample studied failed to accurately reflect the population at large? The voting polls taken prior to the 1992 general elections in the UK were way off the mark in predicting a Labour landslide largely as a result of sampling problems, in addition to a gross underestimation of the 'last minute' factor in voting behaviour. In survey research, the choice of sample is often *the* issue. So how do we ensure that a survey adequately taps the true range of population characteristics? The next section may provide some answers.

3.2.1 Sampling techniques

There are two major methods for obtaining participants for our study, and they differ in terms of cost, effort and the extent to which they will generate samples that are a fair representation of the general population. The first of these is termed probability sampling, or **random sampling**, whereby, as the name suggests, a number of individuals are picked from the population totally at random and in the absence of any selection criteria whatsoever, except – and this is a major exception – that every single member of the population has an equal probability of being selected for the sample. The advantage of this approach is seen in its fairness and objectivity, since everyone in the population has the same chance of being selected. In an ideal world, this would be the social researcher's preferred method of sampling since any group drawn in this way would be truly representative of its population. The only problem is in ensuring that the process of drawing subjects is truly random, that a crofter on the Isle of Skye has as much chance of becoming a subject as a stockbroker in London. In order to achieve this we would require an accurate sampling frame, which is merely a comprehensive list of every member of the population; drawing from this frame would then be carried out using modern computer software or the older, but just as effective, tables of random numbers. In reality – and this is a mistake often made by undergraduates – many so-called random samples have more in common with what is sometimes known as area sampling, a process of restricting the available population to particular areas, clusterings or locations. The undergraduate who randomly samples from his own neighbourhood, rather than travelling the country in his search for subjects, is guilty of this, running the risk that the particular section, or subset, of the population from which he is drawing his sample is in some way unusual; a pre-election opinion poll taken in the west of Scotland for instance would generate very different findings from a similar poll in the English home counties. Having said this, however, most undergraduate studies rely on a highly restricted population for subjects, using, for example, schools in the area, or business premises in the neighbourhood; provided the dangers of using a local population are understood – people in one location being more similar than if people from different locations were considered, or even certain rare characteristics being over-represented – the approach is acceptable, not to mention pragmatic. Most student projects are carried out for illustrative, training or assessment purposes and it is unlikely that any undergraduate would have a sufficiently accurate sampling frame of any population to apply a random sampling procedure – let alone the time, money or resources – and in reality most research of this nature will fall into one or other of the categories in the next section, on non-probability sampling. This type of work is designed to introduce appropriate principles and procedures and supervisors will always make allowance for the often suspect sampling approaches taken by students (everyone in my class, my mum and her friends, all the unemployed men in my street, and so on). Having said this, the random approach is of course the preferred method for drawing subjects from a population, especially in funded research, in that it allows us to gather data from a population even when we know little about the characteristics of that population. However, to prevent us from oversampling from a

particularly rare group, or underestimating common features in a population, sampling has to be extensive with large numbers of subjects drawn. The magnitude of this task makes the approach really only viable for major research, marketing or government organisations, with the unfortunate undergraduate restricted, as we have already intimated, to more local, or convenient populations, with all the attendant problems.

One of the advantages of random sampling mentioned above was that we didn't need to know all that much about a population in order to draw a fair, representative sample from it. However, in many cases we actually know a great deal about populations – how they are structured, the different subgroupings or strata that comprise them and the relative proportions of people who fall into the various categories. We know, for example, that people can be classified by social status, by earning bracket, by educational qualification and so on. Researchers have been able to use this knowledge to modify their sampling procedures such that much smaller samples can be drawn, in which the sample represents a smaller, but arguably more typical version of the population as a whole. The procedure, particularly useful to those involved in survey design, is termed, not surprisingly, **stratified sampling**, in which a population is divided into a number of predetermined subgroups on the basis of existing groupings or strata, or according to some predetermined design characteristic.

In normal random sampling ensuring that particular groups are not over- or under-represented by chance requires that large numbers of people must be drawn (e.g. a random sample could easily comprise a greater proportion of middle-class individuals than exists in the general population). However, knowing how the population is structured (stratified), and knowing the relative membership of each stratum, we can draw a series of random samples based on a separate sampling frame for each subgroup, and drawing the same proportion from each group as exists within the population as a whole. This is a useful development of simple random sampling in that it ensures that important (i.e. important to the research issue) subgroups within the population are fairly represented. It also, as we have indicated, means that smaller samples can be drawn, with all the attendant implications for cost.

The other major approach to sampling, which incorporates a variety of procedures, is non-probability sampling. As the name suggests, this approach does not afford every individual in a given population the same likelihood of being selected. It is important to realise therefore that with this second approach, sampling will not be as representative of the wider population as probability sampling, and consequently our freedom to generalise from sample findings ought to be more limited. Simply because not everyone has the same chance of being selected there is an increased likelihood of sampling bias whereby, for all kinds of reasons, certain groups may become over-represented. On the other hand, it is precisely this bias which, in some situations, makes non-probability procedures appealing.

Quota sampling

On the face of it, this looks a lot like stratified sampling. A population is stratified according to particular categories relevant to the research, a number to be selected from each stratum is decided, reflecting the relative proportion of each group to the whole population, and field workers are sent into the streets to fulfil their quotas. Typically, an interviewer might be charged with obtaining a number of respondents within a particular age group, of a given sex, or occupational status. Where this differs from stratified sampling, however, is that the selection of individuals in any quota group is left to the field worker. Quota sampling is undoubtedly cheaper and speedier than random sampling and, like its stratified counterpart, it ensures that particular groups are represented. However, because the approach is not truly random it is risky trying to generalise too much from quota-determined findings. Consider a field worker charged with finding 100 people in the 18–25 age category. Because they are left to their own devices in how they choose respondents, there is a strong possibility of sampling bias affecting selections. The researcher might decide to base her selections on the users of a university library – a typical undergraduate ploy – where, in the space of a single afternoon the entire quota of 100 might be filled. Much easier, surely, than trying to stop people in the street. Except that all 100 respondents would in this instance reflect one particular and unique social grouping. How typical, you might ask, are university students of the general 18–25 age group? Or even (excuse the cynicism here), how typical of the student population would be a sample drawn from a university library? By and large, quota sampling remains a popular method for exploring certain social and political issues, although largely for its cheapness and (sometimes) the illusion of control it offers the researcher. It is useful certainly for

providing a quick overview of issues but its limitations and the potential for sampling bias must always be kept in mind.

Purposive sampling

Occasionally, particular population subgroups may have demonstrated in the past an uncanny facility for predicting larger population trends. For instance, it is now recognised in political circles that certain constituencies – for whatever reason – often provide typical patterns of voting intention; sometimes predictions on the proportions of Labour or Conservative voters turning out can be quite accurate based on observations of such benchmark constituencies. Therefore, rather than randomly sampling from the entire voting population, election researchers will find it convenient to target those particular regions that have been identified as useful indicators. Similarly, market researchers attempting to gauge responses to new products will tend to target particular groups as being the most typical consumers in certain areas. This could be a specific age group, people within a particular income band or those living within a particular geographic area. Without doubt, purposive sampling runs counter to all the sage advice about randomness and the need for representativeness, yet in certain areas it does appear to work and for those organisations who favour the approach its cheapness, speed and practicality outweigh any disadvantages of a non-probability approach.

Snowball sampling

When an area of social enquiry concerns a particular subgroup with which the researcher has very little contact, snowball sampling presents a method of accessing a larger sample than might otherwise have been possible. In research into criminal cultures or drug networks, a researcher may have contact with only one or two members. Such contacts, however, might be in a position to recommend others from their group or, alternatively, they might act as unpaid assistants and agree to distribute questionnaires among their own acquaintances, with these in turn contacting yet others. This is a useful technique for gaining access to groups which would normally be out of reach of the researcher, either as a means of exploring unknown social networks or as a method of obtaining participants. If the aim of the research is to identify the structure and networks of unusual cultures this is a useful first step since it will offer insight into who knows whom, which subgroups might exist and the relationships among them. As merely a source of participants, on the other hand, the dangers of the approach should be pretty clear in light of our previous discussion. Using untrained confederates not only to select others for inclusion in the sample, but also to administer questionnaires (and give instructions and advice and suggestions, etc.) is an open invitation for sampling bias. Having said this, however, snowball sampling is a popular choice for many undergraduate projects. It would not be the first time a student researcher had sent off a friend or parent to persuade work colleagues to fill in questionnaires and complete surveys. Unfortunately, it would also not be the first time that the student researcher failed to realise how biased such a sample might be.

Accidental sampling

This is sometimes known as convenience sampling and, as the term suggests, this approach makes no attempt at representativeness at all. Everyone – and anyone – that the researcher happens to encounter in a certain place, or between certain times, becomes a member of the sample. Now this is fine so long as representativeness is not an issue, and the approach can be used at the developmental stage of a survey, for instance, when particular items, or modes of questioning are being tried out. And to be frank, it is probably also acceptable for many undergraduate projects in which the aim is more to develop research skills than further social understanding. Just so long as the considerable potential for bias is understood. One of the most irritating things for a supervisor to read in a student project is how a 'random sample' was drawn from students in the library, or the canteen, or the pub.

3.2.2   Samples – how to get them

It's all very well knowing whom you want to take part in your study; getting them is another matter altogether. In the case of an observation study in some kind of natural setting there is really no problem, since everyone in the situation is potentially a subject. Studying people unobtrusively in a bank would automatically incorporate all customers, tellers and bank staff into your sample, although there are certain restrictions on this kind of study that must be understood before it can be implemented. Section 3.7 on ethics is of particular relevance here.

The real problem in obtaining participants is that, with the notable exception of naturalistic observation research, everyone in a study must be participating willingly. Commendable as this notion is, it does give rise to problems of its own. Given the previous discussion on representativeness, how typical can our sample be of the general population if entire subgroups (criminals, illegal immigrants, or heavily stressed individuals) refuse to participate in our study – especially if these characteristics are known to be sources of variation within our dependent variable, or they are of particular interest to us. Having said this, however, all the various codes of practice governing the behaviour of social researchers are in agreement on this point. No one should be a participant in any research without their consent, against their will or without their knowledge. So how are you going to get people flocking to take part in what you might well regard as cutting-edge research but which, from the individual's perspective, is as stimulating as watching newts migrating?

For the majority of undergraduate projects, participants are usually drawn from other undergraduates (recall our discussion in the previous section on convenience sampling), with the keen, first year student taking the brunt of the offensive. Indeed, some colleges and universities make it clear that there is an expectation for students – social science undergraduates in particular – to participate in departmental research, whether carried out by fellow students or academic staff. The argument is that a student of a social science is likely to learn as much about the processes of research by participating as by conducting, providing a detailed de-briefing forms part of the experience. However, true as this argument might be, it is nevertheless at odds with the general principle that participants in research should be willing volunteers. Moreover, making such expectations explicit detracts from the fact that most students are genuinely interested in what other people are up to, and will quite happily volunteer, if only in the knowledge that some day they too will be looking for subjects.

As a population, undergraduates are often suitable as a basis for research. When projects are designed for demonstration purposes or when dependent variables are pretty universal within the population at large (not affected by age, social class, region, etc.) rigorous sampling procedures are unnecessary.

Occasionally though, undergraduates will prove inappropriate as research subjects – in situations where an understanding of certain social phenomena would interfere with the course of a study, you clearly don't want sociology students, or economists, or psychologists. After all, how valid would a study be on criminality if your subjects have detailed knowledge of the effects of industrialisation, population density and housing policy on social problems? There is also the more widespread problem that, as a group, the student population is not typical of the population at large. Students tend to be well educated, bright and highly motivated; if they are also volunteers, then you have an unusual group indeed. Consequently, any findings that emerge from a student-based group might not generalise well to the population at large, simply because of their atypicality – in some respects this can be regarded as an extreme case of a **local sampling effect**. Having raised this point though, sometimes the student population represents the only practical group. A longitudinal study, possibly one requiring repeated measures with the same subjects over a period of time, is unlikely to be popular, let alone possible, with members of the general public; fellow students may represent the only practical group for this type of research. As ever though, the decision on which subjects to use rests with the researcher and must be made based on a judgement balancing the relative importance of design needs, practicality, convenience and by weighing up the extent to which our dependent variables are likely to co-vary with other factors not present within the student sample.

3.2.3 Special groups

When a research project is of the quasi-experimental variety, that is when the design revolves not just around any particular manipulation on the part of the researcher but on the selection of particular types of subject, access to special groups might be sought. In the past it has not been unusual for undergraduate researchers to explore, for example, vocational aspirations among third form school pupils in deprived as opposed to wealthy communities, or to study work motivation among managerial staff in various organisations. Some enterprising individuals might even have obtained access to local maternity units in order to evaluate perceived likelihood of social support among mums-to-be. However, while such creative work has been possible in the past, it is becoming increasingly difficult for researchers of any stature – let alone undergraduates working on final projects – to work with certain special groups. Part of the problem relates to a growing sensitivity towards out-

siders, particularly within educational and health institutions; recent developments concerning changes in status and accountability have made many individuals at managerial level in these organisations extremely cautious about, if not suspicious of any research that might reflect badly on policy, practices and procedures. Indeed, it is now a common requirement that any proposal for research in a health or educational sphere, no matter what the source, be considered by an appropriate committee and assessed on the grounds of ethics, potential disruptiveness and public relations. Moreover, since such evaluation committees tend to meet at irregular intervals, the time constraints on most student projects make the use of such groups impractical.

Occasionally an individual might, by dint of personal background, experience or contacts, have access to groups that might otherwise be inaccessible. Some students work part time in offices, some act as helpers in nurseries or school libraries, and some even offer their spare time up for voluntary work among people with social problems. In such cases it is often possible to carry out a practical study within a special subject group, not as a result of some back-door enterprise, but simply because approval is more likely to be granted to a personal request from someone known, than if a proposal arrived cold, through the post from some anonymous source. It wouldn't be the first time that a tutor, trying to guide a supervisee towards a practical research topic, asks if the student has access to some particular or unusual group. More than a few studies have evolved not from some burning research issue, but simply because of the availability of a particular section of the population.

3.2.4 Ensuring co-operation

In some ways research with undergraduates is the easiest to organise. The population is relatively captive and most of your peers will co-operate with whatever strange research scenario you have devised. When your study attempts to survey members of the wider population, however, problems can arise. Approaching people in the street can be a soul-destroying experience – just recall the deftness with which all of us manage to avoid the desperate looking market researcher in the high street and you will recognise the difficulties. Most of us don't like being diverted from our goals and everyone striding down a busy street is going somewhere – to the shops, to meet friends, to the office after an overextended lunch; much better to catch people whose goals have been attained, or even thwarted. Waiting rooms, queues and libraries will be more likely sources of co-operative subjects than trying to stand in the way of some poor woman, laden down with shopping and children, who just knows she's going to miss the last bus home. At least though, in a face to face situation, once you have caught someone's attention, the chances are they will be reasonably happy to answer your questions or fill in your questionnaire. This is by no means true in the much more anonymous case of postal questionnaires.

Many surveys use the device of postal question-naires because they are cheap – no more than the price of a stamp – and huge sections of the popu-lation can be reached quickly. Unfortunately, the approach is also prone to generating the poorest response rate of all data gathering techniques – with one or two notable exceptions. The problem is that few people see any reason to respond to a 'cold' questionnaire; in the face to face scenario, there are all kinds of subtle pressures and rewards present which make it likely that someone will take the time to answer your questions, no matter how banal. You provide a distraction to a boring wait at the bus stop, they like your face or they are touched by your expressions of relief and deep joy to find someone who isn't running away from them. Either way, despite its own set of problems, the direct approach will usually produce a co-operative response due to factors that are simply not present in the more distant postal approach.

Receiving a questionnaire through the post lacks the warmth and human contact of the direct, one to one approach. Add this to the requirement of not just filling in the questionnaire, but also posting it back – a chore, even if a stamped addressed envelope is pro-vided – and we should be surprised that anyone takes the bother to respond at all. Most people would prob-ably prefer to expend the energy in steaming the stamp off the envelope than to answer questions on a form. The exceptions are when there is a legal obliga-tion, as in the case of the national census (there is the threat of a fine or imprisonment for non-compliance), or when there is a positive reward on offer – as when we fill in forms to obtain credit, or it is implied that answering questions and returning on time will make us eligible to win a million pounds, or when it is clearly in the interests of respondents to comply (see Box 3.2). If none of these conditions can be met then it would seem that another method must be sought to collect data.

Box 3.2   Getting a response

There are three tried and tested methods of increasing response rates to postal questionnaires.

1   **Legal sanctions**
'Failure to comply could result in a fine or even imprisonment.'
(Few undergraduates will be in a position to enforce threats of this nature. This is usually left to national governments or the power companies.)

2   **Offer of financial reward**
'Reply within seven days and you could be entered in our million pound prize draw, or be eligible to win one of our other wonderful prizes.'
(Student loans are unlikely to extend to offering real financial incentives to potential respondents.)

3   **Implication that a response might provide something of benefit, either to the respondent or to others**
'Your responses, and the responses of others in your situation, might help in some day finding a cure for…'
(A cynical sounding statement, obscuring the fact that most people like to be helpful and are willing to share their experiences, especially when those experiences are in some way unusual or abnormal. The abuse of this approach is both unethical and unforgivable.)

3.2.5   How many subjects?

In estimating population characteristics

Along with 'Whom should I choose?' 'How many should I get?' ranks as one of the most common ques-tions asked of tutors. Unfortunately most students are constantly surprised at how such an apparently simple question should stimulate such a variety of complex and sometimes unhelpful responses. 'It depends' is probably the most common response, along with the equally enigmatic 'How many can you get?' Clearly this is not a simple issue, and the following discussion is an attempt to explain the difficulties in, and offer some solutions to, the vexed problem of determining sample size.

What every undergraduate wants to know, of course, is how big should their sample be. They want a number; they want to be told something like, '50 is the number of questionnaire responses (or interviews,

---

Box 3.3 Size doesn't matter

(rumour spread by researchers with small samples)

In an ideal world sample sizes (n) can be precisely calculated, providing that certain things are known by the researcher:

1 The extent to which what we are interested in varies within the population (a measurement known as the standard deviation, SD or σ).
2 The margin of error we are prepared to tolerate when generalising from our sample to the population (me).
3 The level of confidence we require in our estimates of the population (z).

This is worked out using the following formula (apologies, but we really can't do this without some numbers):

$$n = \left(\frac{z \times \sigma}{me}\right)^2$$

Imagine the following scenario. Our continuing interest in the habits of undergraduates (see Chapter 2, Box 2.21, 'Amazing facts about exams') leads us to explore how much time, on average, social science students spend socialising (in the pub, clubbing, with friends, etc.). We

are prepared to accept a margin of error (me) of 1 hour either way and we want to be 95% confident that our estimate will be accurate (i.e. we are prepared to accept that, not only might our estimate be out by 1 hour, but that there is a 5% chance that it will be completely wrong anyway). Assuming we know (don't ask) that socialising time varies within the population with a standard deviation of 4 hours, all of this translates into the following:

$$z = 1.96; \text{SD or } \sigma = 4; me = 1$$

(You will be wondering where on earth we picked this number for z from. In statistical terms confidence can be expressed either as a percentage (95%) or as a transformed z-score ($z = 1.96$). A look at Chapter 4 and our discussion on the normal distribution should make this clearer.)
The formula then becomes:

$$n = \left(\frac{1.96 \times 4}{1}\right)^2 = 7.84^2 = 61.5$$

In other words, given our requirements and the information available, we need 62 students in our sample.

---

or experimental subjects) you need for this study'. Or, to translate from the language of research into the language of student angst, they want to know, 'How many do I need to make this a good study, to get me a good mark', or, 'Just how hard will I have to work?' However, it is simply not possible to answer these questions readily because, as we have said above, it really does depend. It depends on the following factors: level of variability in the population, margin of error and level of confidence.

Any social issue will be characterised by *variability* – be it opinions, actions, beliefs, rituals and so on. This is expected due to the complexity of modern society and the people who inhabit it: opinion on any issue, for instance, will vary depending on age, sex, occupation, income, ethnic background, political affiliation, geographic location, level of industrialisation, other attitudes and so on and so on. This is an extensive list of factors that could influence any number of social issues, and this is only the tip of the iceberg. The point is that if we are hoping to draw a representative sample from a population in which there is considerable variability, then to take this level of variation into account, our sample has to be pretty big. The opposite of course is also true. If what we are interested in is subject to few influences and there is consequently very little variability

in the population, then samples can be smaller. To recall an earlier example, if we were studying cloned newts, where every member of the population was identical and there was therefore no variability whatsoever, then a sample of one would suffice. If our identical newts had been brought up in differing environments, however, we would need more in order to allow for this and, as the possible sources of variability increased, so too would our need for bigger and bigger samples. Consider Box 3.3; the example here shows a formula-based method for estimating sample size (be reassured, this is the only formula that appears in the book) in which variance – the extent to which some aspect of the population varies – is a key element. In our example, what we are interested in (social time) varies on average by only about four hours within the student population. However, if we had found that there was more variation in the amount of time students spent at the pub, or wherever, producing a standard deviation (a measure of variability) of six hours, then our sample size would have to be larger. In fact, the formula would require 138 participants for our study. (You might want to try this relatively simple calculation for yourselves, by substituting the value 6 for the existing value of 4 in the formula in Box 3.3.)

Margin of error is another important determinant of sample size. Whenever a sample is used to estimate some aspect of a population (in a nutritional study we might measure the heights of a sample of pre-school children and estimate average height within the population, for instance), there will always be some difference between the two measures – that of the sample and the actual population parameter – causing error in our population estimates. This margin of error, sometimes known as sampling error, is susceptible to sample size, such that the larger our sample, the smaller our margin of error (the difference between the sample and population characteristics). The reason for this should be becoming clear now in light of our previous discussions on samples. When something varies within the population (there are short people and there are tall people, for example) a small sample might easily over-represent some elements to the detriment of others.

'I have bad news – the human race is shrinking!'
'Ah, no – there are only seven people in your sample, and as it happens none of them is over four feet.'
'Ooh, right!'

With larger samples, extremes will be evened out, sampling bias reduced and the character of the sample will assume a closer and closer approximation to the population. Return again to our example in Box 3.3. We had originally stated that we were prepared to accept a margin of error of one hour in our study on student activity. Supposing we wanted to be more precise and required that our sample predictions came much closer to the character of the whole population: supposing we wanted to reduce our margin of error to 0.5 of an hour. Substituting this new value in our formula would require a dramatic increase in sample size to 245. This in fact represents a general rule in sampling. Whenever we wish to reduce our margin of error by half, we need to quadruple our sample size – a daunting requirement for any researcher.

Level of confidence is the remaining factor in the issue of sample size. An important element of all social research concerns the confidence we have in our research findings. Historically the convention has been to express this in terms of percentages, as in: 'We are 90% confident that this finding is true; that this difference is real', and so on. Another way of looking at this is we are confident that in 90 cases out of 100, this prediction would be supported, or this difference would be observed. Of course, the converse would be to admit that 10% of the time our findings would not be supported, and indeed much research reports its findings in this manner – as in an effect being observed as

significant (real, meaningful) at the 10% level (sometimes expressed as the 0.10 significance level). Over the years social scientists have come to accept that a 95% confidence level is sufficiently rigorous for most applications. Sure, they could be wrong in their claims 5% of the time, but by and large this is seen as an acceptable risk. Occasionally though – when there is risk to life in making a mistake or serious money could be lost by, for instance, implementing potentially damaging policies on the basis of research findings – a researcher wants to reduce the possibility of being wrong. In this instance a confidence level of 99% may be adopted, reducing the possibility of making an inappropriate judgement to 1%. There is, though, a price to be paid. Consider again the example in Box 3.3. Here the confidence level has been set at the usual 95%. Note that this is expressed as the value 1.96, which might seem a little odd but merely represents the transformation of values from a percentage scale to a different scale (known as a z-scale). The process is fully discussed in Chapter 4 and if this current section has lost you it might be worth having a look ahead to our consideration of distributions and z-scores. Otherwise, read on.

A 95% confidence level, when transformed into a different kind of scale (z-score), produces a value of 1.96, and this is the value found in our formula. Increasing our confidence level to 99% would result in a corresponding z-score of 2.58 (trust us) which, when substituted into the formula, would generate a value for n of 107. In other words, if the same study were carried out but the researcher wanted to be extra certain of not making a mistake, he would need a sample size of 107. And finally, if we were to put all of these things together, a measure of variation of 6 hours in social time, a margin of error of only 0.5 hours and a confidence level of 99%, we would need a sample size of:

$$n = \left(\frac{2.58 \times 6}{0.5}\right)^2 = 30.96^2 = 959$$

Clearly the estimation of sample size for any study is a complicated thing. There are a number of elements that have to be considered and as each one varies there is a direct, knock-on effect on sample size. However, the deeper thinkers among our readers may be feeling a little uncomfortable about the previous discussion. How, you might well ask, are we able to include a measure of population variation in our formula when surely the whole point of studying samples is to estimate such population characteristics? Well, it is possible to approximate a measure of population variation by looking at the sample (if what we are interested in varies dramatically within our sample it's a safe bet this will be true of the population also), but by then we have already carried out our study and the question of sample size becomes spurious. So how do researchers get round this?

One solution is to carry out a small-scale, pilot study in which the sample variation can be used as a basis for estimating the variation in the population. We can then apply our formula prior to the full-scale study. This of course takes time and money and besides, to obtain a reasonable estimate from the sample it would have to be of a reasonable size, bringing into question the need to repeat the exercise at all. In reality, much funded research tends to adopt rule of thumb guides to sampling and many of the major survey organisations accept a sample of 1,000 as being acceptable – it is a manageable number (for a large research group), it ought to be representative and any more than this has a minimal impact on margin of error.

For undergraduates it should be apparent that these guidelines on sampling will be inappropriate. No student will be able to gain access to 1,000 possible respondents and the formula for estimating sample size contains too many unknowns. Which is why, returning to the introduction to this section, when a student asks a supervisor, 'How many should I get?' the response is most likely to be, 'How many can you get?' By and large most undergraduate research is carried out using inappropriate samples. We have already intimated that this inappropriateness will be partly due to unrepresentativeness (see Section 3.2.1 on sampling techniques). Now we can add to this the issue of inappropriate sample sizes. Practical constraints and the nature of this kind of research make it unlikely that the average student project will have anything like a suitable sample size but then, arguably, given the function of this work at undergraduate level, does it really matter?

Most undergraduate research is carried out for the purposes of demonstration, illustration and the gaining of experience and it is accepted that samples will be neither representative nor sufficiently large. What is important, however, is that students understand this, that they are aware that findings must be expressed with reservations and that whatever is noted about the sample is unlikely to be true of the population as a whole (see Box 3.4). And having said all of this, it remains for us now to stick our necks out. How many participants should you aim for in your study? A minimum of 30. Unless, of course, your research is

---

Box 3.4   ...with reservations

No piece of research is ever perfect and the researchers will always have some doubts about the accuracy or relevance of their findings. They may not always say so and many a government department or political party has fudged statistics to suit their own ends. In undergraduate research, however, one of the important functions of reporting findings is to demonstrate that you understand the limitations of your work. Whether or not a study has unearthed anything remarkable or even noteworthy, is largely irrelevant. What is important, and what you will be assessed on, is the extent to which you displayed initiative, you were objective and systematic, your approach was ethical and that you were aware of the problems and limitations of the research.

Although the findings of this survey indicated extreme attitudes in the area of new police powers of arrest, the process whereby respondents were drawn raises concerns about how far these results can be generalised: undoubtedly a local sampling effect was present and analysis of the characteristics of participants indicated that four important ethnic groups were not represented. Nor were there any females. Furthermore, given that the sample size was limited to 10, it is clear that findings are likely to be relevant only to this group and not typical of the population as a whole. The range of attitudes expressed within the sample does suggest that the issue generates many viewpoints within the population and that to estimate attitudes reliably here would require a truly random sample of 1,000.

---

qualitative in nature, then different rules apply. Or you intend to conduct a case study, in which case the sample size is determined by the characteristics of the case itself.

Sample size in hypothesis testing

When the purpose of a study is to test specific hypotheses, most of the above discussion on sample sizes applies. Thus, if we aimed to compare two groups on some measure (we might compare a group of unskilled workers with a managerial group on some measure of general health with a view to exploring an hypothesis about the relationship between occupational status and health), we would wish to ensure that both samples were truly representative of their populations, both in terms of number and type. Consequently, all the sampling issues we have already considered above – variability, level of confidence, etc. – are relevant here. We would want to demonstrate that when we support or reject an hypothesis (e.g. that there is no significant difference on a measure of general health between a sample of unskilled and a sample of managerial workers) that this finding is true of the population as a whole, and not merely of the particular groups we sampled in our study. In practice, however, few researchers – and certainly not undergraduates – will draw the usually large numbers of individuals for their study required by conventional sampling guidelines. Instead, they consider the amount of variability in the population and the type of analytical test that will be used to determine whether or not an effect is present (some tests are better than others) and defend this in terms of **power**. There are calculations available to determine precisely how powerful a research procedure is – similar in many ways to our earlier calculations for estimating sample size – and power can be explained simply as the extent to which a procedure or a specific test will correctly identify a significant difference (or effect) where one really exists. It is not our intention to say much more on this topic – power calculations can be complex and are better suited to specialist texts in the area. Any of the statistics texts referred to in our further reading sections should deal with these issues effectively.

It is sufficient for us to make the point that if a study uses only 10 participants in each comparison group we would be less likely to demonstrate the existence of an effect (a difference between the groups, for instance) than if each of our samples comprised 20, or even 30 subjects (see Box 3.5, and accept our apologies in

Box 3.5 Something fishy about statistical tests...

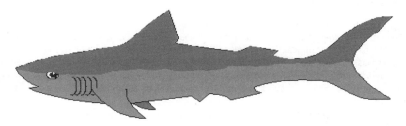

Some statistical tests are more powerful than others in that, with the same information available, one test would say: 'Sorry, mate, nothing doing'; while another might say: 'You're in luck'. Consider the slightly spurious example (though of personal interest to the authors and keen fishermen everywhere) of two groups of trout fishermen working the same stretch of a waterway, but using different lures. The Morpeth to Newcastle-upon-Tyne waterway team are fishing with multicoloured lures, while the Forth and Clyde canal team are using monochromatic bait. Each member is timed on how long it takes to land the first trout and the average times of each group are compared. What we want to know is, if there is a difference between the average catch times (there nearly always is), is this due to a real effect of the different lures, or is this just a chance effect?

For the sake of this example, let's assume the team using the multicoloured lure took on average 3.4 minutes before landing a catch, whereas the monochrome group took 4.6 minutes. One type of test, the Mann-Whitney U test, when finished its little calculations, would claim that this difference was so large that it could not be explained as a chance event. A more powerful test, such as the Student's t-test, would argue that this difference between the average times, based on the number of participants in each group, is easily explained away as a purely chance thing, and that the type of lure made no real (statistically significant) difference. The table below gives the numbers:

Test	Statistic	Probability	Decision
Mann-Whitney U test	$U = 19$	$p = 0.018$	significant difference
t-test	$t = 1.88$	$p = 0.077$	non-sign. difference

Clearly then, demonstrating that an effect or an event is present or not is far from being an exact science. As we have been at pains to mention elsewhere, it depends...

advance). Similarly, research among statisticians demonstrates that using one particular kind of test to demonstrate some effect, such as the *t*-test, will be more likely to demonstrate an effect where one exists, than if another kind of test were used, such as the Mann-Whitney *U* test. Put simply, a study that uses a larger sample will be more powerful than one based on small numbers; a study that uses one kind of statistical test can be more powerful than one that uses a different form of analysis.

Again, in practice, research that aims to test hypotheses can be carried out with relatively small sample sizes. As a general rule you don't want to drop below 30 participants per group, but in fact most statistical tests will allow analyses to be carried out using many fewer, although as sample sizes decline, the chances of correctly identifying a finding also reduce.

See Chapter 5 for illustrations of some of the common forms of analysis and Box 3.6 below for an illustration of the above discussion.

It remains to say that, while most undergraduate studies will not be powerful (in that sampling procedures might be convenient rather than conforming to the requirements of probability research, and sizes will usually be small), it is still expected in any report that these issues are raised, and that the student makes it clear that the limitations of their particular research are well understood. It is also worth mentioning that by the time the junior researcher embarks upon funded social research there will be an expectation of a clear statement of how powerful this research is. After all, if someone is paying you good money they have a right to know how useful (accurate, relevant, valid, powerful) your findings are likely to be.

Box 3.6   The healthy alternative

Imagine a study in which we are examining differences in general health between skilled and managerial workers. We may have postulated that managerial workers earn more, have a better lifestyle and more interesting work than the skilled workforce. Consequently, on a self-rating scale on which individuals are asked to rate their perceived level of health over the previous 12 months, we might hypothesise that average scores of general health will be significantly higher for the managerial group than the skilled group. (By significant we mean that the difference is sufficiently large, or consistent, so as not to be explained away as a purely chance effect. See Chapter 4 for the relevant discussion on probability and statistical significance.)

If we worked with two extremely small samples – say, 5 managers and 5 skilled workers – and observed a difference between their average health ratings of 5.0 and 4.2 respectively, we might feel that with such small numbers of subjects this difference is not meaningful, and could well be explained away by all sorts of things. And in fact, if we applied one of the standard difference tests used in these circumstances, this impression would be confirmed:

Group	Group size	Mean (average) score	*t*-value	Significance
Managers	10	5.0		
Skilled	10	4.2	1.37	0.207

The above table provides all the relevant information on our study. It shows the average health measures being compared, it shows the *t*-value (a transformed measure of the magnitude of this difference) and it indicates how significant this difference is. By convention, unless a significance value is 0.05 or less, then we accept that there is no *real* effect and any observed difference can be explained by chance, or some form of error.

In the above example, the difference between 5.0 and 4.2 is *not* significant. Consider now what happens when a larger sample – say, 20 – is drawn from each population of managers and skilled workers. The observed difference in health scores may stay the same, but when this difference holds true across a larger number of individuals, the outcome of our study is very different indeed:

Group	Group size	Mean (average) score	*t*-value	Significance
Managers	20	5.0		
Skilled	20	4.2	2.31	0.027

3.3 Secondary research

It is a common, if not self-evident, expectation among researchers that they will be involved in all stages of their research – from the initial identification of issues, through the design and implementation of a study, to the analysis of data and reporting of findings. In the social sciences, though, there exists the opportunity to base one's research on work that has been carried out by others, quite legitimately, incurring a huge saving in time, effort and money. This is secondary research. Several agencies – primarily but not exclusively governmental – conduct regular surveys designed to review the nature of society and chart the changing state of the nation. The National Census is one example, providing 10-yearly snapshots of the UK going right back to 1851. The General Household Survey (GHS) is another, an annual survey carried out by the Social Survey Division of the Office for National Statistics, and providing information on some 10,000 households across the country. Typical information found in the GHS concerns income, housing, economic activity, education and health. A survey like this is a huge resource and often provides a basis for preparatory work in primary research. It also serves as a major teaching platform and many readers of this book will be currently working with the GHS as part of their undergraduate training to develop their own analytical skills. However, the use of secondary sources is not without its problems, for while there are some clear advantages to working in this way, there are disadvantages also.

3.3.1 Advantages of secondary research

- Access to secondary information usually incurs some cost, in terms of fees to the relevant research or publishing body. However, such fees rarely come anywhere near the costs of carrying out the primary research.
- Where time is important, it is obviously quicker to consult information that already exists than to design, carry out and analyse a primary study of your own, providing of course the secondary information meets your needs.
- From a teaching or training point of view, secondary data provide an opportunity to practise important research and analytical procedures on a large body of information normally out of reach for the

undergraduate. As we have previously intimated, primary undergraduate research often involves very small samples; what luxury to work with a sample of some 10,000 individuals!

- Secondary data can provide a useful basis for the initial exploration of a population. When samples are large – as they usually are in these big social surveys – they often offer an insight into the character of a group that will be studied later, as part of a primary research project (e.g. we can discover important things about the distribution of age, occupation and marital status of a population; we can determine the political, religious and ethnic structures of a population).
- Although primarily descriptive in nature, secondary information will often lead to the identification of social issues that might be more intensively investigated in subsequent, primary research (e.g. if one of the large-scale social surveys indicated that people in the north made more demands on health and welfare services than those in the south, this could initiate further research into health, education or economic issues for the different regions).

3.3.2 Disadvantages of secondary research

- Because the studies that provide secondary information were designed and carried out by someone else, it follows then that they were intended to meet that someone else's own particular needs. This is probably the biggest drawback of using secondary information, since the original research might not have asked the questions *you* would have liked to ask, or might not have sampled from all the groups you would have liked to look at. Having said this, many of the major social surveys are sufficiently broad to be applicable to a wide variety of studies but it will always be the case that the needs of a particular researcher will never be fully met by secondary information.
- Although most secondary information is usually accompanied by explanatory notes (a **codebook**, detailing what questions were asked and how responses were encoded), it will not always be clear how decisions were made when assigning categories or summarising data. The example below, in which participants are asked to classify themselves on an index of educational attainment, might well reach the secondary researcher as shown:

ATTAIN   Educational attainment

MISSING VALUES   – 9

VALUE LABELS   ATTAIN
                  1 = LOW
                  2 = MEDIUM
                  3 = HIGH

Here, all the researcher knows is that educational attainment was classified into three categories, and unless categorisation was based on some generally accepted and understood system, he has

no idea of knowing whether MEDIUM attainment includes diplomas and first degrees, or whether the category relates only to standard and advanced scholastic grades. Important information if the researcher is interested in educational issues in particular. See Box 3.7 for a fuller example of codebook information.

- Finally, a rather obvious problem with secondary data is that by the time they reach the new researcher it is (often) no longer current. The time factor involved in collecting and analysing primary data means that some social survey data are out of

---

Box 3.7   Cracking the code

When the information from an original study becomes available to later researchers, it is known as secondary data. These later researchers are therefore presented with what is in effect *fait accompli*. The primary study has been carried out, data gathered, variables re-coded and so on. There is almost no opportunity for a later researcher to modify any of the information from the original study, other than by further summarising or re-coding. However, so that use can be made of these secondary data, codebooks are usually provided, which comprise information on all the measurements taken, the questions asked and the types of responses generated by questionnaires. The following is an example of what is found in a typical codebook.

List of variables

Name	Position Label	
NEWT1	1	SPECIES OF NEWT, EITHER COMMON OR GREAT-CRESTED
NEWT2	2	ENVIRONMENT IN WHICH NEWTS WERE OBSERVED
PROB1	3	CYCLING SPEED OF NEWTS ON MAZE 1
PROB2	4	CYCLING SPEED OF NEWTS ON MAZE 2
PERS	4	PERSONALITY SCORES OF NEWT SAMPLE
EDATTAIN	5	EDUCATIONAL ATTAINMENT OF SAMPLE

NEWT1   SPECIES OF NEWT, EITHER COMMON OR GREAT-CRESTED

MISSING VALUES   −1

VALUE	LABEL
−2	N.A.
1	COMMON NEWT
5	GREAT CRESTED NEWT
7	FROG, MASQUERADING AS NEWT

Codebook information of this type is generally useful, and sometimes essential in explaining the contents of research information. For instance, without this explanation, who would ever have guessed that NEWT1 provided profile information on the sample, such that cases identified by the number 1 referred to common newts, while 5 referred to the great-crested variety. However, codebook explanations are not always clear – we do not know, for instance, why there is a gap between 1 and 5 in the categories of newt. Does this mean that there are other varieties which (for reasons not explained anywhere) did not feature in this particular study? Or is it the case that in order to minimise mistakes in entering large amounts of data the researcher chose to select numerical values that were not only quantitatively quite different from one another, but also widely spaced on conventional number keyboards. (This latter explanation is often, though not always, the reason for the apparently odd choice of numbers used to assign categories.) And anyway, where did the frogs come from?

(Note: codebook information is often supplied as a hard copy accompaniment to a data file. It is also usually available as part of the file itself and can be reviewed or printed off to suit the researcher.

date by as much as a year before the secondary analyst gets hold of it. For undergraduates the problem is even worse since poor, under-funded departments will often only acquire older (and cheaper) survey data sets for their students. It would not be unusual for students to be working with material that is as much as 10 years out of date – hardly likely to offer a contemporary picture of 'Living in the UK'.

3.4   Using questionnaires in research

3.4.1   Questionnaire design – how to get information

By this stage in our research, we have hopefully decided on the research issue we are going to explore, we know whom we are going to use and we have decided on the key components of our hypothesis (e.g. we are exploring the relationship between educational attainment on incomes for both middle-class and working-class individuals and we are predicting a causal connection between our variables, moderated by class). We also know what kind of information we want from our subjects, the precise data needed to test our hypotheses and to ultimately explore the research issue in question. So how are we going to get this information?

Some research designs will use standardised instruments to generate information (general health questionnaires, stress measures, personality tests, etc. – see Section 3.5), others will rely on an outcome measure of a laboratory experiment (reaction times, frequency of correct responses to stimuli or changes in decision times). Many designs though will require custom-made procedures to gather information, as researchers devise questionnaires to assess attitudes to numerous issues, to obtain information on what people do in various social situations, to measure opinion on a wide range of social and political issues or to explore the distribution of different categories of person in the population. Gathering information of this sort might appear, on the face of it, straightforward. They are all simple question and answer scenarios, whether they involve interviews or questionnaires. The reality is somewhat more complicated in that the development of a 'good' questionnaire is not just a skill but almost an art in itself. The following sections attempt to make the process a little easier, explaining the pitfalls and offering solutions.

Probably the simplest rule of information gathering is: 'If you want to know something, ask', and, by and large, this is the most useful rule to follow when designing a questionnaire or interview programme. Just ask your subjects to tell you what you want to know. Most people are honest, disingenuous and, once they have agreed to participate in a study, usually willing and co-operative. Unfortunately, a common perception of social science is one of a somewhat sneaky profession, relying on methods of deception and misdirection for its information. Even among students of the discipline, there is a view (especially among the psychologists within it) that subjects have to be tricked in some way into giving honest, objective responses and, unfortunately, such a view will only continue to encourage the sense of suspicion and mistrust directed at elements of the profession by outsiders. Such a lamentable state of affairs has its origins in the type of research allowed before guidelines were established by the sociological and psychological societies and the various educational and medical associations that govern the activities of their members. Contemporary researchers now frown on the needless use of deceptive techniques (see Section 3.7 on ethics). In most instances – with certain qualifiers – the direct approach is best: if you want to know something, ask. The qualifiers however are important.

The general rule of *ask and ye shall be answered* holds true most of the time. Sometimes, though, the nature of response can be influenced by who does the asking and how the asking is done. Consider the following question:

HAVE YOU EVER, AT ANY TIME IN YOUR LIFE, COMMITTED A CRIME?

An apparently simple question, if asked by a social science researcher guaranteeing absolute confidentiality. Imagine though the nature of response if the same question were asked by a serving police officer conducting research into criminal behaviour among undergraduates. So the *who?* of a question is important and what every researcher must ask him or herself is: 'Will the fact that *I* am asking a particular question affect the response?'

The other major qualifier is the *how?* of a question. The example above: *Have you ever, at any time in your life, committed a crime?* can only generate either a Yes or No response. Modifying the question to:

WHAT CRIMES, NO MATTER HOW SMALL OR INSIGNIFICANT, HAVE YOU EVER COMMITTED IN YOUR LIFE?

is likely to produce a very different class of response. Aside from the fact that this could be described as a leading question (it assumes people do commit crime) the asker has no control over the type and quantity of response. Anything from a 'How dare you...', to a two page list of guilt-ridden confession is possible. And so, the *how?* of a question is an important quality consideration. The following section describes the most common ways of asking questions and the kinds of responses each produces.

3.4.2 Types of scale

There are two broad types of question available to the researcher, one in which the compiler controls the nature of the response and one in which the subject is free to respond in any way. Both have their uses and their disadvantages, and the decision as to which method to apply is one the researcher must make in terms of the context of the research and the quality of the information required.

Closed-ended questions

These are questions where the possible range of responses is predetermined by the tester. (The opportunity for free response is closed to the person answering.) There are many forms of this type of item, the simplest of which allows for answers on a **dichotomous scale**, i.e. questions offering only two answer choices.

> Do you like the book?
> YES   NO

The types of data that questions like this produce are in the grand tradition of survey techniques, as outlined in Chapter 1 of this book (Section 1.3.9). Subjects respond by selecting one or the other of the nominally-scaled categories and sample data can be presented simply, by referring to the numbers, proportions or percentages of subjects who selected each category. Table 3.1 and Figure 3.1 demonstrate the economy

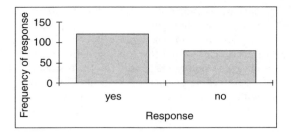

Figure 3.1 Responses of 200 sociology students to an attitude question.

and elegance of this approach. Both the illustrations offer an 'at a glance' summary of the data, and the Yes/No distinction represents one of the simplest – and most common – item formats available to researchers. However, care must be taken not to confuse simplicity with impoverishment. True, the Yes/No response options provide only limited information but, when other variables are introduced, the basic dichotomous distinction suddenly becomes quite sophisticated.

Consider the above example when we wish to further analyse the Yes/No choice in terms of the student's sex, or age group, or study options; suddenly we have more than straightforward descriptive data – we can begin to make comparisons and to make inferences. We have now moved, and quite painlessly at that, to a point where the obsessive number devouring statistician begins to take an interest (see Figure 3.2).

However, the dichotomous example is only one of a variety of closed-response formats. There is no reason why we should stick to just two possible responses when, with most questions we might want to ask, there are invariably several types of response possible. These are then multiple-category scaled items, i.e. questions offering three or more choices for the respondent.

> This year, for a change, are you going to:
> a. do some work   ☐
> b. find a better course   ☐
> c. marry money   ☐
> d. develop a taste for malt whisky   ☐

Just as with the previous example, the response categories are independent of one another, i.e. there is no relationship of magnitude or order between any one category and another, only of difference – the essence indeed of all nominal scales. Similarly, the display of these types of data are equally straightforward, as Figure 3.3 demonstrates.

Table 3.1 Responses of 200 sociology students to an attitude question (%).

Response	N	%
YES	120	60
NO	80	40

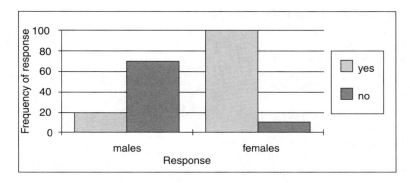

Figure 3.2.

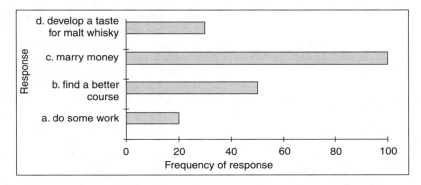

Figure 3.3　Frequency of response to the question: 'This year, are you going to…?'

The third category within the closed-ended question format involves **rating scales**, i.e. scales that rate some attribute from positive to negative, low to high, strong to weak. These move along the continuum of sophistication, but still enable the research to retain control of how subjects can respond. Instead of requiring subjects to choose from a number of response categories that differ in type from one another (as in the dichotomous and multiple examples above), we focus on just one single category and require subjects to indicate their strength of feeling on the issue. In the 'Do you like the book?' example, subjects could only state that, Yes, they did (or No, they didn't). Interesting as such responses are, they nonetheless obscure the range of feeling within either category, i.e. one Yes respondent might be transcendentally ecstatic about the book, whereas another might merely be adopting a 'yeah, it's OK' attitude. This kind of internal distinction is lost in fixed category items, but is accessible in rating scales in which, at its most basic

level, nominally-scaled responses are transformed into ordinally-scaled ones. Consider this restructuring of the previous Yes/No item:

I am enjoying this book:

not at all			tremendously	
1	2	3	4	5

Not only does this provide a more detailed picture of how subjects' strength of feeling varies within an issue, it also moves the relevant information away from the descriptive and towards the more traditionally quantitative. What this means is that, while in the previous examples subjects differed in the *type* of response they could make, now subjects differ in terms of, at the very least, the order, and even *magnitude* of response. It also moves the analysis of data towards a format with which many quantitative researchers feel more comfortable. We now have measures of central tendency (average) and variability to play with; in other words, parametric data.

However, the presentation of more sophisticated data like these should be no less straightforward than for the earlier examples, provided we are familiar with the concepts of sample statistics. Box 3.8 demonstrates this.

As with our categorical examples we can, of course, make our analysis more sophisticated with the inclusion of additional independent profile or subject variables. For instance, we can compare the different sexes on the same scale, or different seminar groups, or whatever. Figure 3.5 demonstrates this.

A special variant of scaled items comes to us from Likert (1932). In this approach, subjects are asked to provide their level of agreement with a statement.

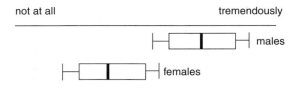

Figure 3.5.

Usually (though not always) corresponding numerical values are absent and appended only later when the researcher converts response categories to quantitative equivalents. For example, in Box 3.9, subjects choose one of the agree/disagree categories. The choice made will ultimately place their attitude on some kind of (assumed) linear scale and means, standard deviations and all kinds of comparisons can be produced in the time-honoured manner of parametric statistics, even though by rights this is actually an ordinal scale, with the numbers referring to categories rather than points on a continuum. Many researchers, especially undergraduate ones, choose to ignore this, however, and continue to treat these types of data as if they were interval and hence, susceptible to parametric analysis. There is debate on the issue and arguments range from the purists who would gladly have their students shot for treating category data as if they were continuous, and the pragmatists who take the line that, 'well, if it's going to show something, why not?' Definitely a case for checking with your supervisor. (Note, if these statistical terms are foreign to you, the next chapter introduces basic statistical concepts.)

A **Likert scale**, therefore, contains a statement with which the respondent indicates the amount of agreement/disagreement with an issue. This method

---

Box 3.8

Table 3.2   Mean response rates to an attitude item.

	μ (mean)	σ (SD)
I am enjoying the course	3.75	0.64

The mean provides a measure of central tendency (average) on the issue and the SD (standard deviation) a measure of how much, on average, scores varied around this value. Chapter 4 explains these concepts in greater detail. Figure 3.4, which accompanies these data, is shown below.

not at all   tremendously
1   2   3   4   5

Figure 3.4.

In this figure the median, or middle value, indicated by the dark bar in the middle of the rectangle (some statistical packages represent this as an asterisk *), is approximately 3.7; the interquartile range (the range of scores from the lower quarter to the upper quarter of the distribution of scores), as indicated by the upper and lower limits of the enclosed rectangle, is approximately 3.2 to 4.2, and the overall range of responses, shown by the upper and lower 'whiskers', is approximately 3.0 to 4.4. This particular method of descriptive illustration is termed a boxplot and is further explained in Chapter 4.

Box 3.9   Using the Likert scale

'Social scientists are nice people'

strongly agree	agree	don't care	disagree	strongly disagree
(+2)	(+1)	(0)	(−1)	(−2)
5	4	3	2	1

Normally, with this type of item, respondents are presented with only the written response options (strongly agree, agree, etc). The numerical scales are shown to indicate how the researcher might transform actual responses to numerical scale values.

whereby actual scale values are obscured can have its advantages. A problem with asking subjects to choose a numerical value indicating a particular view or attitude is that sometimes people are unclear as to how their feelings can convert to a number; or they may be reluctant to select extreme values, or unsure of how one scale value differs from the next. Replacing numbers with choice categories (as in the Likert scale) will sometimes alleviate this problem, in addition to making items more 'user-friendly'. A development of this approach, in which subjects are indirectly placed on some scaled position, is the **semantic differential**, shown below. Here, the respondent rates an issue on a number of bipolar categories. The choice of pole can indicate intensity of feeling on the issue.

> Research projects are (choose one of each pair of response options):
>
> good   bad
> easy   difficult
> useful   worthless
> challenging   problematic
> interesting   boring

In its simplest form, items at one pole can be given a positive value, with items at the other negatively valued. A simple arithmetic count of both positive and negative choices can produce an overall score that will be indicative of the general attitude towards an issue.

Open-ended questions

These are questions where the individual is free to offer any response. With this type of question the researcher is relinquishing control of how the subject can behave. In fact, open questions are not really questions at all. Rather they are scenarios or situations created artificially in which respondents are encouraged to air their views or feelings. In this respect they have much in common with what psychologists call **projective techniques**, as used in a clinical setting, or for the measurement of personality variables. Given free choice, we all tend to project some part of ourselves onto a situation, and this is the principle behind the open-ended question. What we say or write in response to an unrestricted item is an expression of our feelings, values and opinions.

Unstructured questions invite the subject to answer in an unlimited fashion. For example:

> What do you think of the book so far?_____

Note, in a question of this type the researcher does in fact have some control over how much of a response an individual can make, although the content will still remain unpredictable. Leaving the item as it stands invites a very brief response, possibly only a single word. Allowing several blank lines though, or even a page, might encourage a much fuller response.

The second type of open-ended question uses *word association*. The individual is asked to respond with the first thing that comes to mind on presentation of the cue word. For example:

> What do you think of when you hear the following?
> RESEARCH PROJECT   EXAM   STATISTICS

A third type of open-ended question involves *sentence completion*. The participant is offered an incomplete sentence and asked to continue in their own words. For example:

> I chose to study the social sciences because_____

Note that the comment about controlling the length of response, as encountered in the 'What do you think of the book so far?' example above, is relevant here also. The great advantage in not restricting responses is that the full variety of human thoughts and feelings is available to the researcher. The disadvantage is that it is available in a totally unstructured and uncontrolled form. Responses to any of the above can range from a few words to hours of introspective rambling. Accordingly, the approach lies more at the qualitative end of the research dimension (in terms of the type of information generated) but for quantitative researchers the data produced by open-ended questioning are more problematic: given the wide range of possible responses, considerable judgement is required and each subject's response must be inspected for common themes or threads of thought that offer an insight into the unique nature of the individual.

As a general principle, unless the components of an issue and the range of possible responses to a question are well understood, a study would normally be piloted using some form of open-ended enquiry. (Chapter 2 explores this issue in more detail.) This would identify the type and range of responses likely, any sources of ambiguity, overlap among items and so on. Only then would the more direct, closed-type items be used. The rule in closed-type items is simple: you will only get the information you ask for, so you had better have a good idea of what you are likely to get!

3.5 Special techniques for information gathering

3.5.1 Focus groups

Section 3.4 on questionnaire design ended with the sage advice that if you don't ask the questions, you won't get the answers. But how do you know which questions to ask? or how much of an issue is important? or relevant to your sample group?

It would seem then that, even before we consider our very first questionnaire item, we should know in advance what we are looking for. In many cases, this will have been established following an appropriate literature review: issues would have been identified at this stage and hypotheses developed. However, there are certain situations in which a research issue, or its key components (and hence a workable hypothesis), cannot readily be identified in this way; many elements of attitudinal and behavioural research are simply not accessible via the standard route and have to be explored in a more direct manner. One particular method of doing this, which evolved within the marketing sphere, is the **focus group**.

One of the key functions of the marketing process is to find out how people are likely to respond to new products, publicity campaigns and marketing information. If this is done well, we, the consumers, respond positively when a product is released on the market and (so the manufacturers hope) go out and buy it. Poorly done, the result is a marketing disaster and possible bankruptcy. The attempt by Ford to launch America's first small, economical automobile in a culture of gas-guzzling monsters was an abysmal failure, and even today comedians make jokes about their parents being the first in the street to buy an Edsel. Similarly, the attempt by British Leyland in the seventies to persuade us that an Austin Allegro with a square steering wheel was a must, ended in fiasco. (Oddly enough, the square-wheeled Allegro is now something of a collectors' item.)

These examples represent classic marketing disasters – public opinion was seriously misjudged and important informational cues missed. By and large, however, marketing strategists tend to get it right (or right enough), relying on a variety of techniques to gauge opinion, evaluate campaigns and judge consumer response. One of the mainstays of the approach is the focus group.

Much as the term suggests, focus groups are essentially discussion groups comprising in some cases randomly composed, or in others, carefully selected, panels of individuals brought together to discuss, or focus on, specific issues. Discussion can be free-flowing or controlled, but usually under the guidance of a moderator, or facilitator, whose role is to maintain the focus of the group's attention on the issue, and to further probe or develop important themes. As an exploratory instrument, focus groups are superb sources of information, allowing a skilled researcher excellent insight into the values, beliefs, fears and aspirations that comprise most attitudes. Not surprisingly, then, the approach has become an important tool in recent years in social science research. Opinion though is divided as to both the value and the procedures involved in focus groups. In some quarters, the focused approach is seen as a preparatory procedure only, a way of refining ideas, getting to grips with the scope of a particular issue or developing a theory sufficiently to generate hypotheses (as intimated in our discussion of open-ended questions). For others, the focus group is an end in itself, with the information generated providing the essential and necessary data for a study. And certainly, given the vast amount of potential information generated in this format – hours of audio tape, pages of transcriptions, etc. – its appeal as a qualitative research tool is obvious. However, it is in the first context that focus groups are probably of most use to undergraduate researchers, providing as they can a way of coming closer to an issue, of developing a greater understanding of the components of attitudes and of identifying key or relevant issues that will ultimately form the basis of a questionnaire.

With their increasing application within the social sciences, several guidelines have evolved covering the use of focus groups and related procedural issues – how to sample, optimal group sizes, the composition of groups (whether or not members should be strangers or people known to each other) and so on. There are views on the roles of moderators, on how to collect information and whether or not to analyse data in qualitative or quantitative terms. For the majority of undergraduate studies though, a focus group *approach* is probably of more value than adopting a full procedure. In most cases a student is merely interested in identifying or refining important issues so that questionnaire instruments can be designed that will ask the right questions and provide sufficient coverage of an issue to deal appropriately with a given research topic. However, such a scaled-down version will still require planning. Subjects have to be recruited to participate; individual characteristics have to be identified if these are going to be important variables in a study; topics for discussion have to be prepared, along with procedures for guiding or focusing discussion, dealing with awkward individuals and recording data. Equally important, especially if the research is dealing with a sensitive topic, is the thought that must be given to protecting vulnerable members of the group and to dealing with upset or catastrophe. Generally speaking, untrained undergraduates would be discouraged from using a focus approach to explore highly emotive or disturbing issues without a great deal of supervision and forward planning. Indeed, most research ethics committees would reject an undergraduate proposal to explore feelings and attitudes towards sensitive issues when participants of the focus group were themselves the victims of, for example, abuse or assault. Approval of this type of study would only be given if supervisors were present at each focus session and experience of intervention could be guaranteed.

By and large, many undergraduates tend to underestimate this procedure, calling brief, informal discussion meetings with relatively few individuals, failing to control discussion adequately and not recording data in any systematic way. Often this process is seen merely as a precursor to the more important business of interview schedule or questionnaire design; students forget that they will ultimately have to justify every issue covered, and every item contained in any instrument. This can only be done if the issues have been properly explored and understood in advance.

For a more detailed review of focus groups, their history and their application, several excellent references are provided at the end of this chapter. The Asbury (1995) article in particular is a useful review article.

3.5.2 Pilot research

Most of us feel that, by the time we reach the stage of implementing our research design, we have worked everything out to the last detail: we have completed our literature review and therefore know how other practitioners have fared in their research, we have identified all potential sources of bias and we have used an appropriate procedure to focus on the key issues and develop a foolproof questionnaire. However, complacency at this stage is to admit to a poor regard for the vagaries of human nature – misunderstanding instructions, misperceiving the researcher's intent, refusal to co-operate and so on are

all events that can ruin the best conceived study. The solution of course is to pilot your method – try it out on a small sample of the population you will eventually be working with. This is the only way to refine the elements of a design, to identify questionnaire items that are misleading, confusing or offensive. Such pilot work need not be extensive – indeed in designs where subject pools are limited, pilot studies must be constrained – but it should be thorough: a survey or questionnaire administered to a small subset of our sample, in addition to some kind of focused interview, can be useful in identifying limitations and areas for improvement. Mistakes at this stage can be easily remedied; identifying flaws only after a major study has been implemented is hugely wasteful, not to mention demoralising.

3.6 Using standard instruments in research

Many studies will make use of standard scales, existing questionnaires or psychometric tests as part of their data gathering procedure, either as devices for assigning individuals to different conditions, or as a key source of data, as in an outcome measure. This could involve using an existing stress inventory to assign people to the categories of either stressed or unstressed, in a study of job burnout in modern organisations, categories that will comprise the various elements of an independent variable. Alternatively, standard instruments could provide us with our dependent measure, as in a well-being questionnaire measuring the impact of de-industrialisation in particular regions, or an established job satisfaction instrument assessing responses to different supervisory styles in an educational setting. By and large, using existing scales as part of a study can make life a little easier for the researcher. Normally, before a test can be released on to the market, it must demonstrate that it is fit for its purpose – a great deal of preparatory work has invariably gone into the design and construction of a sociometric instrument. This provides the researcher with a useful measurement or classification tool without the need for the lengthy process required in developing a new instrument from scratch. However, using an existing test correctly requires familiarity with the general principles underlying measurement and scaling, in addition to an understanding of the essential characteristics of the particular test or questionnaire itself. Such a level of competence can only be attained through many years of experience with measurement scales; furthermore, the major publishers and distributors of tests have for some years provided training courses in various aspects of assessment while, more recently, in the psychological field, the BPS (British Psychological Society) has introduced an accreditation scheme whereby potential test users are obliged to undertake specific training before they are regarded as qualified to use particular tests. This is an important consideration, since failure to understand how a test has developed, or what specific responses mean, or a failure to prevent bias in administering or scoring, can lead to misinterpretation of scores and misleading – or even damaging – information being fed back to the testee. Equally dangerous is the potential for exploitation when tests are used by unqualified or unscrupulous people and it is largely for these reasons that the BPS introduced its scheme.

The observant reader might have realised by now that most undergraduates are unlikely to have either the experience or training to include existing scales as part of their research repertoire with any personal competence. The assumption though is that it is the competence of the supervisor and the department to which they belong that allows the use of such instruments, not the student, although in all cases the user will be expected to familiarise themselves thoroughly with whichever test they will be using.

3.6.1   What you need to know about established measurement scales

While it would be nice to test every aspect of some social issue under investigation, such that we could explore a group or culture's entire history, or measure every single aspect of an individual's life as it relates to the issue we are interested in, this is clearly impractical. (Any such test would be not only unwieldy, but would probably take a lifetime to administer.) What established instruments actually do is study a small but carefully chosen sample of some topic, issue or behaviour, in the hope that we can generalise from the specific to the global, in much the same way that a survey, while its main interest is the entire population, can only ever explore a small section of that population. Hence, a vocabulary test cannot address every single word in a person's repertoire; rather it deals with a sample of what the individual knows.

To be of any use in predicting or describing what people do in general, this sample of items must be representative of the overall area, both in terms of *type* and *number* of items. An arithmetic test using only five items for instance, or only items on multiplication, would be a poor test of arithmetic skill. A good test on the other hand would have to include items on addition, subtraction, multiplication and division. Furthermore, we might be unhappy if such a test omitted items involving fractions or decimal calculations and we might also expect some measure of computational abilities such as dealing with square roots, power or factorial calculations. The underlying point here is that it would be impossible to develop a good, representative test of any aspect of human endeavour unless the composition of that behaviour had been fully considered in advance.

While we expect test designers to demonstrate a sound knowledge of their particular area, it is equally important that we, as ultimate users of tests, also understand a good deal about the issues we are exploring. How else could we judge whether or not a test was a good one for our purposes, or, given a number of similar tests, how would we know which was the most appropriate?

3.6.2   Standardisation

Even the best measurement scale in the world will be wasted unless we can ensure that scores reflect the whole subject we are interested in, as opposed to some other factor. Notorious 'other factors' that can affect apparent performance on a test are instructions given to subjects, anxiety of the test-takers, motivational factors, methods of collecting data and scoring procedures. Unless every individual who completes a test does so under identical, standardised conditions, any observed effects might simply reflect **procedural variations** rather than actual differences in behaviour. Box 3.10 illustrates the point.

Fortunately, many test constructors are well aware of this issue and are able to employ several procedures to reduce the effects of administration variability. The EPI (Eysenck's Personality Inventory, and a favourite among psychology undergraduate researchers) is a good example – a pre-printed test with restricted response categories and instructions clearly printed on every copy. Even scoring has been taken out of the hands (or judgement) of the administrator, being achieved via standard scoring stencils. Finally, interpretation of individual profiles can be guided by reference to printed norms, a procedure with which all test users must become familiar.

Box 3.10 So what exactly are you measuring?

Instructions given to a group of university students prior to the administration of a standard intelligence test.

Instruction (a)

'The test you are about to complete is one of the most advanced tests of intellectual functioning yet devised. Your scores on this test will be considered by a team of experts and their decision will partially determine whether or not you are allowed to enter the honours stream next session. It is therefore important that you do well.'

Instruction (b)

'I'm afraid today's video presentation is cancelled due to the technician's inability to remove the cling film wrapping from the tape. For want of something better to do, we've found this intelligence test. It's not an especially good test but it might be a bit of fun and it will give you something to do.'

Both of the above instructions are in their own way inappropriate (and also unethical) in that they actively cue respondents to approach the test in a particular way. We would not be surprised to obtain two completely different sets of scores but in this case not measuring intelligence but, more probably, motivation or – especially among those receiving Instruction (a) – test anxiety.

3.6.3 Norms

Contrary to popular belief, there is no predetermined pass or fail level in most tests. It would be nonsense to talk of passing a stress or personality test for instance, although the notion might seem less bizarre if we are dealing with something like arithmetic for which some form of pass level can realistically be set. (Most students will be aware that their various exams, that test their knowledge of or competence in particular subjects, have clearly defined pass and fail levels.) In fact, in the majority of tests, individual scores are compared against other scores that have previously been collated by the test designer. This comparison function is obtained by first administering the test to a large, representative sample of those for whom the test will subsequently be used (the **standardisation sample**). This provides us with a **norm**, which is simply a measure, or series of measures, indicating how people typically (or normally) perform on this test.

Norms can take various forms, although usually they comprise a measure of average performance (being the arithmetic average, or mean of the scores of all the participants in the standardisation sample), and a measure of the extent to which scores tend to vary above and below this average (given as a standard deviation – see Chapter 4). The point of these measures is that, provided the people who tried out the test during these initial stages are representative of the broader population, then what is true for the sample should be true for everyone. And this is a crucial point. For statistical purposes a standardisation sample of 600 or so subjects would be fine, providing what we are measuring is pretty stable in the population. If, however, a test is being designed to measure some trait that is known (or suspected) to be influenced by many factors (it can vary with age, sex, social class, occupation, etc.) then the sample would need to be much larger to allow the different sources of variability to be reasonably well represented. (This issue has been discussed more fully in Section 3.2.5.) In the development of the Eysenck Personality Questionnaire (Eysenck and Eysenck, 1969), one of the better known instruments of its type, Eysenck and Eysenck used a standardisation sample of more than 5,000 subjects. With a sample this large, they were able to explore the major traits of psychoticism, extraversion and neuroticism by age, sex and some 47 different occupational groups, a diversification that would not have been possible with smaller numbers of subjects. The point of this protracted discussion on norms and samples is that if a test is to be used as part of a student project (or indeed for any research purpose), it is important to be aware of how relevant norms are to the group being studied. A standardisation sample that is small, or that does not allow for sources of variation might be of limited value in describing the larger population.

Returning to the Eysenck questionnaire, the large standardisation sample allows us not only to state that the average extraversion score for all males in the sample was 13.19 and for females, 12.6, but also that the average for male students was 13.8, with female students 13.49. Similar information is available for many other occupational categories.

Providing an average measure of performance on a test is a common method of presenting norms, but there are others. Most typical, and more informative in some ways, are norms that are expressed as **percentiles** – a measure of the percentage of the standardisation sample that scored at or below a particular level. Hence, if a test manual informs us that a score

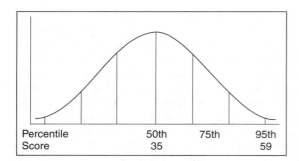

Figure 3.6 Scores and percentile ranks on an abstract reasoning test.

of 35 on an abstract reasoning test is at the 50th percentile, then we know that approximately 50% of the standardisation sample scored 35 or less; if we are told that a score of 59 lies at the 95th percentile, then we know that 95% of the standardisation sample scored 59 or less, and so on (see Figure 3.6).

3.6.4   Test reliability

Every measuring instrument, if it is to be of any use, must possess a number of important qualities. The first of these is that it must be sensitive to whichever aspect of the environment – be it some physical property or a social phenomenon – it is measuring, and accurately detect any changes that might occur. Equally important, it must not indicate change where no change has taken place. This may sound strange, but consider an everyday measuring instrument, such as a ruler. If we measure the height of a table on a Monday and obtain a measure of 1 metre, but on the Tuesday obtain a height of 1.3 metres, there are two things that can have occurred. The first is that the table (for some bizarre reason) has changed its dimensions in the course of a day and is now 0.3 metres taller than it was on Monday, a change that has been accurately detected by our ruler. Alternatively, the table has not changed, rather it is the ruler that has changed – possibly some temperature-sensitive metal was used in its manufacture and the thing actually shrank overnight. The point of this example is that with a standardised test, we always try to ensure that the first case is the typical one. When a change is signalled it must be the aspect of the social environment that is changing and not the instrument itself. In other words, a test must demonstrate consistency, or *reliability*. There are a number of ways in which this might be done:

- **Test–retest reliability**. The simplest and most direct method for demonstrating that a test is behaving consistently is to measure the same thing twice. The same test is administered to the same subjects and the two scores compared, using a form of correlation (a statistical technique for exploring the relationship between two variables or, in this case, two tests. See Chapter 4, Sections 4.10.1 to 4.10.3). Obvious problems here are **practice effects**, which could actually produce a poor comparison between two presentations of the same test simply because our testees were getting better at the task. This could lead us to wrongly assume the instrument is not reliable when in fact the opposite is the case – the test has been sensitive to the change in behaviour. Alternatively, if subjects recall their original responses and attempt to reproduce them, an artificially high correspondence between the two measures might occur, demonstrating more the reliability of subjects' memories than the stability of the test. Only tests not affected by repetition can be assessed in this way.

- **Alternate form reliability**. When there is a danger of straightforward repetition producing a misleading reliability measure – as in the memory issue – two different forms of the test can be given to the same subjects and the scores correlated. Care should be taken to ensure that the two forms of the test are truly equivalent and of course practice can still influence performance.

- **Split half reliability**. This is a method for assessing reliability without the need for two repetitions of the same or parallel forms of the same test. In this variant, a test is administered once only, the items split in half and the two halves correlated. Sometimes a straight split is made, with the first half of a test compared with the second half, while at others, the split is in terms of odd-numbered items versus even-numbered ones. However, this method is not so much a measure of temporal reliability (consistency over time) as of internal consistency (where all the items themselves are measuring in the same direction), and should not be regarded as an alternative to either of the previous approaches; this provides a check of how reliable the individual items are. If a good comparison is achieved, the items are deemed to be consistent and the test largely reliable (insofar as all the items are measuring in the same way).

There are of course a number of problems in attempting to demonstrate reliability, with practice and memory effects having already been discussed. Equally important though are procedural and administration factors. Any variations among successive repetitions of a test will adversely affect reliability measures. Nor is the split half approach without its problems, with the strength of comparisons often varying depending on how the split is made. There are statistical ways of dealing with reliability problems, and the actual correlation between two testings is not the conventional calculation most undergraduates are familiar with, but rather a development that attempts to counterbalance the deficiencies of the reliability procedure in general. The manuals that accompany all tests ought to provide details of the procedures used to establish reliability, together with the associated reliability coefficients. For illustrations on the calculation of these statistics, any of the references dealing with psychometrics at the end of this chapter are suitable.

3.6.5   Test validity

The next crucial quality that a test should possess is validity. This is simply an expression of the extent to which a test is actually measuring what it is supposed to be measuring, although the methods available to demonstrate this quality are often far from simple. In terms of test characteristics validity is possibly even more important than reliability. After all, reliability only tells us that, whatever the test is measuring, it is doing so consistently. It doesn't necessarily inform us about what the test is actually measuring, or how good a job it is doing of measuring it. If a test is demonstrably valid though, we know it is doing what it claims to do. Unfortunately, in the historical development of testing some of the early forms of intelligence test were proven invalid when it was observed that they could not be completed successfully without a conventional educational background. They had more to do with scholastic aptitude than what people regard as pure intelligence (whatever that might be). This is validity, and this example also offers an idea of the scope of the problem. Given that many tests attempt to measure aspects of behaviour that are largely implicit and assumed to exist through indirect observation and inference (creativity, personality, intelligence, etc.) and whose presence remains a subject of fierce debate among theorists, the problem of validity becomes a huge and, some might argue, insoluble one. Having said this though, a number of methods are available that go some way towards demonstrating the fitness of particular tests, and the different types of validity are discussed in the following sections.

Content validity

If a test is to demonstrate **content validity** then the content of the test must accurately and adequately reflect the content of the phenomenon under investigation. In the case of an opinion or attitude measure, for example, the content of the test should be based on a thorough understanding of the attitude, related views, associated measures and likely values expressed; knowledge tests should be a fair representation of the topics that comprise the information base. Your economics exam, for instance, should be a good expression of the course of study, reflecting topic diversity, issues raised and recommended readings given. If it does not fulfil these criteria students have every right to complain about the lack of content validity present in their exam (the content of the test failed to reflect the content of the course). However, many such tests can become overloaded with items that lend themselves to objective testing. While it is easy enough to explore an individual's familiarity with informational aspects of an issue, how do you measure something like critical appraisal? And, as previously mentioned, early intelligence tests comprised primarily items on academic skill rather than abstract reasoning, creativity and the like. Achievement tests in particular will invariably be examined in terms of their content validity.

Face validity

This is often confused with the previous test feature, since, as with content validity, the concern is with the appearance of a test. However, **face validity** is not a true indication of validity, being concerned only with what a test appears to measure, and having little to do with what is actually being measured (on the face of it, what does this test seem to be measuring?). Nevertheless, this represents a useful feature of any test because there will be a relationship between how people view a test and their willingness to participate; if we see an instrument as childish, irrelevant or even insulting, we will certainly not give it our full attention. Box 3.11 illustrates this issue.

In some cases, especially in the area of opinion studies, it is not always possible to ensure face validity. In a situation where a participant may not respond honestly if the true purpose of the test is known, we may be tempted to disguise part of the test content. This of course must be done with extreme caution and only with considerable justification. It should be understood that this approach actively deceives subjects and adherence to ethical guidelines (as

Box 3.11   On the face of it...

Orange ice lollies cost 50p each, raspberry lollies 35p and lemon ones 40p. If a schoolboy has £1.60 to spend in his tuck shop, and he wants to buy at least one of each for his friends, of which flavour of ice lolly can he buy two?

The above problem would be a good (valid) item in a test of general arithmetic reasoning. However, if the item appeared in a test designed for trainee electrical engineers, the response would more likely be derisory laughter than the correct answer (which is raspberry lollies, for the computationally challenged). For this particular group the item would not have face validity and some rephrasing would be in order:

One millimetre cable costs £35 per 100 metre drum, 1.5 mm cable £40 per drum and 2.5 mm cable £50 per drum. If a project buyer needs electrical cable of each size and has £160 to spend, of which diameter cable can he buy 200 metres and stay within his budget?

This is the same item as the previous one except, for this group, it now has face validity. (By the way, the correct answer is 1 millimetre cable, in case you haven't got the idea yet.)

published by the various research governing bodies such as the BSA (British Sociological Association) and BPS) must be ensured. See Box 3.12 for an illustration of the problem, and also Section 3.4 on questionnaire design in which this issue is further explored.

Criterion-related validity

When a test is developed to diagnose something about an individual's present circumstances, or to predict something about a person's future, validation can sometimes be effected by comparing test scores to some other indicator (or criterion) of what the test is trying to measure. This is known as **criterion-related validity**. An occupational selection test, for example, can be checked against later job performance (which is actually how such tests are validated); a neuroticism test can be checked against counsellors' records, or friends' ratings of behaviour. A scholastic achievement test can be checked against assignment ratings, and so on. Within this general procedure of relating test scores to some other criterion though, there is a particular condition concerning the temporal

Box 3.12   How needy?

Armed with a limited budget and charged with identifying the 20% of pensioners most in need of additional subsistence payments, you devise a questionnaire to determine differing levels of deprivation.

Please indicate, on the scale below, how adequate your pension is in meeting your individual needs.

1	2	3	4	5
totally inadequate	inadequate	acceptable	pretty good	wonderful

(Note: the wording used for the response categories would be chosen to reflect the type of question and the nature of the respondent.)

If other items on the questionnaire are like this, approximately 99% of our sample will fall into our most needy category – simply because it is obvious what the questionnaire is about, and what the consequences of particular responses will be. And human nature being what it is...

Modifying the appearance of items, however, might provide a more subtle route to the information you

are looking for. For example, if items appear to be measuring more general behaviour than obvious levels of deprivation:

Please indicate how often you eat a hot meal in the course of a week.
Approximately how much do you spend on fuel in the course of a week?
On average, how many times do you go shopping during the week?

Items like this allow us to infer certain things about respondents, indirectly, and it could be argued that for some types of information this form of deception is the only way of ensuring an honest or accurate response. However, an approach of this type is deceptive and runs counter to the spirit of openness that forms the basis of current ethical principles. Such approaches also tend to encourage the sense of mistrust in which the social sciences are occasionally regarded by others. The question is, is the need for such information so great that the means by which we obtain it are justified?

relationship between the test and its criterion measure (i.e. when we actually obtain this validating information). This relationship is determined by the nature of the test itself – whether or not it is measuring something about an individual's current circumstances, or whether it is predicting something about the future.

- **Concurrent validity**. The criterion against which scores are to be checked is obtained at the same time. This is the type of proof that is necessary when a test is assessing some aspect of a current condition (as in a diagnostic test).
- **Predictive validity**. In a test that predicts something (as with aptitude tests) a follow-up study is carried out to test the strength of the prediction. Most selection tests are obliged to demonstrate criterion-related predictive validity, since everything from an interview to a job sample test is predicting something about job candidates. If a selection test is described as having predictive validity, then during its design phase it might have been administered to job candidates as part of a general selection and recruitment process. Subsequent assessment of individuals actually hired by the company would be compared with the predictions made on the original test, and if a good match is obtained, the test is declared valid. Only then would it be developed for future use in the selection process. A problem here is criterion contamination, in which the independent measure can become contaminated by knowledge of the test results and therefore ceases to be truly independent.

'He looks sick, what do you think?'
'Yeah, now that you mention it…'

This is a tricky problem to overcome in many cases since it is common for the individual responsible for an original assessment to be the same person involved in subsequent evaluations. The only way round this is to ensure that independent assessments are truly that. Subsequent, or follow-up, measures should ideally be taken by individuals who have no detailed knowledge of previous evaluations.

Construct validity

Construct validity indicates the extent to which a test measures some theoretical construct or concept, such as intelligence, creativity or personality. Not surprisingly this represents the most difficult form of validity to demonstrate, since the concepts being measured – as the name suggests – are really theoretical entities whose existence is inferred by observation of related activities. Consequently, validation of such concepts is also indirect – measurements of activities that are believed to be related to, expressions of or caused by some underlying factor.

Age differentiation is one such indirect method of validation. If a trait is expected to change with age, scores on the test should reflect this change. For instance, if the understanding of certain concepts (e.g. prejudice) is part of a developmental process, we should be able to observe this by comparing older children with younger ones.

Correlation with other tests is another commonly used validation method whereby a new test should compare well with existing tests of the same trait. (The Binet test of intelligence – one of the earliest examples of this type of test – and the later Wechsler Adult Intelligence Scale were often used to validate new tests of IQ.)

Administration to extreme groups offers another method of validation, such that if two groups are known to differ on a trait, again the test should reflect this difference (a personality test for instance might clearly distinguish between extreme extraverts and extreme introverts). This is a particularly crude measure, however, since it will only demonstrate that a test is capable of identifying broad differences and not how well it measures fine distinctions.

In fact, in the case of construct validity, a number of independent measures would be used to provide a comparison function, and most manuals for specific tests will offer extensive detail on how precisely the test was validated.

All of the foregoing discussion from Section 3.6 onwards represents essential reading for anyone contemplating using a standard testing instrument as part of a study, but will be of special interest to students pursuing psychology modules. However, for anyone who aims to make use of an existing test it is important to understand how it was devised, how reliable it is and what steps were taken to prove its validity. Familiarity with test norms is also vital, since this information tells us for whom the test is suitable, and what particular scores are likely to mean. Apart from being a major factor in determining your competence to use a given test, you will also be required, in a final report, to fully justify the use of a particular instrument. And none of this is possible unless you *read the manual*.

While standardised tests will often comprise an element of undergraduate research, there will be occasions when no existing test is suitable for a particular design, or in which an issue is being explored using questionnaire or survey methods. This is usually the case when contemporary opinions, values and beliefs are being investigated. In such cases the researcher must develop her own instrument, a task sufficiently demanding that sometimes the development of a measure – with all the attendant requirements of reliability and validity – becomes the study itself.

3.7   Conducting ethical research

It is important to be aware that, before you can inflict a study on an unsuspecting public, you are bound by certain constraints on your behaviour – especially that concerning your willing participants. Aside from the implicit moral obligation of any social researcher to prevent distress among those individuals who give up their time to help out, there exist a number of guidelines that should always be considered in the design and implementation of any study. Developed over many years of research, and based on broadly accepted moral behaviour and ethical values, a number of guidelines have been produced by the various overseeing bodies and are available in full in their many publications, relating both to human and (where appropriate) animal subjects.

A summary of the main points of these guidelines is offered below and students should note that, while they are only guidelines, most supervisors would decline to supervise an undergraduate project if such guidelines were not adhered to. Moreover, as we appear to be evolving into an increasingly sensitive, not to say litigious, society, academic institutions are themselves becoming more cautious about the nature of research carried out in their name. In any event, ignoring these points should only be considered in exceptional circumstances, and with the strongest possible justification since, by and large, they reflect powerful human values and not simply professional ones.

3.7.1   Sampling

Where subjects are to be drawn from specific populations (workers in an organisation, patients in a hospital, pupils in primary schools), you should be aware of any possible disruption to normal institutional functioning that your study may cause. It is therefore

important that approval and/or authorisation be sought from appropriate individuals or bodies before your work commences. Indeed, some institutions (e.g. hospital boards) require research proposals to pass their own form of ethics committee before approval is given. Furthermore, any reporting on the findings of a study must include details of all procedures used to obtain participants, to ensure the consent of subjects and to seek the approval of relevant bodies.

3.7.2   Apparatus

Apparatus refers to any instrument, device or questionnaire that is used to aid the collection of data. In the case of standard equipment, such as a tachistoscope (a device for back-projecting images onto an enclosed screen for predetermined durations), it is important that all operations are fully understood and the regulations governing use are fully adhered to. In the case of standard questionnaires and psychometric tests, the instructions for administration and scoring must be followed. Further, no such instrument should be used without a thorough awareness of norms, limitations, applications, reliability and validity studies, such that in no way can subjects be disadvantaged by a lack of familiarity with the manual. (This issue is covered in detail in Section 3.6.)

In the case of non-standard equipment, full details of, for instance, circuit diagrams, safety precautions and usage should be included in a report. In the case of non-standard questionnaires, a full copy, with a rationale for each item, must also be included as part of the report (see Chapter 7, Section 7.3.8). The reason for so much detail is not simply replicability, although this is often important, but also to ensure that ethical standards are seen to be maintained. If a researcher is unable to provide such depth of information or, worse, is unwilling to do so, then the research is clearly suspect.

3.7.3   Procedure

Participation in any social study is normally voluntary and you must ensure that subjects are aware of this, and that they are able to withdraw *at any time* during a study, without prejudice (i.e. without any fear of sanction and with an assurance of no negative consequences of withdrawal), a right that extends even beyond the data collection stage. At no time must you coerce or use deceit, which is not in itself a part of the study, to obtain co-operation. In the event that some form of deception forms part of the experimental manipulation, you must ensure that subjects are fully de-briefed (i.e. told exactly what has happened and why).

If a situation is encountered in which participants are not able to provide some form of **informed consent**, steps must be taken to protect the individual. If people with brain damage, young children, or individuals exhibiting other forms of cognitive disorder are to be approached as participants, consent must be obtained from those who have the interests of your potential subjects at heart. This could be relatives, parents, carers or medical staff. And even then, unless there is sound reason for pursuing a particular research interest, such individuals should not be used in a study. Increasingly, academic departments are now requiring participants to sign a consent form, stating that they fully understand the purpose of the study in which they are participating and that they are aware of their rights, both legally and morally.

If the data collected in a study are to be confidential (as they should be), you must take steps to ensure that, not only is this so, but that it is seen to be so, especially by your subjects. This is especially true if the data might be considered private and personal to participants. Again, reported research is now expected to include details of how the confidentiality of responses has been ensured.

As a general rule, subjects should never be placed under undue stress. However, should induced stress form a part of a study, advance preparations must be made in terms of controlling such stress, and for preventing possibly catastrophic consequences (both physiological and emotional). Generally speaking, no undergraduate would be permitted to conduct a study along these lines nor, unless in exceptional circumstances, would an experienced researcher. The days of Milgram, in which subjects were placed under great personal stress in the false belief that they were inflicting pain on others, have gone!

3.7.4 General

All of the above are merely guidelines to enable you to conduct yourself and your research in an ethical, humane and fair manner. They should not be regarded as constraints, rather as a series of reminders that when you carry out a piece of research you are dealing not with abstract sources of data, but with real people who have rights of privacy, sympathy, and expectations of fairness of treatment to which all of us are entitled.

3.7.5 Current issues

The importance of adhering to a common set of moral and ethical standards in the treatment of other people is unassailable, and professional bodies like the British Sociological Society and the various psychological societies have an important role in reminding members of their obligations. Recently, the BPS has taken the position that even the use of the term 'subject' is in itself unethical. The view is that it is impersonal and that 'psychologists owe a debt to those who participate in their studies and ... people who are willing to give up their time, even for remuneration, should be treated with the highest standards of consideration and respect.' Consequently, the recommendation in the BPS code of conduct is that more suitable terms are 'participants', 'respondents', 'individuals', or some other non-controversial term. Debate on the issue continues. (See Section 3.11.)

3.8 Review

In this chapter we have considered the practical aspects of carrying out a study. By this stage you should have a good idea of how many subjects you require, how you will recruit them and who they will be. You should also know precisely how you are going to collect your data – whether you will be using an existing measure or devising a measurement scale of your own. If you are developing your own instrument, you should now appreciate the various options available in terms of item design, the advantages of the different approaches and the associated pitfalls. You will also have sufficient familiarity with accepted procedures to ensure that your study will be carried out in an ethical manner.

3.9 Explanation of terms

alternate form reliability a measure of reliability obtained by administering equivalent or parallel forms of a test to the same subjects on separate occasions. Using different forms of a test in this way is seen as a control for memory effects.

closed-ended questions a type of questionnaire or interview item in which the range of responses possible to a respondent is determined by the researcher.

codebook a detailed breakdown (usually accompanying secondary data) of the contents of a research data set, likely to include a description of the variables examined in a study, information on how categories were generated and explanations of the numerical codes used to identify various groups.

concurrent validity a version of criterion-related validity in which the comparison measures are taken at the same time as the test findings become available.

construct validity the type of validation necessary for any test attempting to measure some psychological concept or construct. This is not really a measure in itself and does not describe one single procedure – rather, construct validity is demonstrated using a variety of techniques.

content validity demonstrated when the content of a test – in terms of the type and scope of items – comprises a fair and representative reflection of the opinion, attitude or event that is the focus of interest.

criterion-related validity a method of demonstrating test validity by comparing test findings to some other measure, or criterion.

dichotomous scales measuring scales on which there are only two kinds of response (as in Yes/No).

face validity a characteristic of measurement instruments whereby a test seems to be measuring what it claims to be measuring. This is an aspect of a test's appearance and its apparent relevance to subjects. The term is potentially misleading since it provides no indication of true, objective validity, but it does influence the attitudes of participants and their level of co-operation.

focus groups a type of discussion group established to explore particular issues. They can be used as a primary source of data in their own right, or as a preliminary to a more structured data gathering method.

generalisation the ability to apply findings gleaned from a sample to the population at large. This is only possible when samples truly reflect population characteristics; otherwise findings are situation specific.

informed consent the agreement of a subject to participate in research, based on a full understanding of the aims of a study, and of their own rights in respect of confidentiality and ethical treatment.

Likert scale a type of rating scale in which the numbers are replaced by response categories, usually in terms of how much a subject agrees with a particular statement. Possible responses are typically: strongly agree; agree; don't know; disagree; strongly disagree.

local sampling effect a possible consequence of a practical constraint on some research, describing an effect of restricting sampling to a local community. Inadvertently such samples can become overloaded with unusual or extreme localised characteristics. See also 'sample bias' and 'situation specificity'.

norms measures of typical or normal performance, expressions of attitude or ratings on particular tests, usually measured in terms of mean scores and measures of spread for specific subsections of the population, though sometimes presented as a proportion or percentage of a sample producing particular scores. See also 'percentiles'.

open-ended questions a type of questionnaire or interview item in which there are no restrictions on the range of responses possible to a respondent.

percentiles in psychometrics a cumulative measure of the proportion of individuals who score at, or below, particular points on a measuring scale.

pilot research a small-scale study usually carried out in advance of the main research, the aim being to identify problems before the study proper begins.

population the entire set of entities that comprise the group, or subgroup, of subjects that are the object of study, and in which the entire range of an outcome measure is represented.

power an evaluation and a measure of the extent to which a procedure or test will correctly identify the presence of an effect where one really exists.

practice effects a tendency for performance on certain types of test to improve over time simply as a result of practice. The effect can often lead to artificially reduced measures of reliability.

predictive validity a version of criterion-related validity in which the comparison measures are taken some time in the future, after test findings have become available.

procedural variations an occasional tendency for apparent differences among subjects on particular tests to reflect variations in testing procedures as opposed to actual variations on some quality.

projective techniques methods whereby we 'project' or express some element of our individual nature, attitudes or personality, as when we respond to open-ended questions in a survey, or make up stories about what we see in a Rorschach Ink Blot.

random sampling a procedure of drawing subjects from a population in a totally random fashion; every single individual has an equal probability of being selected.

rating scales measuring scales on which there is a range of numerical responses available to the respondent.

reliability coefficient the statistic that offers a numerical indication of test reliability. The statistic is based on a modified version of correlation, in which such factors as the number of items in a test are controlled for. A common measure here is Cronbach's alpha.

representative a term used in different contexts but meaning the same thing. In psychometrics, it refers to a highly desirable characteristic of tests, in which the item coverage is a fair reflection, or representation, of the area under investigation. In sampling procedures, it refers to the importance of ensuring that subjects comprising a sample for study are a fair reflection, or representation, of the population from which they have been drawn.

sample a subset of a population that forms the subject basis for a study. It is assumed that the sample will be representative of the population from which it has been drawn such that observations on the sample will allow inferences to be made about the population.

sample bias the result of a particular sample being over- (or under-)represented on some characteristic that makes the sample atypical of the population from which it was drawn. This has the effect of limiting the extent to which inferences about the population can be made. Related terms are *situational bias* and *situational specificity*, in which the situation in which a sample is drawn can lead to bias, or the over-emphasis of certain characteristics specific to a particular situation.

semantic differential the responses available lie at two extremes of a single continuum, e.g. good/bad.

situation specificity describes the tendency for many research findings to be relevant only to the sample or situation in which the study was carried out. A function of rigorous sampling and controls that remove a particular study too far from real life.

split half reliability a measure of reliability that measures the relationship among the items of a particular test. By splitting a test into two halves, and comparing the scores of subjects on each half, it is possible to measure the internal consistency of a test.

standardisation in the context of psychological testing, standardisation refers to the process of ensuring identical procedures for administration, data collection and scoring.

standardisation sample the particular subset of a population who first experience a particular test, the aim being to identify typical or normal scores (norms).

stratified sampling a procedure of drawing subjects from a population according to some predetermined strategy. Normally, if a population is seen to comprise certain strata (socioeconomic divisions, ethnic groupings, etc.) a sample should reflect the same structure and in the same proportions.

test reliability a measure, or indication of the extent to which a test produces consistent results across time and situations.

test–retest reliability a measure of reliability obtained by administering the same test to the same subjects on two separate occasions.

test validity an indication of the extent to which a test is actually measuring what it is supposed to be measuring. Unlike reliability, validity is not necessarily demonstrated statistically, although there are instances in which it can be.

3.10 Further reading

Asbury, J.E. (1995) Overview of focus group research. Special Issue: Issue and applications of focus groups. *Qualitative Health Research*, November, **5**(4): 414–420.

Beech, J.R. and Harding, L. (1990) *Testing People: A Practical Guide to Psychometrics*. Berkshire, England: NFER-Nelson.

Bulletin of the British Psychological Society (1985) A code of conduct for psychologists. *Bulletin of the BPS*, **38**: 41–43.

Bulletin of the British Psychological Society (1985) Guidelines for the use of animals in research. *Bulletin of the BPS*, **38**: 289–291.

Cooper, P. and Tower, R. (1992) Inside the consumer mind: Consumer attitudes to the arts. *Journal of the Market Research Society*, October, **34**(4): 299–311.

Eysenck, H.J. and Eysenck, S.B.G. (1969) *Personality Structure and Measurement*. London: Routledge & Kegan Paul.

Likert, R.A. (1932) A technique for the measurement of attitudes. *Archives of Psychology*, **140**: 256.

Sarantakos, S. (1998) *Social Research*, 2nd edition. Basingstoke: Macmillan.

Stewart, D.W. and Kamins, M.A. (1993) *Secondary Research: Information Sources and Methods*, 2nd edition, Applied Social Research Methods Series, Volume 4. Newbury Park, CA: Sage.

Useful websites

Statement of Ethical Practice of the British Sociological Association. At: http://www.britsoc.org.uk/about/ethic.htm

Ethical Standards of the American Sociological Association. At: http://www.asanet.org/members/ecostand.html

The Code of Conduct for Psychologists. At: http://www.bps.org.uk/about/ruled5.cfm

Quantitative techniques

Describing the social world: Introducing SPSS

Cries for help

- *What do all these numbers mean?*
- *Should I be using bargraphs, or boxplots?*
- *What is the Standard Error anyway?*
- *Help!*

Chapter 4 deals with the data generated in quantitative research. What do we do with the numbers produced by a survey or experiment, how do we present them and what is the most appropriate form of descriptive analysis? In particular, how can we use numerical information to make sense of our world?

The initial sections deal with basic concepts in describing data – using tables, graphs and introducing descriptive statistics – while later sections are concerned with the practical issues of setting up data files and working with modern statistical software. In particular, the **SPSS** statistical package will be used to illustrate procedures and outputs, a package that is becoming one of the most frequently encountered quantitative tools in academic and government departments. (SPSS is an abbreviation of Statistical Package for the Social Sciences, although the acronym is sometimes expressed as Superior Performance Statistical Software.) By the end of this chapter you will be able to create a file for your data in SPSS, generate a variety of basic, descriptive statistics, produce appropriate graphs and (hopefully) be able to interpret complex computer output. As with all sections of this book, however, the aim is merely to introduce essential concepts; those interested in more advanced ideas and techniques should pursue some of the articles cited in the further reading section (4.12). This is especially true of statistical concepts since, as we have previously pointed out, this is a research methods book and not a statistical primer: of necessity, we discuss those issues that are important to understanding research but readers interested in mathematical proofs will need to look elsewhere. Again, our further reading will offer some fruitful pointers.

4.1 Using numbers to represent the social world

So, the study is completed and you will now have amassed a great deal of information, and if your research was quantitative in nature, this information will take the form of numbers. The proportion of Yes or No responses to an opinion questionnaire, measures of attitude on rating scales, scores on some kind

Exploring Chapter 4

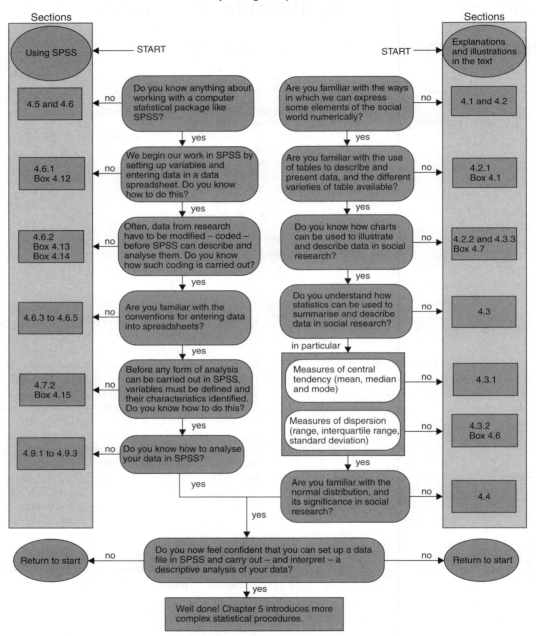

of behaviour measure – these are all typical. In addition, you will also probably have key information on your participants – profile information such as gender, age category, social class and similar. These too will probably be in the form of numbers, and here is an important point – the central philosophy of a quantitative approach is that everything in the universe can be represented numerically. This allows widely diverse elements to be compared using a common classification and measurement system. Hence, the strength of an opinion on a social issue might be expressed as a value between 1 and 7; membership of a particular occupational class as one of five numerical categories (1 = professional; 2 = managerial, etc.) with even a person's sex expressed simply as 1 for males and 2 for females. (Ouch! We can hear the screams already, so let's make that 0 = male and 1 = female.) Once the notion of numbers being mere symbols that represent other things is understood, the next stage in the quantitative process is to make use of the significant characteristics of numbers – they can be added, subtracted, multiplied and divided. In other words, they can be manipulated.

4.2 Making sense of numbers

Choosing to represent the world numerically is only the beginning of the quantitative process. After all, taking a series of measurements on a sample of subjects – be it height, age, membership of particular groups or scores on some attitudinal variable – will only provide you with a list of numbers. And if this is a long list the numbers quickly become meaningless. Yet the quantitative approach is intended to make sense of the world, so techniques have evolved to do this.

When numbers are used to describe, illustrate or summarise aspects of our universe there are always three ways in which this can be done. And we emphasise the term *always*. Irrespective of what we want to do with our numbers, be it to describe (the purpose of this chapter) or to draw inferences, compare groups or explore relationships (the themes considered in Chapter 5), there are always three things we can do with our numbers – we can form our numbers into *tables*, we can generate *charts* from the numbers, and we can calculate *statistics*. This is especially true of the procedures outlined in the following sections, in which techniques are considered for describing, summarising and illustrating the social world through numbers – **descriptive techniques**.

4.2.1 Tables

At their most basic, tables allow us to organise numerical information in a way that imposes some order on our data, and in this way they serve the functions described in the introduction to this section, of summarising and simplifying.

Imagine a research scenario in which we are interested in the performance of skilled versus unskilled individuals on some co-ordination task (readers are alerted to the imminent return of amphibian-based analogies). As part of our study we may feel it relevant to report on, or describe, the key characteristics of our sample, and what better way to do this than in a table.

Table 4.1 in Box 4.1 is a good example of a simple table which reduces, summarises and describes

---

Box 4.1 Lots of tables

Tables and their uses: *gender* (sex of subject)

Table 4.1 The distribution of males and females.

	Value	Frequency	%	Cum.%
Male	1	14	46.7	46.7
Female	2	16	53.3	100.0
Total		30	100.0	100.0

More tables and their uses: *skill* (cycling skill level of participants)

Table 4.2 The distribution of skilled and unskilled subjects.

	Value	Frequency	%	Cum.%
Skilled	1	15	50.0	50.0
Unskilled	2	15	50.0	100.0
Total		30	100.0	100.0

Table 4.3 Distribution of male and female cyclists by skill level.

Sex of participant * cycling skill Crosstabulation
Count

		cycling skill		Total
		skilled	unskilled	
sex of participant	male	8	6	14
	female	7	9	16
Total		15	15	30

information in a way that is both easy to follow and meaningful. In the examples in Box 4.1 tables have been used to organise information in a way that both summarises and describes, a particularly appropriate technique for nominally-scaled information. Tables 4.1 and 4.2 are known as **frequency tables** (the frequencies with which subjects fall into each category are reported) while Table 4.3 is slightly more sophisticated, being a contingency table. Contingency tables are combination tables whose contents are the result of a **crosstabulation**, a procedure whereby frequencies are reported across two different variables – in this case we are presented with information on individuals who were both male and skilled, etc. (For the sake of completeness, the placing of any one individual in the table is contingent upon both their gender and their skill level.) (See data set M&K.dat2)

While most studies require that the researchers report on the characteristics of their subjects, this is especially true of survey-based research, in which the disposition of a sample is often the whole point of the study: how many subjects claimed they would support the Conservatives at the next election, as opposed to Labour; how many respondents voted Yes on the issue of a single European currency; of these, how many were male, middle class and living in rural communities, and so on. However, tables are not the only way to represent this type of information, which can sometimes have a more immediate impact when presented graphically.

Box 4.2   Picture this

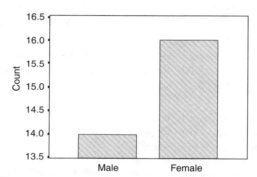

Figure 4.1   The distribution of males and females.

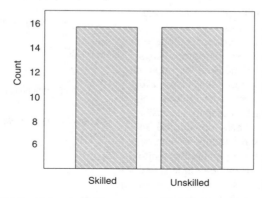

Figure 4.2   The distribution of skilled and unskilled cyclists.

continued

Box 4.2 *continued*

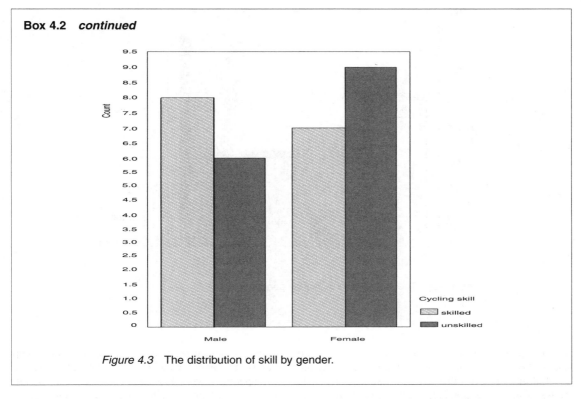

Figure 4.3 The distribution of skill by gender.

4.2.2 Graphs

While no one would deny the importance of tabular illustrations, it must be said that not everyone is comfortable with this approach. Aside from the fact that many of us seem to have an inherent fear of numbers, causing us to shy away from even the most informative of table, presenting information pictorially often has more immediate impact. Graphs can be colourful, striking even; moreover, apart from appealing to an apparent liking for visualisation, they can often emphasise effects which could easily be overlooked in the dry world of tabulation. The figures in Box 4.2 reproduce the information displayed in the preceding tables.

Each of the figures has been produced using the extensive range of display options usually available to the user of modern computer software, to achieve a pleasing but uncluttered effect. Generally speaking most researchers tend to shun over-embellishment, partly as a matter of taste, and partly because over-complexity in an illustration might obscure those very characteristics of the data the figure is attempting to demonstrate. On a practical note, complex, multi-coloured illustrations are also expensive to reproduce

and many publishers of papers, journal articles and book chapters will often prefer a simpler way to make a point. Consequently, in this particular textbook you will find the majority of graphs and charts presented in a relatively straightforward manner. And forget colour – the publishers wouldn't spend the money.

Many undergraduates, especially those new to sophisticated presentational software, find the range of illustrative options irresistible (Figure 4.4 – don't copy this!). Tempting as it is to play with styles and chart options, the best advice is, keep it simple and be consistent – don't keep changing the format of figures and tables.

4.2.3 Statistics

The third method for making sense of our universe is quite different from the previous two: tables and graphs both tend to provide a broad view of the data, with illustration and description being their primary function. Statistics on the other hand can express and summarise substantial amounts of data with a single value. This is what a statistic is – a numerical value

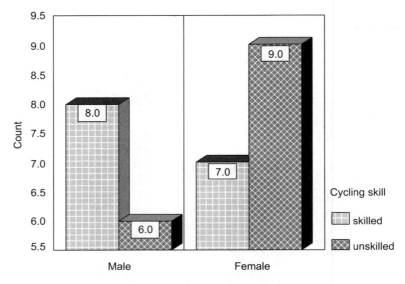

Figure 4.4   The distribution of skill by gender.

which represents a body of data according to certain established conventions, plus (usually) an associated symbol that identifies the particular aspect of our data being expressed. Moreover, a statistic is often merely the first step in a more complex analysis, in the way that a measure of average can often be used as the basis for comparison with other measures of average. The next section illustrates the point, while Box 4.11 later in this chapter presents common statistical symbols and their associated meanings.

4.3   Using statistics to illustrate and describe

4.3.1   Statistical measures – central tendency

When trying to describe or illustrate the typical characteristics of a variable, we often opt for some measure of central tendency (jargon for average) which best represents our information. Consequently we describe the heights of a group of undergraduates in terms of an arithmetic average and, because we are used to using this kind of statistic in our everyday lives, we readily understand that average is only a part of the story; while most people will cluster

around some central measure, we nonetheless accept that some people will score higher than this, and some people lower. Observing that the average height of a group of undergraduates is 5'9" recognises the fact that there will be some students who measure 5'10", or even 6'. Similarly, there will be some people who measure 5'8" or 5'7", but by and large, most of the people will measure round about the 5'9" mark. This is what average is all about, the almost universal tendency for anything we care to observe to cluster around some central or typical measure. (Some readers may be uncomfortable with our use of old-style imperial measures, preferring metres and centimetres. It is, however, an age thing and we like feet and inches.)

The term 'average' is usually taken to represent the arithmetic average, in which all the scores or values in a set of observations are summed, then divided by the number in the set. Statistically, this is known as the arithmetic **mean** (symbolised by $\bar{x}$) and it is the most precise of all the different measures of centrality based, as it is, on actual scores. However, there are situations in which the mean, irrespective of its accuracy, may not fulfil the function of indicating typicality. This can occur when a distribution contains one or more extreme scores, or outliers, as in the example in Box 4.3.

In example (i) in Box 4.3, the arithmetic mean works out as 8.3, which is fairly typical of the way

---

Box 4.3 The mean as a measure of central tendency

(i) the mental age scores of male undergraduates

      5, 6, 7, 7, 8, 8, 8, 9, 9, 10, 11, 12   mean = 8.3

(ii) the mental age scores of female undergraduates

      5, 6, 7, 7, 8, 8, 8, 9, 10, 11, 120   mean = 18

---

scores are clustered in this group. In example (ii), however, the mean is 18, which clearly is typical of none of the members of this particular group. (If you are wondering, by the way, how such an extreme score as 120 could find its way into a group whose real average is closer to 8, admittedly this is unusual. Perhaps a passing alien of outstanding intelligence joined the class to see what we humans were up to, or perhaps we made a mistake in measuring our subjects. Either way, the calculated mean is going to be misleading.)

To deal with such problems, which are really quite common (not the part about the alien), an alternative measure of central tendency is available to us which is not so sensitive to extreme values. This is the **median**, which is simply the middle value in a range of scores (arranged in order from lowest to highest that is,

rather than simply jumbled up). In example (i), the median would be 8. In case (ii) the median is also 8, a much more representative value than the arithmetic average, and a statistic not in the least influenced by the extreme score of 120.

This tendency for the middle value in any range of scores to provide a good measure of average is a universal phenomenon, allowable by the fact that the measurement of every human characteristic will always produce a clustering of observations that will typify the majority. Height, shoe size, intelligence, income, whatever – there is invariably a measure, or range of measures which is most typical of that particular trait. Hence, the middle value will invariably fall within this common, or most typical cluster, which is why the median is usually a good measure of average.

There exists a third measure of central tendency, which is really a 'rule of thumb' indicator, termed the **mode**. The mode, or modal value, is the most frequently occurring score in a series of observations and as such, often provides the simplest and speediest estimate of average. Providing the trait or characteristic being measured is of the kind where most people are scoring around some typical level, the mode will give a similar value to the other two measures. In both the examples in Box 4.3, the mode is 8. Box 4.4 illustrates all three measures of central tendency.

Box 4.4 The mean, median and mode compared

If people are drawn at random from the general population and their shoe size measured, the following arrays of scores might be produced:

(i)   2, 2, 2, 3, 3, 4, 5, 5, 5, 5, 5, 6, 6, 7, 7, 8, 9

Each of the three measures of average is suitable here, with the mean, median and mode giving a typical score of 5.

(ii)   5, 5, 6, 7, 7, 7, 8, 8, 9, 9, 10, 10, 10, 10, 11, 11, 12, 13, 14

Here, the mean is 8.95, the median 9 and the mode – in fact, there are two modes, making this measure of average inappropriate here. Both the mean and median are the most useful measures of central tendency in this case. And if you are wondering why there appear to be two groupings of 'typical' sizes, this could be attributable to the fact that this particular sample comprises a mixture of males and females, and that their shoe sizes are sufficiently different to give two distinct clusters.

(iii)   5, 5, 6, 7, 7, 7, 8, 8, 9, 9, 10, 11, 25, 37

In this final example, the occurrence of two extreme scores at the top end of the range will artificially pull the calculated arithmetic average towards this extreme. Hence, the mean here would be 11. The median, however, immune as it is to the effects of such extreme scores, would be the much more reasonable 8, with the mode not far away at 7.

(Note: in the event that a median fails to land on an actual middle value, as will be the case with all even-numbered arrays, the procedure is to take the average of the two adjacent scores. Thus, a median falling between the values of 5 and 6 would become 5.5.)

Finally, most contemporary statistical software, if it is good enough, will make allowances for the fact that extreme scores are possible in any study. The SPSS output shown in Box 4.5 is a typical example, in which the true arithmetic mean is printed alongside an adjusted mean, which has removed the top and bottom 5% of values from its calculations (5% trim). This serves the purpose of eliminating much of the influence of extreme scores. It also, however, reduces the size of the data set, which must be taken into consideration, especially where sample sizes are already small.

4.3.2 Dispersion

In describing the characteristics of a variable it should now be clear that relying solely on measures of central tendency provides only part of the picture. Much of the discussion in the previous section involved problems associated with how widely, or unevenly, scores varied around some central measure, and this aspect of any variable or distribution is of considerable interest to researchers.

Much in the same way that even the layman has an intuitive grasp of the concept of average, so too do most of us have a working understanding of dispersion, even if we lack the statistical skills to generate appropriate measures.

Think back to school days and class exams: if you scored 46 in an arithmetic test and stated that the class average was only 45, you would be more likely to impress parents and friends by pointing out that the top mark was 47. Alternatively, if you scored 50 to the same mean of 45, you might just keep quiet about the fact that the total range of marks was from 0 to 100!

What we have been applying here is the simplest measure of dispersion, the **range**, which is a statement of the lowest score to the highest. Table 4.4 illustrates this, with SPSS providing both the range and a minimum and maximum value. (Note: as with central tendency there are several measures of dispersion.)

As we have already discovered with central tendency, trying to reduce a large amount of information to a typical, representative value is not without its problems, in particular the misleading effects caused by extreme scores. In much the same way, a simple range, or a statement of minimum and maximum values, can be equally inappropriate when extreme scores are present. Table 4.4 illustrates the point: the minimum and maximum values are given as 5 and 37 respectively, with a corresponding range of 32. This implies a broad spread of scores, yet we know that the majority of subjects in this group had shoe sizes in the 5–11 range (see Box 4.4). Fortunately, just as with measures of average there exist alternative ways to represent spread that are not susceptible to extremes.

One such measure is related to the median and is known as the **interquartile range**, or IQR. Just as any array of scores can be divided in two by the median, or middle value, so can it be further subdivided: if we

---

Box 4.5   Big foot and how some averages are better than others

Descriptives

		Statistic
shoe size	Mean	5.0714
	5% Trimmed Mean	5.0794
	Median	5.0000
moreshoe size	Mean	8.5000
	5% Trimmed Mean	8.5000
	Median	8.5000
evenmore shoe size	Mean	11.0000
	5% Trimmed Mean	9.8889
	Median	8.0000

The three examples are extracts from SPSS outputs based on the data shown in Box 4.4, relating to measurements of different shoe size. While a great deal of information is typically shown in response to a request for descriptive statistics, since our concern at the moment is with measures of central tendency only, the normal output has been curtailed. In each example SPSS has provided three measures of average – a mean, a median and a trimmed mean, in which scores at either end of the range have been eliminated. In most cases this has little effect, except for reducing the range of values on which the average has been calculated, as in the first two examples. In the third illustration, however, where there are two extreme scores, the mean becomes inappropriate as a typical measure of average. The 5% trim gives a more representative value, as confirmed by the similar median value.

(Note: a useful hint for embryonic statisticians is to compare the mean and median values in a distribution. If the distribution is normal, as in a typical clustering around some middle score with a few cases tailing off at either side, the median and the mean will be close to one another. However, when extreme scores are present the calculation of the mean will be influenced and noticeable differences will be observed in comparison to the median. The evenmore shoe size example above illustrates this.)

Table 4.4 The spread of feet.

Descriptives

			Statistic	Std. Error
evenmore shoe size	Mean		11.0000	2.3950
	95% Confidence Interval for Mean	Lower Bound	5.8258	
		Upper Bound	16.1742	
	5% Trimmed Mean		9.8889	
	Median		8.0000	
	Variance		80.308	
	Std. Deviation		**8.9615**	
	Minimum		5.00	
	Maximum		37.00	
	Range		**32.00**	
	Interquartile Range		**3.5000**	
	Skewness		2.432	.597
	Kurtosis		5.639	1.154

take the lower half of a distribution and divide this in turn by half, we obtain two quarters. Similarly, if we take the upper half and further divide this, we also obtain two quarters. These two further subdivisions are known as the lower quartile and the upper quartile (or Q1 and Q3). See below.

```
5 5 6 7 7 I 7 7 8 8 9 I 9 10 10 10 10 I 11 11 12 13 14
      Q1          Median          Q3
       7             9            10.5
```

All we need to do is subtract the value at the first quartile from the value at the third (Q3 – Q1), and we have the interquartile range, which is a measure of spread in which the top and bottom quarters have been removed, thus eliminating any extreme values. In the above example the IQR would be 3.5.

There exists a third measure of spread which, like the mean, is based on the actual scores or values found in a distribution. Termed the **standard deviation**, this provides an indication of how much, on average, scores deviate from the mean. Because it is based on actual values it is a very accurate and powerful statistic. For the same reason, however, it is also susceptible to extreme values and if a distribution becomes too skewed in one direction, the standard deviation ceases to be of value in representing a distribution. Box 4.6 completes our review of dispersion.

4.3.3 Graphs

We have noted previously how useful graphs can be for illustrating large amounts of data. The bargraphs at

Figures 4.1, 4.2 and 4.3 (Section 4.2.2) are informative and high impact illustrations of their respective nominal categories, not only clearly describing the characteristics of each group, but allowing an immediate, visual comparison of different groups. Similarly, the type of data on which means and standard deviations can be calculated (i.e. interval data) is also susceptible to graphing techniques, again allowing alternative methods for presenting the same information.

The examples shown in Box 4.7 are further illustrations of how SPSS produces a range of charts in support of underlying numerical data.

4.4 The normal distribution

A major characteristic of the social world is the tendency for certain patterns to repeat themselves. One such pattern, observed whenever we measure an event, attitude, response or behaviour, is the tendency for most people to congregate around some middle value, with fewer and fewer people falling into more extreme categories. This always happens if the group we are observing reflects the 'normal population' – normal in that there is the expected variation among individuals in the group we are measuring. Putting it another way, this is the pattern we normally see whenever we observe any human or social phenomenon. When we fail to observe this typical outcome we talk of a distribution being skewed (see Box 4.8).

We have already witnessed this effect with our previous examples on shoe size (see Boxes 4.4 and 4.5)

Box 4.6   Calculating the standard deviation

Consider the example of the shoe sizes of a group of undergraduates, shown below:

2, 2, 2, 3, 3, 4, 5, 5, 5, 5, 5, 6, 6, 7, 7, 8, 9

The calculated mean (obtained by adding up the individual sizes and dividing by the number of observations) is 4.9. To find out how much each score varies, or deviates from this value, we perform a simple subtraction:

Mean	Score	(Mean-score)
4.9	2	2.9
4.9	2	2.9
4.9	2	2.9
4.9	3	1.9
.	.	.
.	.	.
.	.	.

In approximately half the cases, taking each score from the mean will produce a positive value, as above. Because, however, about half of the scores in a distribution will be greater than the mean, the results of some of these calculations will be negative values, as below:

Mean	Score	(Mean-score)
.	.	.
.	.	.
.	.	.
4.9	5	−0.1
4.9	6	−1.1
4.9	7	−2.1

In many statistical calculations, negative values are irritations. In the calculation of the standard devia-tion, they are eliminated by squaring the result of each subtraction:

Mean	Score	(Mean-score)	(Mean-score) squared
.	.	.	.
4.9	5	−0.1	0.01
4.9	6	−1.1	1.21
4.9	7	−2.1	4.41
.	.	.	.

The total deviations can now be obtained by adding up all these squared values, but what we really want is an average of these, obtained simply by dividing by the number of observations. However, just when we thought we had the answer, we mustn't forget that we are currently dealing with squared scores and not the original values, and this must be rectified. Taking the square root will finally pro-vide the statistic known as the standard deviation.

In summary, the standard deviation is obtained by: subtracting each score from the mean; squaring this value; summing these values and taking an average; taking the square root.

Alternatively, for those comfortable with statistical expressions, this can be shown as a formula:

$$SD = \sqrt{\frac{\Sigma(x-\bar{x})^2}{N}}$$

Referring to Table 4.4, the standard deviation for the evenmore shoe size example is shown, and the exagger-ated measure caused by the extreme scores is apparent. (Note: a breakdown of the expressions in the above for-mula can be seen in Box 4.11.)

---

but the notion holds true for most other factors, such as age, education level, income or indeed any aspect of existence in which there is variation.

Studies of general intelligence, for instance, show that most of us will cluster around some average measure, usually given the arbitrary value of 100 (based on Louis Terman's development of the original Binet mental age and chronological age relationship). As with height, there will be some people who will score in higher ranges (105–110), but there will be fewer of these. At more extreme ranges (110–120) there will be fewer still. This typical pattern is illus-trated in Figure 4.8, a histogram in which the heights of each bar represent the number of observations giv-ing particular scores.

This pattern, of course, will only occur providing the group being measured is normal. (Recall that this use of the expression 'normal' is a statistical one, referring to a typical, or expected pattern.) If, by some chance, the observations on intelligence were made on an unusually bright group (who mentioned our students?) there would be more than the usual (or normal) proportion of intellectually superior people in our sample. Therefore the distribution of scores would reflect this '**skew**', as illustrated in Box 4.8.

In most instances the kind of skewness illustrated in Box 4.8 will not occur if the group we are observ-ing is typical, or normal, or the sample an honest reflection of the population at large. You might recall the discussion in Chapter 3 in which sampling issues were considered: in particular, the problem of inad-vertently over-representing particular groups was noted, a problem that could easily give rise to a

Box 4.7   At a glance

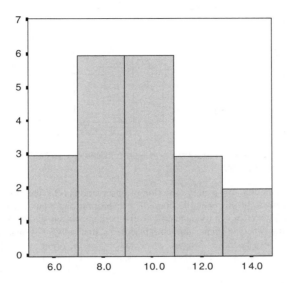

Figure 4.5.

Figure 4.5, a **histogram**, provides an 'at a glance' representation of the moreshoe data shown in Boxes 4.4 and 4.5. Immediately apparent is that the most frequent shoe sizes are occurring around some central value between 8 and 10, and that the range of shoe size is from 5 to 15. (The actual values were mean = 8.9 and range 5–14, making our visual judgement on the basis of the histogram pretty impressive.)

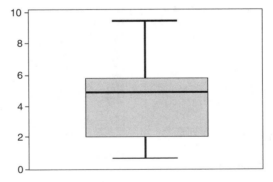

Figure 4.6.

Figure 4.6, based on the shoe size data shown in Boxes 4.4 and 4.5, is known as a **boxplot** and is another frequent illustrative chart, utilising the measures of median, IQR and overall range. Many people new to this mode of presentation find boxplots unintelligible, yet once their principle is understood, they quickly become a useful tool for the researcher.

The median value is indicated by the black bar running through the shaded box (in previous versions of SPSS this was shown by a simple asterisk). The upper and lower quartiles are shown by the upper and lower limits of the rectangle itself, while the overall range of values is shown by the horizontal lines resembling the plunger on a syringe (actually termed the 'whiskers' of the plot).

Inspection of this chart would suggest that the average shoe size is just over 5, the interquartile range about 3 and the overall range of sizes going from 2 up to 9. (The actual values were median = 5; IQR = 3.5; range = 7 – again, an impressive judgement from a chart.)

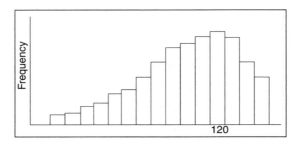

Box 4.8   Skewness

Figure 4.7 Histogram showing a skewed distribution of IQ scores.

When a distribution contains more than the usual proportion of observations near one of the two ends of the measurement scale, it is said to be skewed. In this example, there is a disproportionate number of observations close to the higher end of the distribution. This is known (counter-intuitively, perhaps) as a negative skew. This tendency for some distributions to deviate from the expected shape can be represented statistically, as shown below.

Mean	112.5000	Std Err	.6270	Min	70.0000	Skewness	−.9191
Median	115.0000	Variance	176.9321	Max	135.0000	S E Skew	.1151
5% Trim	113.2778	Std Dev	13.3016	Range	65.0000	Kurtosis	.8212

The skewness statistic of −.9191 is calculated using a formula that considers how much each score deviates from the mean, and interprets these differences in terms of the standard deviation. Fortunately, SPSS does all this for us and all we need to do is inspect the coefficient of skewness for magnitude. If necessary, a simple rule of thumb method for estimating skewness is to compare the mean with the median, reminding yourself of the tendency for the mean to be affected by extreme scores in a way in which the median is not.

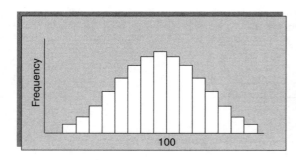

Figure 4.8 Histogram showing the distribution of IQ scores around a mean of 100.

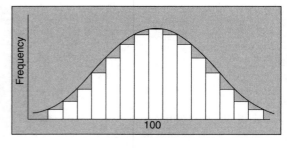

Figure 4.9.

skewed distribution. If sampling is carried out properly though, and if what we are measuring conforms to the typical human pattern, the type of distribution we obtain is called a **normal distribution**. Statisticians usually prefer to display such trends, not in the form of histograms, but in the form of a 'bell-shaped' or 'inverted U' curve, as in Figure 4.9.

All normal distributions share this typical shape, and they also share similar characteristics:

1   The shape of the distribution is always symmetrical.
2   The highest point of the distribution represents the mean. (And because this distribution is so symmetrical, this point will also represent the median and the mode.)
3   Furthermore, due to this symmetry, each half of the distribution will account for 50% of the scores (see Figure 4.10).
4   Dividing the normal distribution into equal halves is only the beginning of the descriptive potential

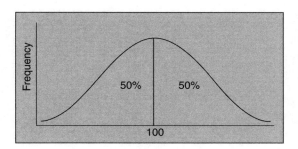

Figure 4.10.

for this particular shape: e.g. we can identify the particular score below which only 25% of the sample falls (Figure 4.11). Likewise, we can identify a similar score at the other end of the distribution, above which 25% of the sample falls. This is a procedure we have already considered in the section on dispersion, when the concept of quartiles was introduced (see Section 4.3.2).

In case no one's noticed, it's worth pointing out that we have actually progressed from looking at specific examples involving a sample, some kind of measure of average and a range of scores, to what is in effect a theoretical model of just about any human characteristic one might think of. Just as the mean is simply a useful statistic that typifies or symbolises a range of scores, so too the **standard normal distribution** (as it is termed when it serves as a model, rather than a representation of some concrete measure) merely offers a general picture of the way most aspects of human endeavour within society look – a lot of people clustering around some middle value, with the number of cases declining the further removed they are from this point.

The significance of this evolution from the real to the theoretical is that if most actual human characteristics conform to an approximation of this normal shape, then whatever can be deduced from the standard normal distribution (i.e. the theoretical model) will hold true for real life. Consequently, because all normal distributions share the same symmetry, it is possible to identify standard distances from the mean, and to know what proportions of scores fall on either side of these points. For this, we use the formula for the standard deviation (SD) already encountered at Box 4.6:

$$SD = \sqrt{\frac{\Sigma\,(x - \bar{x})^2}{N}}$$

This formula allows us to divide our distribution into three equal proportions on either side of the mean: 1, 2 and 3 SDs above the mean, and -1, -2 and -3 below the mean, as in Figure 4.12.

In case we are in danger of losing anyone at this point, it is worth recalling that in this perfectly balanced distribution, a line down the centre will divide the distribution into two equal halves. Similarly, a distribution based on some real social element, be it income of a particular group, a measure of stress within certain occupations or levels of weekly spending, so long as it conforms pretty well to the now typical shape, will also be divided in two by some measure of centrality – in other words, the mean. By way of illustration, if the weekly family spending bill in a given region is normally distributed, with a mean of £100, we know therefore (because of our increasing understanding of the characteristics of this kind of shape) that 50% of the families measured have spent close to or below this value, while the other 50% spent close to or above £100 per week.

Developing from here we can now return to the notion of the standard deviation, recognising that what this particular statistic does is divide a distribution (providing it approximates the characteristic shape of the normal curve) into six segments, or intervals, based on the absolute range of scores. And because all normal distributions are symmetrical, we can expect to

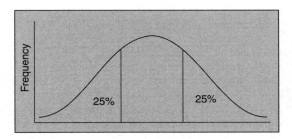

Figure 4.11 Subdividing the distribution.

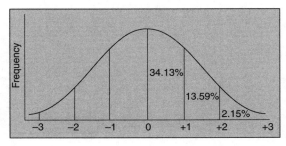

Figure 4.12 Standard deviations from the mean.

find that about 34% of the scores are between the mean and one SD above. Another 34% are between the mean and one SD below. Since the number of cases decline the further away we travel from the mean, the interval between the first and second SDs will comprise 13.59% of all observations, with the third and last interval containing the remaining 2.15%.

For example, if we discovered that our family spending distribution had a mean of £100 and a SD of £5, we would know that the dividing points above the mean are £105; £110; £115. Similarly, the dividing points below the mean are £95; £90; £85.

Actual (raw) spending amounts (£)

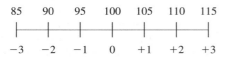

Equivalent standard deviation values

Thus for any normal distribution, if we divide the distribution into three equal parts above and below the mean, we know that the proportion of scores falling between the particular values will always be: 34.13%; 13.59% and 2.15%. While these proportions remain constant, the actual values that represent the different standard deviation positions will obviously change.

For example, Figure 4.13 is based on a distribution of weekly family spending ranging from £85 to £115 overall. If we conducted a similar study in a different region, we might find that, although our mean was again £100, the range of weekly spending might be broader, as in £70 to £130. With individuals spread out across this more extensive spending range, then our standard deviation value would be different, i.e. 10. Figure 4.14 illustrates this point.

Therefore, while the shape of our new distribution would be the same as in the original example, and while the proportion of scores falling between any

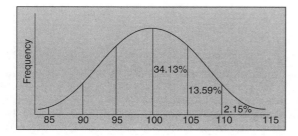

Figure 4.13 The proportion (percentage) of observations falling between SD subdivisons.

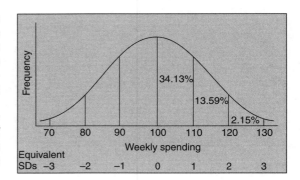

Figure 4.14 Normal distribution of spending, ranging from £70 to £130.

given standard deviation points would be the same, the actual raw scores reflecting these standard units would be different.

To calculate where any individual score falls in a distribution, we need to transform it into the same kind of score as standard deviation scores, reminding ourselves that the standard deviation allows us to divide up a distribution in terms of percentages. Known as a **z-score** this tells us how many SDs a score of, say, 103 is above the mean, or how many SDs a score of, say, 94 is below the mean. The significance of this information is demonstrated in Box 4.9.

To summarise this section we restate that all societal elements possess the same approximate characteristics. Most observations will congregate around some central value, with decreasing numbers falling above and below. Presenting these common characteristics graphically invariably produces an approximation to the normal distribution, a theoretical distribution that nonetheless allows us to predict the proportion or percentage of observations that will fall between any two points, irrespective of the actual scores that comprise the real distribution, as the example in Box 4.10 will hopefully illustrate.

To conclude this part of Chapter 4 we return to the subject matter of earlier sections in which we introduced the concept of statistics – a set of values which expressed or summarised data in various ways, along with associated symbols that allow us to identify the particular aspects of our world they represent. There are many such statistics and readers will inevitably encounter them at some point in their research. Box 4.11 presents the most common of these, along with appropriate explanations.

Box 4.9 What are *z*-scores?

To understand the relationship between a single score and a distribution of scores of which it is a part, the score must be transformed into a form that can be interpreted in terms of our standard normal distribution. Once this transformation has taken place, we can now view our score in terms of percentage differences above or below the mean.

Transforming a score into a *z*, or standardised, score can be achieved via the formula shown below:

$$z = \frac{x - \bar{x}}{\text{SD}}$$

With a mean of 100 and an SD of 10, a raw score of 103 converts to a *z*-score of $+0.3$, and a raw score of 94 has a *z*-score of -0.6. With a mean of 100 and an SD of 5 (as in Figure 4.13), a raw score of 103 has a *z*-score of $+0.6$, and a raw score of 94 has a *z*-score of -1.2, and so on. However, aside from offering a visualisation of how far a particular score deviates from its mean, more precise information can be offered. Recalling that normal distributions can be subdivided into standard deviation units, each with its own known percentage of observations, it ought to be possible to interpret any individual score also in terms of percentages. This is precisely what can be done with *z*-scores.

Consulting the statistical tables that invariably form an appendix to any modern statistics textbook will identify the tables of proportions of area under the normal curve. Such tables state the proportion, or percentage of cases which, for a given mean and standard deviation, will fall between a *z*-score and its mean, or which will fall beyond *z*.

By way of example, if our score of 103 above generated a *z*-score of $+0.6$, the appropriate statistical tables indicate that 22.57% of all the scores that made up that particular distribution fall between this score and the mean. Alternatively, the same tables will indicate that 27.43% of all scores fell above this score. See Figure 4.15.

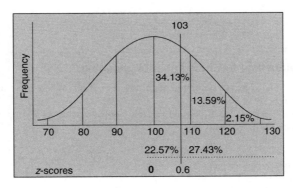

Figure 4.15 The position of an individual score on the standard normal distribution.

4.5 Computer analysis and SPSS

In the last decade the advances in statistical computing have been extremely rapid, with numerous systems proliferating in an attempt to capture a section of a huge market. Initially available only as mainframe facilities in large academic departments, such systems became progressively accessible to owners of small portable machines until today, anyone with a half-decent PC or Macintosh computer now has at their disposal the type of analytical power once only available to major universities.

Software too has undergone a revolution with the once cumbersome command-driven packages giving way to the more user-friendly, menu-driven approach. This method of manipulating files and carrying out complex operations has proven extremely successful and now, with the advent of Windows software for PC owners, advanced statistical software is now in reach of us all. (Windows is either a registered trademark or trademark of

---

Box 4.10   I can't take any more of this

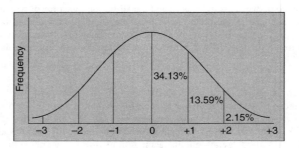

Figure 4.16.

A study among the readership of this book identified a mean reading time (average time anyone can stand to read any of this before nodding off or suddenly remembering an urgent engagement elsewhere, like cleaning the bathroom) of 7 minutes, with an SD of 2 minutes. We therefore know that approximately 68% of our readers can manage between 5 and 9 minutes at any time.

Box 4.11   Common statistical symbols and their meaning

x	a score, or the column heading for a variable in univariate analysis. Where more than one variable is present, the notations become x_1, x_2 ... x_n.
y	a score, or the column heading for the second variable in bivariate analysis. Also the variable heading for the dependent variable in 3-group comparisons.
Σ	the sum of ... (whatever follows)
Σx	the sum of the scores
x^2	the square of the score, or scores
Σx^2	the sum of the squared scores
$(\Sigma x)^2$	the sum of the scores, which is then squared
$\sqrt{}$	the square root
!	factorial (e.g. $!5 = 5*4*3*2*1 = 120$)
$\bar{x}$	a sample mean. Obtained by $\Sigma x/n$
s	a sample standard deviation, used as an estimate of the population standard deviation
μ	a population mean
σ	a population standard deviation
n	the number of observations in a sample
N	the number of observations in a population
s^2	sample variance

Microsoft Corporation in the United States and/or other countries.)

There are many different varieties of statistical software and departments, and individuals within those departments all have their own preferences. However, increasingly, one particular system has been developing – at least in Europe – as the academic industry standard, the system known as SPSS (Statistical Package for the Social Sciences). It is this particular system that will form the basis for the following illustrations.

4.6   The basics of working with SPSS

Let us assume that the superb piece of research that you so painstakingly designed has been completed and now you find yourself staring at a small mountain of data – numbers, ratings, responses or reams of dialogue. The chances are that for many, the thoughts that accompany such piles of information go along the lines of 'What am I going to do with all these numbers?' The answer couldn't be simpler. These numbers are going to be sorted, simplified and summarised, they will be reduced to statistics that will impose meaning on the factor or behaviour they represent and they will be used to draw inferences and test hypotheses. They will also form the basis for a variety of graphs and charts that will illustrate, highlight and describe. But before any of this is possible, we must create a space to store our information – we must create an SPSS data file.

Those new to computer statistical software might be daunted by the scale of a package like SPSS, but in its use, nothing could be simpler, as the following sections will demonstrate.

4.6.1   Setting up variables and data entry

The first contact with SPSS takes the form of a blank spreadsheet, a kind of template that opens automatically when the programme is activated (by clicking or double-clicking on the SPSS icon similar to that in Figure 4.17). At this stage the spreadsheet comprises merely a grid of empty cells, devoid of data and not even titled, but forming the basis of a file in which all the information from any study can be stored. However, the SPSS spreadsheet is more than simply a bin for information; it offers the capacity to manipulate data

Figure 4.17   The SPSS icon.

and perform complex analyses via the symbols and menu options that form a part of it. Figure 4.18 illustrates the major elements of a typical blank spreadsheet: there are a number of empty cells (many thousands of these in fact, although only a screen's worth will be visible at any one time). This particular image is based on version 10 of SPSS, currently (at the time of going to press) the most up to date of the releases. Moreover, the layout is similar to earlier versions (back to version 6) and is relevant to both Macintosh and PC equipment.

The title of the particular spreadsheet or data set is always shown, although initially this appears as a file called 'untitled'. Not until you actually enter some data into the spreadsheet and save your work are you given the opportunity to give your data set, and your file, an appropriate name.

Beneath the title area is a ribbon of buttons, a series of small symbols that when selected (by a single mouse click) perform various functions. Some switch the view from the data spreadsheet (containing all the numbers and values generated in your research) to the variable view spreadsheet (showing each variable in your file), along with explanatory information. Some change the way the data appears and one initiates printing (Figure 4.19).

Not all of these buttons will be available until the spreadsheet contains data, and in fact when the first untitled file is opened several of the symbols will be 'greyed out', indicating that they are currently deactivated. In the sample empty spreadsheet in

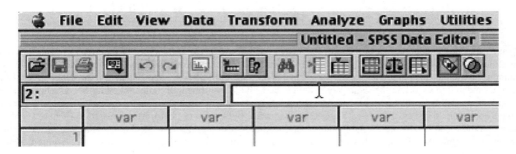

Figure 4.18   An SPSS spreadsheet.

Figure 4.19   The printer icon.

Figure 4.18 for instance, the printing symbol is unavailable, and will not become active (as in Figure 4.19) until there is something to print.

The final part of this window (a window is whatever is currently on the screen) is the menu bar running along the top. Opening any of these menu items (by clicking and holding the mouse button depressed, or simply clicking in the PC versions) will display the various functions available under each heading. Generally speaking the main categories of operation are File Handling (opening new files, saving, etc.), Editing (copying, pasting and moving information about), and statistical functions. Box 4.12 offers an example of the menu items at work.

4.6.2   Coding data

Once a study is completed you will have available large amounts of data. Some of these will be what are termed **profile** or **subject data**, which comprise descriptive information on the individuals who participated in the study. For example, you will probably have numbered your subjects to enable you to identify cases while at the same time ensuring the anonymity of the actual participants. You are likely to know, for instance, if they were male or female, how old they were, whether married or single, working or unemployed, users of private or NHS health facilities, and whether they cycled or not (or whatever was relevant to the particular study). If the study took the form of a true experiment, you will also have information on which experimental condition subjects were assigned to (e.g. control or experimental). And finally, you are likely to have a number of outcome measures – responses to questions on a survey, scores on a number of questionnaire items or performance measures on some experimental task.

Box 4.12   Using menus in SPSS

All operations and functions within SPSS are accessed in the same way – using the mouse and selecting any of the menu items with a single button click will explore all the operations available under each heading.

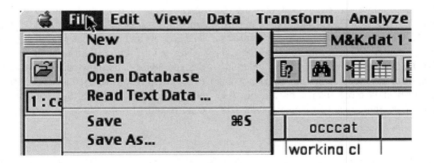

Opening the file menu at the top of the data spreadsheet will allow access to the types of functions shown. Selecting a particular function is achieved by dragging the arrowhead over each option until the desired one is selected. Releasing the mouse button at this point automatically selects this option and SPSS will happily perform the desired activity. All the other menu items work in the same way although, as with the assortment of toolbar symbols beneath the menu, not all operations will be available at any particular time. It is also worth noting that many operations can be carried out using a combination of keystrokes (e.g. Ctrl+O to open a file, or Command+O for Macintosh users). These are always shown on the menu if they are available and experienced users often prefer to work this way because of its speed. In the above example the File menu has been opened and you will see that the keystroke shortcut for saving updates is Command+S, or ⌘S

Box 4.13   It depends on how you look at it

When we create a data file to hold all the information on our research there is more than one way in which we can display it. The most basic level of display is known in SPSS as the **data view**, which shows (not surprisingly) the actual numerical data we have gathered. The illustration below is an extract from the M&K data set 1 which presents the findings of a hypothetical social survey.

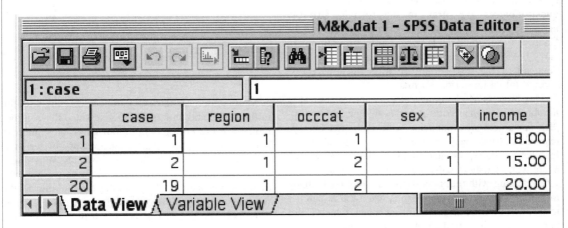

To remind ourselves what all these numbers mean we can choose what SPSS terms the variable view, a separate part of the display in which we can enter descriptions and explanatory information about our variables. See below.

	Name	Type	Width	Decimals	Label
1	case	Numeric	8	0	case id number
2	region	Numeric	8	0	major uk region
21					

◄ ► \ Data View ⅄ **Variable View** /

In this view we can type in relevant information, such as that the variable 'region' is a numeric variable, the numerical value used to identify particular regions has no decimal places and the variable itself stands for 'major uk region'. There are more options for customising your variables, as explained in later sections, but for the moment it is useful to appreciate that when presented with a data set (especially when encountering secondary data for the first time) we can readily discover what all the variables are and all the numbers mean by choosing the variable view. In a final refinement, we can combine some of the variable information with the basic data. When in data view, selecting the label symbol 🏷 switches the numerical codes to the categories they represent.

	case	region	occcat	sex
1	1	scotland	working cl	male
2	2	scotland	middle cla	male

Not all of this information though will necessarily be numerical. The respondent profile details are likely to be simply categories into which individuals can be placed (male or female; control or experimental). Likewise response or outcome data will often be in a non-numerical format – much survey data are in the form of nominal categories chosen by respondents (yes/no/don't know). Likewise, scaled responses on questionnaires are often in the format 'strongly agree/agree/uncertain/disagree/strongly disagree'(see Chapter 3, Section 3.4). However, if the intention is to carry out some form of quantitative analysis on your data, all of the relevant information must be transformed into a numerical format.

This process of changing category information into numbers is known as **coding**, and nothing could be simpler. A subject who happens to be male can be represented in the 'gender' variable by the value '1'; females can be represented by the value '2', and so on. Moreover, statistical software is at its most contented when dealing with numbers so the procedure has many merits; in fact, the only problem is when the researcher loses track of what all the numbers mean, which is not uncommon, although SPSS allows a record to be kept of such explanatory information in what it terms the variable view, as illustrated in Box 4.13. Alternatively, a full record of all the variables and numerical codes used in a data set can be obtained using one of a number of special commands, as demonstrated in Chapter 3, in Section 3.3 on secondary research. The actual logic and the processes behind coding are shown in Box 4.14.

4.6.3   Entering data and naming variables

Each variant of statistical software has its own set of preferences concerning data handling, but all share certain conventions, the most fundamental of which relate to how data are entered. The typical format – and that required by SPSS – is that all cases are identified by a subject or case number, in a single column. Traditionally this is the first set of data entered into any data set, although with the current version of SPSS this is no longer strictly necessary, since all the rows in its spreadsheet are numbered, and actually identified by the system as case numbers. However, the authors have found it a useful discipline to begin all data entry by identifying, numerically, each subject who participated in a study. This sets the scene as it were and makes it easier to deal logically with subsequent data entry and to correct errors.

Table 4.5   Average weekly supermarket spending (£) on luxury items for middle-class and working-class families.

Middle-class families	Working-class families
25	15
22	12
19	18
21	14
22	19
—	—
—	—

Many undergraduates experience difficulty with this initial stage, and understandably so since the common method of presenting data in journal articles and textbooks distinguishes among participants in terms of group or category, as Table 4.5 illustrates. When dealing with data in this format the intuitive way to enter them into a statistical spreadsheet is to mimic this two column table. While this is fine for publication or illustration purposes, it is not the way most statistical software works, as the next section demonstrates.

4.6.4   Data entry – between-group designs

The trick in error-free data entry is to begin, as mentioned in Section 4.6.3, with a single column listing of every subject or observation that comprised a particular study. Each successive column contains information relevant to its associated subject, whether it be subject or grouping characteristics, or outcome measures on some experimental task. Table 4.6 illustrates the point, presenting data for an experimental study in which one group of families participated in a health education programme emphasising dental care. Average spending on dental products was monitored following the programme, and compared to a control group of similar families who did not participate in the programme. (Note: this particular design conforms to that of a true experiment, as opposed to a quasi-experiment, and if you've no idea why, a look at Chapter 2 might help.)

All between-group data are organised in this way, with a separate column devoted to each variable as it relates to individual cases. In Table 4.6, Family 1 participated in the control condition and returned a weekly spend of £1. Family number 3 was in the group that participated in the dental education programme and returned a weekly spend of £4, and so on. The approach

Box 4.14   Coding data

When collecting data during the course of a study it is sometimes not possible, and occasionally undesirable, to record information numerically. Subject profile information is invariably presented in terms of specific categories (male/female; married/single), while some response variables are often more comfortably expressed qualitatively. Many subjects for instance are happier when allowed to respond to descriptive categories rather than numerical scales. Compare the examples below.

1   How satisfied are you with your course of study so far?

completely unsatisfied	unsatisfied	neutral	satisfied	completely satisfied
☐	☐	☐	☐	☐

2   Please rate on the scale below your level of satisfaction with the course so far. Selecting 1 indicates complete dissatisfaction; selecting 5 indicates complete satisfaction.

1	2	3	4	5
☐	☐	☐	☐	☐

While qualitative categories might be preferable for some subjects, if the ultimate aim of a study is quantitative analysis, such descriptive categories must be re-coded, which simply means replacing category information with an appropriate numerical value.

Item   **Code**

Subject no.   7

gender   M   F
                                          ☐   ☑   2

marital status   single   married
                                          ☑   ☐   1

condition   control   experimental
                                          ☐   ☑   2

How do you feel about the book so far?

brilliant	good	limited	awful
☑	☐	☐	☐

4

In the above example, all the items offer descriptive, qualitative responses to subjects. However, in order to analyse the data in terms of, for example, the percentage of males and females responding to a particular attitudinal category, or even to determine the number of single versus married subjects who participated in the control and experimental conditions, it is necessary to convert this information into a format that is more accessible to conventional statistical software. Hence, male subjects are coded with the value '1', and females '2'. (One of the contributors to this text wishes to point out that the convention of using 1 = male and 2 = female should not convey any sense of order or magnitude; the numbers merely differentiate between the classes on a **nominal scale**.)

continued

Box 4.14 *continued*

Likewise, other profile information can be coded numerically – *married* can be represented by the (arbitrary) value '2', with *single* coded as '1', or the other way around; it doesn't really matter, providing it makes sense and we are consistent. Responses on outcome measures are coded in the same kind of way, with the proviso that when response alternatives indicate degree, as in 'greater than' or 'less than', the numerical codes must reflect this. Consequently, coding of an item along the lines of: 'to what extent do you agree with…?' would generate an **ordinal scale** (1 2 3 4 5) in place of the categories 'strongly agree', 'agree' and so on. Many researchers take the additional step of regarding ordinally-scaled categories as representative of points on a continuous scale. This allows for a number of operations to be carried out, such as calculating a mean response across a number of related categories, as in the example below:

1   What do you feel about the book so far?

brilliant   good   limited   awful

☑   ☐   ☐   ☐   4

2   How good do you feel the statistical explanations have been?

brilliant   good   limited   awful

☐   ☐   ☐   ☑   1

3   How effective do you feel the graphical illustrations are in this text?

brilliant   good   limited   awful

☑   ☐   ☐   ☐   4

If we represent the descriptive terms of *awful* to *good* by the numbers 1 to 4 (with the higher values reflecting a more positive attitude) then an average value of 3 would represent the above responses. Overall, the attitude towards the text-book is positive.

Table 4.6   Monthly spending on dental care products for two groups of families.

Family	Condition	Spending on dental care (£)
1	control	1
2	control	2
3	education programme	4
4	education programmme	5
5	control	3
6	education programme	6
7	education programme	5
8	control	2
9	control	1
10	education programme	3

can of course be extended to allow for any number of variables, as is the case with traditional social science research. Much survey data and a great deal of government statistics are based on considerable quantities of information, such that for each individual participant or case there can be several dozen associated measures.

4.6.5   Data entry – within-group designs

When entering data for a within-subjects design, the general principle of one subject column followed by separate columns for each related variable still

Table 4.7 Monthly family spending on dental care products before and after a health education programme.

Family	Spending before (£)	Spending after (£)
1	1	4
2	2	5
3	3	6
4	2	5
5	1	3

holds. For example, if in the health education experiment outlined in Table 4.6 we decided that differences between the control and experimental groups were being confounded by the effects of individual differences (i.e. the families were just different and differences in dental care spending had nothing to do with the education programme), we might opt instead for a within-subjects design in which the same subjects participated in both conditions, as in Table 4.7.

Here again, there is a single column devoted to identifying the family or case number, with successive columns providing information relevant to each case. By way of example, Family 1 spent an average of just £1 on dental care products prior to the health education programme and £4 after.

4.7 Setting up data in SPSS

4.7.1 Working with SPSS

The first step in setting up a data file in SPSS is to recognise that all computer-based analytical systems appear initially dim, unhelpful and occasionally intransigent. Of course, software producers and distributors emphasise user-friendliness and sophisticated help functions yet the truth is that all such systems are designed not to be nice or awkward, but to obey. Few systems will make suggestions, none will make allowances and all of this makes life difficult for the novice. However, providing we appreciate that no statistical package will do any more than we tell it to do, then we are on the way to developing an effective working relationship.

Translated into actions this means that we must always explain what we are doing and what we expect in response. The majority of errors can usually be traced back to a failure to adequately, or fully 'explain' what is required. The next section,

and Box 4.15 in particular, demonstrates the main steps in setting up a data file in SPSS.

4.7.2 Naming and defining variables

For any analytical system to be able to work with a set of data – generate tables, draw graphs, make comparisons – it needs to be able to identify the variables that comprise the data set. This is the first task in data entry and it is initiated by clicking, or double-clicking (using the mouse button) on the column heading cell found at the top of the first empty column of data cells, or by selecting the **variable view** window at the bottom of the data window. See Box 4.15 for a full illustration of these procedures.

4.8 SPSS and descriptive statistics

So far in this chapter a large number of tables and graphs have been used to illustrate various points about measures of central tendency, dispersion and the general presentation of quantitative information. The remaining sections now deal with the procedures for generating this type of descriptive information, based around a hypothetical example of a study in which male and female students were asked to provide measures of their attitudes towards various issues. These could have been anything from the siting of contraceptive machines in the toilets to a liking for small, green amphibian creatures. The actual measures themselves are not important, serving only to provide a platform for the illustrations that follow. And in fact, this is an important point: there exists a set of procedures for describing and analysing data that doesn't distinguish among different possible research contexts. So, we could have opted for a sociological example, one from economics, a psychology study or an illustration from education. We have in fact opted for the one about small, green amphibians and Box 4.16 demonstrates the procedures for describing data.

As we have already explained, tables represent one of the most common methods of describing numerical data and most types of modern software – word processing, database and spreadsheet packages – offer excellent facilities for the production of high quality tables. For most purposes though the table facilities within SPSS are adequate, as Table 4.8 – based on our newt study – illustrates.

Box 4.15   Defining variables in SPSS

	Name	Type	Width	Decimals	Label	Values	Missing	Columns	Align	Measure
1	var000	Nu ⋯	8	2		None	None	8	Right	Scale ▼
2										

Selecting the variable view in SPSS activates an (initially) empty spreadsheet into which we can type details of the variables in our research, as in the above illustration. This example shows the default settings for all data (i.e. the way SPSS describes variables until we do something to change this description). Intimidating at the outset, the variable window quickly becomes a straightforward tool for the novice, once all its parts are explained, as follows.

The settings above refer to the first variable in our analysis (1) and SPSS has assigned it the Name var0001. Our first action would be to replace this with a **variable name** of our own choosing (case, gender, group, family, score, or whatever) with the proviso that our name does not exceed eight characters, which is the maximum allowed in any SPSS cell. We don't know why. The Type of variable is currently shown as Numeric, which will suit most of the variables you are likely to use, although you could have other types, such as string (this would be people's names, or towns, or countries) or date. These other options become available by clicking at the top of the Type column. The Width of our numeric variable is set at eight characters and whatever number we type in SPSS will automatically round it to two decimal places (2 Decimals).

The next setting is an important one: since our variable name will often comprise an abbreviation or some personal code (remember we can only use eight characters) we often wish to attach a more usefully descriptive label. For example, our variable name might be simply 'reg', and we expand on this in the Label column by typing in 'major uk region'.

Sometimes a variable will be of the category type, with the variable name being a collective for a number of groups or categories. For instance, the variable 'gender' will be made up of two groups (male and female); the variable 'class' might have five, and so on. However, recall that, like most analytical packages, SPSS does not actually work with alphabetic information (words) although it will display it. Categories then, such as male and female, have to be represented by some numerical value (e.g. 1 and 2) and the next settings column, Values, allows us to tell SPSS which numerical values stand for which categories.

The Missing column is another important one in SPSS; from time to time and for various reasons, some of our data for some of our subjects will be missing. Sometimes a survey respondent will refuse to answer a particular item on a questionnaire (they might object to the intrusive nature of an item, or question its relevance), some items will be omitted by accident and some will so obviously have been misunderstood that a response to a particular item might have to be ignored (as when a subject selects two options from a response scale). Similarly, the researcher can make mistakes in recording or transcribing responses – all expressions of a natural human fallibility which result in the occasional finding that some of our data are missing.

Most undergraduate researchers, not familiar with the peculiarities of computer software, or the significance of missing pieces of data, might take the line: 'So what?' So there is a piece of missing information, so subject number 24 forgot to complete item 19, so I'm not sure if the response to this particular item is a '3' or a '5'. Just type in a zero or leave the cell blank and go on to the next one.

Neither of these options is recommended. A blank space, while it will be picked up by SPSS as a zero value in a list of values, might actually be caused by the person entering the data inadvertently mis-keying, and SPSS will not discriminate between a genuine missing value and incompetence on the part of the operator – they all look the same, as it were. Using a zero is not a good idea either, since zero is itself a value, or represents a category within a coded variable. However, it is important to let SPSS know if any values have been omitted. Even a simple calculation like the arithmetic average will be undermined by miscounting the number of cases or values. Moreover, it is sometimes useful for the researcher to be able to identify cases or subjects who did not respond to particular items in the event that they represent an interesting subgroup of the population.

The convention for dealing with missing values is to enter an extreme, or bizarre value which could not form part of a conventional set of values within a specific variable, and which is clearly distinguishable from them. Hence, if a response to a given item is of the nominal Yes/No variety (typically coded 1 and 2 respectively) then no response at all could be represented by the value 9, or 99, or whatever. Providing SPSS is informed that whenever it encounters '99' it is to treat this as a missing value, then calculations won't be affected and any such cases can be readily spotted.

Columns is a throwback to the early days of computing when data was stored on punchcards. Each punchcard was divided up into 80 columns and every piece of information on a case allocated a certain number of these columns. Our own variable has been allocated a space of eight columns (characters).

continued

Box 4.15   *continued*

Align is self-explanatory, in that our data can be centred, left or right aligned in the column.

Measure is the final setting and allows us to describe the kind of scale on which our variable is measured, be it nominal, ordinal or interval.

The example below is taken from the M&K.dat1 data set, showing how two of the variables have been set up.

	Name	Type	Width	Decimals	Label	Values	Missing	Columns	Align	Measure
1	case	Numer	8	0	case id nu	None	None	4	Right	Scale ▾
2	region	Numer	8	0	major uk	{1, scotland}..	None	8	Right	Nominal

In this instance our second variable is 'region'; it is a numerically defined variable and the full descriptive label describes it as 'major uk region'. In its composition, the variable comprises a number of different regions, each represented by its own numerical value. For example, Scotland is represented by the value 1. There were no missing cases, and the variable was measured on a nominal scale.

Box 4.16   **Descriptive statistics and SPSS**

Descriptive statistics in SPSS are easily obtained through the **Analyze** menu at the top of the data spreadsheet. (In earlier versions of SPSS this was shown as a Statistics item on the menu.) When selected, a number of statistical operations are offered:

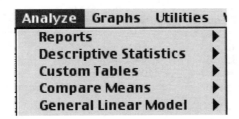

Generally speaking the options available within these menus remain constant irrespective of which version of SPSS is used, but there are some differences. We have already mentioned that this Analyze menu was previously known as a Statistics menu. The General Linear Model was also previously found as ANOVA models. The important thing is not to be intimidated by such variations – simply try them and see what they offer.

The next step in our analysis is to choose what we want from the available options. In this instance, we want Descriptive Statistics:

Analyze	Graphs	Utilities	Window	Help
Reports	▶			
Descriptive Statistics	▶	Frequencies...		
Custom Tables	▶	Descriptives...		
Compare Means	▶	Explore...		
General Linear Model	▶	Crosstabs...		

continued

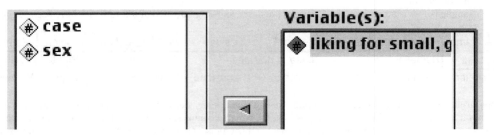

Box 4.16 *continued*

The basic descriptive options are shown above, and selecting any one of them will open a further window which allows us to select which variable we intend to describe. Selecting Frequencies, for instance, would produce the following:

Selecting variables for any kind of analysis in SPSS follows the same general sequence. All the variables in a data set are displayed in a scrolling box on the left part of the window, where one or more can be selected using conventional mouse clicks. In the above example, a number of variables from our hypothetical green amphibian study are shown – the subject identification number, the individual's gender and their attitude score. An arrow button ▶ transfers the selection to a variables window on the right from where, depending on the particular analysis being carried out, a number of additional options can be selected. A final OK will produce an appropriate output which will be tabular, graphical or both.

Table 4.8.

SEX

		Frequency	Percent	Valid Percent	Cumulative Percent
Valid	male	19	55.9	55.9	55.9
	female	15	44.1	44.1	100.0
	Total	34	100.0	100.0	

The **Frequencies** command is suited to the analysis of a single variable that comprises category data – the number of males and females in a sample (as in Table 4.8), the number of experimental subjects participating in a control or experimental condition, or the frequency with which respondents to a questionnaire item opted for a Yes as opposed to a No response on some issue. However, in the event that tables are not as informative as they might be – and this is a problem common to many statistical outputs – the option of seeing the same data presented graphically is usually offered (see Figure 4.20). This bargraph presents the same information as in Table 4.8, showing the distribution of males and females who participated in our study. As with most charts it offers a visual illustration of the data that is often more immediate and easier to grasp than tabulated information. It often does this, of

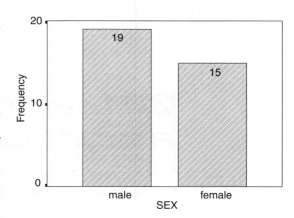

Figure 4.20 Frequency of males and females in the 'newt' study.

Table 4.9.

Descriptive Statistics

	N	Minimum	Maximum	Mean	Std. Deviation
liking for small, green amphibians	34	13.00	28.00	19.3529	3.9303
Valid N (listwise)	34				

course, at the expense of precision yet it is the preferred method of presentation in many fields. Newspaper articles, in particular, and various trade publications writing for a diverse readership will opt for this approach, although it should be said that academics tend to prefer tables, for their very precision.

When the data are continuous, or interval-scaled, the **Descriptives** command is appropriate, offering relevant parametric statistics on central tendency and dispersion. As with most SPSS operations numerous options are available, allowing the user to determine how much information will be displayed. In our current example, asking for descriptive statistics of the 'newt' variable (measures of liking for small, green amphibians), the Descriptives command produces Table 4.9.

Considerably more information, however, is available via the **Explore** command which provides not only an extensive statistical breakdown of a given variable, but also a number of graphical views. Moreover, unlike the Descriptives command, Explore allows us to inspect a variable by different categories, broken down by the sex of the individual. Consequently there are really two outputs, one for males and one for females. Box 4.17 offers the entire output generated on the newt data.

The final option in the Descriptive Statistics submenu is the Crosstabs command. Concerned with nominal- or ordinally-scaled data, Crosstabs provides frequency counts of pairs of related variables. A crosstabulation is performed in which a count is made of the number of events that occur across two categories. For instance, in our 'newt' study, how many of the males were also skilled cyclists; how many of the females were also unskilled cyclists; and so on. Table 4.11 presents the typical tabular output. In this instance for the two category variables in the 'newt' data set – cycling skill level and gender. (All will be revealed presently.)

Table 4.11 is termed a 2 × 2 contingency table, there being two variables in the analysis, each comprising two categories. Occasionally the more informative notation of 2R × 2C is used, making it clear how the data are laid out – with two categories in the *R*ow variable, and two in the *C*olumn. In its basic format each cell displays only the number of observations or cases

applicable to its particular categories, such that in this illustration we can see that, in the novice group, there were 10 males and 7 females. More useful for descriptive purposes is the translation of cell counts or frequencies into percentages, thus reducing the sometimes misleading effects of uneven subject numbers represented in each category. In the setting up of this example, a sub-command allowed the specification of what actually appears in the various cells: percentages were selected for the column variable and the cells now provide the additional information that, for the novice cyclist condition, 52.6% of the cases were male and 46.7% female (see Figure 4.24).

The 2 × 2 case is the simplest of the crosstabulation relationships possible for, as we are aware, variables can be subdivided into many components. We could measure preference for beer or lager among different astrological signs for instance, and this would give us a 12 × 2 contingency table; we could obtain an impression of political bias in newspapers by equating the political affiliation of subjects with their most frequently read newspapers. If there are three major parties, and six possible national papers, we would generate a 3 × 6 contingency table, and so on. Box 4.18 offers a sophisticated application of crosstabulation in addition to providing a word of caution in the use of this procedure.

4.9 Interval data and correlation

4.9.1 Describing two continuous, interval variables

The above discussion has concerned itself with the descriptive analysis of single continuous variables (e.g. liking for amphibians), single nominally-scaled variables (gender) and pairs of nominally-scaled variables (region and political party). However, as we considered in Chapter 2, some research will involve exploring the relationship between two interval-scaled variables. Relating working hours to stress levels is an example of such an approach, since both measures

Box 4.17 Full descriptive output in SPSS

The Explore command in SPSS provides the most comprehensive analysis of continuous data – detailed tables providing information on average, spread and skewness, stem and leaf tables and a variety of pictorial representations. In Table 4.10, the newt data have been examined by the nominal variable of sex. (We are interested in whether or not liking for green amphibians depends on whether you are male or female.)

Table 4.10 Descriptives

	SEX			Statistic	Std. Error
liking for small, green amphibians	male	Mean		17.9474	.9381
		95% Confidence Interval for Mean	Lower Bound	15.9766	
			Upper Bound	19.9182	
		5% Trimmed Mean		17.6637	
		Median		17.0000	
		Variance		16.719	
		Std. Deviation		4.0889	
		Minimum		13.00	
		Maximum		28.00	
		Range		15.00	
		Interquartile Range		4.0000	
		Skewness		.996	.524
		Kurtosis		.601	1.014
	female	Mean		21.1333	.7676
		95% Confidence Interval for Mean	Lower Bound	19.4870	
			Upper Bound	22.7797	
		5% Trimmed Mean		21.0926	
		Median		21.0000	
		Variance		8.838	
		Std. Deviation		2.9729	
		Minimum		17.00	
		Maximum		26.00	
		Range		9.00	
		Interquartile Range		4.0000	
		Skewness		.321	.580
		Kurtosis		−.837	1.121

The table produced by this command is undoubtedly comprehensive. There are several measures of central tendency (mean; trimmed mean; median), of dispersion (range; interquartile range; variance; standard deviation), of normality (skewness; kurtosis) and a number of crude descriptive measures (minimum; maximum). The choice is impressive – how much more would anyone ever want to know about a measure? The choice is also – especially to an undergraduate new to statistics – intimidating. In reality, few researchers would pore over a table such as this attempting to squeeze every piece of information out of the data. Most of us are content to inspect the mean values of the different groups along with the standard deviations to give an impression of how spread out scores or measures were. Only if we felt there was something unusual about our data – the distributions were not normal; there were extreme scores – would we start looking at the other descriptive measures. (Note: if any of these statistical terms are giving cause for confusion, a review of the earlier sections of this chapter would be useful. Section 4.3 explains central tendency and dispersion, while Section 4.4 deals with normal distributions.)

The next part of the typical Explore output takes the form of graphical presentation of the data. Figures 4.21 and 4.22 are histograms, one each for the groups of male and female subjects. If our study had investigated an issue in terms of three groups (e.g. young, middle-aged, elderly), there would have been three histograms offered. In our examples we asked for the additional option of having a smoothed distribution curve fitted to the histogram, which allows us, at a glance, to estimate averages and also obtain an impression of skewness, if present. From the graph alone, we would estimate the male and female means as approximately 17 and 21 respectively (a pretty good estimate when compared to the actual values that are shown beside each chart). Both distributions also exhibit slight positive skewness.

continued

Box 4.17   *continued*

Histogram
For SEX=male

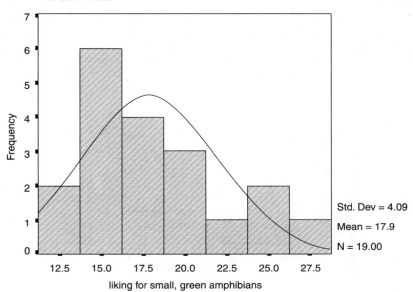

Figure 4.21.

Histogram
For SEX=female

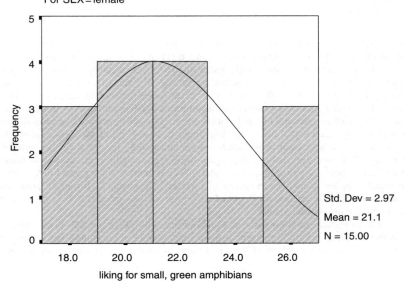

Figure 4.22.

continued

Box 4.17 *continued*

In the final illustration offered by this particular package a single chart (Figure 4.23) directly comparing the distributions of both groups is offered, in the form of boxplots. Figure 4.23 is extremely useful in that, at a glance, we can estimate averages (median values) for each group, in addition to the measures of interquartile range, minimum and maximum and crude range. The differences between the groups are clear and more immediately appreciated than they would be were we to consult the descriptive statistics table only. For more information on the boxplot, see Box 4.7.

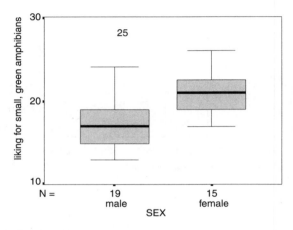

Figure 4.23.

So far our discussion has concentrated on the major aspects of the data being described (central tendency and dispersion). However, in the interests of completeness the **standard error** – short for the standard error of the mean – provides a measure of the extent to which the sample mean in question is likely to be close to the mean of the population from which it has been drawn. In general terms, the smaller this value is, the less error there is; moreover, the standard error is partly a function of the sample size, so the larger the sample the less error there will be. In terms of describing the characteristics of a variable this is not particularly important, but if we are interested in the extent to which a sample is a fair reflection of a population, the standard error becomes an essential piece of statistical information. 95% Confidence Interval for Mean (sometimes termed merely **Confidence Interval**, or CI) is, like the standard error, concerned with estimating population characteristics. The values given here indicate the range within which we are 95% confident that the population mean lies, which works out as two standard errors above and two standard errors below the mean (approximately). The obsessive among you might wish to consult Table 4.10 and demonstrate this for yourselves. A review of Chapter 3, in which we discussed estimating sample sizes might also be of interest, as will sections of Chapter 5, in which we look more closely at the role of the standard error in estimating population characteristics.

The remaining statistic to be considered is **kurtosis**; as with skewness, this measure relates to the physical shape of a distribution being, in this instance, an indicator of how steep or shallow is the curve comprising the normal distribution. Aside from that, the measure of kurtosis is of little real value in analysis, apart from being a pretty piece of statistical terminology.

Table 4.11. A 2 × 2 contingency table.

SKILL * SEX Crosstabulation

			SEX male	SEX female	Total
SKILL	novice	Count	10	7	17
		% within SEX	52.6%	46.7%	50.0%
	experienced	Count	9	8	17
		% within SEX	47.4%	53.3%	50.0%
Total		Count	19	15	34
		% within SEX	100.0%	100.0%	100.0%

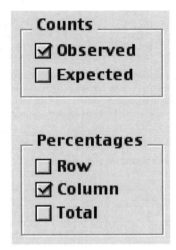

Figure 4.24 Determining the appearance of a contingency table.

can vary along their own continua. Matching measures of conservatism to age is another and equating weight to different measures of blood pressure is a third. All these examples are similar in that they represent pairs of linked observations of continuous data, in a procedure termed **'correlation'**.

4.9.2 Correlation

Correlation refers to the relationship between two variables (co-relationships). Specifically, the variation in one variable is said to be associated with the other in some way, and the following example shows this.

Imagine we have observed that in Scotland as temperature rises the reported incidence of road rage also rises, i.e. we have two variables that appear to be related:

X	temp.	10	12	15	15	20	25	26	28	29	30
Y	road rage	5	4	5	6	6	10	20	19	25	26

Merely by inspection we can see there is a relationship between the two variables, i.e. as X (temperature) increases, Y (incidents of road rage) also tends to increase.

By convention, this type of relationship is presented graphically, and usually in the form of a scatterplot, where each plot on the graph represents a pair of values. In the example in Figure 4.26 every plot represents a temperature value and its corresponding road rage value.

In our previous discussion of descriptive statistics we explained that there were three ways in which variables can be effectively described – by tables, by graphs and by statistics – and this is precisely the case with the data from correlational studies. The twin rows of data for temperature and road rage represent the conventional tabular presentation of correlated variables, and it is important to realise that each pair of values actually represents a single observation, in which two measures were taken at the same time:

Observation	Temperature	Mean no. of road rage incidents
1	10	5

Inspection of the tabulated data clearly suggests that some kind of relationship exists for as scores on one variable (temperature) increase, so do scores on the other (incidence of road rage). As we have observed, however, trends are not always immediately apparent through tables, sometimes requiring the simplified but more immediately illustrative effect of a chart or figure to identify pattern. Hence the **scatterplot** in

Box 4.18 Crosstabulation explored

In a hypothetical study exploring aspects of political support, a sample of 500 subjects is drawn from three regions – Scotland, the Midlands and the South of England (see M&K.dat1). Political affiliation is assessed by questionnaire and respondents' sex is noted, allowing a breakdown of the basic two-variable relationship by a third, control variable, as is shown in the three tables below.

In Table 4.12, political support is presented simply in terms of geographical region. It can be seen, for instance, that Labour is likely to do best in Scotland at the next election with Conservative support strongest in England.

Table 4.12.

major uk region * political partyvoted at next election Crosstabulation

% within major uk region

		political partyvoted at next election				
		labour	conservative	sdp	other	Total
major uk region	scotland	40.8%	14.9%	18.4%	25.9%	100.0%
	midlands	31.3%	25.3%	26.0%	17.3%	100.0%
	s.england	15.3%	41.3%	28.0%	15.3%	100.0%
Total		30.3%	25.9%	23.6%	20.2%	100.0%

In Table 4.13 voting intentions have been further broken down by a control variable, as it is known, that of the individual's sex. Thus we have voting intentions by geographic region for males, and voting intention by region for females. This is quite a sophisticated development and allows us to explore our data in more detail. We could for instance determine whether or not women's voting intentions reflect the general trend, or is there perhaps something unusual about this group?

Table 4.13.

major uk region * political partyvoted at next election * SEX Crosstabulation

% within major uk region

SEX			political partyvoted at next election				
			labour	conservative	sdp	other	Total
male	major uk region	scotland	37.8%	11.7%	17.1%	33.3%	100.0%
		midlands	28.9%	31.3%	20.5%	19.3%	100.0%
		s.england	16.7%	46.2%	21.8%	15.4%	100.0%
	Total		29.0%	27.6%	19.5%	23.9%	100.0%
female	major uk region	scotland	44.9%	19.1%	19.1%	16.9%	100.0%
		midlands	34.3%	17.9%	32.8%	14.9%	100.0%
		s.england	13.9%	36.1%	34.7%	15.3%	100.0%
	Total		32.0%	24.1%	28.1%	15.8%	100.0%

We could continue this process of further subdividing our data and it might be of interest to explore voting intention not only by region and sex, but also by occupational category. However, if we do continue with this process we begin to encounter problems.

While initially a sample size of 500 might have seemed adequate, when this is subdivided by six occupational classes, three regions and two sexes, a random distribution would leave us with only about 13 cases per category. If numbers were further diluted across three age groups, the likely numbers falling into any cell are further reduced with some combinations (e.g. male, professional, middle-aged, England) only sparsely distributed among all the possible cells. This problem is intensified when we rely on percentage values alone in cells – 4% of a sample of size 50 is only two people.

A related problem, which will be considered at greater length in Chapter 5, concerns the use of crosstabulations to analyse the distribution of observations. In a search for patterns among responses, or in an attempt to judge whether actual observations deviate substantially from our expectations, certain statistical techniques can be applied to crosstabulated data. However, to be effective these techniques impose certain conditions on the data, one of which concerns minimum numbers of cellular observations, or rather, minimum numbers of what we would expect in particular cells – when this becomes small, the data are no longer susceptible to statistical analysis.

continued

Box 4.18 *continued*

An obvious solution to the problem of numbers is to increase the sample size. However, often this is not possible, especially in undergraduate research, so an alternative solution would be to reduce the number of subdivisions. In the above example, ignoring the regional differences would make more cases available for each cell (and more expected values, which is important from the point of view of further analysis), as would collapsing occupational categories. Opting for two or three groups – such as managerial, white collar and blue collar – would considerably increase the pool of subjects available for each cell and might produce the added gain of achieving the requirements for statistical analysis. Of course, the disadvantage of taking this approach is that important distinctions among subjects can be lost and it is up to the individual how important this is in terms of the overall research issue.

A final point brings us back to the essential purpose of descriptive statistics – that they are intended to summarise, describe and illustrate. Unfortunately, contingency tables, while they do meet these requirements, sometimes fail to do so immediately and with clarity. They provide too much information for the 'at a glance' effect and often require close inspection for any patterns to emerge. Consider again Tables 4.12 and 4.13: there is no question that they contain relevant data, and in a precise format, but gaining an overall impression of how individuals are distributed across the various cells will not be immediate. On the other hand, consider Figure 4.25, a combination barchart showing similar information. Here we can see the overall level of support for each party, broken down by the sex of the voter.

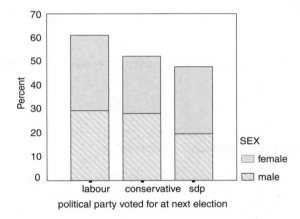

Figure 4.25.

It looks like Labour will do rather well.

Figure 4.26 demonstrates the general nature of the relationship – that as one variable increases, so does the other. Moreover, this pattern of change reflects a close link between the two variables since, for a given increase in temperature, there is a proportional – as opposed to a random or unpredictable – increase in reported rage. (Note: these data are clearly hypothetical, as anyone who has lived in Scotland will appreciate; after all, when was the last time anyone in the frozen north experienced temperatures in the 30s?)

In the language of correlation, the above example demonstrates a strong, positive correlation: strong, because as one variable changes, the other changes by a similar amount, and positive since as one variable changes the other changes in the same direction (i.e. as one increases, the other variable also increases). Box 4.19 illustrates the different kinds of correlational relationships.

So far we have demonstrated two of the common methods for describing correlated data – tables and graphs. The third and final approach is that which attempts to represent and describe relationships through the use of symbols, and their related numerical values, in the form of statistics.

The most common version of representing the relationship between two variables statistically uses the symbol r, which is an expression for the coefficient of correlation, from Pearson. In numerical

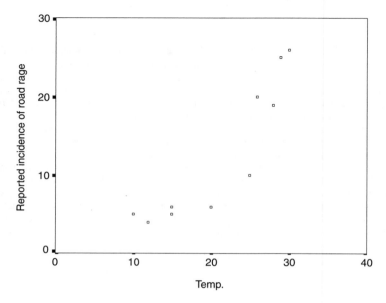

Figure 4.26   The relationship between temperature and road rage.

Box 4.19   Different types of correlational relationships

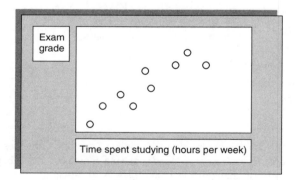

Figure 4.27   A positive correlation.

Given the language of correlation introduced so far (i.e. strong, positive) it can be rightly assumed that correlations can also be weak, and negative. Generally speaking we would expect that those who indulge in regular weekly study time will perform better come examinations than those of us whose idea of research is investigating how many pints of beer we can lift from a standard pub counter in a given evening. Compare Figure 4.27 with the next in the sequence (Figure 4.28). In this second example there is still a strong relationship between the two variables, insofar as when one variable changes the other changes by a similar amount. However, while one variable increases (social/pub time) the other *decreases*. This will probably come as a great surprise to the majority of undergraduate students.

continued

Box 4.19   *continued*

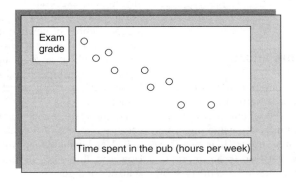

Figure 4.28   A negative correlation.

The final example (Figure 4.29) shows a very poor, or weak relationship. Not surprisingly, taking varying amounts of exercise will have little or no effect on examination performance, indicated by the absence of any kind of pattern, or correlation above.

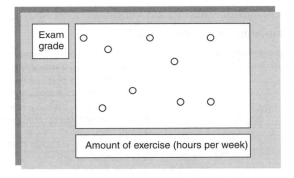

Figure 4.29   A weak correlation.

(Note: these examples have been chosen to illustrate particular points – with large databases it is not always possible to detect an obvious pattern from a scatterplot alone.)

terms the co-efficient of correlation is a value ranging from −1 through 0 to +1, with the strength of a particular relationship indicated by how close the calculated value approaches to 1 (or −1). Weak relationships will of course be indicated by values closer to zero.

Aside from providing a measure of the magnitude of a relationship, *r* also describes the direction of a relationship. If the calculated value for *r* is positive, this signifies that as one variable increases, so too does the other. Figure 4.27 in Box 4.19 is an example

of a positive relationship. In fact, by inspecting the plots on the graph we can see that this is also a strong relationship, and the actual calculated value for *r* in this instance is +0.87.

Negative values for *r* indicate that, as one variable increases, the other decreases, as in Figure 4.28 in Box 4.19. Here, as the time spent on social indulgence increases, exam performance, as expected, decreases. The actual value in this hypothetical example is −0.9.

Figure 4.29 demonstrates a poor relationship. As one variable increases (exercise) the other variable seems to vary independently. The value of r here is +0.002, an extremely weak relationship in which the sign (+ or −) is largely irrelevant.

4.9.3   Beware of correlations

In all of the above it is important to note that none of the relationships described necessarily imply causality. Certainly, study time and exam performance could well go together, but this relationship might be purely coincidental or even spurious; it is possible that studying in itself does not lead to an improvement in exam performance, but rather it is the type of person who studies a lot who does well in exams, which is not the same thing. In fact the danger is in assuming that just because we can correlate two variables there must be some kind of relationship. When

in reality pairs of variables may be easily linked purely on the whim of the researcher, rather than in any logical expectation that they might be related. For instance, it would be perfectly feasible to correlate the number of newts run over by careless cyclists on particular days with sun-spot activity for the same periods, without anyone suggesting that any kind of causal relationship existed between the two, even if, by accident, a strong correlation coefficient could be demonstrated.

The problem is that many people assume that just because two sets of measures can be linked, they *are* linked, and in more than simply a coincidental manner. However, this takes us into the realm of inferential statistics and goes beyond the scope of this particular chapter. It is enough to make the point that correlational relationships are not in themselves causal relationships, a point that many undergraduates, new to research, often overlook. A more detailed look at this

---

Box 4.20   When is a relationship not a relationship?

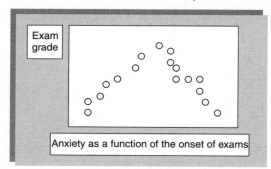

Figure 4.30

Figure 4.30 demonstrates a phenomenon understood by undergraduate students everywhere – the tendency for exam preparation to be closely linked to individual anxiety levels. The typical undergraduate experience is for studying to be minimal when exams are far in the mists of the future. However, with the onset of deadlines most students can settle down to some studying: the odd book is read, journal articles might be applied for and, occasionally, a lecture might be attended. As exam pressure mounts, more and more time is spent in the library, studying at home and turning down social opportunities, reflecting growing anxiety levels and expressed by improved

motivational levels. For each individual there will probably be an optimal distance from assessment periods which is associated with peak studying performance – for some it will be months, for some weeks, and for a few, possibly, only a few days prior to exams. However, if study is delayed beyond this optimal period and a hapless student doesn't open a book until the day before an examination, performance will seriously decline. Anxiety will be present of course, as will motivation, yet the consequences of too high levels of stress – fear, panic, frustration, anger – are likely to interfere with any attempt to concentrate on studies and performance will inevitably deteriorate.

This is precisely the case with Figure 4.30: there is an initial rise in performance as anxiety increases, followed by a sharp decline when anxiety levels become extreme. Without doubt then there is a very strong relationship between these two variables, initially positive and subsequently negative. Yet, if the relationship were considered only statistically, the calculated coefficient of correlation would be misleading, since the positive elements in the calculation would be obscured out by the negative ones. The moral to this illustration is that, while statistics are often the most convenient method of exploring and describing data, they can be misleading; the wise researcher will always want to view the appearance of information. (The other moral is, of course, don't leave your studying too late.)

(Note: there are ways in which non-linear relationships can be explored but these are not considered here.)

issue, in addition to more complex applications of correlation, is presented in Chapter 5.

A final point to be made here is a general caution about the use of statistics. So far in this chapter the impression has been given that tables, charts and statistics are alternative methods for describing data, each with its own particular strengths. While this statement is largely true there will be instances in which reliance on purely statistical descriptive techniques can be misleading – as when a real relationship becomes obscured by the computational processes on which statistics are based. Box 4.20 makes the point.

4.10   Review

The aim here, as in all chapters of this book, has been to introduce general principles and provide examples of those principles in operation. Moreover, the chapter has attempted to provide an introduction to one of the commonest statistical packages available to students. Students should now be able to create a data file in SPSS, enter data correctly, format the data and perform elementary descriptive analyses. For an overview of what has been covered we suggest a review of the flowchart at the beginning of this chapter.

4.11   Explanation of terms

analyze   in the context of SPSS this is a menu item which makes available the various commands for describing data.

boxplot   a type of graph used to represent interval-scaled data, emphasising the median, the IQR and the minimum and maximum values.

central tendency   the frequently observed phenomenon whereby measurements of any trait or behaviour tend to cluster around some typical or central value, such as an average.

coding   the process of transforming information into a numerical value. Typically, males might be identified by the value 1, and females by the value 2.

confidence interval   the range of values within which we are confident that a population mean is likely to lie. Confidence is given as a probability, usually 95%.

correlation   a measure of the association between two variables. Expressed as a statistic r, which indicates both the strength and direction of a relationship.

crosstabulation   a procedure in which the proportion of cases or observations falling across two nominal or ordinal variables is noted. The type of table in which the outcome of this procedure is presented is a contingency table. This is also an option under the Descriptive Statistics menu of SPSS.

data view   The particular view of a data file in SPSS in which we can enter data and in which we have access to the various commands for describing and performing analyses.

descriptives   An option in the Descriptive Statistics menu of SPSS which provides a limited range of measures on a single, interval-scaled variable. Typically the mean and standard deviation are offered.

descriptive statistics   In the context of SPSS, one of the sub-commands available in the Analyze menu, which offers various ways of describing our data.

descriptive techniques   a series of procedures whose aim is to describe data in a manner that effectively summarises, simplifies and illustrates.

dispersion   the tendency for scores in a distribution to vary around some middle value.

explore   An option in the Descriptive Statistics menu of SPSS which provides the full range of measures of central tendency and dispersion for a continuous, interval-scaled variable. Moreover, these measures are available for different levels, or categories of a corresponding nominal variable (e.g. average and range of income can be explored by the sex of the individual).

frequencies   An option in the Descriptive Statistics menu of SPSS which offers a simple count of the number of cases falling into different categories (e.g. the number of males and females in a sample).

frequency table   a table in which the frequency of cases, subjects or observations is presented, either as a number, a percentage of the whole, or both. Such tables are useful for describing the distribution of cases across the categories of a single, nominal or ordinal variable.

histogram   a type of graph, similar to a bargraph, used to represent interval-scaled data.

interquartile range (IQR)   the difference between the values at the lower and upper quarter of an ordered array of values.

kurtosis   a measure of the steepness or shallowness of the curve that forms part of the shape of a distribution.

mean   the arithmetic average of an array of scores or measurements, calculated by summing all the scores and dividing by their number. This is the most powerful measure of central tendency because of its precision.

median the middle value of an ordered array of scores. This statistic is sometimes used in preference to the mean when extreme scores are present.

mode the most frequently occurring value in an array of scores.

nominal scale a scale in which the participants of a study are distinguished by the group or category to which they belong. Differences between or among categories are qualitative and imply no sense of magnitude. Gender is a nominally-scaled variable, with two categories, male and female.

normal distribution a term describing the characteristic arrangement of observations on any variable, with most scores clustering around some central value and fewer and fewer observations occurring with the distance from this average measure.

ordinal scale a scale in which the participants of a study are distinguished by the group or category to which they belong. Differences between or among categories are quantitative but only at the level of 'greater than' or 'less than'. Assigning research participants to an age category (young; middle-aged; elderly) places them on an ordinal scale.

profile data (sometimes known as **subject data**, or **descriptors**) descriptive information on the subjects who participate in a study. Typically the subject's sex, age group, social category and so on.

range a simple measure of dispersion, being merely the difference between the lowest and highest values.

scatterplot a type of graph that shows the relationship between two variables. Each plot on this type of chart represents one observation at which two measures have been taken (as in a particular level of road rage associated with a particular temperature).

skew a measure of the extent to which a real distribution deviates from the normal distribution shape, as influenced by an unusual number of cases falling at one particular end of a distribution.

SPSS a modern statistical computer package developed to organise, describe and analyse research data.

standard deviation the most powerful measure of - dispersion, based on the extent to which each individual score in a distribution varies from the mean.

standard error (of the mean) a statistic based on the standard deviation of a (theoretical) group of sample means, which provides a measure of how close the sample mean might be to the population from which it has been drawn.

standard normal distribution the term given to the theoretical distribution that serves as a model for all real, normal distributions.

statistic a symbol, along with its numerical counterpart, that represents, summarises or defines important characteristics of a variable. The symbols themselves are usually taken from the Greek alphabet.

value label additional information used to describe and explain the coded values that represent the different categories in a variable. When identifying the sex of an individual in SPSS for instance, males might be assigned the value 0, while females are identified by the value 1.

variable label additional information used to describe a named variable in SPSS. In variable view of the current SPSS release, abbreviated variable names can be expressed in more detail here.

variable name the name used to identify a variable in SPSS – usually limited to 8 characters and requiring expansion under the variable label element.

variable view the particular view of a data file in SPSS in which we can define and describe important characteristics of our variables. We can provide a fuller explanation of variables, assign numerical values to categories and so on.

variance a measure of dispersion based on the actual values in a distribution and describing the average squared deviation of scores around a mean.

z-scores the numerical values produced when actual scores in a distribution are transformed into the same scale and system of measurement as the standard deviation.

4.12   Further reading

Dometrius, N.C. (1992) *Social Statistics Using SPSS*. London: HarperCollins.

Howitt, D. and Cramer, D. (1997) *An Introduction to Statistics for Psychology*. London: Prentice Hall.

Kinnear, P.R. and Gray, C.D. (2000) *SPSS for Windows Made Simple: Release 10*. Hove: Taylor & Francis.

Robson, C. (1997) *Real World Research: A Resource for Social Scientists and Practitioner-researchers*. Oxford: Blackwell.

Making inferences about research

Statistical analysis using SPSS

Cries for help

- *I've got two independent variables, six conditions and two outcome measures. Which test should I use?*
- *All I want is a straightforward t-test. But what's this equal and unequal variances stuff?*
- *I've got a probability of 0.5. Is this significant?*
- *My ANOVA tells me I've got a significant effect – but it won't tell me where it is!*
- *Help!*

Chapter 5 goes beyond the description of data, which formed the basis of Chapter 4, and considers how these data can be used to make decisions. Do the skilled employees in our study really have different voting preferences to the managerial staff? Did one group perform better than another on an experimental task? Do these observed differences in purchasing signify a genuine difference between middle- and working-class families? Do these results support my hypothesis? Was the theory correct? The major statistical tests for answering these kinds of questions will be demonstrated and the procedures for making statistical decisions explained. As with Chapter 4, examples and guidance

for analysis using SPSS will be given at various points throughout.

5.1 Inferential statistics

Descriptive statistics are in themselves important means to understanding the characteristics of data and, consequently, describing the social world. However, those very parameters usually taken to represent our environment – specifically, measures of spread and central tendency – can be further used to draw important inferences, to test hypotheses and develop theory. Comparing the means of two samples can be the first step in demonstrating that a genuine difference exists between two groups, or that a particular intervention has had a real effect on some attitude or opinion measure. And this is what inferential statistics are all about – making deductions and drawing conclusions. In the very first chapter of this book the purpose of research was defined as describing, explaining and predicting aspects of the world in which we live. Describing and, to some extent, explaining have been considered in the previous chapter. Understanding the world and the people in it, however, requires a more detailed appreciation of the

Exploring Chapter 5

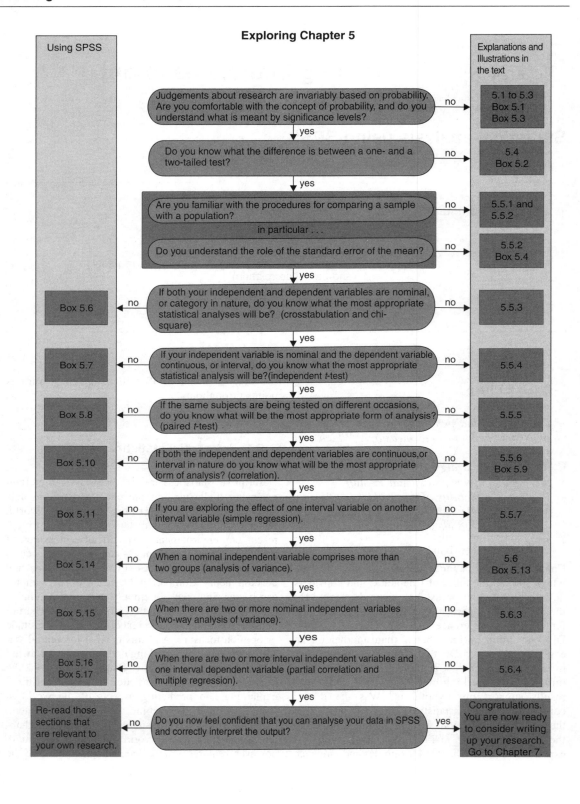

Using SPSS

Explanations and Illustrations in the text

Judgements about research are invariably based on probability. Are you comfortable with the concept of probability, and do you understand what is meant by significance levels? — no → 5.1 to 5.3 / Box 5.1 / Box 5.3

yes

Do you know what the difference is between a one- and a two-tailed test? — no → 5.4 / Box 5.2

yes

Are you familiar with the procedures for comparing a sample with a population? — no → 5.5.1 and 5.5.2

in particular . . .

Do you understand the role of the standard error of the mean? — no → 5.5.2 / Box 5.4

yes

Box 5.6 ← no — If both your independent and dependent variables are nominal, or category in nature, do you know what the most appropriate statistical analyses will be? (crosstabulation and chi-square) — no → 5.5.3

yes

Box 5.7 ← no — If your independent variable is nominal and the dependent variable continuous, or interval, do you know what the most appropriate statistical analysis will be?(independent *t*-test) — no → 5.5.4

yes

Box 5.8 ← no — If the same subjects are being tested on different occasions, do you know what will be the most appropriate form of analysis? (paired *t*-test) — no → 5.5.5

yes

Box 5.10 ← no — If both the independent and dependent variables are continuous,or interval in nature do you know what will be the most appropriate form of analysis? (correlation). — no → 5.5.6 / Box 5.9

yes

Box 5.11 ← no — If you are exploring the effect of one interval variable on another interval variable (simple regression). — no → 5.5.7

yes

Box 5.14 ← no — When a nominal independent variable comprises more than two groups (analysis of variance). — no → 5.6 / Box 5.13

yes

Box 5.15 ← no — When there are two or more nominal independent variables (two-way analysis of variance). — no → 5.6.3

yes

Box 5.16 / Box 5.17 ← no — When there are two or more interval independent variables and one interval dependent variable (partial correlation and multiple regression). — no → 5.6.4

yes

Re-read those sections that are relevant to your own research. ← no — Do you now feel confident that you can analyse your data in SPSS and correctly interpret the output? — yes → Congratulations. You are now ready to consider writing up your research. Go to Chapter 7.

information we gather and a sophisticated ability to manipulate it, which goes beyond the purely descriptive. And if we ever hope to be able to make predictions about what people do – how they will vote, how they will respond to policy changes or what demands they are likely to make on health care provision – we need to demonstrate that events we observe or effects we encounter during the course of a survey or observational study are not mere chance occurrences. Not surprisingly then, inferential statistics rely heavily on the concept of probability.

5.2 Probability explained

Whenever a researcher attempts to make a point, support an hypothesis or test a theory, she is trying to show that a particular set of observations is not merely a chance occurrence. This is not an easy task, due to the astonishing richness and variety of the countless elements that comprise our society. No two people are ever alike. Even identical twins, as we know, cannot share the same physical space and are therefore subjected to differing experiences and influences throughout their lives. Consequently, selecting any two people at random and looking for differences in measurable characteristics will produce a breathtaking lack of commonality. But this is normal. Each of us inherits a unique genetic pattern, which contribution to individual singularity is further enhanced by particular parental interactions, selective exposure to peer influences, attitudes, values, education, nutrition, opportunities, social and cultural forces. The wonder of this is that there exists any common ground in our social world whatsoever.

The point we are trying to make here is that whenever we look at any two individuals, or groups of individuals, we should *expect* there to be differences between them, and this is the researcher's problem. If an educational researcher devises a study to demonstrate that a new form of teaching strategy is more effective than traditional methods, how do we know that any differences between a sample using the new techniques and a sample using the traditional strategies are nothing more than a reflection of the very human tendency for variation. The groups might have been different anyway, so how do we know that the new approach had a *real* effect?

The answer lies in probability.

Every event in the world, every occurrence, happens with its own particular level of likelihood, or

probability: the chance of someone having a puncture while driving home from work is pretty unlikely in these days of modern tyre technology, but it can happen (and often does, at the busiest junctions). Having two punctures is even less likely (less probable), while experiencing three flat tyres is unusual in the extreme. And if our hapless driver discovered four flats – and the spare – he could quite reasonably assume that something was going on.

Making decisions about the outcome of research operates in a similar manner. Comparing two groups on any measurable characteristic – be it height, shoe size or opinion – will always produce differences. In fact, given what we have just said about human variability, we would *expect* differences. Moreover, we would be prepared to accept that such differences might reasonably range from the marginal to the moderate, purely by chance and without anything sinister going on. Comparing the average heights of two groups of undergraduates, for example, could easily produce the heights of 1.9 metres and 1.8 metres respectively, showing a very slight difference between the two. We could, however, discover mean heights of 1.9 and 1.6 metres, and still not be too surprised. After all, while this difference of 0.3 metres is less likely than our previous finding, it is still possible, given this known tendency for variation in all things human. Values of 1.9 and 1.4 might start us wondering though, while 1.9 and 1.0 would make us extremely suspicious – just like the driver with all the punctures. And this is how statistical – and subsequently research – decisions are made: when an event occurs that is so unlikely that, even within the bounds of human variability, it is remarkable, then we can claim that a discovery has been made or an effect demonstrated. Three simultaneous punctures might be possible, but four is a conspiracy. A difference in heights between 1.9 and 1.6 metres might be unusual, but that between 1.9 and 1 metre might suggest that our samples have not been drawn from the same population.

The question now to be addressed is 'How unusual is unusual?' Certainly we all have an intuitive idea of what is unusual-but-possible as opposed to what is downright impossible, but this is a subjective thing, based on feelings, beliefs and, occasionally, misperceptions about the laws of chance. The example in Box 5.1 is a good illustration.

The rule, which has become the accepted norm for making statistical decisions, is that if an event occurs (a difference between groups, the outcome of an intervention), when the chances of it occurring naturally are less than five times in a hundred, then this event is

---

Box 5.1   Probably improbable

Certainty		Every day it will rain somewhere
	↑	Most students will forget the distinction between Type 1 and Type 2 errors
		Every day it will rain somewhere in the UK
		Frogs will eventually develop intelligence equal to humans
		Some day pigs might fly
Impossibility	↓	There will come a time when all students devote all their time to study

---

deemed too unusual to be plausible, or within the acceptable range of variability. The event is then given the status of being **statistically significant**.

This cut-off – known as the 5% or 0.05 significance level – is deliberately far removed from high probability events (it will rain somewhere on any given November day in Britain for instance) to ensure as far as possible that when we decide an effect is present, a change has occurred or whatever, that we are not merely seeing an unusual but not completely out of the ordinary event. The astute reader though will have noticed the essential flaw in this approach. Even an event so unlikely that we might expect to see it, naturally, only 5% of the time, is still possible in an infinitely variable universe. And because of this, we can be led to false conclusions in our research, as the next section demonstrates.

5.3   Scope for errors

Every event in the universe exists on an imaginary continuum running from certainty to impossibility, with the full range of probabilities in between (see Box 5.1). The convention is to view events as 'different' only when their probability of occurrence is as unlikely as 0.05 or less. However, the danger here is that such events, though rare, could still occur by chance alone. In fact, according to the rules of probability, events of this rarity could actually occur by chance 5% of the time. Or to put it another way, if we use this level of probability to identify events as significantly different from what we might normally

expect, we will be wrong approximately 5% of the time.

In research terminology this is known as a **Type 1 error** – the possibility that an apparently significant finding can actually be explained in terms of unusual but nonetheless valid variations and individual differences. Alternatively, a **Type 2 error** can occur when we wrongly accept that an unusual event is merely an extension of chance occurrences when in fact we have a significant finding. Expressed more simply, whatever we decide in research, there is always some chance that we will be wrong.

One solution to this problem of course would be to push our cut-off point further along the continuum of probability, not accepting a finding unless it is even less likely than the 5 times in a hundred level. (This is what our suspicious researcher did in the coin tossing example illustrated in Box 5.3 below, being reluctant to end a friendship unless there was clear and unambiguous evidence of cheating.) And indeed, some researchers anxious to avoid Type 1 errors do just that, refusing to accept a finding as being significant unless its probability of occurrence is 1 in a hundred or less (known as the 1% or 0.01 significance level). Unfortunately, while a finding significant at this extreme level is more robust, it will also be more difficult to demonstrate due to the need for a really clear cut effect; a study in which families living in the proximity of a nuclear reactor are compared with families living elsewhere on a measure of childhood leukaemia, for instance, would have to generate truly huge differences between the groups before we could argue a statistically significant finding at this 0.01 level.

5.4   One- and two-tailed tests

An added complication to this problem of when an observation or finding indicates significance concerns whether or not our hypothesis (and our test) is one-tailed or two-tailed. This is an issue that often causes difficulties in comprehension for those new to statistical analysis, but it needn't, once the principle is understood.

Suppose we were concerned with an industrial process of some kind, say the brewing of a particular variety of ale. To ensure that a new batch measures up to what we normally expect from this brew, we take a number of bottles off the production line and subject them to analysis – looking at flavour, strength, colour and so on. We might even invite a few friends round to assist in the assessment process.

While modern production methods are now well controlled and the chances of a particular sample deviating from the norm are slim, this was not always the case. In the past it would have been quite likely in this kind of study to find samples deviating quite markedly from the expected norm. The point of this particular study would be to determine whether or not variation is within acceptable ranges, or whether the sample characteristics are so far removed from what would normally be expected of this brew that the batch would be recalled.

From the way this hypothetical example has been expressed, it should be clear that when we are comparing our sample to the expected characteristics of the population as a whole, we are prepared for differences to be in either direction, i.e. that the new batch will merely be different from our expectations; it might be stronger or weaker, it might be fuller flavoured, or insipid. Figure 5.1, displaying a distribution of hypothetical flavours, illustrates this.

The figure can be taken to represent the known characteristics of the particular brew we are interested in. There will be a mean, or norm for this population and variation about this mean. When we compare our sample statistics to these population parameters, we could find that our sample is placed somewhere beyond the mean (stronger, fuller flavoured, etc.). But equally, we could find our sample falling below the mean (weaker, less flavourful, etc.). Since the ends of this kind of distribution are known as 'tails', our sample could lie at either tail, and therefore any test that allows for this either–or case is termed a **two-tailed test**.

This allowance for observations to fall at either tail of a distribution requires further explanation in probability terms. So far we have argued that an event will be deemed statistically significant if it occurs with a

probability of 0.05 (5%) or less. However, if we try to test this in a two-tailed manner, we would be wrong to examine the 5% cut-off point at each tail, since what we would be doing is checking for the occurrence of an event that appears only 5% of the time in one direction and 5% of the time in the other direction. In reality we end up using a 10% significance level!

To ensure then that we evaluate an event in terms of only the 0.05 level, this measure of extremeness must be spread between the two ends of a distribution, meaning that the *actual* cut-off point of a two-tailed test is 2.5% in either direction. See Box 5.2 for a fuller explanation.

Hopefully by now the notion of events being evaluated in terms of their probability of occurrence is understood, but if there is still some puzzlement over this, Box 5.3 should illustrate the point.

5.5 Statistical analysis

5.5.1 Comparing samples and populations – an overview

Most social research (unless you happen to be a government) works with samples, since it is generally speaking impractical to observe, interview or test every single member of a population – a point we have made a number of times now. However, it is usually our ultimate intention to generalise our sample findings to the wider population. We want to argue that what is true for the few will be true for the many. All of these issues have been extensively explored in Chapter 3 and anyone unclear about sampling issues might wish to review Section 3.2 on sampling.

In order that we *can* generalise from the few to the many it should be clear now that this is only possible if we can demonstrate that our sample actually belongs to the population we are ultimately interested in. In a zoological study aiming to learn something about social hierarchies within the great crested newt population, we would be in serious trouble if the sample we in fact studied comprised common newts. (Well, they do look much the same to the uninitiated.)

By the same token if our study were aimed at investigating the spending habits of a particular age group (say the 18 to 25 year band), we might well wonder how useful a sample would be whose mean age were 16. The problem is that no matter how rigorous our sampling procedures, the characteristics of a sample will always differ to some extent from the population from which it was drawn. The question therefore

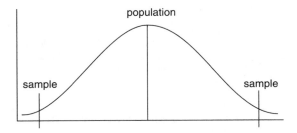

Figure 5.1 Any sample drawn from a population is likely to differ in some way from the typical characteristics of that population.

Box 5.2 One- and two-tailed tests explained

A quality control chemist with statistical leanings suspects that a current batch of dark ale will not be typical of the usual brew, due to a problem during the production process. Making a number of selections at random from the current production line, our closet statistician has colleagues rate the liquor on an index of flavour. His expectation, and hence his hypothesis, is that the sample drawn from this current batch will be different from the known characteristics of this particular beer. However, he does not know in what way the sample will differ so he proposes an hypothesis that covers all eventualities – specifically, the sample could differ from the known characteristics of all previous batches (the population), but it could differ in either direction (i.e. more flavour than or less flavour than). This is a two-tailed hypothesis.

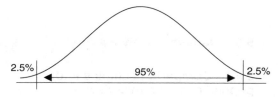

Figure 5.2.

If our embryonic statistician selects the usual 0.05 cut-off for his test then he is proposing that the sample batch cannot be considered unusual unless it differs from the expected range of flavours in a way that would only ever happen 5% of the time. Another way of looking at this is that 95% of the time variations from the population average will be within an acceptable range. If the new batch, however, falls outside that 95% limit, then it must be considered statistically different from the expected norm. Figure 5.2 shows the range in which the sample must fall to be considered different. Also apparent is the way in which the remaining 5% of rare differences has to be divided between the two extremes of the distribution. In practical terms what this means is that to be considered significant within a two-tailed context, a particular event must be further out along the rarity continuum than we might have expected; it is almost *as if* we are using a 2.5% cut-off level rather than the 5% one, although in probability terms this is not the case.

All of the above is relevant only if the researcher is unsure of the way in which his sample might differ from the population. If, on the other hand, he was pretty sure that the new batch would not be perceived as so flavourful as the normal brew then in his comparison with the population he would only be looking at the lower end of the distribution, or at one tail.

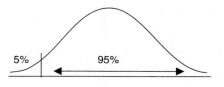

Figure 5.3.

Clearly, while he is still working within his 5% boundary, all of our researcher's scope for unusualness is at the same end of the continuum. Comparing Figure 5.3 with the previous one, it should be clear that betting only on one tail of a distribution is more likely to produce a result than if he had to consider both ends – but only if he gets the direction right. And this is the problem with one- versus two-tailed tests: two-tailed tests are more difficult to prove, but will nonetheless pick up a significant finding no matter at which end of the continuum it falls. One-tailed tests, on the other hand, while easier to produce a result are only effective if the researcher has chosen the right direction to explore.

Returning to our beer tasting study now, on averaging judgements across 30 observations, a mean measure of 153.2667 is obtained. (Totally meaningless, but representing flavour for the purpose of this example!)

In the past, and using similar measures, this particular ale has produced a score of 156 on the same flavour index. Clearly the two averages are different, but what our researcher must now decide is whether or not the sample is too different from the population to be considered *really* different (a statistically significant difference).

An appropriate test here is the one-sample *t*-test, in which a sample statistic (sample mean) is compared with a known population parameter (population mean) and a formula applied to ascertain the likelihood that the sample comes from this population. (The precise formula for this calculation can be inspected in any standard statistics textbook.) Applying SPSS to the problem produces the following output:

One Sample t-tests

Variable	Number of Cases	Mean	SD	SE of Mean
SAMPLE	30	153.2667	8.913	1.627

Test Value = 156

Mean Difference	95% CI Lower	Upper		t-value	df	2-Tail Sig
−2.73	−6.062	.595		−1.68	29	.104

continued

Box 5.2 *continued*

The above SPSS output is more fully explained later in this section, but for the purposes of our demonstration the important information is that, given all the other information about the sample (its size, the spread of scores around the mean), the observed difference of 153.2667 from the population mean of 156 would occur with a probability of 0.104 (or 10.4% of the time). Large as this difference is, it is not large enough to be statistically significant, i.e. it does not fall at or beyond the conventional cut-off level, as Figure 5.4 demonstrates.

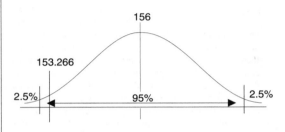

Figure 5.4.

However, had our researcher been convinced that the new batch of ale would score lower on the index of flavour, then he could have applied a one-tailed test, whereby he could concentrate his attention only at one end of the continuum. In this instance, the observed difference suddenly approaches statistical significance (see Figure 5.5).

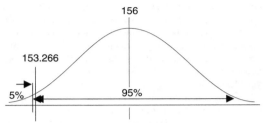

Figure 5.5.

By way of a final demonstration, returning to the SPSS output, we observe that the two-tailed probability of obtaining this difference at either end of a distribution is 0.104. Converting this to a one-tailed probability is achieved simply by halving the two-tailed value. Thus the probability of obtaining this observed difference, below the population mean, is 0.052.

(Note: this example is based, somewhat loosely, on the life of Gosset, employee of a well-known Irish brewing family and occasional statistician, known more familiarly as Student, originator of the *t*-test in its various forms.)

becomes, how different does our sample have to be from the population before we have to say, 'the sample was not drawn from that population'?

While the relationship between samples and populations is a central one in social science research, there are other areas of human endeavour in which it plays an important role, in particular in the industrial sector.

Industrial processes today are highly organised, usually automated and incorporating sufficient checks and balances to ensure a consistent quality of product. However, given the potential for variability that exists in our universe (not to mention Sod's Law) there is always some chance that a current process (and therefore product) will differ slightly from previous standards. And sometimes, not so slightly. Consider the unfortunate owner of what has become known as a 'Monday morning car', a vehicle that in all respects looks like every other of the same model, yet in which nothing works. This is a readily understood factor of modern industrial life and nowadays most manufacturing processes contain a quality control element. A steel foundry will compare a current smelt with the quality of previous output; a pharmaceutical company will check the purity of medicines against previous standards; and a brewer will test a current batch of ale against earlier brews.

Because, as we have already stated, samples are rarely a perfect match with the population from which they are drawn, industrial processes tend to make similar allowances to the social researcher. Hence, a Trabant can still be called a Trabant providing it conforms to, or falls within, a specified range of variability on certain characteristics set by the manufacturer. A current batch of malt whisky can still be called malt whisky as long as it matches – within particular tolerances – certain malt characteristics, and so on. As with social research though, the question is, how far can our sample deviate from the known population characteristics before we have to reject the batch? There would come a point at which the flavour, strength or colouring of our whisky is too different from the norm to be accorded the brand label. Thus our question has expensive connotations, when a rejected product might run

Box 5.3 Taking a chance

Imagine you and a close friend are constantly disagreeing about what to do at weekends – where to go, whom to go with and so on. To resolve these differences, a coin is usually tossed. It's your friend's 'lucky' coin, and invariably the fall is in her favour. She doesn't call it her lucky coin for nothing! However, you are now becoming suspicious that there might be something more sinister behind your friend's luck since you can no longer remember any occasion when you got to do what you wanted. In short, you suspect your friend is using a bent coin; you suspect your friend of cheating.

Stealing into her room one night you retrieve the questionable coin and prepare to carry out an experiment: you will toss this coin 100 times and observe the outcome. Your recollection is that in resolving differences your friend always calls heads, and nearly always wins. Therefore your expectation is that in this experiment there will be an unusually high number of heads. The problem is, what constitutes unusual?

If this coin were fair, then at each toss there would be two possible outcomes, head or tail, with each equally likely. In 100 tosses then, you might expect 50 heads and 50 tails. Of course, due to variations in a variety of factors (wind speed, hand used to flip coin, height of flip) you would accept some deviation from the expected distribution. 55 heads and 45 tails for instance might pass

without remark, as might 60 heads and 40 tails. But what about 70 heads and 30 tails? Would this be unusual enough to convince you that your friend is a cheat? Would you risk a friendship of many years standing on a 70–30 distribution? Perhaps not – this is unusual but not impossible. But what about 90 heads and 10 tails? Surely this event is rare enough to prove our suspicions?

This is how statistical decisions are made: we do not live in a perfect universe and so will always accept that actual events will vary somewhat from our expectations. However, when an event occurs that is so unusual that we might expect to witness it by chance only 5% of the time, we argue that such an event is no longer within the accepted range of variability. This event, whether it be the extent to which a sample mean differs from a population parameter, or the observed choices on a questionnaire differ from what is expected, can be regarded as statistically significant. As with our surreptitious coin tosser there comes a point beyond which we will no longer accept events as being attributable to chance alone. In statistical terms this is known as the point of statistical significance. (In fact, in this particular example, a split of 60–40 would be rare enough in statistical terms to state that the coin was biased, although in defence of our friendship we would probably still make allowances for our friend and choose a much more remote event as our cut-off point.)

into hundreds of motor vehicles, or many thousands of litres of sub-standard malt whisky. So how do we make this judgement?

5.5.2 Comparing samples and populations – the standard error of the mean

The following attempts to explain some of the theoretical background to the procedures that allow us to compare samples with populations and, in particular, answer the question: 'Does this sample come from that population?' In social research (although not exclusively so, as the previous section on industrial quality control illustrates) this is an important question. In some instances it represents the starting point for quantitative research. A study on low income families, earning on average £200 per week, may involve interviewing a sample whose average worked out at £175 per week. The researcher would want to know whether this sample actually comes from the wider population of families earning £200, or whether this sample in

fact represents a completely different – and much more disadvantaged – group. Specifically, is this difference between £200 and £175 an acceptable variation from the population average, or is the difference too great?

In other instances, rather than representing a starting point for further research, as in the above discussion, the extent to which a sample differs from a population is the central issue in the research. Consider a typical educational question in which a headteacher wants to know if this year's pupils (the sample) really are performing more poorly than those of all previous years (the population). The number of standard grades achieved may be fewer than in the past, but is this difference marginal and part of acceptable variations in performance, or are this year's pupils really different? This type of question may be part of the normal monitoring process typical of all educational establishments, in which case the aim is largely descriptive, or it might reflect a more investigative, inferential stance in which the headteacher is concerned that a change in teaching strategies, a decline in teacher morale, or a revision of recruitment standards has affected pupil performance.

In either event the question remains the same: does this sample belong to that population? The answer lies in an understanding of a statistic known as the standard error of the mean, or sometimes simply the **standard error**.

The standard error reflects the extent to which an element within a population varies. Specifically, if a population characteristic varies widely, any sample drawn from that population could itself deviate markedly from the population average yet still be regarded as reasonably coming from the population. If, on the other hand, variation within the population is only slight, then a sample that differs markedly probably doesn't belong to the population. It should be no surprise then to note that the formula for calculating the standard error is based partly on the population standard deviation:

$$SE = \sigma/\sqrt{n}$$

Where SE is the abbreviation for standard error of the mean
σ is the population standard deviation
n is the sample size

The standard error informs us how far a sample can deviate from a population before we can claim it was drawn from a different population. The full procedure for determining the standard error is outlined in Box 5.4, but for the moment it is sufficient to state that once we have calculated the standard error we are in a position to state that if our sample mean is greater than two standard errors beyond the known population mean (either greater than or less than), then this sample does not come from that population. More accurately, we are 95% confident that the sample does not belong to the population. Yet remember our previous discussion on Type 1 errors; we could be wrong, and in fact 5% of the time we would be.

Returning to our hypothetical study on low income families (population mean = £200; sample mean = £175), suppose the standard error calculation produced a value of £20. According to what we have said above, providing our sample mean falls between two standard errors on either side of the population mean, the sample was drawn from the population. In this instance, the range within which we are confident that samples might reasonably fall (given what we know about variation within the population) would be £160 to £240. Thus our sample with a mean of £175 could well have been drawn from the population with a mean of £200.

For the sake of completeness, this range of acceptability derived from the standard error is termed the confidence interval, and expresses the range of population values within which we are 95% confident that sample means will fall. Table 5.1 shows how this is expressed in SPSS, based on the shoe size data in Chapter 4. In this example, a sample of schoolchildren had their shoe size recorded. The calculated mean is given as 4.94, and SPSS informs us that the standard

---

Box 5.4   The standard error of the mean, and what it is

The following is a step-by-step guide for calculating the standard error of the mean, and includes an explanation of how this particular statistic is used to compare samples with populations.

Consider a hypothetical situation in which we draw a large number (hundreds) of samples from a particular population. For each of these samples we calculate a mean score. If we create a distribution of all these sample means, the following will be observed:

- The distribution of these sample means is normal in shape.
- The calculated mean of the sample means (MSM) = the population mean.
- The standard deviation of these sample means is called the standard error of the mean (SE).
- The standard error is calculated thus: $SE = \sigma/\sqrt{n}$

- 95% of all the sample means fall between two SEs of the MSM (see Figure 5.6).

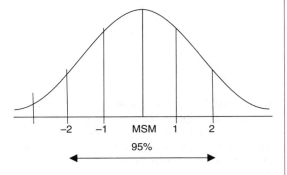

Figure 5.6.

continued

Box 5.4   *continued*

- Most importantly, because the MSM and the population mean are the same, 95% of all sample means fall between two SEs of the population mean.
- Example: A tutor learns that this year's social science students have scored an average of 58 in their term examination. Since the mean exam marks for previous years is 55 (with a standard deviation of 5) the tutor wants to know whether this year's students are really just like all the previous years' and the difference between the marks is merely part of chance variation, or are these students really different from previous years'? If there are 20 students in this year, the calculation of SE would progress as follows:

$$SE = \sigma/\sqrt{n}; \quad = 5/4.47; \quad = 1.118$$

If we now use this information to interpret the distribution of means, we find Figure 5.7.

According to our calculations, 95% of all sample means are likely to lie between 52.76 and 57.23. Since

our current year mean of 58 lies outside this range, we assume it does not come from the population whose mean is 55. This year's students are really different.

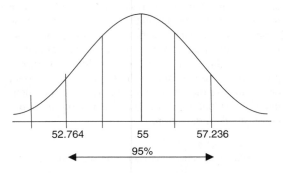

Figure 5.7.

Table 5.1.

Descriptives

			Statistic	Std. Error
Shoe size	Mean		**4.9412**	**.5107**
	95% Confidence Interval for Mean	Lower Bound	**3.8585**	
		Upper Bound	**6.0238**	
	5% Trimmed Mean		4.8791	
	Median		5.0000	
	Variance		4.434	
	Std. Deviation		2.1057	
	Minimum		2.00	
	Maximum		9.00	
	Range		7.00	
	Interquartile Range		3.5000	
	Skewness		.178	.550
	Kurtosis		−.641	1.063

error is 0.5107. If our interest was in whether or not this sample of children came from a particular population, we could determine whether or not our sample mean of 4.9 falls within the range of 1.0214 above and below a known population mean (0.5107 × 2). Alternatively, we would be 95% confident that the population from which this sample was drawn came from a population whose mean lies between 3.8585 and 6.0238.

5.5.3 Category (nominal) independent variables and category (nominal) dependent variables: the application of chi-square

Some examples might be:

- Labour and Conservative voters are compared on their preference for cracking the big or little end of boiled eggs.

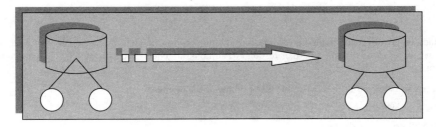

Figure 5.8 Category independent variables and category dependent variables.

• Rural and urban dwellers are compared on their support for a total ban on fox hunting. Responses are Yes – No – Unsure to a questionnaire item.

Many survey- and questionnaire-based studies are of the nominal–nominal design. That is the independent or causal variable comprises a number of categories, and the dependent or outcome measure is also composed of categories; as when the choice of response to an item (Yes/No) is determined by the sex of the respondent (male/female). (Note: while both these examples refer to nominally-scaled variables, the following discussion relates equally well to cases in which either or both variables are ordinally-scaled. Note also that if these terms – nominal, ordinal – are unfamiliar, you will find complete explanations in Chapter 2, Section 2.4.2.)

In this type of design the most appropriate form of analysis is by a combination of crosstabulation (previously illustrated in Chapter 4) and chi-square (χ^2). The **chi-square** (pronounced ki-square, as in kyak) test of association, to give it its full title, compares actual observations with what would be expected were chance alone responsible for the distribution of events. As the difference between observations and expectations increases, this is reflected in the magnitude of the statistic. In the example above, if there was no sex effect in the choice of response to a particular item, we would expect a random, and more or less equal, distribution of male and female responses in each of the Yes/No categories. If this is not the case, then there would be evidence for a sex effect in choices.

A problem with this particular statistic is that it merely informs us that there is an effect of some kind within the associated variables, but not where. This is why a crosstabulation is useful since inspection of the cells that comprise a contingency table can often identify the source of an effect. Box 5.5 provides an illustration.

The output in Box 5.5 is typical of SPSS – informative but hugely intimidating to anyone not totally familiar with this type of statistical table. However, there is a trick to dealing with any mass of information, and that is to take it a piece at a time.

The first part of the output that interests us is the information relating to the difference between actual observations and expectations; specifically, did people living with a partner or on their own make random choices among the two response categories?

In Table 5.3, headed 'Chi-Square Tests', are 'Pearson Chi-Square' followed by a range of other ways of evaluating the relationship between the variables. All of these different measures have their uses and a fuller appreciation of their application can be obtained either via the SPSS help facility, or by consulting a comprehensive reference book, such as Kinnear & Gray (2000). For most purposes, however, the first (Pearson) is sufficient and the others can be ignored. Next, and reading across the table, the value of the calculated chi-square is presented, followed by the degrees of freedom (df) and, finally, a significance value. This last value is the one on which decisions will be made, since it represents the probability that the actual observations match our expectations, assuming chance were the only factor in determining our subjects' responses. In this instance the probability that observations and expectations are the same is so high that there is no suggestion that people living alone or with a partner are answering differently to the questionnaire item. (We would expect this distribution of yes/no responses, by chance, approximately 60% of the time, as indicated by the 'sig.' value of 0.602.) It is only when the probability falls on or below the conventional 0.05 level that we can claim an effect of some kind. (Note: extremely low probability values, indicating hugely significant effects, are shown by SPSS as 0.000. Many students wrongly

---

Box 5.5

During a study on the effects of changing relationships within society a number of individuals identified via questionnaire as either living alone or with a partner respond to an item on general life satisfaction. The particular item asks the question:

Do you feel satisfied with the course your life is taking at the moment?

           Yes   **No**

A sample SPSS output is shown below:

Table 5.2.

living with partner or alone * life satisfaction Crosstabulation

| | | | life satisfaction | | |
			yes	no	Total
living with partner or alone	partner	Count	**140**	**103**	243
		Expected Count	**137.1**	**105.9**	243.0
		% within living with partner or alone	**57.6%**	**42.4%**	100.0%
		Adjusted Residual	.5	−.5	
	alone	Count	**141**	**114**	255
		Expected Count	**143.9**	**111.1**	255.0
		% within living with partner or alone	**55.3%**	**44.7%**	100.0%
		Adjusted Residual	−.5	.5	
Total		Count	281	217	498
		Expected Count	281.0	217.0	498.0
		% within living with partner or alone	56.4%	43.6%	100.0%

Table 5.3.

Chi-Square Tests

	Value	df	Asymp. Sig. (2-sided)	Exact Sig. (2-sided)	Exact Sig. (1-sided)
Pearson Chi-Square	.272[b]	1	.602		
Continuity Correction[a]	.186	1	.666		
Likelihood Ratio	.272	1	.602		
Fisher's Exact Test				.651	.333
Linear-by-Linear Association	.272	1	.602		
N of Valid Cases	498				

a. Computed only for a 2 × 2 table
b. 0 cells (.0%) have expected count less than 5. The minimum expected count is 105.89.

interpret this as meaning there were no significant findings.)

In our example chi-square tells us that respondents in the two relationship categories are not choosing in particular ways between the response alternatives. However, it does not tell us much more than whether or not the pattern of responses was statistically significant. If we want to find out more about how participants actually responded we need to look at the actual pattern of responses itself, as illustrated in the contingency table (Table 5.2). This is why chi-square is rarely used on its own; the addition of a **crosstabulation** is needed to further explore the relationship between the two variables.

It is easy to appreciate how the contingency table shown can appear scary to the novice. There is a multitude of information on offer but again, provided it is considered a piece at a time, it becomes manageable. (Note: in the setting up of this analysis we deliberately chose a complex output to aid our discussion. In fact, many users would opt for something simpler, the procedures for which are outlined in Box 5.6.) The contingency table is divided into a number of discrete blocks, or cells as they are known. The most important of these we have highlighted in bold type, and they are the four middle cells that provide numerical information on the actual pattern of yes or no responses on the life satisfaction question. To the left of this middle section is the descriptive information on what all these numbers actually signify. For each of the respondent categories, partner and alone, the following is presented.

- Count – the actual number of respondents who answered yes, living with a partner (140) and those who answered no (103).
- Expected count – if responses were largely random and not reflecting any real differences in preference between the groups, these are the number of responses we would expect in each category, i.e. yes (137.1) and no (105.9). (Note: expected counts in any one cell are calculated as Row total * Column total/Grand total. For the first cell – partner/yes – this would work out as: $243 \times 281/498 = 137.1$.)
- % – the count has been converted to a percentage value, such that 57.6% of those living with a partner chose the yes response, and 42.4% chose no.
- Adjusted residual – a transformed measure of the difference between the expected and the actual number of responses in each cell. When this value reaches 2 and above (approximately) the difference between actual and expected observations for that particular cell is probably too great to be explained as a chance patterning. In our example we already know (from inspection of the chi-square statistic) that our overall pattern of responses reflects no significant response preference. Consequently, the adjusted residual values are all less than 2.

The remaining sections of the table – the cells at the bottom and the extreme right – offer information on totals. For example, we are told that the total number of respondents in the living with a partner category was 243, and the total number of respondents selecting the yes response was 281.

This concludes our consideration of the nominal–nominal type of relationship in which we have attempted to present the tabulated and statistical output from the typical mode of analysis for these types of data, namely the contingency table and

the chi-square statistic. Needless to say this represents an introduction only and the crosstabulation procedure can be used for more sophisticated applications than we have offered here. For instance, our example has only considered two variables in its analysis – participants' relationships and response to a questionnaire item. We might have further analysed the link between these variables by a third, control variable, such as the person's sex. Hence we would have obtained outputs examining the partner–response relationship for males and the partner–response relationship for females. Finally, it should be noted that the variables used in our example reflect the simplest of category types, in which each variable comprises only two categories. The crosstabulation procedure is equally relevant when our variables comprise more than two categories. We may, for instance, have explored people's life satisfaction by their astrological sign, in which case our independent variable would comprise 12 categories. Similarly, instead of a simple yes–no response, we might have opted for a yes–no–don't know composition, making our dependent variable a three category measure. For further details on crosstabulations, and how to perform them in SPSS, please refer to Box 5.6.

5.5.4 Nominal (category) independent variables and interval (continuous) dependent variables: between-group comparisons and the independent *t*-test – two group comparisons

Some examples might be:

- Blue and white collar workers are compared on earned income.
- Skilled and unskilled cyclists are compared on the time taken to complete a cycling circuit.
- A control group and an experimental group are compared on a learning task.

One of the most common experimental designs involves the exploration of the effects of a single category variable on some continuous measure. Comparing males and females on some measure of attention span at lectures might be one example; investigating the differences in the price paid for consumer goods by shoppers in the UK as opposed to Germany would be another. In both examples the

Box 5.6   Crosstabulation and Chi-Square in SPSS

The procedure for carrying out the analysis that produced Tables 5.2 and 5.3 is as follows (actual procedure based on the M&K.dat 1 data set):

In DATA VIEW

- Analyse
- Descriptive statistics
- Crosstabs

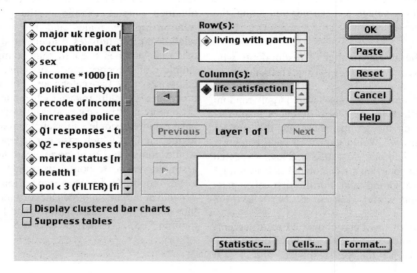

With the above window now displayed, the 'living with partner' variable is placed in the Row(s) box, and the 'life satisfaction' variable in the Column(s) box. (We could have switched the row–column position for each of the variables without affecting any of the calculated statistics. The tables would have a different appearance though and we would need to take care when selecting our percentages. This is worth trying yourself to see the effects.) From here the next option we selected was: 1v. Cells...

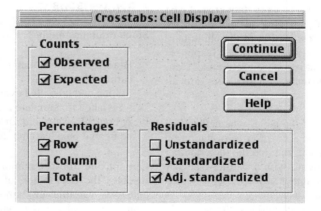

From the cell display window we selected the following options which determined what information would be displayed in each cell of the contingency table:

continued

Box 5.6   *continued*

- Observed counts
- Expected counts
- Row percentages
- Adjusted standardised residuals

Selecting Continue and returning to the main Crosstabs window, the final option selected was: Statistics:

From here our final selection was: Chi-square.

This comprised the full sequence of actions required to produce the output shown for our nominal–nominal example. However, there are some additional points to be made here. First, by changing the selections we make while setting up commands in SPSS, we change both the appearance and the content of the corresponding output. Consider the following example, again based on the M&K.dat 1 file. In this instance we have chosen to explore a possible relationship between political party supported and whether or not individuals favoured increased police powers. This time though we opted for a reduced analysis, as follows:

- Analyse
- Descriptive statistics
- Crosstabs
- 'Party' in Row(s)
- 'Police powers' in Column(s)
- Cells – select Observed counts
- Statistics – select Chi-square and Lambda

The following output is obtained:

political partyvoted at next election * increased police powers Crosstabulation

Count

		increased police powers		Total
		yes	no	
political partyvoted	labour	53	98	151
at next election	conservative	79	52	131
Total		132	150	282

continued

Box 5.6 *continued*

With the corresponding chi-squared analysis shown as:

Chi-Square Tests

	Value	df	Asymp. Sig. (2-sided)
Pearson Chi-Square	17.899[b]	1	.000

The much reduced contingency table is the result of asking for only the actual observations (counts) to appear in each cell. However, given that, in this instance, the chi-square is highly significant (0.000 is a much lower probability than our usual cut-off of 0.05, a probability so remote in fact that no value could be printed), we would actually prefer more information here in order to identify the precise nature of the significant effect.

It remains to consider one final refinement. A closer look at the Statistics window above will show that, in addition to the chi-square, we also selected something called **Lambda**. This is known as a proportional reduction in error statistic (PRE) and there are many types – some relevant for nominal data (as this is) and some for ordinal, as indicated in the Statistics window. PRE measures indicate the proportion by which error in predicting one variable is reduced, when we know something about another variable. In the current example we might be interested in knowing by how much our ability to predict support for increased police powers is improved by knowing the individual's political affiliation. Let's have a look at the lambda output:

Nominal by Lambda	Symmetric	.202
Nominal	political partyvoted at next election Dependent	.198
	increased police powers Dependent	.205

For a relationship in which both the independent and dependent variables are nominal (nominal by nominal) lambda offers three values. We merely select the one that fits our analysis – in this case 'increased police powers' is our dependent variable – and note the associated value, which is .205. We interpret this by stating that error in predicting how people respond on the police powers item is reduced by 20% if we know the person's political affiliation. Alternatively, our ability to predict responses increases by 0.205 when we know how a person intends to vote. This and the other PRE measures are more fully explored in the Dometrius (1992) reference at the end of this chapter.

To conclude, when crosstabulation is used to test hypotheses, the formal presentation would be as follows:

1 Null hypothesis: there is no statistically significant association between political party supported and support for increased police powers.
2 Alternate hypothesis: there is a statistically significant association between political party supported and support for increased police powers.
3 Test: Pearson's chi-square test of association, 0.05 significance level.
4 Outcome: chi-square = 17.899; $df = 1$; $p = 0.000$.
5 Decision: reject the null hypothesis and accept the alternate hypothesis.
6 Reservations: usually a Type 1 error, but as our significance value is so small this would seem unlikely and our decision to accept the alternate hypothesis is robust.

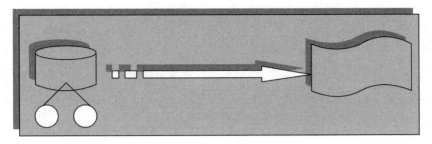

Figure 5.9   Category independent variables and continuous dependent variables.

independent variable is nominal, with gender comprising the two categories of male and female on the one hand, and shoppers made up of either the UK or German categories on the other. Similarly, the dependent, or outcome variables are interval-scaled variables, with measures able to vary continuously on their respective scales.

Studies using this approach are often of the quasi-experimental variety, in which different (but naturally occurring, or already existing) groups are selected and compared on some measure, but the design is equally at home with the traditional experimental set-up common to much psychological research in which the categories being compared are a control and an experimental group. The following example illustrates this.

A sample of male undergraduates is drawn from the student population and divided at random into two groups. Group 1 attends a presentation from a male 'nutritionist' extolling the gastronomic virtues of members of the genus *Rana* (frogs). In particular the legs, shallow fried in garlic and butter, are supposed to be delicious. Meanwhile, Group 2 is attending an identical presentation though in this instance from an attractive female 'nutritionist'. Both presentations conclude with the information that this particular delicacy would be available that day in the campus dining hall (the result of an unfortunate earlier study involving cyclists of questionable skill). As part of a marketing exercise, the participants in both groups are asked to rate how likely they would be to sample the new menu, on a seven-point scale running from 'No way' to 'Somebody try and stop me!'

This particular scenario is typical of early research in the persuasive communication field in which the covert purpose of the study is to investigate the impact of the source of a communication, rather than the communication itself. Specifically an experiment of this sort would be exploring the hypothesis that male subjects would respond differently to a message originating from an attractive female source than to the same message from a male source. The type of analysis ideally suited to a design of this nature is the *t*-test.

The dedicated reader, interested in the historical development of statistical procedures, might recall that Gosset, in his guise of the statistician Student, developed an approach for comparing the characteristics of a sample with those of a population (known as the one-sample *t*-test and a development of the standard error procedure outlined in Box 5.4). In particular he developed a formula for determining how far away a sample mean had to be from a population parameter to be able to say that this sample did not come from, or did not represent, that population. In an extension to this work, Student produced a variant of his *t*-test that could be applied to two samples, according to the following logic.

If two samples are drawn from a particular population, and measured on almost any variable, the first and most likely finding is that the means of both samples will be very similar. (Imagine selecting two groups of students at random and comparing their average heights.) However, the second – and necessary – finding is that they will not be the same. This might appear a contradiction, but it is not; we are continually reminding ourselves that the scope for human variability is vast and that no two people can ever be truly identical since, even for identical twins, they cannot occupy the same space. Consequently, no two groups can ever be truly identical, even if drawn from a **homogeneous** population (one in which all individuals share similar characteristics). Therefore while we might expect any two samples to be similar in some measurable way, we would also expect them to be different.

Were we to take numerous pairs of samples from our population our expectation would be that, in the majority of cases, the differences between each pair would be minimal. However, because of what we know about human variability, we would also expect to find some instances where the differences between the pairs of samples were larger than marginal, but there would be fewer cases in which this occurred. Similarly, because the universe allows for considerable variety, we would encounter some cases in which the differences between pairs were moderate, but there would be still fewer of these. And just occasionally, we would expect to see a pair of samples between which differences were considerable. And this would be rare.

It is this rare finding that is the important one. If the difference between two sample means is so rare that it is only likely to ever occur 5% of the time, we are in a position to argue that it is more likely that the two samples are not in fact drawn from the same population. Alternatively, if we draw two samples from a single, homogeneous population we might assume (without actually testing for it) that they will be similar on some key characteristic. If one group is subjected to some kind of intervention or to an experimental treatment and then the groups are compared, any observed differences between them can be attributed to the intervention. An education authority keen to try out a revolutionary teaching programme might introduce the new scheme to one particular school then compare exam results against another school in the same area using conventional methods. This is a similar scenario to the above example on persuasive communications: initially both groups of male subjects – if properly sampled – might be expected to share similar views on the eating of frogs' legs. However, after the persuasive presentations from the different sources (the intervention, or experimental treatment), these views might have diverged. Which is the whole point of the study.

The **independent** *t*-test (unpaired *t*-test; independent samples *t*-test, unrelated *t*-test) compares the means of two different samples and provides a probability that these means are the same (or that they come from the same population). SPSS output from our hypothetical frog-eating study is shown in Table 5.4. Recall that respondents indicated on a seven-point scale how much they were likely to try the new, gourmet product. The higher the score, the more likely they were to try it.

In true SPSS fashion, the *t*-test output in Table 5.4 contains a great deal of information, yet again contributing to possible confusion, not to say intimidation, among novices. We will begin therefore by attempting to disentangle the information we need from all of the information that SPSS has helpfully provided.

Table 5.4.
(a)

Group Statistics

	source of communication	N	Mean	Std. Deviation	Std. Error Mean
attitude to trying new product	male source	50	2.7600	1.4507	.2052
	female source	49	4.6531	1.6652	.2379

(b)

Independent Samples Test

		Levene's Test for Equality of Variances		t-test for Equality of Means					95% Confidence Interval of the Difference	
		F	Sig.	t	df	Sig. (2-tailed)	Mean Difference	Std. Error Difference	Lower	Upper
attitude to trying new product	Equal variances assumed	.437	.510	−6.035	97	.000	−1.8931	.3137	−2.5157	−1.2705
	Equal variances not assumed			−6.026	94.659	.000	−1.8931	.3141	−2.5167	−1.2694

Let's begin by stating the obvious – the output for the t-test comprises two separate tables. To be honest it is only the second of these (Table 5.4(b)) that is necessary for the purpose of deciding whether or not our groups differ significantly, but Table 5.4(a) nevertheless provides useful additional information. In almost every case, when this computer programme performs a statistical analysis, it will include as part of that analysis a table of descriptive information. Hence, the first of our two tables merely describes the data on which the t-test is performed; we see that there were 50 participants in our male source sample, and 49 in our female source sample. We are also given the mean attitude values that are to be compared in our test, along with other descriptive information. The means are given as 2.76 and 4.65. While all of this is of use, and will be required at the write-up stage of a report, it is the second table that draws our main interest.

Although the t-test table appears as a single table it in fact comprises a number of distinct elements that should be considered separately. Specifically, the table presents a test for equality of variance, the results of two different t calculations and related statistical information.

The t-test, while designed to test for differences between the means of two samples, nevertheless assumes that the distributions within each sample, and hence the average variation about the means, are similar. If this is not the case – and this in itself can be an interesting finding – a modification to the t-test formula is necessary. The decision is made with relative ease, merely by comparing the variance within one sample with the variance within the other. **Levene's test** for the equality of variances does exactly that, and provides a probability that the two variances are equal. We can see that in our example the F-value (the statistic used to express the ratio of one measure of variance to another) is given as 0.437, with an associated probability of 0.510. This indicates that approximately 50% of the time we would expect a difference of this magnitude by chance alone. Consequently we assume that the distributions comprising each sample are similar. Indeed, just by inspecting the standard deviations of both samples (from the group statistics table) we would have come to this conclusion. Had the probability value dropped below 0.05 though, we would have had to accept that the variances were clearly unequal and apply the alternative formula.

The final part of the table relates to the t-test itself. Selecting the 'Equal variances assumed' option (based on the previous Levene's probability) we note the t value of -6.035 (which is merely a transformed meas-

ure of the difference between the sample means), and the associated significance value of 0.000. What this is telling us is that the likelihood of obtaining such a difference between two sample means by chance alone is so remote that the probability value falls off the end of the scale as it were – certainly well below our conventional 0.05 cut-off and less even than the more remote 0.01. (It is worth reminding ourselves that when the probability of an observed difference between means is so remote, SPSS prints the value 0.000. This does not mean that the probability of this particular occurrence is zero, nor does it mean that the observed difference was not significant, both common errors among undergraduates, as we have already intimated.) In other words, the source of the communication made a statistically significant difference to subjects' responses to the attitude item.

Note: when working with t-tests there are two points to be appreciated. The first is that the value of t reflects the magnitude of the actual difference between the two sample means being compared. The bigger this difference, the bigger will be the t value and the more likely that this difference will be significant. The second point concerns the fact that t values can be both positive and negative, a possible source of anxiety for some students. In practice, the sign is unimportant, merely reflecting the difference between the sample means being compared. If the larger mean is subtracted from the smaller, the difference will of course be a negative value. It is the magnitude of the t value that is important, not its sign.

The precise sequence for performing a t-test in SPSS is given in Box 5.7.

5.5.5 Nominal (category) independent variables and interval (continuous) dependent variables: within-group comparisons and the paired t-test

Some examples might be:

- A measure of approval for government policy is taken from a group of voters both before and after they view a political broadcast, and the measures compared.
- Measures of blood pressure are taken before and after the administration of a new hypertension drug treatment.
- A group of social science students is examined in research methods before and after reading this book.

Box 5.7   Comparing two samples with the *t*-test in SPSS

Imagine a study exploring regional variations in lifestyle, in which among a number of questions respondents are asked to state their annual earnings. As part of the analysis workers in Scotland are compared with those in the South of England (see M&K.dat 1). Data are collated and an independent *t*-test carried out. The procedure is as follows:

*   Analyse
*   Compare means
*   Independent samples *t*-test

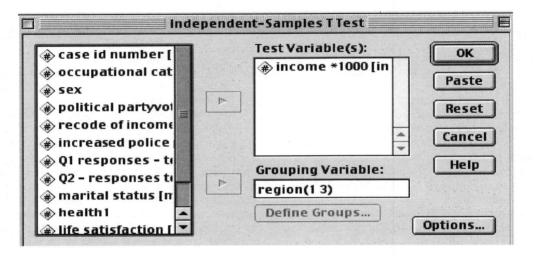

*   With the *t*-test set-up window visible we select from the main variables area on the left the variable that will be our dependent, or outcome measure for our analysis (termed the 'test variable' in SPSS).
*   Select the independent or causal variable in our analysis (termed the 'grouping variable' in SPSS).
*   Define Groups – this is to enable us to inform SPSS how we have identified (defined) the different groups in the data set. It wants to know what numerical value has been used to identify participants living in Scotland, etc. In the Define Groups window (below) we specified the values 1 and 3 to identify people living in Scotland and the South of England respectively. (In our main data set the value 2 was used to identify people living in the Midlands, in case anyone is wondering.)

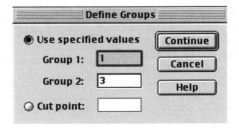

On clicking Continue in the Define Groups window, followed by OK when we are returned to the original *t*-test window, the analysis is carried out and the following output produced.

continued

Box 5.7 *continued*

Independent Samples Test

		Levene's Test for Equality of Variances		t-test for Equality of Means						
		F	Sig.	t	df	Sig. (2-tailed)	Mean Difference	Std. Error Difference	95% Confidence Interval of the Difference Lower	Upper
income *1000	Equal variances assumed	4.645	.032	−3.005	349	.003	−2.6694	.8883	−4.4165	−.9223
	Equal variances not assumed			−3.099	346.800	.002	−2.6694	.8615	−4.3637	−.9750

We have reproduced only part of the output here, overlooking the table of Descriptive Statistics and emphasising only the *t*-test output. Immediately it should be apparent that the outcome of this analysis is quite different from that of the independent samples example shown in the text (Section 5.5.3). In the present instance the Levene's test indicates that the variances of the two samples being compared are significantly different ($F = 4.645$; $p = 0.032$). In other words, the chance of finding a difference of this magnitude is less than our conventional 0.05 cut-off point. For statistical purposes then, we assume the variances are unequal and consult the appropriate part of the *t*-test output. The 'equal variances not assumed' calculation generates a *t*-value of −3.099, with an associated probability of 0.002 (SPSS states this as sig., short for significance level, which is the same as a probability value, for those in danger of becoming confused at the varying terminology favoured by this particular package). In other words, there is a significant difference in earnings between people living in Scotland and those in the South of England. If we were to express this formally, we would do so as follows:

1 Null hypothesis (H_0): the mean income of a Scottish sample will equal the mean income of an English sample.
2 Alternate hypothesis (H_1): the mean income of a Scottish sample will not equal the mean income of an English sample.
3 Test: *t*-test for independent groups; 2-tailed; 0.05 significance level.
4 Outcome: t(unequal v) $= −3.099$; $df = 346.8$; $p = 0.002$.
5 Decision: reject H_0 and accept H_1.
6 Reservations: possibility of a Type 1 error, though given the large sample sizes and the small probability value associated with the *t*-test, this is unlikely.

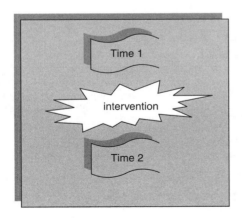

Figure 5.10 Repeated measures.

In Chapter 3 a particular type of design was outlined that had some advantages over the conventional two-group comparison. Rather than use different individuals in each category (e.g. one set of subjects in a control group and another set in an experimental group), the same people can be used in two or more conditions. The advantages of this approach are that fewer subjects are needed in a study, and the complicating effects of individual differences are minimised.

It is worth reminding ourselves that taking repeated measures on the same individuals requires a different approach to data entry from the usual one – or at least, that's how it appears. In Chapter 4, the rule for entering data into a conventional statistical programme was that cases or observations were identified first (by, for instance, a subject number) and then each associated piece of information in turn. For subjects tested on two different occasions, then, data entry into a package like SPSS would appear as shown in Table 5.5.

Consider a medical study in which a group of hypertensive patients are put on a novel regime of daily aerobic exercise to try to reduce their blood pressure (BP) without the use of drugs. BP readings are taken before, and then six weeks after, the introduction of the exercise regime. The before and after measures are subjected to analysis using the **paired *t*-test** (also known as the repeated measures *t*-test; correlated *t*-test; within-groups *t*-test; dependent *t*-test). The output is shown in Table 5.6, and relates to resting, or diastolic blood pressure.

In this example we have printed the descriptive statistics associated with our study, and it can be observed that the average blood pressure reading of our sample was 94.0667 before the introduction of the exercise scheme, and 89.5 afterwards. Clearly there is a difference, but

whether or not this difference is real, or simply a chance variation, must be determined by inspection of Table 5.7 containing the *t*-test output. It must be pointed out that we have modified the appearance of the output in Table 5.7 using the 'pivot' controls available in SPSS for the purpose; the output in its original format would not have fitted onto the page without shrinking it to the point where all definition would be lost. (A useful tip for anyone planning on using SPSS output in a report.)

The relevant information here is the *t*-value of 2.595, which reflects the magnitude of the difference between the two means. The significance value of 0.015 is the probability that these two means are derived from the same population (that they are the same, in other words, with any differences being attributable to chance factors).

The decision made in this example is that exercise did significantly affect blood pressure. Of course it is quite possible that during the time between the first and second readings blood pressure might have fallen anyway (leading us to make a Type 1 error), in addition to the possibility of other repetition effects occurring. These issues have been discussed in Chapter 2, Section 2.5.3, and this might be a good time to review the particular problems of this type of within-subjects research. In the meantime, Box 5.8 demonstrates the procedures for carrying out this kind of analysis.

Table 5.5.

Case number	Time 1	Time 2
1	score	score
2	score	score
3	score	score
4	score	score

Table 5.6.

Paired Samples Statistics

		Mean	N	Std. Deviation	Std. Error Mean
Pair 1	pre-exercise diastolic BP	94.0667	30	8.1830	1.4940
	post-exercise diastolic BP	89.5000	30	6.5482	1.1955

Table 5.7.

Paired Samples Test

			Pair 1
			pre-exercise diastolic BP – post-exercise diastolic BP
Paired Differences	Mean		4.5667
	Std. Deviation		9.6372
	Std. Error Mean		1.7595
	95% Confidence Interval	Lower	.9681
	of the Difference	Upper	8.1652
t			2.595
df			29
Sig. (2-tailed)			.015

Box 5.8 Comparing two measures on a single sample using the paired *t*-test

In a study examining the impact of student loans, one measure relates to the amount of money students spend on books. A measure of spending is taken before loans are introduced, and another after. The procedure for carrying out the paired *t*-test is as follows:
- Analyse
- Compare Means
- Paired-Samples *t*-test

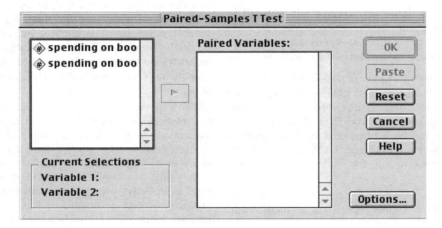

From the *t*-test window we select the pair of variables we wish to analyse. Clicking OK produces the following output:

Paired Samples Test

			Pair 1
			spending on books before loans – spending of books after loans
Paired Differences	Mean		.1905
	Std. Deviation		3.0760
	Std. Error Mean		.6712
	95% Confidence Interval	Lower	−1.2097
	of the Difference	Upper	1.5907
t			.284
df			20
Sig. (2-tailed)			.780

We have modified the above table from the original SPSS format in order to display it on a single page. The important information is that the *t*-value of 0.284 has an associated probability of 0.780. Thus, any difference in book spending before and after the introduction of student loans is not significant. Whatever our students are doing with the extra money, it is not going on books. The formal expression of this is as follows:

1 H_0: there is no difference in the mean spending on books before and after loans.
2 H_1: there is a difference in the mean spending on books before and after loans.
3 Test: paired samples *t*-test; 2-tailed; 0.05 significance level.
4 Outcome: $t = 0.284$; $df = 20$; $p = 0.780$.
5 Decision: accept H_0 and reject H_1.
6 Reservations: the possibility of a Type 2 error, since a sample size of 20 might be too small to demonstrate a genuine, if small, effect.

5.5.6 Interval (continuous) independent variables and interval (continuous) dependent variables: relationships and correlation

Some examples might be:

- The decline in the frog population is linked to the increase in cyclists.
- Variations in exam performance are observed as study time changes.
- Mortality rates within an elderly population are linked to variations in outside temperatures.

When both major elements in a study are continuous, interval-scaled in nature (as in relating variations in road rage incidents to changes in population density), the type of study being described is correlational. This particular methodology has been considered in some detail in Chapter 2 (Sections 2.6.1 and 2.6.2), and it is worth reminding ourselves of the main features of the approach.

1   Correlation simply describes a relationship between two variables.
2   The correlation statistic (r) demonstrates whether or not this relationship is strong or weak, and identifies the direction of the relationship.
3   The correlation statistic is a positive or negative value ranging from 0 to 1.

The most important of these points is the reminder that, at its simplest level, correlation is purely a descriptive device. It informs us that two things may vary together in a particular way, but it does not allow us to say much more than that. It certainly doesn't allow us to say that one variable causes changes in the other, although many researchers – even experienced ones – often mistakenly argue that it does. Certainly the temptation to do this is strong; we are all used to making assumptions about our world and about things that go together. In many instances though such assumptions are unwarranted, reflecting more our unsophisticated perception of the world, rather than any real cause and effect relationships.

Consider the widely held view among undergraduates that ratings in a test will be directly related to the number of hours spent in study. A perfectly reasonable assumption one might think, except for the occasional appearance of the individual – much loved by her fellow students – who seems to spend minimal time in study yet consistently outperforms all others in her class.

The explanation here is quite straightforward for the relationship between study and performance in assessments is not simply a matter of time but of comprehension. The student who spends several hours every night preparing for an exam but ultimately fails to understand key concepts will not perform effectively, whereas the person who quickly grasps important principles and understands how they are applied will probably do well, even with less studying. This is not to say that there will be no relationship between study time and exam performance, since in many cases the time spent on a topic will often result in an improved understanding of that topic. The point is that the relationship between the two variables is not as straightforward as most people think. And this is the problem with correlations – we can readily demonstrate relationships between pairs of variables, but understanding the nature of such relationships is often more tricky. Box 5.9 further explores this issue.

Whilst it is important to recognise the dangers in reading too much into the relationship between

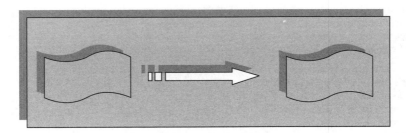

Figure 5.11   Continuous independent variables and continuous dependent variables: correlation.

two variables, it is also useful to appreciate that correlation is often only the first step in what can become a number of more sophisticated forms of analysis.

One of the more useful features of a correlation can be found in the **coefficient of determination** (R^2, or r-squared), a statistic that allows us to state the proportion of variation in one variable which can be predicted by another. This particular statistic can be readily obtained by squaring the relevant correlation value. Hence if we had found that a correlation between temperature levels and road rage incidents, for instance, was 0.902 we could further state that 0.815 (0.902*0.902), or 81%, of the variability in rage incidents could be predicted by temperature levels. This is a useful piece of information and moves correlation away from the purely descriptive to something more sophisticated. We are now in a position to argue that temperatures probably have a strong causal effect on incidents of road rage. However, even with a correlation of 0.9 the relationship is not clear cut since, depending on the r-squared value, about 20% of variation in road rage is caused by some other factor, or factors. Or to put it another way, 20% of the variation in road rage incidents – a substantial amount – cannot be predicted by temperature.

In Chapter 1 one of the important functions of research was identified as prediction, yet correlation on its own is not a good predictor. If we take our temperature and rage example, we could suggest, within a range

---

Box 5.9   As we always suspected...

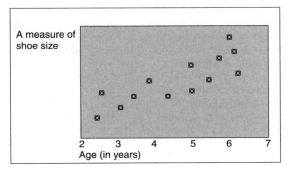

Figure 5.12   A strong positive correlation.

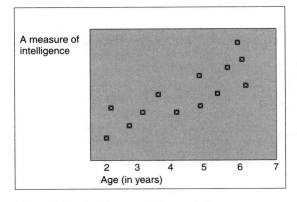

Figure 5.13   A strong positive correlation.

continued

Box 5.9 *continued*

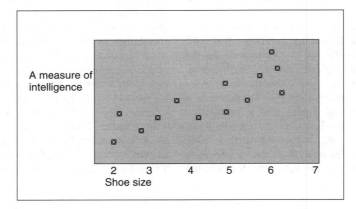

Figure 5.14   A strong positive correlation.

The relationships expressed in Figures 5.12 and 5.13 are much as we would expect, reflecting the often intuitive nature of correlations. However, the relationship shown in Figure 5.14 is clearly – and the authors are being in no way footist about this – nonsense. Yet because both shoe size and intelligence correlate with age it becomes inevitable that they will correlate highly with one another. The difference is that while we happily accept the first two, along with the implication that age is acting as a causal factor, the third relationship we perceive as purely spurious. And this is the problem with correlations – the relationships between the twinned factors in Figures 5.12 and 5.13 seem perfectly reasonable yet we laugh at any implication that Figure 5.14 demonstrates anything more than coincidence. However, if we consider the nature of both intelligence and shoe size we quickly realise that mere age changes are not in themselves sufficient explanations: the real factors responsible for physical and intellectual growth are the complex maturational processes responsible for human development from birth into adulthood. As expressions of these fundamental influences, then, both intelligence and shoe size will be related but not in any causal manner – both are simply expressions of underlying processes that affect many things.

of values, the likely number of rage incidents for a particular temperature. However, this would only ever be a vague approximation since the related observations do not form a straight line; in Figure 5.15, based on the temperature and rage example in Chapter 4, while there is clearly a relationship between the two variables, selecting a temperature value of, say, 22° we would be hard pressed to predict the number of people likely to be charged for hurling abuse (or worse) at other road users.

If though we could replace the information on our graph with a straight line that best fitted the observations, we could make a more precise estimate of one variable from the other. This is exactly what simple regression allows us to do, which is the topic of the next section. In the meantime, the procedure for performing correlation is outlined in Box 5.10.

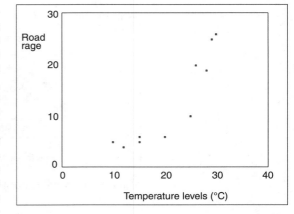

Figure 5.15.

Box 5.10 Correlation in SPSS

Correlation provides a measure of both the strength of a relationship between two variables and the direction of the relationship (positive or negative).

Visualise a study on changing attitudes within society (M&K.dat 1). A questionnaire exploring various opinions and social values asks, among others, the following questions:

1 To what extent do you feel that there are higher levels of crime today than 10 years ago?
2 To what extent are you in favour of arming the police?

One might reasonably expect that those respondents who felt crime was on the increase would be more in favour of arming the police. To perform a correlation analysis of responses to these two items, the following procedure is applied:

- Analyse
- Correlation
- Bivariate

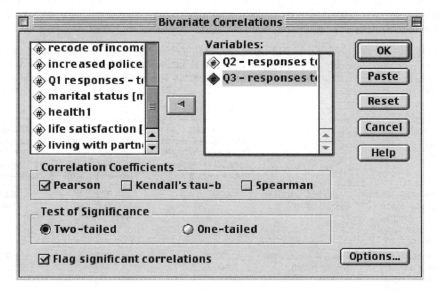

The two variables to be correlated are selected from the main Variables window on the right hand side and without further changes to the other options, OK is selected, producing the following output:

Correlations

		Q2 responses – 'to what extent do you agree that there are higher levels of crime today than 10 years ago?'	Q3 responses – 'to what extent do you agree that the police should be armed?'
Q2 responses – 'to what extent do you agree that there are higher levels of crime today than 10 years ago?'	Pearson Correlation	1.000	.873**
	Sig. (2-tailed)		.000
	N	501	501
Q3 responses – 'to what extent do you agree that the police should be armed?'	Pearson Correlation	.873**	1.000
	Sig. (2-tailed)	.000	
	N	501	501

**. Correlation is significant at the 0.01 level (2-tailed).

continued

Box 5.10 *continued*

The above output is one of the most straightforward in SPSS, once you understand that this program helpfully (or unhelpfully) performs a correlation on every possible combination of variable pairs. This means that in the simple two-variable (bivariate) case, the first variable is correlated with the second; the second variable is, somewhat unnecessarily, correlated with the first; the first variable is correlated with itself; the second variable is correlated with itself. Since any variable correlated with itself produces an $r = 1$, and is meaningless anyway, we can ignore the cells in which this information appears. We need then only consult either one of the remaining cells (it doesn't matter which, since they offer the same information). And no, we don't know why SPSS does all this.

Having cleared that up, the information in the relevant cell really is pretty clear (honest). The cell contains the correlation between the two variables ($r = .873$); the significance of this relationship ($p = .000$); the number of cases on which the correlation was based ($n = 501$). Somewhat redundantly, we are also given the information that SPSS will print an asterisk (*) at every correlation coefficient that is significant at the 0.05 level, and two asterisks (**) for coefficients significant at the 0.01 level. In our present example we can clearly see within the cell that our correlation is highly significant ($p = .000$), but if we had correlated several variables together, searching a complex cellular matrix is probably easier when we're just looking for asterisks, as opposed to trying to interpret the contents of a large number of cells.

It remains to point out that while this type of relationship is termed a bivariate correlation (relationship between two variables), the procedure is readily applied to any number of continuous variables. For example, if we were to add a third variable to our analysis of attitudes towards the police, SPSS will perform a series of bivariate analyses, as in the output table below.

Correlations

		Q2 responses – 'to what extent do you agree that there are higher levels of crime today than 10 years ago?'	Q3 responses – 'to what extent do you agree that the police should be armed?'	Q1 responses – 'to what extent do you support increased powers of arrest for the police?'
Q2 responses – 'to what extent do you agree that there are higher levels of crime today than 10 years ago?'	Pearson Correlation	1.000	.873**	.906**
	Sig. (2-tailed)	.	.000	.000
	N	501	501	501
Q3 responses – 'to what extent do you agree that the police should be armed?'	Pearson Correlation	.873**	1.000	.806**
	Sig. (2-tailed)	.000	.	.000
	N	501	501	501
Q1 responses – 'to what extent do you support increased powers of arrest for the police?'	Pearson Correlation	.906**	.806**	1.000
	Sig. (2-tailed)	.000	.000	.
	N	501	501	501

**. Correlation is significant at the 0.01 level (2-tailed).

In this example we now have three correlations: between Q1 and Q2 ($r = .906$); between Q1 and Q3 ($r = .806$); between Q2 and Q3 ($r = .873$), all of which suggest a certain consistency in attitude among our sample.

1　H_0: there is no significant relationship between perception of current crime levels and attitude towards increasing police powers.
2　H_1: there is a significant relationship between perception of current crime levels and attitude towards increasing police powers.
3　Test: correlation; 2-tailed; 0.05 significance level.
4　Outcome: $r = 0.873$; $n = 501$; $p = 0.000$.
5　Decision: reject H_0 and accept H_1.
6　Reservations: Type 1 error, though given the large sample size and the high significance level this would seem unlikely.

5.5.7 Simple regression – predicting one continuous variable from another continuous variable

Some examples might be:

- What proportion of variation within the newt population can be predicted by changes in global temperature?
- By how much can increases in work satisfaction scores be accounted for by income?
- What is the predicted incidence in road rage incidents for a temperature of 22°C?

In the previous section the value of replacing the plotted observations in a correlation with a single line was outlined. Providing the line is a good fit of the data we should be able to read the value of one variable corresponding to the other simply by inspecting the line. The trick of course is to ensure that our line is a good fit.

One way of generating a line to symbolise our data would be to draw one using only our judgement of what looks appropriate. However, any two people performing the same task would invariably produce very different drawings. Fortunately there is a more precise method for achieving the best fitting line, based on the mathematical formula: $y = a + bx$.

Many of you will recall coming across this formula as part of the standard school maths curriculum. It is the formula for a straight line. In plain English, what this formula does is identify the corresponding value on the y variable for any given value on the x variable. As a formula for a straight line then, this is clearly misleading since to draw any line we need two points – a starting point and another point to join up with. In days gone past stu-

dents would be expected to calculate the values for a and b from the original correlated data, and most current statistics texts still provide the means to carry out these calculations. For the modern student, though, computer packages are more than happy to do this for them, as Table 5.8 shows.

Returning to our temperature and road rage example, the regression command in SPSS produces the output in Table 5.8. It is worth noting that, while the analysis of interest is a simple regression, this is presented as a special case of a much more complex procedure, that of multiple regression. Consequently, much of the content is designed to explain the effects of several (multiple) independent variables on a single outcome variable, and because of this some of the information in Table 5.8 is redundant for our one predictor variable case. For the moment we are using regression to predict how much rage will be associated with temperature.

As usual SPSS offers a wealth of information that is of considerable interest to statisticians, but a likely source of confusion to undergraduates. In fact, the regression output comprises several tables, from which we have extracted the two in Table 5.8. The full output from regression analysis can be seen in Box 5.11 but the average researcher can be more selective and the relevant parts of the output are as follows:

- The correlation between the two variables is shown by the R statistic in the Model Summary table (5.8(a)) ($r = .903$). The coefficient of determination is given by the R Square value of .815. This is the proportion of the variance in the outcome measure which is explained by the predictor variable.
- The values required to interpret our $y = a + bx$ equation are shown in the second table, headed

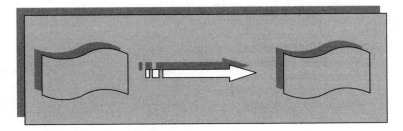

Figure 5.16 Continuous independent variables and continuous dependent variables: regression.

Table 5.8.
(a)

Model Summary

Model	R	R Square	Adjusted R Square	Std. Error of the Estimate
1	.903[a]	.815	.791	4.06

a. Predictors: (Constant), TEMP

(b)

Coefficients[a]

Model		Unstandardized Coefficients		Standardized Coefficients		
		B	Std. Error	Beta	t	Sig.
1	(Constant)	−9.800	3.992		−2.455	.040
	TEMP	1.067	.180	.903	5.927	.000

a. Dependent Variable: reported incidence of road rage.

Coefficients (5.8(b)). Specifically, the value for *b*, which is a measure of the slope of our regression line (how steep or shallow this line is), is given in the column headed B and adjoining the variable name. Thus *b* in the equation is 1.067. The value for *a*, known as the y-intercept, and representing the point on the y-axis that is cut by the regression line, is given in the same column and identified as the Constant. In this case *a* is given as −9.8.

We now have all the information we need to create our best fitting line and by substituting the regression values for the symbols in the straight line equation, $y = a + bx$ becomes: $y = -9.8 + 1.07x$.

Armed with this information we can now do two useful things. First we can draw our best fitting line; by selecting any two values of x we can apply the formula to identify the corresponding y values – giving us the two points needed for any line. For example:

For $x = 0$: $y = -9.8 + 1.07(0) = -9.8$

For $x = 30$: $y = -9.8 + 1.07(30) = 22.3$

We can now produce our best fitting line, as shown in Figure 5.17.

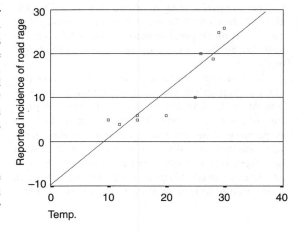

Figure 5.17.

The second application of our newly developed formula is that for any one measure of the independent variable we can now predict a corresponding dependent value. Thus, if temperature was 20° our estimate of road rage incidents would be 11.4 ($y = -9.8 + 1.07(20) = 11.4$). The procedure for performing simple regression is shown in Box 5.11.

Box 5.11   Simple regression in SPSS

Consider a topic that has previously been of interest to us, that of blood pressure. It is now understood that many factors influence standing blood pressure but let us assume that a medical practitioner wishes to explore the effects of weight in particular. A number of patients attending a hypertension clinic have their post-exercise BP recorded and a note is taken of their individual weights (M&K.dat7.BP). The procedure for carrying out a simple regression analysis is as follows:

• Analyse
• Regression
• Linear

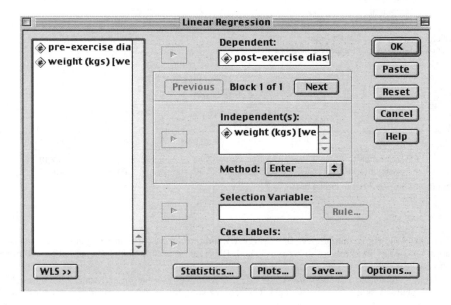

In the Linear Regression window we select the outcome, or dependent, variable in our analysis, placing it into the Dependent box. We then choose from the Variables window the causal factor, placing this in the Independent(s) box. The other options are left untouched and OK selected, producing the following extensive output:

Variables Entered/Removed[b]

Model	Variables Entered	Variables Removed	Method
1	weight (kgs)[a]	.	Enter

a. All requested variables entered.
b. Dependent Variable: post-exercise diastolic BP.

continued

Box 5.11   *continued*

Model Summary

Model	R	R Square	Adjusted R Square	Std. Error of the Estimate
1	.646[a]	.417	.397	5.0870

a. Predictors: (Constant), weight (kgs)

ANOVA[b]

Model		Sum of Squares	df	Mean Square	F	Sig.
1	Regression	518.940	1	518.940	20.054	.000[a]
	Residual	724.560	28	25.877		
	Total	1243.500	29			

a. Predictors: (Constant), weight (kgs)
b. Dependent Variable: post-exercise diastolic BP

Coefficients[a]

Model		Unstandardized Coefficients		Standardized Coefficients	t	Sig.
		B	Std. Error	Beta		
1	(Constant)	50.433	8.773		5.748	.000
	weight (kgs)	.483	.108	.646	4.478	.000

a. Dependent Variable: post-exercise diastolic BP

A cursory glance at the above output inevitably brings to mind the word 'scary' and we defy anyone faced with a full regression output for the first time not to be intimidated. However, as we frequently advise, take it a bit at a time and all will become clear.

The first table – 'Variables entered/removed' – offers descriptive information and states which variable has been entered into the analysis as a predictor (weight). The relative straightforwardness of this information though is confounded by the fact that the simple regression procedure is carried out within a much more complex analysis designed for scenarios in which there are several causal factors (multiple regression – considered in the next section). Hence 'weight' is the only variable in a cell headed 'Variables Entered'.

The next table provides the Model Summary. We note that the correlation between weight and resting blood pressure is .646, with a corresponding r-squared value of .417. From this information we can now say, first, that as weight increases, blood pressure goes up. Second, we can state that approximately 42% of variation in blood pressure can be explained by weight.

The third table is the ANOVA table (analysis of variance) and for the moment it is sufficient to inspect the significance value (.000) which indicates that the predictive relationship between weight and BP is a significant one. ANOVA itself is explained in later sections of this chapter.

The final table – 'Coefficients' – contains the information we require to produce our best fitting line and to make precise predictions. Recall that, in the column headed B, the (Constant) value is the y-intercept, or a in the formula, $y = a + bx$. The weights value is b in the equation and provides a measure of how much blood pressure changes for each unit change in weight. In this case, for every kilo, blood pressure changes by .483 units of pressure. The formula for this particular relationship is $y = 50.433 + 0.483(x)$. For a patient weighing in at 80 kilos, we would predict a blood pressure reading of 89.1. The corresponding plot, with its fitted line, is shown in Figure 5.18.

continued

Box 5.11 *continued*

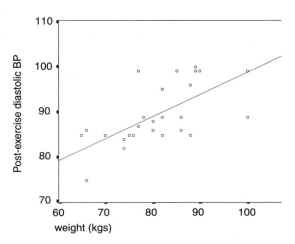

Figure 5.18.

Note: the observant reader will be wondering why this best-fitting line does not cross the y-axis at 50.433, as the formula above indicates. A closer look at the scatterplot will show that SPSS has truncated the scales on both the horizontal and vertical axes. Had the scales been drawn with zero origins, the regression line would indeed have intersected the y-axis at 50.433. Readers will find this an extremely useful piece of information!

5.6 Complex analyses (analysis of variance, regression and partial correlation)

5.6.1 One nominal (category) independent variable and one interval (continuous) dependent variable: between-group comparisons and analysis of variance (ANOVA) – comparisons among more than two groups

Some examples might be:

- Measures of service satisfaction are compared among passengers travelling on the North, North East and North-North East networks.
- Post-operative recovery times are compared for patients taking no, occasional, and regular exercise.
- People born under the 12 astrological signs are compared on their attitude towards a single European currency.

In the previous section (5.5) the typical analytical procedures likely to be used by the novice social researcher were introduced, and for most introductory courses an understanding of crosstabulation, *t*-tests and correlation are more than sufficient. However, as designs become more sophisticated, issues more complex and our research aspirations rise, there is a need for an understanding of more advanced procedures. The next few sections build on the basic techniques already covered and the reader will (hopefully) recognise that advanced procedures, far from being different and requiring a grasp of totally new concepts, merely expand on what has gone before. And we begin with the analysis of variance.

In Chapter 2, it was explained that while the two-category independent variable was typical of many research designs (employed sample vs unemployed sample; male vs female; control group vs experimental group), there were many instances in which a causal factor would comprise a number of components (see Section 2.4.3). Comparing the general health of the five different occupational classes is

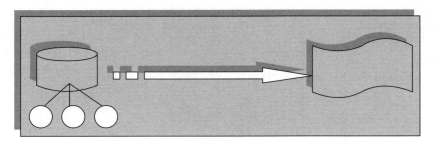

Figure 5.19 Category independent variables and continuous dependent variables: more than two groups.

one example previously cited; measuring the personal incomes of people born under the 12 different star signs would be another. In fact there are many situations in which an independent variable will not fit conveniently into the two-group scenario, and this has particular implications when it comes to analysing the data from such a study. In Section 5.5.4 above the *t*-test was presented as a powerful group comparison test. However, its application is limited to the two-group case and the *t*-test is really unsuitable here. For more complex comparisons of the kind described, what is needed is analysis of variance.

Developed by Sir Ronald Fisher, an agricultural scientist of considerable renown and influence, **ANOVA**, as it is more commonly termed, is an extremely sophisticated analytical tool. As such it is ideally suited to the many category case. However, the procedure is also complex and requires a little explanation, although for a fuller review one of the many statistical texts recommended in Section 5.11 should be consulted.

5.6.2   Analysis of variance

In the previous section (5.6.1) it was argued that real life investigations don't always fall neatly into the two-group comparison outcome. The social class example for instance contained five groups while the independent variable in the astrological sign case comprised 12 categories. These are all merely extensions of the two-sample situation, however. They still involve only one independent variable (class, star sign, or whatever) and differ only in the number of elements into which the independent variable can be subdivided.

In ANOVA terminology, the independent variable is usually called a **factor**, and the various subdivisions,

levels. The above examples would be called single factor or one-way ANOVAs (one independent variable). Furthermore, if different subjects are used for each condition or level, they would be termed unrelated or between-groups ANOVAs; had a repeated measures design been used, they would be related or within-groups ANOVAs. (In case anyone's forgotten the difference between repeated measures and different subjects designs, a review of Chapter 2, will help, especially Sections 2.4.2 and 2.4.3.)

The next question most newcomers to advanced statistics ask is, apart from the opportunity to learn new jargon, what advantage does ANOVA have over *t*-tests? Why not just carry out a series of *t*-tests on all the various pairs of conditions? The example in Box 5.12 shows why not.

For one thing, ANOVA explores all these relationships in a single step, rather than in the multiple repetitions that would be required by the *t*-test. For

---

Box 5.12

In a study hypothesising that personal income depends on star sign, the following paired comparisons (*t*-tests) would be required:

Aries vs Taurus	Aries vs Gemini
Aries vs Cancer	Aries vs Leo
Aries vs Virgo	Aries vs Libra
Aries vs Scorpio	Aries vs Sagittarius
Aries vs Capricorn	Aries vs Aquarius
Aries vs Pisces	Taurus vs Cancer
Taurus vs Gemini	Taurus vs Virgo
Taurus vs Leo	etc.

To complete this analysis in which every possible pairing is compared would require 66 *t*-tests.

another, in a situation in which lots of *t*-tests are carried out, chance alone would throw up the occasional, apparently significant finding and lead to a misplaced interpretation of the data (the risk of a Type 1 error increases). And finally, the single factor ANOVA is merely the beginning of what this sophisticated technique can do.

Unfortunately there is a cost. In SPSS ANOVA will only tell us that a difference exists *somewhere* among the various comparisons being made, not necessarily where. However, since there are ways round this, it is a small price to pay for the considerable rewards offered by this approach. So why analysis of *variance*? We already know that when data are collected from some sample on an outcome measure, the mean provides the most common descriptive statistic. However, we also know that scores vary around this mean, a variance that is due to two things:

1 Individual differences among participants.
2 Error (mistakes in measurement; misclassification of individuals; random occurrences, etc.).

This variance within a sample and around the sample mean is known as the **within-group variance** and is one of the key ANOVA measures.

Consider an example in which we hypothesise that the general well-being levels of a number of university undergraduates will be determined by the amount of physical exercise they take (based on the healthy body–healthy mind notion). If three groups are compared, one taking no exercise, one taking occasional exercise and one taking regular exercise, we might observe the distributions as shown in Figure 5.20. This shows the distribution of response on a well-being questionnaire for each of the three groups. Mean scores are positioned for each group on a well-being scale running from low to high.

Here we can see that each of the groups is represented by a mean score somewhere along our well-being continuum. We also observe that, within each group, there is variation about the respective means – there is within-group variance for each sample. Moreover, because the

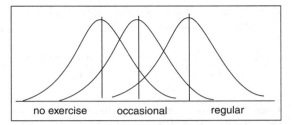

Figure 5.21.

sample distributions are different, there will also be variance between the subjects in one group and subjects in another group. This is known as **between-group variance**, another important ANOVA measure, and attributable, this time, to three things:

1 Individual differences.
2 Error.
3 A real difference, or treatment effect.

Such between-group variance can be considerable, as in the above well-being example (where the samples are clearly scoring at different levels on the outcome measure), or negligible, as in Figure 5.21.

In this example, while there is still considerable within-group variance, the differences between the groups are much smaller. What ANOVA aims to do is determine whether or not the observed differences among these distributions are significant, or perfectly acceptable, given the effects individual differences and errors have on measurement. More specifically, if subjects were in different groups, would the differences between them be greater than if they were in the same group? In our first well-being example clearly the well-being score of any given individual will be nearer that of another in the same exercise group than to an individual in either of the other two groups. In the second example though, there will be many instances when individuals in different groups are closer to one another than some who are in the same group. The significance of these differences is tested using Fisher's *F*-statistic:

$$F = \frac{\text{(average) between-group variance}}{\text{(average) within-group variance}}$$

The logic of this is that when we compare individuals, whether in the same group or in different groups, much of the variation between them is due to the same

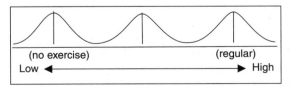

Figure 5.20.

things – individual differences and error. Applying the F-ratio procedure then we have:

$$\frac{\text{Individual differences} + \text{Error} + \text{Treatment effect}}{\text{Individual differences} + \text{Error}}$$

Once the common sources of variance are eliminated from both the numerator and the denominator, anything left over must be attributable to the treatment effect (where the treatment effect is that which separates participants into the different groups, be this exercise level, star sign, experimental condition or whatever). If this is small (expressed as a small F-value), then assigning subjects to one group or another has little impact on the variability among them. However, if this is large (expressed as a large F-value), then this signifies that belonging to one group as opposed to another makes a real difference, and one that cannot be attributable to either individual differences or error (since these common elements have now cancelled one another out).

There is a third measure of variance used in ANOVA, and this is termed the *total variance*. This is obtained by treating individual subjects as if they belong to one single distribution as opposed to their own particular group. A *grand mean* can be calculated for all subjects, irrespective of sample, and the measure of variance for the combined subjects provides the total variance, a measure that forms part of the calculation of the F-ratio.

In the language of ANOVA, variance is given as the average of the *sums of squares*, or SS (the sum of the squared deviations from the mean), such that the within-group variance is known as MSwithin, between-group variance as MSbetween and the total variance, TotalSS. Box 5.13 illustrates the derivation of these terms.

Continuing with our exercise and well-being example, the SPSS output for such a study is shown in Table 5.9. (Note: SPSS allows for one-way ANOVA calculations via the Compare Means menu, and not just under the ANOVA heading, which is normally reserved

for more complex designs.) The information most immediately relevant to the researcher, and the element that is usually inspected before anything else, is the F probability value (Sig., short for significance). This is a measure of the likelihood that there is no difference in well-being scores between any of the three groups. In this case the probability value is 0.000, which is well below our 0.05 cut-off value, pointing to a significant difference somewhere in the comparison. (See Box 5.14 for further discussion on this topic, including an explanation of multiple group comparisons.)

The rest of the ANOVA table (5.9) might appear complicated but if the reader would take a moment to consult Box 5.13, on the key elements of analysis of variance, the terms and their meaning will soon become clear.

All ANOVA tables begin with a description of the analysis being carried out – in this case we see that the dependent variable 'wellbeing' is being explored in terms of the different groups that comprise our study.

In the analysis itself, each of the sources of variance is presented – 194.667 (between); 268.000 (within); 462.667 (total), with each value representing the sum of the squared deviations from the relevant mean. Degrees of freedom (df) for each source of variance are presented next: 2 in the between variances case (df for categories are given as $k - 1$, or the number of groups less 1. There are three exercise levels, hence $df = 2$).

Mean squares are shown next, being merely the sums of squares for each source of variance divided by the appropriate degrees of freedom.

Finally, the F-statistic itself is shown (16.343), a calculation that requires that the mean squares (between) is divided by the mean squares (within). The more ambitious student might wish to attempt this and the other calculations manually to confirm the SPSS version, in which case the data can be found in M&K.dat8.exercise.

On a practical note, when inspecting the output from an ANOVA special attention should be paid to the degrees of freedom (df). If an analysis was

Table 5.9.

ANOVA

wellbeing scores

	Sum of Squares	df	Mean Square	F	Sig.
Between Groups	194.667	2	97.333	16.343	.000
Within Groups	268.000	45	5.956		
Total	462.667	47			

Box 5.13   The language of ANOVA

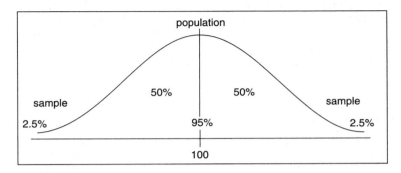

Figure 5.22.

The measurement of any variable generally produces a conventional type of distribution (see Figure 5.22). This typical arrangement of scores is usually expressed in terms of a measure of central tendency, such as the mean, but it is clear that this is an artificial measure since all the scores that comprise this distribution vary to a greater or lesser degree from this middle value. Moreover, while many forms of analysis rely heavily on the mean, analysis of variance, as the term suggests, is more concerned with how scores vary or deviate from the mean. This is calculated as follows:

1   Once the mean has been established, each individual score in a distribution is compared with this central value:

Mean	Score	Difference (Mean − Score)
50	25	+25
50	60	−10
50	48	+2
50	55	−5
.	.	.
.	.	.
.	.	.

2   In order to eliminate negative values from our calculations, each score is squared:

Mean	Score	Difference (Mean − Score)	Difference^2
50	25	+25	625
50	60	−10	100
50	48	+2	4
50	55	−5	25
.	.	.	.
.	.	.	.
.	.	.	.

3   Adding up all these values gives us a measure of the total variation (squared) within a distribution. Another way of expressing this is that we now have a sum of the squares (sum of the squared deviations) or, as ANOVA terminology prefers it, SS.

To compute the F-statistic, which tells us whether or not a manipulation or treatment has had an effect, we need to generate a number of different measures of variation. We need to know the amount of variation within each group – SSwithin; we need to know the variation between the groups – SSbetween; and we also need to know the total variation for the combined groups – TotalSS.

However, just when we think we have got the hang of ANOVA, there is one additional step required before calculation of Fisher's F-statistic can be carried out. Specifically, analysis of variance is concerned not with the total variation for each of the within and the between conditions, rather it is based on measures of *average* variation (for which the statistical term is variance). Hence, the within variance used in calculations is based on within/df (the within-group variation divided by the appropriate degrees of freedom for each sample); the between-group measure is based on between/df (between-group variation divided by the number of groups − 1); the total variances measure is based on total/n − 1.

This may appear complex but all it does is provide a measure of average variation for each component. At the end of this exercise we would be left with:

Mean Squares within (Mean SS within or MSwithin)
Mean Squares between (Mean SS between or MSbetween)

The one-way ANOVA output presented in this chapter demonstrates the application of the analysis of variance terminology.

based on three groups, the particular degrees of freedom would be $(k - 1) = 2$, as in the current example. Similarly, if a sample comprised 48 participants, the relevant degrees of freedom would be $(n - 1) = 47$. In ANOVA, inspection of the between-group *df* is to be strongly recommended: it would not be the first time that, in the setting up of the data for analysis, one of the groups to be compared is omitted. The only clue that this has occurred would be in the degrees of freedom, which in the between-group case would be one less than it ought to be. Unfortunately this is often overlooked in our eagerness to get to the *F*-statistic. As is the convention for this book, the procedure for performing analysis of variance is outlined in Box 5.14.

Box 5.14 One-way ANOVA and SPSS

For this illustration we return to our main source of data – M&K.dat1 – which contains the results of a hypothetical social survey exploring a number of issues, some descriptive, some attitudinal and some behavioural. For our ANOVA we have chosen to analyse the responses to the question 'To what extent do you support increased powers of arrest for the police?', by the UK region in which the various respondents lived. There were three regions – Scotland, the Midlands and the South of England – making the *t*-test inappropriate and the ANOVA the preferred method.

The one-way analysis of variance is one of the most straightforward to set up in SPSS, as the following steps illustrate:

- Analyse
- Compare Means
- One-Way ANOVA

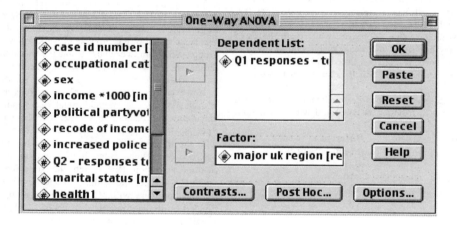

In the usual way, our outcome measure is placed in the Dependent List box (we could have several dependent variables in here and SPSS would perform a whole series of tests). Our independent variable is placed in the Factor box and we could at this point go straight to the ANOVA output by clicking OK. (Note: in previous versions of SPSS the user would be required to define the groups by typing in the numerical values used to identify each of the levels, much as is still required for the *t*-test). However, as we have already intimated in the main text of this chapter, one of the inherent drawbacks of analysis of variance is that the procedure will happily tell us if there is indeed some effect present – there may be a significant difference somewhere among the various groups – but it will not tell us where. There are various ways round this; we could, for example, request an output of the mean scores for each group and inspect them for likely effects (we make a guess). This can be achieved via the Explore command in the Descriptive Statistics sub-menu or, alternatively, it can be obtained as part of the ANOVA set-up itself. Selecting Options… in the One-Way ANOVA window (above) produces the following in which we can check the box marked Descriptives:

continued

Box 5.14   *continued*

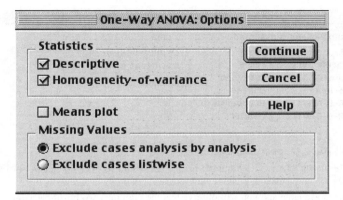

Alternatively, and this is often the preferred method for number-shy undergraduates, we can generate descriptive boxplots through the Graph menu.

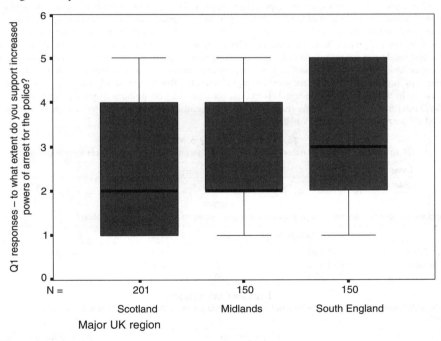

Figure 5.23

Inspection of Figure 5.23 might lead us to think that, if a difference exists among our groups, it would most likely be between Scotland and the South of England, although possibly also between the Midlands and the South of England. The point is we would be guessing when in fact we could be precise.

Referring to the ANOVA window again, you will note that another of the available options is termed Post Hoc. This provides the opportunity for carrying out a series of paired comparisons between all the possible combinations of groups. These are like the *t*-tests we have already encountered, but with various corrections to prevent the possibility of Type 1 errors (which is what could happen if we simply performed a series of *t*-tests).

continued

Box 5.14 *continued*

```
╔═══════════════════════════════════════════════════════════════════╗
║           One-Way ANOVA: Post Hoc Multiple Comparisons              ║
╠═══════════════════════════════════════════════════════════════════╣
║ ┌─ Equal Variances Assumed ──────────────────────────────────────┐ ║
║ │  ☐ LSD           ☐ S-N-K          ☐ Waller-Duncan              │ ║
║ │  ☐ Bonferroni    ☑ Tukey          Type I/Type II Error Ratio: [100]│ ║
║ │  ☐ Sidak         ☐ Tukey's-b                                   │ ║
║ │  ☐ Scheffe       ☐ Duncan         ☐ Dunnett                    │ ║
║ │  ☐ R-E-G-W F     ☐ Hochberg's GT2 Control Category:  [Last  ▲▼]│ ║
║ │  ☐ R-E-G-W Q     ☐ Gabriel        ┌─ Test ──────────────────┐  │ ║
║ │                                   │ ◉ 2-sided  ○ < Control  ○ > Control │ ║
║ └──────────────────────────────────────────────────────────────┘ ║
║ ┌─ Equal Variances Not Assumed ──────────────────────────────────┐ ║
║ │  ☐ Tamhane's T2   ☐ Dunnett's T3   ☐ Games-Howell   ☐ Dunnett's C│ ║
║ └──────────────────────────────────────────────────────────────┘ ║
╚═══════════════════════════════════════════════════════════════════╝
```

There are several options available and you will observe that they fall into two broad categories which we encountered earlier during our consideration of the *t*-test – equal variances assumed and not assumed. As with the *t*-test, if the variances among the groups being compared are not equal, adjustments to the calculations are made. From the user's point of view we merely select a comparison test from the appropriate category. The decision on whether or not variances are equal is based on Levene's test, shown as part of the ANOVA output, and selected by checking the Homogeneity-of-variance box in the Options window (see above). The decision as to which of the paired comparison tests to use, however, is more complicated. All of the tests offered differ in the ways in which comparisons are made and how conservative they are. (A more conservative test might not accept an observed difference as being significant when a less conservative test will.) The arguments for choosing one test over another are complex and statisticians themselves are often in disagreement. For practical purposes though, and certainly for most undergraduates, the **Bonferroni test** is adequate, or the Tukey HSD test (shown as Tukey in the list of available tests). However, for those of you wishing to pursue these matters further, the Howell (1987) reference at the end of this chapter provides a useful introduction to paired comparison tests.

The full SPSS output for the ANOVA is given below.

Test of Homogeneity of Variances

Q1 responses – to what extent do you support increased powers of arrest for the police?

Levene Statistic	df1	df2	Sig.
.744	2	498	.476

ANOVA

Q1 responses – to what extent do you support increased powers of arrest for the police?

	Sum of Squares	df	Mean Square	F	Sig.
Between Groups	17.427	2	8.713	3.966	.020
Within Groups	1094.178	498	2.197		
Total	1111.605	500			

Multiple Comparisons

Dependent Variable: Q1 responses – to what extent do you support increased powers of arrest for the police?

Tukey HSD

(I) major uk region	(J) major uk region	Mean Difference (I–J)	Std. Error	Sig.	95% Confidence Interval Lower Bound	Upper Bound
scotland	midlands	−.26	.16	.227	−.64	.11
	s.england	−.44*	.16	.015	−.82	−6.81E-02
midlands	scotland	.26	.16	.227	−.11	.64
	s.england	−.18	.17	.544	−.58	.22
south england	scotland	.44*	.16	.015	6.81E-02	.82
	midlands	.18	.17	.544	−.22	.58

*. The mean difference is significant at the .05 level.

continued

Box 5.14 *continued*

The output we have displayed comprises three tables. The first to claim our attention is the middle one, the ANOVA table. The most important element is the significance value of .020. This is the probability of obtaining the observed differences in questionnaire responses among respondents in the three regions. As this is below .05 we know that – somewhere among the three groups – a significant difference exists. To determine the precise nature of this effect we requested a *post hoc* analysis in which all pairs would be compared. The Levene's test for equality of variance produced a non-significant result ($p = .476$) allowing us to choose one of the tests from the Equal Variances Assumed list. We selected the Tukey test and the corresponding output indicates that when the mean difference in questionnaire responses between all pairs of regions is analysed, the only significant difference is observed between Scotland and the South of England (and the South of England and Scotland). We could examine the actual probability values shown in the Significance column, but SPSS helpfully identifies with an asterisk (*) those comparisons that demonstrate a significant difference.

The outcome of the analysis is that, when respondents in the three regions are compared on their responses to the questionnaire item, a significant difference is observed between those living in Scotland and those living in Southern England. There were no significant differences between the Scots and the Midlanders, or between the Midlanders and the Southernes. A formal setting out of this analysis is shown below.

1 H_0: there are no significant differences in response to a questionnaire item among respondents in three major UK regions.
2 H_1: there are significant differences in response to a questionnaire item among respondents in three major UK regions.
3 Test: one-way ANOVA; 2-tailed; 0.05 significance level.
4 Outcome: $F(2,498) = 3.966$; $p = 0.020$.
5 Decision: reject H_0 and accept H_1.

(Note: it is a convention when reporting ANOVA findings to state the degrees of freedom for both the between- and the within-subjects variance. This is usually presented in brackets after the F, as shown above. The appropriate values can be extracted from the output table.)

5.6.3 More than one nominal (category) independent variable and one interval (continuous) dependent variable: between-group comparisons and two-way analysis of variance (ANOVA) – comparisons among more than one causal factor, each comprising two or more groups

Some examples might be:

- A study is designed to test whether or not income is determined by a combination of an individual's sex (male or female) and social class (middle or working).
- Examination performance is analysed in terms of pupils' community (urban vs rural) and gender (male vs female).
- The decline in the newt population is examined in terms of cyclists' skill level (novice vs experienced) and their age group (young, middle-aged, elderly).

Just as it is common for independent variables to comprise more than two categories, so it is often the case that a study comprises more than one independent variable. In Chapter 2, Section 2.4.7 considerable discussion was offered on this issue, with particular attention paid to the problem of whether the existence of several independent variables should be dealt with by controls, or by incorporating them into the design. In the event that we decide that more than one factor is having an effect on some outcome measure, and providing these factors are nominal or ordinal in character, we are led once again towards analysis of variance.

In the case of more than one causal factor, successive one-way ANOVAs are as inappropriate as repeated t-tests would have been to test a single factor containing more than two categories, and for the same reasons – sooner or later, successive tests will throw up an apparently significant finding which is really a naturally occurring though rare event (Type 1 error). Moreover, when two or more factors are impinging on a dependent variable, it will often be the case that they will not do so independently, having rather an interactive effect. Once again, the notion of interacting factors is discussed

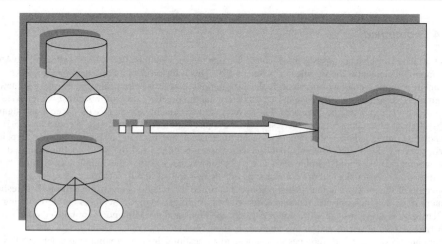

Figure 5.24 Category independent variables and continuous dependent variables: more than one causal factor.

in Chapter 2, Section 2.4.7 and ought to be reviewed if this idea is causing confusion.

If our design is of this more complex variety, the type of ANOVA required is termed a two-way ANOVA, or sometimes factorial or multi-factor analysis of variance. An example follows.

Assume that in a health and welfare study we are interested in post-operative recovery times. We know from previous research in the area that exercise plays an important role in the length of time it takes patients to recover from certain classes of operation. However, suppose disturbing evidence is emerging that recovery rates vary from health authority to health authority and we now wish to incorporate this new element into

our research. Our dependent variable here would be a measure of recovery time (days) to a predetermined level of health or mobility. We have, however, two independent variables – exercise level (none, moderate, intensive) and health authority (A and B). Our analysis then is a two-way, 3 by 2 ANOVA. (There are two (or more) causal factors, the first comprising 3 levels and the second 2 levels.) The ANOVA logic is the same as in the one-way case, with multiple groups being compared in terms of variance, and the output of our present study is shown in Table 5.10. (This output is based on M&K.dat8.exercise.)

The output of a **two-way ANOVA** differs slightly in appearance from that of the one-way, although the

Table 5.10.

Tests of Between-Subjects Effects

Dependent Variable: post-operative recovery time

Source	Type III Sum of Squares	df	Mean Square	F	Sig.
Corrected Model	232.381[a]	5	46.476	8.476	.000
Intercept	2781.085	1	2781.085	507.220	.000
EXERCISE	184.130	2	92.065	16.791	.000
HOSPITAL	30.561	1	30.561	5.574	.023
EXERCISE * HOSPITAL	7.153	2	3.577	.652	.526
Error	230.286	42	5.483		
Total	3284.000	48			
Corrected Total	462.667	47			

a. R Squared = .502 (Adjusted R Squared = .443)

information is essentially the same. There is just more of it. The important point to remember is that when we interpret SPSS output, not all of it will be relevant to our particular study. Moreover, of the information that is relevant, some is more important than the rest.

In Table 5.10 there are two things we are interested in. First, is there a **main effect**? A main effect refers to the influence, on its own, of each independent variable on the outcome measure. In this example we have two independent variables (exercise regime and hospital authority) and the table shows that both variables have a significant impact on recovery times. On its own, there is a significant difference on recovery time among the three different exercise levels, with a probability less than .01 (shown as .000 in the output). Also, on its own, there is a significant difference in recovery time between the two different hospital authorities, with a probability of less than .05 (shown as .023 in the output).

The second element of this output that is of interest is whether or not there is an interaction between the two independent variables, i.e. might the effects of a particular intensity of exercise depend on which hospital authority the patient is under? In this case there is no interaction effect with the probability of .526 being given.

As with the one-way ANOVA, we can take our analysis further, especially as – typical of ANOVA – we are told merely that effects were observed, but not where. This is never a problem when a factor comprises only two levels (as with our hospital authority), since we need only inspect the two mean values to identify which is the higher. The ANOVA has already demonstrated that this observed difference is significant and we need go no further. Where factors comprise more than two levels (as with our exercise variable) *post hoc* **tests** can be applied in the same way as for one-way analyses. There is an option for this in the two-way set-up window. Dealing with interactions, however, is more problematic. SPSS has not been able to solve the problem of two-way interactions and a rather convoluted procedure is required – data must be re-coded such that our two independent variables are reduced to just one, as in Table 5.11. In this format we can proceed to carry out a one-way ANOVA, along with appropriate *post hoc* tests to identify significant paired comparisons. It is certainly a clumsy procedure and we would not recommend this unless the ANOVA identified a significant interaction. However, it does work.

A more immediate way perhaps of illustrating ANOVA data, and one that we strongly recommend for undergraduates, is a simple line chart. In this format changes in the outcome variable are immediately

Table 5.11.

Group	Recovery time
No exercise/hospital A	days
No exercise/hospital B	days
Mild exercise/hospital A	days
Mild exercise/hospital B	days
Intensive exercise/hospital A	days
Intensive exercise/hospital B	days

obvious in terms of the different levels of the independent variables. Moreover, in the event of an interaction, the graph shows quite clearly where and how this occurs (see Figure 5.25). It clearly shows the general trend is for recovery time to decline the more exercise our patients take. It also clearly demonstrates that hospital authority A is lagging behind B at all levels, with longer recovery times irrespective of the amount of exercise taken. More interestingly, under intensive exercise, recovery times in A begin to increase again, a finding that would normally warrant further study.

This ends our consideration of analysis of variance, although it should be noted that this is by no means the end of what the procedure can achieve. We have not, for instance, developed the within-group design, in which

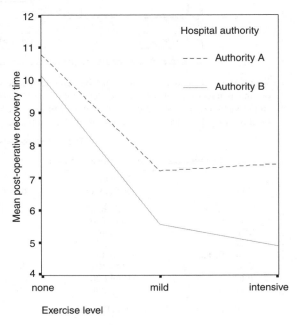

Figure 5.25.

Box 5.15 Two-way ANOVA in SPSS

Imagine a study, a favourite of the authors, that is concerned with the varying fortunes of the **newt** population. In one scenario we argue that the declining population of this species of amphibian has to do with the numbers of cyclists using our country lanes. We hypothesise that there will be two factors linked to the numbers of squashed newts, namely an individual's cycling skill, and their sex. If each variable has two levels (male vs female; novice vs skilled), a two-way ANOVA is carried out as follows:

- Analyse
- General Linear Model
- Univariate

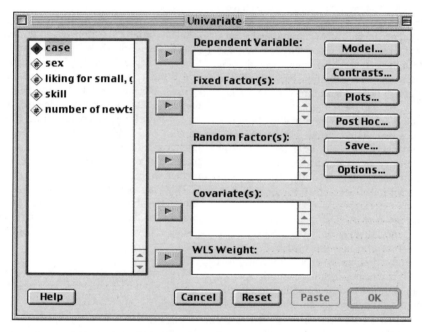

We select our dependent variable from the Variables window as usual and place it in the Dependent box. We next select our independent variables and place them in the Fixed Factors box. This identifies these variables as the factors responsible (we believe) for variations in the number of newts run over. None of the other options is of interest to us for this level of analysis so we merely select OK and await the output.

Tests of Between-Subjects Effects

Dependent Variable: number of newts run over

Source	Type III Sum of Squares	df	Mean Source	F	Sig.
Corrected Model	157.879[a]	3	52.626	10.955	.000
Intercept	1647.773	1	1647.773	342.998	.000
SEX	20.441	1	20.441	4.255	.048
SKILL	14.343	1	14.343	2.986	.094
SEX * SKILL	128.436	1	128.436	26.735	.000
Error	144.121	30	4.804		
Total	1968.000	34			
Corrected Total	302.000	33			

a. R Squared = .523 (Adjusted R Squared = .475)

continued

Box 5.15 *continued*

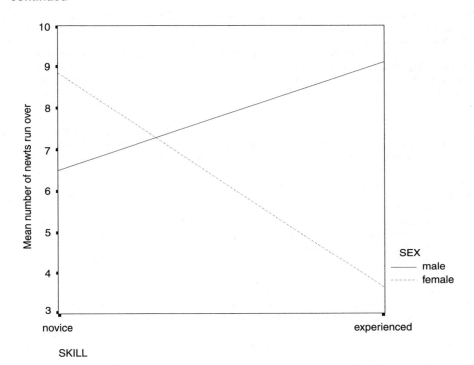

Figure 5.26.

Multiple Comparisons

Dependent Variable: number of newts run over
Tukey HSD

(I) GROUP	(J) GROUP	Mean Difference (I–J)	Std. Error	Sig.	95% Confidence Interval Lower Bound	Upper Bound
male&novice	male&experienced	−2.6111	1.0071	.066	−5.3495	.1272
	female&novice	−2.3571	1.0801	.151	−5.2942	.5799
	female&experienced	2.8750*	1.0397	.045	4.800E-02	5.7020
male&experienced	male&novice	2.6111	1.0071	.066	−.1272	5.3495
	female&novice	.2540	1.1046	.996	−2.7495	3.2574
	female&experienced	5.4861*	1.0650	.000	2.5902	8.3821
female&novice	male&novice	2.3571	1.0801	.151	−.5799	5.2942
	male&experienced	−.2540	1.1046	.996	−3.2574	2.7495
	female&experienced	5.2321*	1.1344	.000	2.1476	8.3166
female&experienced	male&novice	−2.8750*	1.0397	.045	−5.7020	−4.8004E-02
	male&experienced	−5.4861*	1.0650	.000	−8.3821	−2.5902
	female&novice	−5.2321*	1.1344	.000	−8.3166	−2.1476

*. The mean difference is significant at the .05 level.

continued

Box 5.15   *continued*

The full ANOVA output is given above, indicating that there is a main effect for sex ($F[1,33] = 4.255$; $p = .048$), but no main effect for skill level ($F[1,33] = 2.986$; $p = .094$), although this is clearly heading in the direction of significance. There is, however, an interaction effect of sex * skill ($F[1,33] = 26.735$; $p = .000$). In plain English what this means is that, if you look at the main factors on their own, the sex of the cyclist has a significant effect on how many newts are squashed, but the skill level, on its own, does not. However, the magnitude of this sex effect does depend on whether the cyclists were skilled or novices. Or to put it another way, the skill of the individual only has an effect on the newt population when you also consider whether they are male or female.

So far this is a good story and we have learned a lot about what influences the newt population, but we can refine our understanding further. Recall that ANOVA tells us if there is some kind of effect, but not where it is.

A visual presentation of the relationships might help and, indeed, if we consult Figure 5.26, we see that for female cyclists there is a huge difference in their newt count depending on whether or not they are experienced. Novice female cyclists kill a lot more newts than experienced ones. This effect – although not so marked – is reversed for male cyclists: novice males kill fewer newts than experienced ones. We have no idea why.

For our final table we computed a new Group variable by combining the sex and skills variables. This allowed us to carry out a one-way ANOVA as a stepping stone to multiple paired comparisons. (The procedure is complex and will require some assistance from supervisors, but the outcome is rewarding. As a starting point the process is carried out in the Transform menu using the Compute command.) Inspection of the table indicates that the significant differences are between female experienced cyclists and male novice, male experienced and female novice.

---

repeated measures ANOVA allows us to compare several measures on a sample, and not just the two that the paired *t*-test allows. Neither have we considered mixed designs in which the effects of several repetitions are considered by some between-groups variable. For instance, we might explore the effects of a new drug treatment on males and females, measured over four different occasions. However, tempting as it is to continue developing this procedure we are mindful of the introductory nature of this book. ANOVA is a powerful analytical tool and we have already progressed our discussion to a sophisticated level. There is more than enough here for most undergraduates and we would be surprised if the majority of student research designs failed to fit in to one of the models we have discussed. However, in the event that a particular design goes beyond what we have presented, the recommended texts at the end of this chapter offer further discussion.

5.6.4   More than one interval (continuous) independent variable and one interval (continuous) dependent variable – multiple regression and partial correlation

Some examples might be:

• Do attitudes towards government policy on abandoning the state pension vary as a result of both age and income?

• What are the combined effects of extraversion, introversion and a measure of locus of control on a speed decision task?

• Can variations in the newt population be explained by variations in temperature and rainfall?

Other examples might be:

• What is the true relationship between temperature and the incidence of road rage once we have controlled for the effects of population density and the neuroticism of drivers?

• Can we predict absenteeism rates within a production organisation from hours worked, once we have eliminated the effects of income?

• We know that opinions on arming the police force are based on many complex and interrelated factors, such as a person's age, their personal values, anxiety levels and so on. Can we examine the effects of age only on this issue, without these other factors obscuring the relationship?

Once we understand that any event in the social world (an outcome measure, or dependent variable) is unlikely to be determined by just one causal factor (independent variable, or predictor), we are closer to appreciating the real world than when our explorations were based on the single independent variable/single dependent variable scenario. Accepting this level of complexity in life requires an equally complex method of analysis. We have already encountered one such sophisticated

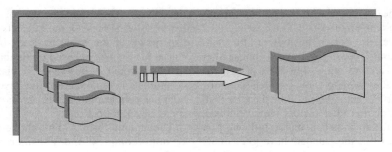

Figure 5.27 Continuous independent variables and continuous dependent variables: more than one causal factor.

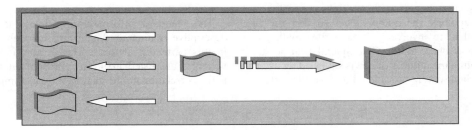

Figure 5.28 Continuous independent variables and continuous dependent variables: one causal factor and many extraneous factors removed.

approach in the two-way ANOVA, which has the potential for exploring the effects of many predictors on some outcome measure. ANOVA, as we now appreciate, is the preferred approach when our predictors are nominal or ordinal (category) in nature. When our predictors are interval (continuous) in nature, we are in the realm of correlation and regression.

There are two approaches we can adopt to the many predictor/one outcome case, and the decision on which to choose is based largely on what the researcher is trying to do. For example, returning to our road rage study, we may have ascertained from various sources (previous research, an exploratory study or issues raised during a focus group session with convicted offenders) that a number of things are likely to be linked, causally, to incidents of aggressive driver behaviour. These might be: vehicle density; temperature; personality; driving experience. If the point of our study is to explore the combined effects of all these factors on road rage, or to determine the relative contributions of each on the outcome measure, then our approach is that of multiple regression. We have already observed that, in simple regression (Section 5.5.7), we can state how much variation in an outcome measure is predicted by an inde-

pendent variable. Multiple regression allows us to do the same, but with many (multiple) predictors. Similarly, we have noted that, in simple regression, the regression coefficient (b, in the regression formula) provides a measure of how much a dependent variable changes for a given change in a predictor. The same is true for multiple predictors – with multiple regression we can identify the relative contribution of each factor, in addition to determining whether or not such contributions are statistically significant.

Supposing, however, that our research aim differs from the multiple predictor case of the preceding discussion. Imagine that a city planning department, charged with developing a new traffic system which, among other things, would minimise the incidence of dangerous road rage, identifies the same factors as likely contributors to aggressive driving behaviour. Undoubtedly driver experience will play a part, as will personality. There is evidence that rage also varies with temperature, but these are all factors outside the control of the planning unit. So what if research indicates that high scoring extraverts feature most often in incidents of road rage. Are the planners going to insist that drivers take the EPI before being allowed inside the city boundaries? Or will traffic barriers go up when temperatures rise above 20 degrees? Unlikely. However, it is within the ability of the planners to control traffic density, via speed limits, filter systems, CCTV and warning signs. To justify the expense though, they need to know the precise contribution of the density factor. Would it be the case that, once the effects of the other factors were removed, traffic density still remained a major influence on road rage? To test this the planners have to examine the correlation between density and rage, with all the other factors removed. The procedure is termed **partial correlation**.

This section begins with multiple regression and without apology the authors decided that the first example had to involve their favourite small, green amphibians once more. Consequently, in a study investigating the number of newts squished by cyclists three variables were considered as possible influencing factors. They were the age of the subjects, the extraversion scores of the subjects and the cycling experience of the subjects. Each of these potential causal factors was selected on the basis of arguments that they would all in some way relate to the levels of co-ordination required to circumnavigate hordes of hopping and leaping newts across a standard cycle route. See Table 5.12.

The output from a multiple regression analysis is both complex and considerable, and Tables 5.12(a), (b) and (c) represent only a part of what is available with this analysis. In the interests of clarity some elements of the typical output have been omitted.

The standard information available is initially descriptive, telling us what variables were involved in this particular analysis. The various independent variables are listed in turn. Following on from this is the correlational information, the most important of

Table 5.12.
(a)

Variables Entered/Removed[b]

Model	Variables Entered	Variables Removed	Method
1	cycling experience (years), age of riders, extraversion scores[a]	.	Enter

a. All requested variables entered.
b. Dependent Variable: number of newts run over.

(b)

Model Summary

Model	R	R Square	Adjusted R Square	Std. Error of the Estimate
1	.753[a]	.566	.553	1.7473

a. Predictors: (Constant), cycling experience (years), age of riders, extraversion scores

(c)

Coefficients[a]

Model		Unstandardized Coefficients		Standardized Coefficients		
		B	Std. Error	Beta	t	Sig.
1	(Constant)	5.697	1.210		4.710	.000
	age of riders	$-4.680E-02$	.028	$-.117$	-1.647	.103
	extraversion scores	.206	.050	.314	4.123	.000
	cycling experience (years)	$-.515$	.075	$-.515$	-6.876	.000

a. Dependent Variable: number of newts run over

which is the *r*-squared value. Standing at .566 the implication is that 57% of the variance in newts run over can be explained by a combination of the various causal factors. However, since these factors *are* acting in combination it is quite possible that the effects of one particular factor are being obscured or exaggerated by the effects of others. Therefore it is possible that one or more of the independent variables is having a greater or lesser impact on the decline of the newt population than at first appears.

Looking at the coefficients table (5.12(c)), we observe a number of columns of data. The first of these simply identifies the various variables in the analysis. The second column, headed 'B', refers to the value *b* in our old friend $y = a + bx$, where *b* is a measure of the slope of the regression line or, alternatively, the amount of change in the *y* (outcome) variable for every unit change in the *x* (independent) variable. Hence, for every increase on the extraversion scale of 1, there is a corresponding change to the number of newts squished of 0.206, and so on.

The next important section here is found under the **BETA** column heading, the values here being the standardised coefficients encountered in the B column. This is to deal with the problem of different predictors being measured on different scales and to allow us to compare directly the effects of several independent variables with each other. For completeness, values are standardised by multiplying the value of *b* for a given predictor by the ratio of the standard deviation of the independent variable to the standard deviation of the dependent variable, as in the formula:

$$B = b\,\frac{sx_i}{sy}$$

If this is all a bit too much, however, a general rule of thumb is that the larger the BETA value, the more important is the variable in predicting or determining the dependent variable. Accordingly, it would appear that the variables responsible for the decline in the newt population are cycling experience, extraversion scores and age, in that order. The final two columns describe *t*-values and their associated probabilities. The information given here measures the improvement in the predictive power of the independent factor as each variable is added to the equation. Thus, adding cycling experience and extraversion to all the other variables produces significant *t*-values (the

probability that the inclusion of this variable made a difference), while adding age as a predictor fails to add significance to the equation. Therefore we can state here that of all the independent variables that could be included in an attempt to predict the number of newts run over, experience and extraversion of the rider were the only ones that made a significant difference. In other words, when it comes to accounting for the decline in the newt population, experience and personality are the dominant factors. See Box 5.16 for a review of the procedure for carrying out multiple regression analysis.

In the event that the research aim is not to explore the effects of a number of predictors on some outcome measure, but rather to consider the influence of a single factor on a dependent variable, with the other predictors controlled for, the approach is partial correlation.

Conventional bivariate correlation explores a relationship between two variables, expressing this as a correlation coefficient (*r*). For example, we may note that the incidence of muggings seems to rise every time there is an increase in sunspot activity. If this relationship is noted over a 10 month period and a correlation performed, we might demonstrate an $r = 0.895$. This is highly significant and, if squared, would allow us to argue that approximately 0.80 (80%) of variation in muggings can be explained by changes in sunspot activity. Impressive, one would think. (See M&K.dat10.muggings.)

Supposing, however, that it is pointed out to us that the rate of muggings also varies with temperature ($r = 0.903$), and moreover, that sunspot activity also varies with temperature ($r = 0.938$). This presents us with something of a problem, since all three variables are intercorrelated, it is possible that the apparent relationship between any two is overexaggerated. More specifically, since temperature correlates with sunspot activity, and sunspot activity correlates with the rate of muggings, some of the variation in muggings presumably can be explained by temperature. Figure 5.29 might clarify this. It shows that the amount of variation in muggings explained solely by sunspot activity is in the region A. That explained by temperature is in the region B. The variation within region D is explained by a combination of sunspot and temperature. Therefore, the correlation between sunspot and muggings is overexaggerated by the region D, part of which is attributable to temperature. Thus, if we were to remove the obscuring effect of temperature we would find that the true sunspot effect is much less than the original A + D, comprising merely A.

Box 5.16   Multiple regression and SPSS

Consider a previously encountered problem for a department of city road planners. It is believed that incidents of dangerous road rage are caused by a number of factors – temperature, personality and traffic density. In a study to determine the relative importance of each of these factors, a multiple regression procedure is followed:

- Analyse
- Regression
- Linear

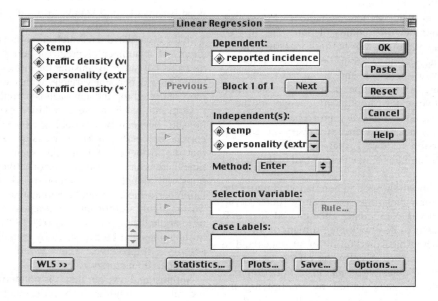

In the Regression window, we select from our list of variables the outcome measure (reported incidence of road rage) and place this in the Dependent box. Our causal factors – temperature, personality and traffic density – are placed in the Independent box. Since we are concerned with the combined effects of all these factors, we leave the pre-set method for the analysis as Enter (enter all variables simultaneously). Clicking OK produces the following output:

Variables Entered/Removed[b]

Model	Variables Entered	Variables Removed	Method
1	traffic density (*100)/hour, personality (extraversion), TEMP[a]	.	Enter

a. All requested variables entered.
b. Dependent Variable: reported incidence of road rage

Model Summary

Model	R	R Square	Adjusted R Square	Std. Error of the Estimate
1	.920[a]	.846	.817	3.78

a. Predictors: (Constant), traffic density (*100)/hour, personality (extraversion), TEMP

continued

Box 5.16 *continued*

Coefficients[a]

Model		Unstandardized Coefficients		Standardized Coefficients		
		B	Std. Error	Beta	t	Sig.
1	(Constant)	−9.415	3.628		−2.595	.020
	TEMP	.235	.207	.195	1.136	.273
	personality (extraversion)	.111	.339	.054	.327	.748
	traffic density (*100)/hour	5.251	.925	.744	5.677	.000

a. Dependent Variable: reported incidence of road rage

The first output table informs us of the variables used to predict our outcome measure, and the method whereby the regression analysis was carried out – all variables were entered simultaneously to assess their combined effects. The next table shows the *r*-squared value: .846. In other words, an impressive 84% of variation in road rage incidents can be predicted by a combination of temperature, personality and traffic density. The third table provides specific information on the relative contribution of each variable: in particular the B column shows the unit change in our outcome measure for each change in a predictor. The BETA column indicates the order of importance of each factor, and the t and Sig. columns demonstrate that only traffic density has a significant impact on incidents of rage.

The full regression formula is:

$$Y = -9.415 + 0.235 \text{ (Temp.)} + 0.111 \text{ (Personality)} + 5.251 \text{ (Traffic density)}$$

In statistical terms we can see in Table 5.13 first the **zero-order correlation** between muggings, sunspot and temperature (termed zero-order since this is the basic correlation with nothing removed, or controlled for). (Note: this example is presented for illustrative purposes and we would suggest that, practically, such a small sample would not contribute to a credible analysis.)

If we now remove the effect of temperature from the sunspot–mugging relationship, we generate what is termed a first-order partial correlation, as shown in

Table 5.14. (Note: had we removed two factors we would term the resultant correlation a second-order partial, and so on.)

The remarkable observation that can now be made is that, by removing the effects of temperature, the original strong correlation between sunspot and muggings disappears. We see now that there is no direct relationship between these two factors and that

Table 5.13.

Partial Correlation Coefficients

Zero Order Partials

	MUGGINGS	SUNSPOT	TEMP
MUGGINGS	1.0000 (0) P = .	.8951 (8) P = .000	.9025 (8) P = .000
SUNSPOT	.8951 (8) P = .000	1.0000 (0) P = .	.9384 (8) P = .000
TEMP	.9025 (8) P = .000	.9384 (8) P = .000	1.0000 (0) P = .

(Coefficient/(D.F.)/2-tailed Significance)
' . ' is printed if a coefficient cannot be computed

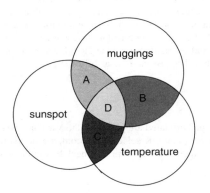

Figure 5.29.

Table 5.14.

Partial Correlation Coefficients

Controlling for..		TEMP
	MUGGINGS	SUNSPOT
MUGGINGS	1.0000	.3234
	(0)	(7)
	P = .	P = .396
SUNSPOT	.3234	1.0000
	(7)	(0)
	P = .396	P = .

(Coefficient/(D.F.)/2-tailed Significance)
' . ' is printed if a coefficient cannot be computed

what we were led to believe at the outset was largely the result of a third factor – temperature.

This has to be an upsetting revelation for most undergraduates – suddenly nothing is certain any more. Relationships between variables are no longer straightforward and what were previously thought of as statistically rigorous findings now depend on the influence of other factors. However, we should try not to become too disturbed. After all, since the first chapter of this book we have been at pains to point out that nothing in the social world is simple and that for any event there may be numerous causal and contributory factors. The trick has always been to identify what those other factors are and to make a judgement about which

are important and which can be ignored. The success with which we can do this will often determine the ultimate value of our research. Box 5.17 demonstrates the procedure for carrying out partial correlation.

5.7 Review

In Chapter 5 we have discussed a number of methods for analysing data that go beyond the descriptive, allowing us to make inferences and predictions. In so doing we have hopefully provided sufficient tools for quite sophisticated undergraduate designs, although it should be remembered that most of the material here serves primarily as an introduction. With the more advanced procedures, such as complex ANOVA and multiple regression, there are various cautions that apply, concerning the conditions under which some tests are more (or less) appropriate than others. Similarly, although we haven't touched upon it, there are situations in which some types of analysis are interchangeable, with the researcher opting for the one that best suits both the data and the overall research aim. The point we are trying to make is that our discussions and illustrations so far represent only the beginnings of a huge and complex field. It is our hope that by reading and understanding this chapter you will feel confident enough to take the first steps in exploring quantitative research.

Box 5.17 Partial correlation and SPSS

Consider a proposed research study by an industrial sociologist into the causes of absenteeism in modern industrial organisations. Contemporary views argue that income will be directly related to absenteeism rates, as will the number of hours worked per week. Our researcher though feels the key variable is job satisfaction, since previous research has suggested that workers with high satisfaction demonstrate increased levels of commitment to their work. Consequently, in a correlational study, our researcher performs a second-order partial correlation in which the effects of income and hours worked are removed from the satisfaction–absence relationship. The procedure is as follows:

- Analyse
- Correlation
- Partial

With the Partial Correlation window active, the pair of variables to be correlated are placed in the Variables box. The variables to be controlled for are entered into the Controlling For box, and OK selected. To compare the partialled correlation with the original zero-order relationship, select Options and click the appropriate check box in the window that appears (not shown here).

continued

Box 5.17 *continued*

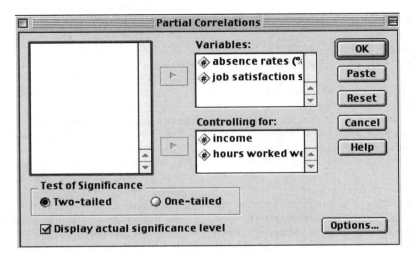

Zero Order Partials

	ABSENT	JOBSAT	INCOME	HOURS
ABSENT	1.0000	−.6704	−.7580	.6646
	(0)	(18)	(18)	(18)
	P= .	P= .001	P= .000	P= .001
JOBSAT	−.6704	1.0000	.6745	−.3782
	(18)	(0)	(18)	(18)
	P= .001	P= .	P= .001	P= .100
INCOME	−.7580	.6745	1.0000	−.3775
	(18)	(18)	(0)	(18)
	P= .000	P= .001	P= .	P= .101
HOURS	.6646	−.3782	−.3775	1.0000
	(18)	(18)	(18)	(0)
	P= .001	P= .100	P= .101	P= .

(Coefficient/(D.F.)/2-tailed Significance)
' . ' is printed if a coefficient cannot be computed

Partial Correlation Coefficients

Controlling for.. INCOME HOURS

	ABSENT	JOBSAT
ABSENT	1.0000	−.2834
	(0)	(16)
	P= .	P= .254
JOBSAT	−.2834	1.0000
	(16)	(0)
	P= .254	P= .

(Coefficient/(D.F.)/2-tailed Significance)
' . ' is printed if a coefficient cannot be computed

We observe from the zero-order correlations that the researcher's suspicions would seem to be confirmed – a strong correlation exists between satisfaction and absence rate. However, once the interfering effects of income and hours worked are removed, the correlation between satisfaction and absence becomes very weak, and indeed, ceases to be significant. Our researcher was wrong.

5.8 Explanation of terms

ANOVA the common expression of the technique of analysis of variance.

BETA a value given in the coefficients table in regression analysis. BETA weights are standard-ised values and are the semi-partial correlation coefficients between the associated predictor and the dependent variable in the equation. When there is only one independent variable, the BETA value is the same as the correlation as it appears in the Model Summary table of the regression output.

between-group variance a measure of the variation among individual scores when subjects are com-pared across two or more groups.

Bonferroni procedure a technique for reducing the possibility of a Type 1 error when multiple com-parisons are made among a number of group means. This is part of the process of identifying exactly where an effect has occurred in an analysis of variance.

chi-square a procedure for comparing the observed frequency of response with expected frequencies in a nominal–nominal study, i.e. when both the independent and dependent variables comprise categories. The difference between what is observed and what is expected is evaluated in terms of the likelihood of obtaining particular discrepancies by chance. This test is used in between-subjects designs.

coefficient of determination a statistic that describes the proportion of variance in one variable that can be predicted from another. Based on the correlation coefficient which is squared to provide this value and shown as r-squared in SPSS output.

correlation A procedure whereby relationships between pairs of interval-scaled variables can be explored. Correlation is expressed by the symbol r, and provides a measure of both the strength and direction of a relationship.

crosstabulation a procedure for tabulating nominally and ordinally scaled variables.

factor The term given to the independent variable in analysis of variance.

homogeneous a description applied to a population in which the members share consistent and similar characteristics.

independent t-test a test that compares the means of two different groups measured on some outcome variable. The magnitude of the observed difference is evaluated in terms of probability. This test is used in between-subjects designs and is also known as: unrelated t-test; unpaired t-test; between-groups t-test; independent samples t-test.

inferential statistics forms of statistical analysis that allow predictions to be made and hypotheses to be accepted or rejected.

interaction effect a term given to a finding in ANOVA in which the effect of one independent variable on an outcome measure is influenced by a second independent variable.

lambda one of a number of PRE measures (propor-tional reduction in error) used as part of the crosstabulation procedure.

level The term given to the categories or conditions that comprise an independent variable in analysis of variance.

Levene's test a test for equality of variance. Used in the independent t-test to determine which of two outputs is appropriate.

main effect the effect on an outcome variable of a series of independent variables, each treated on its own and without the influence of any other.

multiple regression a procedure whereby the pre-cise influence of several interval-scaled variables on some outcome measure can be determined.

newt a tailed amphibian of the salamander family.

one-tailed test an analysis based on a specific or directional prediction of the outcome of a study, e.g. that the mean of one group will be greater than or less than the mean of another. See also 'two-tailed test'.

partial correlation A procedure whereby relation-ships between pairs of interval-scaled variables can be explored, while holding the effects of other variables constant.

paired t-test this test compares the means of two different measures on a single outcome variable taken from a single group, usually on two different occasions. The test is commonly applied to within-subjects designs in which comparisons are made on a before treatment and after treatment basis, or in a no treatment/treatment study, or a treatment 1 treatment 2 study. Related terms include: corre-lated t-test; within-groups t-test; related t-test; repeated measures t-test; dependent samples t-test.

post hoc tests a term applied to tests made after an analysis of variance, the purpose of which is to identify the exact source of a significant effect. See also 'Bonferroni procedure'.

regression a procedure whereby the precise influence of one interval-scaled variable can be determined on another.

standard error standard error of the mean is the standard deviation of a distribution comprising many sample means. Usually calculated from a single sample and used to estimate population parameters.

statistically significant a term applied to an event when its likelihood of occurrence is so rare as to exceed a predetermined probability level, usually taken as the 5% or 0.05 level.

two-tailed test an analysis based on a non-specific, or non-directional prediction of the outcome of a study, e.g. that the mean of one group will be different from the mean of another. See also 'one-tailed test'.

two-way ANOVA analysis of variance in which the effects of more than one nominally-scaled independent variable on an outcome measure are explored.

Type 1 error said to occur when an observation or event is deemed to be statistically significant, when in reality it falls within the bounds of acceptability. An example might be when we accept that an observed difference between the means of two groups is significant, when in fact what we are observing is a naturally occurring, if extremely unusual, event.

Type 2 error said to occur when an observation or event is deemed to be only rare but within the bounds of acceptability, when it is in fact significant. An example might be when we accept that an observed

difference between the means of two groups is a naturally occurring, if unusual, event, when in reality we are observing a significant difference.

within-group variance a measure of the total variation among individual scores within a group or sample.

zero-order correlation a term describing a bivariate correlation in which no other variables have been removed or controlled for.

5.9 Further reading

Diekhoff, G. (1992) *Statistics for the Social and Behavioural Sciences: Univariate, Bivariate, Multivariate*. Dubuque, IA: Wm. C. Brown Publishers.

Dometrius, N.C. (1992) *Social Statistics using SPSS*. London: HarperCollins.

Howell, D. (1987) *Statistical Methods for Psychology*. Boston: Duxbury Press.

Howitt, D. and Cramer, D. (1997) *An Introduction to Statistics for Psychology*. London: Prentice Hall.

Huck, S.W. and Cormier, W.H. (1996) *Reading Statistics and Research*. London: HarperCollins.

Kinnear, P.R. and Gray, C.D (2000) *SPSS for Windows made Simple: Release 10*. Hove: Taylor & Francis.

Qualitative research

Cries for help

- *I want to really understand this group of people, not just hand out a questionnaire.*
- *I'm no good at statistics; perhaps I should do something qualitative.*
- *What do I do with all these interviews?*
- *Can I take these documents at face value?*

Chapter 6 offers an introduction to qualitative research. The aim is to introduce readers who are new to qualitative research to the main approaches and methods, and then to point them in the direction of more detailed texts. We acknowledge from the outset that it is not possible to cover such a broad and diverse topic in a single chapter in more than the most general of terms. In this chapter, therefore, we present brief descriptions of some key approaches, including ethnography, grounded theory, discourse analysis, interpretative phenomenological analysis, hermeneutics, action research and participatory research. We then discuss some of the practicalities of conducting qualitative research, including those associated with using observation, interviews and focus groups. Finally, we consider aspects of analysis and writing up.

6.1   What is qualitative research?

Qualitative research is often introduced in terms of the ways in which it differs from quantitative research: that it does not rely on theory, for example, or that it does not involve statistics. However, to presume a simple dichotomy does neither form of research justice. First of all, there are many different types of qualitative research, encompassing quite distinct approaches, methodologies and philosophies, and it is difficult or impossible to make generalisations. Second, the demarcation lines between qualitative and quantitative methods are not as fixed as they might appear; the extent to which one can say, for example, that a quantitative approach is 'scientific' or 'objective' has been strongly debated (see Potter, 1998). Finally, although again this is open to argument, quantitative and qualitative approaches need not be in direct opposition to one another; they can happily co-exist, or even overlap, within the same study. However, there is a crucial experiential difference between the two forms of research: a qualitative study relies on the skills and abilities of the researcher in a way that is not normally acknowledged or expected in quantitative research. This is made clear in Parker's (1994) definition of qualitative research as

Exploring Chapter 6

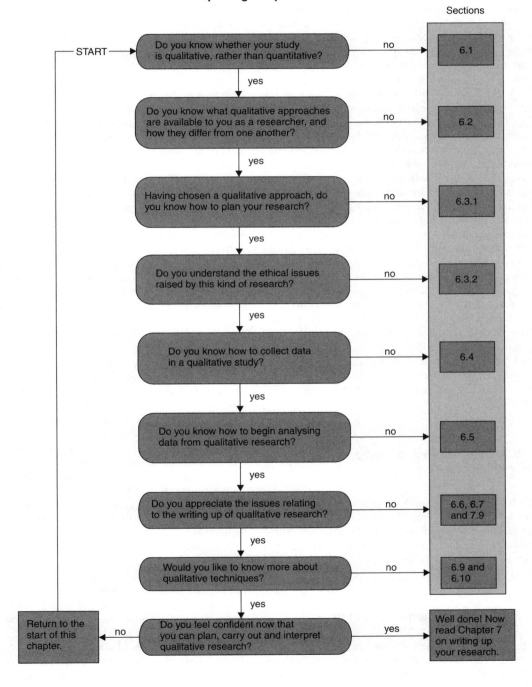

'the interpretative study of a specified issue or problem in which the researcher is central to the sense that is made' (p. 2). Being 'central' in this way is hard work, and it can be very time consuming; qualitative research demands an extra level of involvement on the part of the researcher. Having said this, it can also be both rewarding and exhilarating, particularly if the end result offers even a glimpse of an experience that was not previously well understood.

While there are differences across the social sciences, qualitative research generally involves collecting data in at least one of the following ways: conducting interviews, running discussion or focus groups, informal discussions, observing a situation or individuals, writing field notes, and reading documents. All of these data may be analysed. What you actually do, and which approach you take, depend upon a number of factors, ranging from the philosophical to the severely practical. Whatever approach is taken, qualitative researchers still have to provide a much more thorough rationale for their methodology than those taking a quantitative approach, and this means that they have to understand, and present, something of the underlying philosophy of the approach they have chosen. This may seem unfair, but the knowledge gained by this can be helpful, particularly when analysing and reporting the results. On a practical note, students should know from the outset that social scientists tend to be divided on the subject of qualitative research; it is worth finding out the views (and knowledge) of your supervisor before proceeding too far.

6.2   An overview of some approaches

Each of the approaches described below has a different history or pedigree. In some cases, alternative forms have developed within a single approach. These histories and alternatives are not covered in detail here but we recommend the reader to other more detailed texts in each case.

6.2.1   Ethnographic research

Ethnography is one of the central qualitative approaches, and it employs a variety of techniques. Ethnography is concerned with describing social groups or situations; delineating, for example, behav-

iours and shared beliefs of a particular group of people, and through this gaining an understanding of how and why the participants function and behave as they do within their culture. Typically, the researcher or ethnographer joins a group of people for a period of time to find out as much as possible about the group. The aim is to understand something of participants' lives from the inside (as opposed to observing from afar), to find out what goes on and why, and all with reference to the social context.

An ethnographic approach might be taken to study what happens in particular well-defined environments, such as a classroom, a hospital ward, or a factory; or in a particular group with a common purpose, such as a football team, a town council, or a local action group. The approach is essentially phenomenological in that the aim is to represent the 'world view' of the target group. Typically, theories and hypotheses are generated and explored during the research process and there is an assumption that researchers will put aside their own beliefs and values before exploring those of the target group. In most cases, ethnographic research can only succeed with the full co-operation of the participants; to infiltrate a group or situation and to deceive the participants raises important ethical issues, and we do not recommend such deception to students.

The research starts as soon as the researchers go into the new situation. The methods used to collect data will be varied and suited to the context: the researchers may read any available documentation, observe what appears to be happening, talk to the people involved both formally and informally; later, they may use more structured methods to explore the issues, theories or hypotheses that have arisen. They will gather information about the context, about their target group, and about what happens. The study of 'e-moderating' described in Box 6.1 could be undertaken using an ethnographic approach. What follows is an example of how the researchers might set about their study.

The researchers spend some time before the introduction of the change getting to know the context by sitting in on formal and informal discussions of staff, finding out about the module, talking with the students who will be affected by this change, finding out about their use of and access to computers, and looking at the computing facilities on campus. The researchers take notes during their visits, write up detailed field notes following their visits, reflect on their observations and ask appropriate questions at appropriate times.

Box 6.1   The problem of e-moderating

A university is to introduce tutoring by e-mail (e-moderating) on one of its modules. Seminar groups and tutorials are to be replaced by online group discussions and e-mail communication between students and tutors. This is not a distance learning module. All students are expected to attend lectures in the usual way. The module attracts around 170 students and is run by four tutors. Each student submits two pieces of coursework which count towards the final mark; coursework submission, marking and feedback are all to be conducted using e-mail. While two of the tutors are very enthusiastic about this change, the other two are unsure about the costs and benefits to themselves and to their students. The researchers set out to find out what happens, and why, when the change is introduced.

The first meeting of tutors centres on practical issues: for example, how to keep track of e-mail correspondence and online discussions, how to provide structured comments on coursework electronically, and the location of websites providing useful material for online discussion. However, the researchers notice the various behaviours of the tutors during these meetings: one (Tutor A) is very enthusiastic about the change but he tends to brush aside the concerns of the others; the second (Tutor B) seems comfortable with the change, but she raises most of the practical problems, and she seems prepared (unlike Tutor A) to acknowledge the concerns of the other tutors; and the remaining two tutors are unhappy about the change, but in different ways. Thus Tutor C keeps coming back to one point: that his students will miss out on the social interaction afforded by seminar groups and that they will therefore fail to benefit from this change. Tutor D, on the other hand, seems much more concerned about the amount of work that she will have to do to provide students with individualised feedback. When the researchers follow up these differences, they find that Tutor C seems uncomfortable with computers, and that he makes little use of the one in his office. Tutor D seems to work from home more often than other members of staff, but seems perfectly comfortable with computers. Tutor A uses his desktop computer mainly for administration. Tutor B already uses computers with large groups of students; she seems to be the only one who is aware of the recent problems students have experienced with computer 'crashes' in the open-access laboratories.

While trying to understand the individual reactions of the four tutors, the researchers also become aware that the individuals in this small group are also part of at least two wider communities: their department, and the university. When this line of thought is investigated, the researchers find that Tutor A is firmly embedded in the decision making committees at university level; Tutor B is part of a university group interested in innovative techniques; Tutor C sees himself primarily as a teacher and identifies strongly with students; and Tutor D is relatively isolated in the department, seeing herself mainly as a researcher who has to teach.

The other group involved in this change are the students. Clearly, the researchers cannot interview every one of the potential students. However, they try to talk to as many as they can, both informally in the students' union bar and refectory, and in a more structured way through focus groups. They aim to find people with different outlooks and ideas about the change; they need to gain the confidence of a few key or representative students to find out their feelings and expectations before the module begins, and to track their progress.

The researchers set out to experience the change from the perspectives of students and tutors. For example, they join in the online discussions, and they observe and participate in the electronic collection and evaluation of coursework. Over time, they observe the experiences of the tutors: Tutor A underestimates the amount of work involved and falls behind; Tutors B and D keep on top of the work, but only Tutor B feels comfortable with the experience; and Tutor C is surprisingly successful, taking a student-centred approach to the problems he experiences. Within the student group, some opt out at a very early stage, some struggle on but with increasing feelings of resentment and confusion, and some seem to prefer the new methods. The researchers consider the extent to which the students' experiences can be linked with various factors, including feeling 'comfortable' with computers, the experiences of the tutors, and the available computing facilities.

This example is almost certainly beyond the scope of an undergraduate project, as would be most traditional ethnographic studies. It takes a long time to get inside a group, and to understand the complex social worlds group members inhabit. However, many researchers adopt some of the techniques and ideas from the ethnographic tradition to suit their own purposes. This might also apply to the adoption of the underlying assumptions. For example, it is not always possible to assume that researchers can discard their own ideas and values during research in the way pre-scribed by the pure ethnographic (and phenomeno-logical) tradition: students studying other students, or nurses studying other nurses, do not enter the context as neutral observers. Different points of view are held on this subject, but at least some of those writing in the area suggest that it is perfectly acceptable to adopt some strategies and discard others to develop a methodology that exactly suits a particular research topic (e.g. Tesch, 1990). Useful descriptions of ethnography are provided by Fielding (1993); Hammersley and Atkinson (1995); and Rachel (1996).

6.2.2 Grounded theory

Grounded theory is an approach to research whereby a theory is grounded in actual data rather than imposed *a priori* (i.e. in advance of the data collection). Grounded theory was first described by Glaser and Strauss (1967) and it represented a reaction within soci-ology against the unwarranted or haphazard imposition of existing theories upon situations or contexts. It has its roots in symbolic interactionism, so that the empha-sis within this approach is on the symbolic meanings that people attribute to events, and the ways in which these meanings interact with the social roles that people fill. The relationships among people's percep-tions, the roles or categories with which they associate themselves, and the wider social context, are of central concern within this approach. Data are gathered from similar sources to those used in ethnography. The analysis, however, is typically focused on the search for the kinds of patterns and relationships that can generate theories and hypotheses, with processing continuing until adequate theories emerge to explain the phenom-enon under investigation. As with ethnography, researchers are assumed to come to the study without preconceived ideas.

The grounded theory approach is probably most appropriate in situations that are bounded in some way, and when the central issues are salient or impor-tant to the participants: individuals lacking in involve-ment may generate thoughts and ideas (in the broadest sense) during the research process to appease or please the researchers, who may then find themselves in the position of reproducing, in a painstaking manner, the theories generated by the participants. A grounded the-ory approach could be taken to the study described in Box 6.2 (the use of medication amongst people with asthma), since the issues involved are likely to be per-tinent to the participants.

> **Box 6.2   Why don't asthmatics comply?**
>
> People with asthma do not always comply with the reg-imen of medication and treatment prescribed for them by their doctors. Some people therefore experience more problems with asthma than in theory they need do. Doctors at a local asthma clinic, keen to find out more about non-compliance, have asked patients to complete self-report questionnaires and to keep diaries of medica-tion use. However, the doctors suspect that some of their patients overestimate compliance. The main aim is therefore to find out something about the use of med-ication from the patients' perspectives – to generate theories that might explain the extent of compliance.

Our imaginary researchers start, as they might do in an ethnographic study, by finding out about the medi-cations taken by the patients, by sitting in on formal and informal discussions among doctors and other health care professionals, by sitting in on some con-sultations, and by talking informally to patients who turn up at the clinic. They need to find out exactly what the doctors are asking the patients to do. They find, for example, that some patients are asked to use up to three inhalers daily, with different patterns of use for each (e.g. Inhaler 1 morning and evening, Inhaler 2 three times a day, and Inhaler 3 as required). It becomes clear to the researchers that only some of the inhalers bring immediate relief of symptoms; other inhalers require regular use to bring longer-term bene-fits. Some patients have been instructed to take other medications at fixed times of the day (e.g. 7 am and 6 pm). Most of the patients have been told to use a 'spacer' with their inhalers (a plastic device, around 25 cm in length, which enhances the benefit of inhala-tion). Those with more serious symptoms use a nebu-lizer (a device which pumps the medicine to a mask or mouthpiece using compressed air). All of this background information helps the researchers to understand the everyday experiences of patients.

Following this, the main emphasis is on interview-ing patients. In this particular study, it becomes appar-ent that some participants use inhalers effectively and as recommended in certain situations (for example, when in hospital or during a severe attack) but not in others (when at work, or with the family). Through semi-structured interviews and informal discussions, the researchers develop theories that relate the use of medication to the participants' social roles or social identities: when a participant sees herself primarily as an asthmatic or as a patient, she will follow the 'rules' of that role, one of which is to take the medication as instructed. However, she doesn't follow the regimen when she is at work or when she is socialising (and she certainly doesn't take her 'spacer' out of the house). When she is at home with her family, she is not strict about keeping to the regimen: she doesn't like her children to see her use the inhalers, and would certainly not use a nebulizer in front of her children unless she was very ill. For her, being a mother means being in control and 'keeping going' – to take the medication at home means that she is not adequately fulfilling her role as a mother. The use of medication has different symbolic meanings in these various social contexts. Thus the researchers eventually develop a theory about compliance which is grounded within their own findings. Detailed accounts of grounded theory are given by Charmaz (1995); Pidgeon (1996); Pidgeon and Henwood (1996); and Strauss and Corbin (1994).

6.2.3 Discourse analysis

Broadly speaking, discourse analysis entails a close analysis of a text, transcript or interaction, with the aim of highlighting the social structures and assumptions embodied in the language. The language is taken to be a reflection of a wider social phenomenon. However, it is difficult to find a single definition that does justice to all variations of discourse analysis: 'it is a field in which it is perfectly possible to have two books on discourse analysis with no overlap in content at all' (Potter and Wetherell, 1987, p. 6). This comment reflects the extent of the current debate about the nature and scope of the technique.

Discourse analysis is carried out using either a piece of text or a transcript of spoken words, and it can be combined with other qualitative methods. Within an ethnographic or grounded theory study, for example, documents and speech can be subjected to discourse analysis, and this analysis can aid understanding of the actions of participants within the social context.

A discourse analysis could be applied to the study of non-compliance amongst people with asthma described in Box 6.2. The phenomenon under investigation is in itself allied to a particular form of medical discourse: the word compliance comes from a domain in which one group (doctors) tells another group (patients) what to do. One possible line to follow would be the extent to which the discourse used by people with asthma was medical: for example, inhalers

can be described in 'technical' terms (e.g. salbutamol, fluticasone); by trade names (Ventolin, Flixotide); in the current patient-friendly terms fostered by practice nurses and drug companies (reliever, preventer); or in particular lay terms (blue puffer, orange puffer). Different terms might be used by the same individual at different times; this would tell the researchers something about the ways in which the use of inhalers was understood by the individual in the various social roles he or she filled.

Discourse analysis could also be used in the study outlined in Box 6.1. For example, do the university tutors use language in a way that indicates alliance with management or alliance with the students? Are the different factions amongst the students made apparent in their speech? Do the tutors use different ways of speaking to or about some students than they do to or about others? The answers to these and other questions can then be fed into the research process. It is possible, for example, that tutors whose discourse aligns them with students rather than with management are actually more successful at engaging students in online discussions, even though these tutors were initially less enthusiastic about making the changes.

Historical documents can be subjected to discourse analysis, and this application of the technique highlights many of the issues researchers have to consider. Traditionally, it might be thought that historians search after facts, which means that they must take into account the extent to which the author of the document is a reliable source, and the extent to which the document is authentic. By subjecting a historical document to discourse analysis, the researcher deals with the words on the page. The other questions – who wrote this, when and why? – do not disappear, but they become part of a more complex question: what are we to make of these words? To understand a document from the past, the analyst must learn the rules of the available discourses. This means that historical documents are not read in isolation: the analyst has to learn the conventions, the vocabularies, the forms of the various discourses open to people writing at that time. This can be difficult at first, because of the need to fight the impulse to impose a familiar meaning on a familiar word. However, the same problems can be faced by those trying to analyse a contemporary text, particularly if it is written, or spoken, by someone from a different culture or subculture to their own; the middle-aged, middle-class white analyst may have difficulties comparable to those faced by the historian when trying to analyse the discourse of young, working-class girls from a different ethnic group to his own. For further reading, see Burman and Parker (1993); Edwards and Potter (1992); Munslow (1977); Nikander (1995); Parker (1994); Potter (1998); Potter and Wetherell (1987); and Tosh (2000).

6.2.4   Interpretative phenomenological analysis

Interpretative phenomenological analysis (IPA) has a similar pedigree to that of grounded theory, since it emerged from the traditions of phenomenology and symbolic interactionism. However, it centres on the analysis of speech, language or dialogue, typically obtained through interviews and discussions. The material on which the analysis is based is therefore comparable to, or identical with, that used in discourse analysis. The approaches differ in important ways, however: at the risk of overgeneralisation, discourse analysis remains at the level of language in the broadest sense, while IPA attempts to uncover the cognitions or thought processes that underpin that language. There is therefore an acknowledgement of what the researcher brings to the situation; the researcher interprets the participant's speech and behaviour through his own conceptions and preconceptions.

Returning to the example of the patients with asthma, the IPA researcher might try to say something about the meaning, at the individual level, of medication use; of what it symbolises in different social contexts; and of how medication is understood in terms of the illness, of being asthmatic. The researcher might note the expressions of frustration, resentment and anger when the individual talks about the impact of asthma on her life, noting that she talks of withdrawing from others, while expressing shame and guilt when she talks about failing to take her medication regularly: the researcher interprets the patterns and conjunctions of the expressed emotions, cognitions and beliefs.

It is interesting to conjecture whether or not historical documents may be subjected to IPA. The question in itself is a useful one, because it brings to the fore the bugbear of unwarranted imposition of meaning by the researcher. With a text from another era, the analyst has to familiarise herself with the prevailing assumptions, values and attitudes of that era – but this is often a necessary task for the contemporary analyst too. We do not have a simple answer to our question, but perhaps those setting about the analysis of diaries or letters from the past would find the tenets of IPA

useful. For more on IPA, see Conrad (1987); Smith (1996); Smith, Flowers and Osborn (1997); Smith, Jarman and Osborn (1999).

6.2.5   Hermeneutics

Hermeneutics is concerned with language, or rather the process of using language to make experience understandable or comprehensible. Within this approach, it is assumed that the researcher's own background will have a bearing on the investigation and interpretation. Thus there is an assumption of consciousness, and awareness and knowledge of the phenomenon or situation under investigation, and in this respect hermeneutics differs from phenomenology, in which the researcher is required to lay aside his own values and knowledge.

Within the hermeneutic interview, themes are introduced by the researcher but the participant's views and responses are not constrained in any way by the researcher. Reflexivity is central, in terms of conscious and conscientious reflection on the process and on one's own role within that process. Interpretation depends upon the insight, openness and patience of the researcher: again, the emphasis is very much on the personal qualities of the researcher rather than on any objectivity that they might bring to bear. The assumptions, knowledge and insights of the researcher are made explicit as she continues a circular or spiralling process of analysis and interpretation. Starting with global perceptions, the researcher follows and interprets emerging themes, attempting to capture meaning at different levels. Any of the studies outlined in this chapter could involve hermeneutic interviews and analysis, particularly if the researchers have prior knowledge or experience of the topic under investigation. For further details of hermeneutics, see Kvale (1983), and Leonard (1989).

6.2.6   Action research

Action research involves identifying problems in particular settings, generating hypotheses about the causes and 'cures', acting on these and evaluating the impact. The process can take different forms, depending upon the extent to which the researchers rely on participants to generate the hypotheses and implement the changes. It differs from ethnographic research in that changes are implemented and their effects evaluated during the period of research: note that, in the example described in Box 6.1 (e-moderating), the researchers might have used action research had they been concerned with the success of the new scheme. In many cases, action research will be beyond the scope of the undergraduate project; however, the approach is interesting in its own right and it may be possible to incorporate aspects of action research into a small-scale study.

The extent to which the researcher exerts control over the target group in order to effect change can vary considerably, depending on the extent to which the participants are involved in generating ideas and implementing strategies for change themselves. Many factors will be relevant here, including the extent to which group members are of one mind, the power structure within the group, and the organisational constraints upon it. For example, nurses wishing to make changes to a particular ward may be constrained by a lack of unanimity amongst themselves, by the actions of the charge nurses, by the hospital management, and by the layout of the ward itself.

The whole process of action research is interactive, participative and dynamic. Ideally, it is based upon co-operation and collaboration, between the researcher and the group, and amongst members of the group. Problems can arise if the researcher does not share central values with the participants, if the researcher is perceived to be in some way critical of the group or its members, or if the factions within the group have different agendas. The researcher may therefore have to go to some lengths to demonstrate that he has the interests of the group at heart. Although ideally the role of the researcher would be more observational or collaborative than coercive, sometimes structured assistance in effecting change is called for, particularly if the existing routines are of long standing. Similarly, the researcher may be called upon to provide emotional and practical support for the participants during the process of change. This can be time consuming and draining, but the process can be deeply satisfying if the end result is positive.

Action research could be used to explore the problems faced by ex-residents of a long-stay institution, as described in Box 6.3. Our researchers begin by collecting any available documentation on the closure of the institution. They organise meetings of ex-staff, carers and families to find out more about the problems and the possible remedies. Other points emerge through informal conversations: for example, the researchers uncover resentments, fears and sorrows amongst families regarding what has happened to their relatives and the impact that it has had upon their

> **Box 6.3 The closure of a long-stay institution**
>
> A local long-stay institution has closed and the residents have been relocated in various settings within the community. Some of these people appear to be showing signs of distress or unhappiness. Families and carers have expressed a great deal of concern about this, but their ideas about the causes and remedies appear to vary considerably. The aims of the research are to find out the causes of unhappiness amongst the ex-residents, and to find effective ways to reduce that unhappiness.

own lives. The researchers also interview, converse with and observe the ex-residents in different settings to find out what they think and feel about what has happened to them, and to find out exactly what problems have emerged. The intervention could be planned by any one group of participants, or by the researchers with the co-operation of participants. Changes are evaluated through interviews, meetings, reports, conversations and observations. However, in this kind of study it is always possible that one group benefits from an intervention at the expense of another group: the solution that reassures the families may not have any impact upon the well-being of the ex-residents. There is no simple answer to such a problem, but it helps to clarify the objectives of the study at the outset to all groups of participants. For reviews of action research, see Argyris, Putnam and Smith (1985); Rheinharz (1992); Tappen (1989); Taylor (1994); and Whyte (1984).

6.2.7 Participatory or emancipatory research

With this approach, the participants themselves take a central role; they are involved to a greater or lesser extent in setting the research agenda, designing the study, and collecting the data. The named researcher, therefore, acts more as a facilitator, helping the participants in effect to conduct their own study. The extent to which research is participatory can, of course, vary. For example, university lecturers faced with a change in teaching methods could be consulted about the issues they would like to see addressed in the research, they could conduct observation sessions, and they could act as interviewers. This approach has a number of benefits: participants dictate the agenda, reducing the chance of exploitation, and ensuring that the questions or issues that are most important to them are those that are addressed. It also gives the research the kind of credibility or face validity that is vital to ensure full co-operation and involvement, and the quality of the data may be greatly enhanced as a result. On the other hand, participatory research can be difficult to set up if the research population consists of different factions with different agendas: there may not be a single or central way of viewing the issue or topic. For example, the subjective experiences or views of people who join a support group for asthmatics may be very different from those who passionately avoid such groups. Finally, it may not always be easy to steer participants away from 'unresearchable' topics; the researcher's role here can demand more tact and diplomacy than is usually required. For more information, see Reason and Heron (1995); and Whyte (1991).

6.3 Preparing to conduct a qualitative study

6.3.1 Planning the research

At the outset, the researcher has to consider the time and resources available to collect, analyse and interpret data, and to maintain involvement with participants – important issues to the undergraduate with only a limited time to implement and write up a study. There is, of course, much argument about the extent to which the researcher should go into the field with preconceived ideas or even questions, but the inexperienced qualitative researcher should probably have an idea about the boundaries of her project (Miles and Huberman, 1994): a researcher working on her own to a tight time schedule (such as the date by which the work must be handed in) may only be able to collect data from some of the relevant people on some of the relevant topics.

Having clarified as far as possible the research domain and the likely constraints on the study, the researchers then have to consider the possible approaches: for example, the extent to which they have prior knowledge of a setting, and the implications of that knowledge; or the extent to which they are interested in examining the impact of change; or the extent to which they are interested in the perceptions or understandings of individual participants.

The approach and the focus of the research go hand in hand, although qualitative researchers may find themselves changing or adapting the approach during the course of the research in line with events. Ways of collecting data or information should also be considered ahead of time, although again changes may be made at a later stage. Sometimes the researcher has to exclude methods, and therefore approaches, because of certain constraints: there is no point in attempting a discourse analysis of interactions, for example, if it is not possible to make recordings of the interactions.

Miles and Huberman (1994) suggested a useful series of steps to help plan a study. First, the researcher could try to map out a conceptual framework: drawing boxes or 'bins' that encompass the constructs of interest. The bins in the first instance might be simple and descriptive: the medication used by asthmatics, the benefits they bring, and the side-effects they have. This may be problematic for researchers wishing to limit the imposition of their own preconceptions, but it can help mark the scope of a project. The second step is to formulate some research questions that are consistent with the conceptual framework: for example, what conditions seem to promote the most effective use of medication, and what seem to be the barriers to that use? This may be a rather circular process involving a redrawing of the framework as the questions emerge. The research questions may of necessity be rather vague, but formulating the questions can help the researcher to understand his own preconceptions and biases; these can then be made explicit, a crucial underpinning to much qualitative research. More pragmatically, the process of formulation can highlight problems: some questions may not in fact be 'researchable' and although it is not always possible to spot this at an early stage, the more thought and deliberation that goes into planning the less likely it is that the study will fail.

The third step is that of clarifying the boundaries of the research, perhaps in terms of time, participants, location, or the data: for example, it may be decided to interview consecutive outpatients on a series of days. Finally, the ways in which information might be gathered and recorded should be considered, taking into account all of the previous steps. Again, the plans might be quite vague at first, but will serve to point the researcher in at least one direction before piloting the methods.

Piloting, in whatever form, is important. The researcher needs to know if the proposed methods of collecting data 'work' in terms of achieving the goals. However, piloting may not take place until the research is actually under way. It thus becomes part of the process in a way not usually found within quantitative research. It may not even be described as piloting, but at some stage most researchers have to find out whether or not their chosen methods actually produce data or information that can be used. This applies to the more open-ended or unstructured methods as well as to the more structured. For example, it may be that sitting in on meetings provides the researcher with information about the relationships among the various members of a group but not about the ways in which decisions are implemented. The piloting issues involved in the use of observation and interviews are discussed below; in all forms of piloting, however, it is crucial to keep detailed notes, to record all the factors, both situational and personal, that informed the decisions about methodology. These notes can then be submitted as part of the final write-up of the project.

6.3.2   Ethical issues

As with all forms of research, it is essential that ethical issues are addressed at the planning stage of a qualitative study and that ethical guidelines are adhered to. Generally speaking, potential participants should be provided with information about the study ahead of time, in writing and in person, and they should be asked to read and sign consent forms. Every effort should be made to keep participation anonymous (so that the recording of names and addresses is kept to a minimum) and confidentiality must be maintained at all times.

There is an art to writing information sheets and consent forms, and it is worth getting representatives of the target population to read early versions. These representatives can point out ambiguities, jargon and omissions. Information should be as clear, straightforward and honest as possible, detailing the demands that will be placed on participants (e.g. the topics to be covered in an interview and the time it will take). Sensitivity should be used because not everyone can read and write: in this case, the researcher should explain the study to potential participants in a relatively neutral way, allowing them to ask questions, and indeed to refuse to participate.

People cannot be interviewed without their permission, but they can be coerced into doing so. In a sense, an interview is based on a contract between the researcher and the interviewee, and this should be negotiated explicitly. Even if someone agrees to be interviewed, she should be given the opportunity to terminate the interview at any point. The interviewee should also be told who will have access to the record of the interview and the methods used to ensure anonymity and confidentiality. These issues are important: they are related not just to potential exploitation of interviewees but also to the development of trust, and thus to the quality of the research.

A number of points should be considered before observing participants, or before delving into archive material. These include the extent to which people should be observed without their knowledge, the extent to which stored information should be accessed without consent, confidentiality, and feedback on results to participants. While it may seem relatively harmless to make video recordings of students using computers, it may not seem so to the people involved. Advice should be sought not only from ethical committees but also from representatives of participants. Sometimes researchers wish to observe people's behaviour in settings where knowledge of being observed might change the behaviour. In such cases, the researcher should consider the extent to which this might cause embarrassment or distress to unwitting participants; it is often unnecessary to take video recordings, for example. For further reading, see Cartwright (1993); Kvale (1996); Moustakas (1994); and Rogers (1996).

6.4   Collecting data

6.4.1   Observation

Observation is used in both qualitative and quantitative research in a number of different ways. It can be used to establish what actually happens in various settings, to generate hypotheses and theories, to illuminate findings or examine situations more closely, and to evaluate the impact of interventions. It is in some ways a straightforward and easily understood way of collecting data, but it requires as much preparatory thought as any other method. Decisions must be made before beginning the observations (or during the piloting phase) and in qualitative research at least, the nature and causes of these decisions should be made explicit. The example in Box 6.4 of observing students' use of computers in a laboratory provides a means of illustrating these decisions.

Box 6.4   Observing students using computers

Participants
A laboratory may accommodate 10–20 students. Are particular students to be targeted? If so, why?

Setting
The researchers may focus on the use of a particular computer, or they may observe the actions of target students using any of the available computers. Such decisions will be partly dependent upon the observational method chosen and the resources available to the researchers.

Deciding what to observe
This is a crucial question. What do the researchers mean by 'using the computer'? Is it sufficient or necessary for students to be sitting in front of the computer? Must the computer be switched on and operational? Must the keyboard be used or the mouse moved? If a student observes others using the computer but does not speak or touch the computer, are they 'using' it? These issues must be addressed at an early stage. The target acts must be clearly defined and these definitions must be justified.

Deciding when and how to observe
These are essentially sampling issues. If the researchers are concerned with observing specific behaviours, they can choose time sampling or event sampling. Time sampling involves choosing different periods of time during which to observe, and recording all behaviours or events that occur during that period. This is useful if the researchers are interested in commonly occurring behaviours, or in what happens in a particular situation at different times of day. It would be less useful if the target events or behaviours did not occur frequently. Event sampling, on the other hand, involves recording the relevant details about a target event, although this clearly requires that the researchers know at least roughly when and where this event is likely to take place. The methods chosen to record the observation should obviously be consistent with the aims, but there may be situational and other constraints. Video or audio recording may seem ideal, but may provide an incomplete record of events: for example, people may move about and obscure the behaviours of others, and voices may not be audible. Checklists, notes, stopwatches and event recorders can all be used: none will provide a perfect record of everything that happens.

6.4.2   Conducting observations: practicalities

Consider the ethical issues surrounding your proposed observation. Make contact with the relevant committees and official organisations, and also discuss your plans with representatives of those you wish to observe.

Do a number of 'informal' observations to begin with. Use these to make decisions about whom, where and what you are going to observe. Think about where you should position yourself or where to position equipment. If you are going to use a video recorder, try it out: can you clearly see the behaviours or events that you are interested in? These activities will also make your presence (and that of your equipment) more familiar to the people to be observed.

Prepare detailed descriptions or definitions of the events or behaviours that are to be observed. These may be refined later but it is important to be as clear as possible from the outset.

Conduct a pilot study. Is the equipment reliable? Are you observing what you planned to observe? Can you record all the necessary details in the time allowed? If you are conducting the study alone, you can enlist the help of colleagues to investigate the reliability of your interpretations: if another person interprets the events or behaviours in different ways then your descriptions of behaviour or events should be reconsidered. If you are working with another person, spend time at this stage in establishing agreement and make full records of the decisions made.

Keep records of observations. Make these as detailed as possible, including details of times, the situation and context, the potential range of participants, and anything else that was going on at the time of the observation. Also keep records of your own reflections about what happened. For example, the behaviour of students in a laboratory might be affected by a party held at the students' union the night before. If you think that something was influencing the situation under observation, talk to the people concerned: there may be an explanation.

Start your analysis or interpretation of observations as soon as possible. You may become aware of flaws in your approach that could be remedied before it is too late.

6.4.3   Interviewing

The term 'interview' is used here to describe anything from informal chats with someone to highly structured question and answer sessions. In qualitative research, interviews are generally semi-structured at most, meaning that the interviewer has a set of questions or topics but goes into the interview prepared to deviate, to a greater or lesser extent, from that set.

Depending upon the nature of the study, the researchers may have to choose their potential interviewees from a larger population. This involves the identification of key people, or representatives of different groups or factions. Since perceptions are likely to vary, it is useful to interview a number of people rather than relying on just one person, even when looking for information rather than individual experiences. Most interviews, however, are not conducted purely to gain information but to discover something about the individual's perceptions of, and feelings about, an event or situation. Again, a number of decisions must be made before the interviews are conducted.

The interview is a social event, an interaction between two or more people. As such, it can vary in terms of intimacy and power between the participants. Emphasis is increasingly placed on the responsibilities of the researcher to the interviewee, and many of these are associated with the distribution of power between the two. In parallel with this is an emphasis on equality within the interview in terms of intimacy, such that the interviewee has the right to ask the researcher questions. Typically, the interviewee will look to the researcher for some guidance on this, at

---

Box 6.5   Interviewing people with asthma

Participants
Are you going to interview a representative sample from the people who have attended the asthma clinic (taken from medical records)? Those who attend the clinic on a specific day? Those who respond to a notice posted in the asthma clinic? The decision will depend upon the resources and time available to interview and the extent to which access to medical records is permitted or thought appropriate. Researchers should decide on the extent to which they wish their sample to be representative, and on the appropriate criteria to use to select their sample.

Purpose of the interview
What questions are to be asked and what topics or themes are to be explored? What is the format or structure of the interview? Interviews can be highly structured, using set questions to be phrased in exact terms and in an exact order; semi-structured, where the researchers have some set questions or topics and an idea about the order in which they could be covered, but are prepared to deviate from the order according to the flow of the interview; or loosely structured, where the researcher introduces a topic in general terms and then follows the lead of the interviewee. The format or structure of the interview should reflect the general aims and ethos of the research, but decisions should be made and justified before beginning the interviews.

A semi-structured format would probably be the most suitable approach to take with the asthma study. The researchers want to find out about the person's use of medication and his or her feelings about this; the researchers also want to understand more fully what it means to that individual to have asthma: some of the interviewees may need prompting to discuss these topics. The researchers could therefore delineate a list of open-ended questions, starting out with the more factual questions about the person's experience of asthma and moving on to the more delicate issue of 'non-compliance' after some trust or rapport has been established. However, people's feelings about asthma could emerge at any point during the interview: the researchers have to decide whether or not to follow up on such disclosures as they are made, abandoning the structure in favour of the disclosures.

Clearly, piloting and careful preparation are vital to interviewing. This helps establish the most appropriate ordering of questions or topics, the ways in which questions should be phrased, and whether or not the interview actually elicits the information required.

Setting
It is usually best to start out with the intention of interviewing people in private, although this can be difficult if interviews are conducted in people's homes. These decisions should be discussed with the interviewees beforehand: they may prefer to be interviewed at home or they may wish a more neutral setting, depending upon the topics to be covered. It is important therefore to tell the interviewee ahead of time about the content and purpose of the interview, and the length of time it is likely to last.

Recording the interview
As with observation, there is no one perfect method. Audio and video recorders can be used, although most researchers would use audio recording rather than video recording. Either method has to be negotiated with the interviewee, and their wishes adhered to. Alternatively, the interviewee's responses can be recorded on paper during the interview. While this is less intrusive on the one hand, it can interfere with the process of the interview, since the researcher has to interrupt eye contact occasionally. It also limits the analysis to one that is essentially thematic.

least initially, and will expect them to begin the interview. The researcher can do much to establish the tone of the interview in the first few minutes, in terms of seating, posture, appearance and language. While informality and equality might seem ideal (and may indeed be so for many people) some interviewees may be more comfortable with a more formal approach, and their wishes should be respected.

The researchers should discuss or consider beforehand the issue of disclosing personal information within the interviewing setting. Self-disclosure can help establish a comfortable and open relationship between researcher and interviewee and it can facilitate certain topics: for example, if the interviewee with asthma learns that the researcher also has asthma the interview may open up considerably. However, personal information can also be intrusive and off-putting to the interviewee. A researcher who expresses their own point of view or their own experiences at every turn can inhibit the flow of the interview, particularly if the researcher and interviewee do not share common values or experiences. Some interviewees will not want to know anything about the person who is interviewing them. Although decisions such as these often cannot be made in advance, the issues should be considered before interviewing commences.

6.4.4 Conducting interviews: practicalities

Decide on your potential interviewees. Consider how many interviews you would like to do and how many you are actually able to do. Decide on the criteria to be used in selecting your interviewees. Consider the ways in which you can gain access to the names of potential interviewees, and negotiate these as soon as possible: ethics committees and decision making boards can take a while to grant permission.

Draw up information sheets and consent forms. Indicate the nature and purpose of the research, and the broad aims of the interview. Give a contact name, address and telephone number. Indicate the process of recruitment. If information sheets and consent forms are to be mailed to potential interviewees, enclose a stamped addressed envelope.

Consider the ethics of your study, and the steps you should take to ensure that you do not cause unnecessary upset or distress to your interviewees. Consider confidentiality and anonymity: for example, you should ensure that tapes or transcripts are identified by number only, that they are stored in a safe place with a lock,

and that the documentation linking name to subject number is stored elsewhere (also in a locked place). Consult representatives of your target group as well as any relevant ethics committees.

Make sure that you have done your preparatory work. Draw up a provisional interview schedule with any topics or questions you wish to explore. Pilot this and continue to adapt or change your interview schedule until it easily elicits the information you are looking for. Make sure that at least some of your pilot interviews are with people representative of your target group. Use these pilot interviews to establish a style of interviewing that suits the purpose of your research, and with which you and your interviewees are comfortable. By interviewing people in similar situations to those you are interested in, you will discover problems and difficulties with the way in which you have structured your questions, and you should be able to establish a convenient way of recording people's responses. You will also gain a sense of the time required of the interviewee: this is important when fixing up a time for the interview. Consider the issues associated with power and intimacy within an interview. Try out your audio or video recorder if you intend to use one, and make sure that it works. Record all the decisions you make during this phase of your research and provide justification for the decisions.

Plan a timetable for interviewing and begin to contact your potential interviewees. At this stage you can tell them how long the interview is likely to last and can negotiate a place in which to interview them. If you are interviewing in a particular setting, you could try to find a private room in which to interview people. However, you should respect the wishes of the interviewee: they may prefer to be interviewed at home.

An interview is a social interaction. Do what you can to make a person comfortable. Explain the research again and ensure that the interviewee knows that the interview can be stopped at any time. Negotiate the use of a tape-recorder and respect the interviewee's wishes. If the interviewee initially agrees to the use of a tape-recorder but then seems uncomfortable with that decision, offer to switch it off. If the interview becomes difficult, or if the interviewee becomes upset, switch off the tape-recorder and take some 'time out'. You may both decide to terminate the interview at this stage. Take time at the end of the interview to address any issues that have arisen and to allow the interviewee to ask questions of you.

When you are doing your interviews, keep records of where and when the interview was conducted and how long it took. As soon as possible after the interview, check that your tapes are audible or that your notes are legible, and write out full notes, including your own thoughts and reflections about the interview. If your recording equipment failed in some way, you may still be able to salvage something from the interview if you do this quickly enough.

6.4.5 Focus groups

Focus group methodology emerged from studies of the effects of mass communications or mass media, using 'focused interviews' (Merton and Kendall, 1946). Focus groups represent another way to collect data: a group of people are brought together to discuss a specific topic, under the direction or guidance of a moderator, and the resulting conversation is recorded and/or observed. The decisions to be made about focus groups, and the practicalities, are similar to those surrounding the use of interviews, but there are some additional issues to be taken into account.

Focus groups can be useful at various stages of a project: they can provide the researcher with background knowledge of an area, they can help generate interview topics or questionnaire items, and they can help the researcher judge the adequacy of an analysis or interpretation of a situation. However, the focus group is not an easy way to interview a group of people at once. There is a vast amount of evidence from the field of social psychology to show that people are changed in the company of others: what people say and do, and even perhaps what they think, will be affected by the presence of other people. Sometimes this social influence will work in favour of the researcher, such that other people may spark off a line of thought or an interaction that yields more than would emerge from an individual interview. However, it may also hinder the research process. It takes experience to be able to tell the difference.

The quality of the data gathered from a focus group will depend on the make-up of the group and the skills of the moderator. Obviously, the members of the group should have an interest in, or experience of, the topic under discussion: if you want to know about the problems faced by asthmatics when using inhalers outside of the home, ask asthmatics who have faced these problems, not those who are housebound. But a good group will not compensate for a poor moderator. Even when all group members are willing to talk, a good moderator is required, if only to ensure that

people speak in turn (and can therefore be heard or recorded). The most important point to remember is that the focus group is not an easy option. Having said this, we can recommend a number of useful and practical guides: Greenbaum (1998); Morgan (1988); and Morgan and Krueger (1998).

6.5 Dealing with qualitative data

The analysis of qualitative data is an ongoing process that is best begun early, as soon as the data collection begins in fact. Writing up should also be started early on: analysis and writing up are closely intertwined in qualitative studies. Typically the process of analysis is very arduous and the researcher often goes through a phase of feeling disheartened in one way or another. Although this might not seem like a particularly helpful comment, it is worth knowing that it is a common experience and that it does not signify failure. Perseverance usually pays off.

6.5.1 Field notes

Field notes are the notes made (or scribbled) during and immediately after visits to the location and they cover events, information and the thoughts and reflections of the researcher. The best way to approach the analysis of field notes is to write them up in some structured way; the most useful structures will depend on the focus and orientation of the research (see Miles and Huberman, 1994). One way to go about this would be to start with a description of the contact with participants on that day, giving details of the people involved and the events or situations that were witnessed. Following this, details would be given of the main themes or issues that emerged. The researchers would then indicate their own part in the activities, their reflections, and any other potentially relevant observations. If the researcher has conducted a recorded interview, the field notes should include reflections on the process which could be added to the interview transcript when it becomes available. These remarks might cover the researcher's perceptions of the relationship formed with the interviewee, thoughts on what was said and how it was said, thoughts on the quality of the interview, and reactions and 'mental notes'. When remarks are added to the transcript, they can be made available to others for scrutiny.

6.5.2   Observational data

Observational data can be analysed in different ways. If the observations include discrete behaviours or events, then it might be possible to create categories. For example, if the observation was focused on interactions between people, then it would be possible to discriminate between different forms of interaction. It would then be possible to examine the frequencies of these different forms of interaction, as well as considering the situations in which these occurred, and the outcomes and implications for those concerned. Categorisation is generally a process during which the researcher has to consider the extent to which new events or behaviours can be slotted into existing categories or whether it is necessary to create a new category. Categories should be meaningful in terms of the aims of the research: it becomes difficult to deal with a large number of categories, but collapsing events into a small number of categories can mean that important or relevant variation is missed. A large 'miscellaneous' category usually means that the category system is flawed in some way. It is important to keep clear and detailed records of the process of categorising: the criteria used to select categories, and to assign an event to one category rather than another, should be made explicit in the final report.

Categorisation is the point at which the overlap between a quantitative and a qualitative approach can become apparent: frequencies can be reported, numbers can be applied. Many researchers prefer not to submit their observations to strict categorisation. This can be because they are interested in a sequence of behaviours or events that unfolds during the observation. However, others may resist attempts to apply an implicit interpretation of events, preferring an explicit interpretation during which they and others have access to the process. The categorisation of people and social situations is essentially a flawed and subjective process: for example, mistakes can be made when categorising people according to social class or ethnic origin, and it is better to describe people rather than to ascribe labels that may not be accurate.

6.5.3   Interview data

Burman (1994) pointed out that researchers dealing with interviews have to decide on the precise source of their 'raw data': is the analysis to be conducted on the transcript (such that the transcript becomes the source) or on the interview, including the social context in which the interview was conducted? This is not always an easy distinction (or decision) to make but it may be helpful to consider the extent to which the major focus is on the language used by the interviewee or on the interaction between interviewee and interviewer. Important decisions have to be made, therefore, about the way in which interviews are transcribed, including the extent to which pauses and other speech acts are represented. Various ways of systematising transcripts have been developed (e.g. Jefferson, 1985) which take account of pauses, inflections, intonations and stresses. A full transcription will be a necessary condition for certain forms of analysis, and it makes other forms of analysis much easier to undertake. It is, however, time consuming – Potter (1998) estimates that it could take around 20 hours to transcribe one hour of tape. Sometimes the necessary information can be extracted by listening to audio-tapes, but this leaves the analyst in a rather vulnerable position, since the basis of the analysis is not available to others.

Analysis is likely to involve a search for consistencies on the one hand and variations on the other. The level at which these qualities are sought will vary and it is common for the researcher to consider different levels within the same analysis. Thus the analysis might focus on the use of particular words or phrases, or a response to a particular question, or a narrative on a particular issue. In addition, the researcher might be looking for both individual and group consistencies and variations, moving between the different levels in an effort to find meaning.

One way to begin the process is to focus on a particular question: how do people with asthma feel about their condition, for example, or how do ex-residents feel about their experiences of leaving a long-stay institution? What kinds of expressions were used during the interviews? Are there ways to link these expressions together, or to distinguish one form of expression from another? Some researchers find that metaphors help them at this stage, although there is a danger that the metaphors will gain an unwarranted 'reality'. With the asthma study, metaphors capturing isolation, loneliness and fear might be appropriate, or those describing different ways of understanding health. However, the researcher has to be vigilant in noting aspects of the interviews that are inconsistent with the metaphors.

As mentioned above, the units of analysis can vary. Some researchers prefer to take several copies of transcripts and then to impose order in different ways – using, for example, different highlighters, or cutting up the transcripts and sorting them into different piles. Computer software (e.g. NUDIST or HyperQual) is available to help with this process: different units of text can be tagged and ascribed to any number of different files representing themes or categories. While this may be a more tidy way of doing things and can certainly help with the management of the analytical process, the software does not ascribe any meaning to the categories and it can take the new researcher some time to become familiar with the software. Often, at undergraduate level, that time would have been better spent on the analysis itself. See Miles and Huberman (1994) for a discussion on the ways in which computer software can be used effectively to manage and analyse qualitative data.

6.6   Points to consider when writing up

There is no one 'correct' way of writing up a qualitative study and many different formats can be used to impart the relevant details to the reader. It may make more sense to discuss the findings as they emerge, rather than have a separate discussion section, so that the reader can follow the process of interpretation more closely. Some researchers write up their work almost as a narrative, telling the story of the study from its inception, including details of key decisions in chronological order. Whatever the format, it is important to describe key decisions relating to methodology in detail. This includes decisions about the research agenda, the framing of the research questions, and methods of analysis and interpretation. Given the central role of the researcher in a qualitative study, the researcher's thoughts, feelings, reflections and reactions are relevant. All of these details will help the reader to understand and evaluate the study.

As with any study, the final report should be adequately referenced and should take the work of other authors in the field into account. However, because each qualitative study is unique in some way, extra care should be taken to justify the approach taken. In addition, the role of the researcher should be clearly described so that the reader is made aware of the extent to which the researcher, for example, imposed the agenda or interfered with existing routines. The

procedure used to analyse the data should be carefully explained. In the same vein, sufficient original data should be provided to enable the reader to evaluate the interpretation. Further guidance is provided in Chapter 7.

6.7   Other issues relating to the quality of the research

There is much debate around the question of judging the quality of qualitative work. Some authors have argued that the criteria used to judge quantitative research are not always appropriate here (e.g. Tindall, 1994). This does not mean, however, that the quality of the work is unimportant. In fact, many qualitative researchers are committed to improving and maintaining quality, not only for their own peace of mind, but also because of the responsibility they feel towards their participants. For a recent debate on this topic within psychology (although it would also apply to the other social sciences), see Elliott, Fischer and Rennie (1999); and Reicher (2000).

Since qualitative research typically centres on a particular context, event or situation, and since each researcher brings to the study her own orientations, qualities and skills, there are no grounds for expecting consistencies across studies. However, there are grounds for expecting the researcher to provide sufficient information about the process to permit others to assess the extent to which the interpretation might be idiosyncratic. One of the problems faced by qualitative researchers is that they are subject to the same biases as everyone else. For example, a particularly vivid event or description tends to be remembered and recalled more easily than the more mundane (the availability heuristic; see Tversky and Kahneman, 1973). This is a problem when the vivid description is not particularly representative of the remainder. Researchers should take the time to pull back and consider the extent to which they are reporting the whole picture and not just the aspect to which they are attracted. Miles and Huberman (1994) stressed the importance of considering outliers, or cases that appear to disconfirm interpretations; they should be discussed rather than ignored. Similarly, alternative explanations and interpretations should be fully explored in the report.

Triangulation is the term usually used to describe the ways in which the reliability of a study can be assessed. The term describes the way in which a second point of view on a phenomenon creates a tri-angle. Triangulation can be used in different ways: to assess the extent to which different participants or sources provide the same information; the extent to which different researchers perceive the phenom-enon in the same ways; the extent to which different methods, such as observations and interviews, pro-vide consistent information; and the extent to which different theories or explanations provide adequate accounts of the same data. Useful accounts of the ways in which triangulation can be used are pro-vided by Miles and Huberman (1994) and Tindall (1994).

Validity is an important component of qualitative research to the extent that the researchers should be aiming to provide an adequate account of the phe-nomena under investigation. At the very least, they owe this to their participants. In fact, it is often good practice to show the participants the findings before finalising the report; if they disagree with the inter-pretation then this should be taken fully into account. The field notes and observations made by the researchers during the process of research are vital to assessing the validity or 'trustworthiness' of a report. Readers should have access not only to the ways in which all important decisions were made but also to the reflections of the researchers on their role in the study. Such detail is not generally included in reports of quantitative studies, but with qualitative work it is important to provide clear indications of the ways in which the work might have been weakened (or strengthened) by the researchers' involvement. It is also important to indicate honestly the limitations of the work.

6.8   Review

This chapter has briefly described some of the main approaches to qualitative research, ways of col-lecting data, and the points that should be taken into account before commencing such a study. We acknowledge that those of you who wish to con-duct qualitative research will have to go elsewhere for the fine detail, but we hope that we have given you a starting point, and we recommend that you fol-low up at least some of the references we have pro-vided. We hope that we have not deterred anyone from trying out these methods: qualitative research is time consuming, but it can be very involving and deeply satisfying.

6.9   References

Argyris, C., Putnam, R. and Smith, M.C. (1985) *Action Science: Concepts, Methods and Skills for Research and Intervention*. San Francisco, CA: Jossey-Bass.

Burman, E. (1994) Interviewing. In P. Banister, E. Burman, I. Parker, M. Taylor and C. Tindall (eds), *Qualitative Methods in Psychology: A Research Guide*. Buckingham: Open University Press.

Burman, E. and Parker, I. (eds) (1993) *Discourse Analytic Research: Repertoires and Readings of Texts in Action*. London: Routledge.

Cartwright, A. (1993) *Health Surveys in Practice and in Potential: A Critical Review of their Scope and their Methods*. London: King Edward's Hospital Fund for London.

Charmaz, K. (1995) Grounded theory. In J. A. Smith, R. Harré and L. Van Langenhove (eds), *Rethinking Methods in Psychology*. Thousand Oaks, CA and London: Sage.

Conrad, P. (1987) The experience of illness: recent and new directions. *Research in the Sociology of Health Care*, **6**: 1–31.

Edwards, D. and Potter, J. (1992) *Discursive Psychology*. Thousand Oaks, CA and London: Sage.

Elliott, R., Fischer, C.T. and Rennie, D.L. (1999) Evolving guidelines for publication of qualitative research studies in psychology and related fields. *British Journal of Clinical Psychology*, **38**: 215–229.

Fielding, N. (1993) Ethnography. In N. Gilbert (ed.), *Researching Social Life*. London and Thousand Oaks, CA: Sage.

Glaser, B.G. and Strauss, A.L. (1967) *The Discovery of Grounded Theory*. Chicago: Aldine.

Greenbaum, T.L. (1998) *The Handbook for Focus Group Research*, 2nd edition. Thousand Oaks, CA: Sage.

Hammersley, M. and Atkinson, P. (1995) *Ethnography: Principles in Practice*, 2nd edition. London: Routledge.

Jefferson, G. (1985) An exercise in the transcription and analysis of laughter. In T.A. van Dijk (ed.), *Handbook of Discourse Analysis, Vol. 3*. London: Academic Press.

Kvale, S. (1983) The qualitative research interview: a phenomenological and hermeneutical mode of understanding. *Journal of Phenomenological Psychology*, **14**: 171–196.

Kvale, S. (1996) *Interviews: An Introduction to Qualitative Research Interviewing*. London: Sage.

Leonard, V. (1989) A Heideggerian phenomenological perspective on the concept of the person. *Advances in Nursing Science*, **11**: 40–55.

Merton, R.K. and Kendall, P.L. (1946) The focused interview. *American Journal of Sociology*, **51**: 541–557.

Miles, M.B. and Huberman, A.M. (1994) *Qualitative Data Analysis*, 2nd edition. Thousand Oaks, CA and London: Sage.

Morgan, D.L. (1988) *Focus Groups as Qualitative Research*, Qualitative Research Methods Series 16. Newbury Park, CA and London: Sage.

Morgan, D.L. and Krueger, R.A. (1998) *The Focus Group Kit, Volumes 1–6*. Thousand Oaks, CA and London: Sage.

Moustakas, C. (1994) *Phenomenological Research Methods*. Thousand Oaks, CA: Sage.

Munslow, A. (1977) *Deconstructing History*. London: Routledge.

Nikander, P. (1995) The turn to the text: the critical potential of discursive social psychology. *Nordiske Udkast*, **2**: 3–15.

Parker, I. (1994) Qualitative research. In P. Banister, E. Burman, I. Parker, M. Taylor and C. Tindall (eds), *Qualitative Methods in Psychology: A Research Guide*. Buckingham: Open University Press.

Pidgeon, N. (1996) Grounded theory: theoretical background. In J.T.E. Richardson (ed.), *Handbook of Qualitative Research Methods for Psychology and the Social Sciences*. Leicester: British Psychological Society.

Pidgeon, N. and Henwood, K. (1996) Grounded theory: practical implementation. In J.T.E. Richardson (ed.), *Handbook of Qualitative Research Methods for Psychology and the Social Sciences*. Leicester: British Psychological Society.

Potter, J. (1998) Qualitative and discourse analysis. In N.R. Schooler (ed.), *Comprehensive Clinical Psychology, Vol. 3: Research and Methods*. Oxford: American Book Company.

Potter, J. and Wetherell, M. (1987) *Discourse and Social Psychology: Beyond Attitudes and Behaviour*. London: Sage.

Rachel, J. (1996) Ethnography: practical implementation. In J.T.E. Richardson (ed.), *Handbook of Qualitative Research Methods for Psychology and the Social Sciences*. Leicester: British Psychological Society.

Reason, P. and Heron, J. (1995) Co-operative inquiry. In J.A. Smith, R. Harré and L. Van Langenhove (eds), *Rethinking Methods in Psychology*. Thousand Oaks, CA and London: Sage.

Reicher, S. (2000) Against methodolatry: some comments on Elliott, Fischer and Rennie. *British Journal of Clinical Psychology*, **39**: 1–6.

Rheinharz, S. (1992) Phenomenology as a dynamic process. *Phenomenology and Pedagogy*, **1**: 77–79.

Rogers, J. (1996) Ethical issues in survey research. In L. DeRaeve (ed.), *Nursing Research: An Ethical and Legal Appraisal*. London: Bailliere Tindall.

Smith, J.A. (1996) Beyond the divide between cognition and discourse: using interpretative phenomenological analysis in health psychology. *Psychology and Health*, **11**: 261–271.

Smith, J.A., Flowers, P. and Osborn, M. (1997) Interpretative phenomenological analysis and the psychology of health and illness. In L. Yardley (ed.), *Material Discourses of Health and Illness*. London: Routledge.

Smith, J.A., Jarman, M. and Osborn, M. (1999) Doing interpretative phenomenological analysis. In M. Murray and K. Chamberlain (eds), *Qualitative Health Psychology: Theories and Methods*. London: Sage.

Strauss, A.L. and Corbin, J. (1994) Grounded theory methodology: an overview. In N.K. Denzin and Y.S. Lincoln (eds), *Handbook of Qualitative Research*. Thousand Oaks, CA and London: Sage.

Tappen, R. (1989) *Nursing Leadership and Management: Concepts and Practice*. Philadelphia, PA: F. A. Davis.

Taylor, M. (1994) Action research. In P. Banister, E. Burman, I. Parker, M. Taylor and C. Tindall (eds), *Qualitative Methods in Psychology: A Research Guide*. Buckingham: Open University Press.

Tesch, R. (1990) *Qualitative Research: Analysis, Types and Software Tools*. New York: Falmer Press.

Tindall, C. (1994) Issues of evaluation. In P. Banister, E. Burman, I. Parker, M. Taylor and C. Tindall (eds), *Qualitative Methods in Psychology: A Research Guide*. Buckingham: Open University Press.

Tosh, J. (2000) *The Pursuit of History*, 3rd edition. Harlow: Longman/Pearson Education.

Tversky, A. and Kahneman, D. (1973) Availability: a heuristic for judging frequency and probability. *Cognitive Psychology*, **5**: 207–232.

Whyte, W.F. (1984) *Learning from the Field*. London: Sage.

Whyte, W.F. (1991) *Participatory Action Research*. London: Sage.

6.10   Further reading

Atkinson, P. (1990) *The Ethnographic Imagination*. London: Routledge.

Banister, P., Burman, E., Parker, I., Taylor, M. and Tindall, C. (eds) (1994) *Qualitative Methods in Psychology: A Research Guide*. Buckingham: Open University Press.

Bryman, A. (1988) *Quantity and Quality in Social Research*. London: Unwin Hyman.

Bulmer, M. (ed.) (1982) *Social Research Ethics*. London: Macmillan.

Dex, S. (ed.) (1991) *Life and Work History Analysis*. London: Routledge.

Hammersley, M. (ed.) (1993) *Social Research: Philosophy, Politics and Practice*. London: Sage.

Henwood, K. and Pidgeon, N. (1992) Qualitative research and psychological theorizing. *British Journal of Psychology*, **83**: 97–111.

LeCompte, M.D. and Goetz, J.P. (1982) Ethnographic data collection in evaluation research. *Educational Evaluation and Policy Analysis*, **4**: 387–400.

Richardson, J.T.E. (ed.) (1996) *Handbook of Qualitative Research Methods for Psychology and the Social Sciences*. Leicester: British Psychological Society.

Shaughnessy, J.J. and Zechmeister, E.B. (1994) *Research Methods in Psychology*, 3rd edition. New York: McGraw-Hill.

Silverman, D. (1993) *Interpreting Qualitative Data: Methods for Analysing Talk, Text and Interaction*. London: Sage.

CHAPTER 7

Writing up your research

Cries for help

- *What's an abstract?*
- *How does a design differ from a methodology?*
- *What do I do with all this raw data?*
- *Which is the independent variable again?*
- *What do I do with all these words?*
- *Was this a qualitative study or a quantitative study?*

This chapter considers, in the first instance, all the important elements that comprise a proper report and offers guidance on clear and concise methods for writing up the various activities involved in any piece of research, be it quantitative or qualitative. Points covered include what should go into a report, why it should be there and where it should go. Issues of style are discussed and various ways of reporting results are considered, along with the perennial problem of referencing. For students of the social sciences everywhere, the procedures outlined here represent the final stage in a lengthy process of research. Moreover, because what is being presented is of a much more practical nature than the material covered in previous chapters, a great deal of what follows is of the *what to do/what not to do* variety. It is hoped

that the inclusion of a number of checklists will be of particular use to everyone about to write up their research.

Undoubtedly the emphasis, at least in the early part of this chapter, is on writing up quantitative research, when the aim has been to test hypotheses or support theories. However, since this book has attempted to offer a rounded introduction to social research we have endeavoured to balance what is essentially a positivistic tradition in the field with more qualitative philosophies. Indeed, the preceding chapter (Chapter 6) focused exclusively on qualitative research and it will be worth reviewing this when considering your write-up. Moreover, since many of our readers will in fact have carried out some form of qualitative study (the research may have been exploratory and descriptive in nature, rather than experimental and predictive; there may have been a small number of cases to work with; the area might have been completely novel with no tradition of previous work; or the supervisor might simply have had a preference for this approach), they will find the rigorous structure of a typical scientific report too restrictive for their type of data. There is a need therefore for guidance in writing up qualitative research, and in the latter sections of this chapter we attempt to offer what help we can.

Exploring Chapter 7

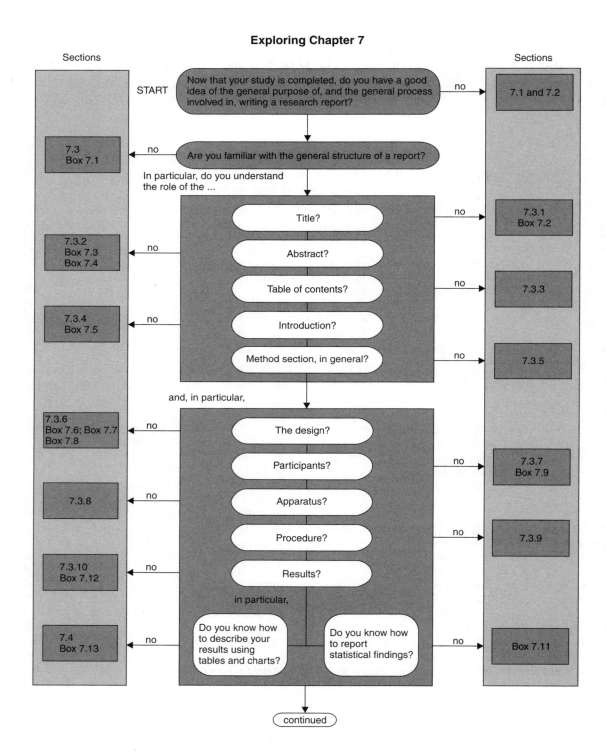

Exploring Chapter 7 *continued*

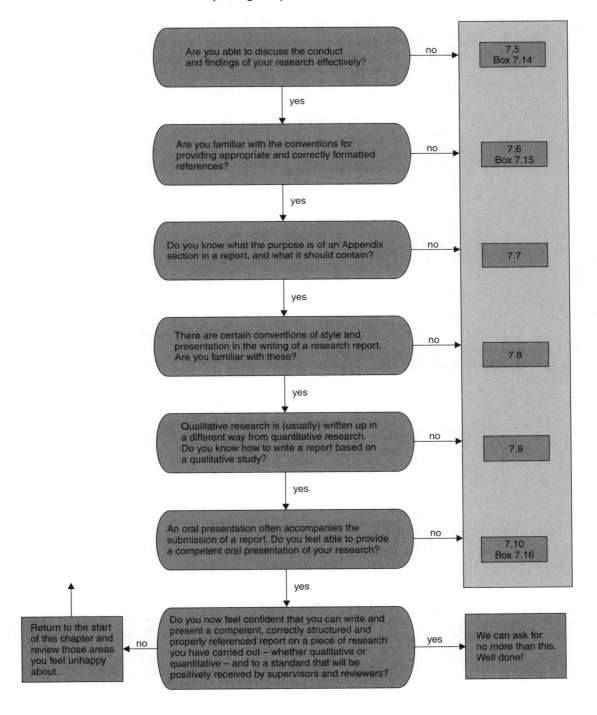

Are you able to discuss the conduct and findings of your research effectively? → no → 7.5 Box 7.14

yes ↓

Are you familiar with the conventions for providing appropriate and correctly formatted references? → no → 7.6 Box 7.15

yes ↓

Do you know what the purpose is of an Appendix section in a report, and what it should contain? → no → 7.7

yes ↓

There are certain conventions of style and presentation in the writing of a research report. Are you familiar with these? → no → 7.8

yes ↓

Qualitative research is (usually) written up in a different way from quantitative research. Do you know how to write a report based on a qualitative study? → no → 7.9

yes ↓

An oral presentation often accompanies the submission of a report. Do you feel able to provide a competent oral presentation of your research? → no → 7.10 Box 7.16

yes ↓

Do you now feel confident that you can write and present a competent, correctly structured and properly referenced report on a piece of research you have carried out – whether qualitative or quantitative – and to a standard that will be positively received by supervisors and reviewers? → yes → We can ask for no more than this. Well done!

no → Return to the start of this chapter and review those areas you feel unhappy about.

A flowchart to direct your reading through this chapter is given here although, as with all previous chapters of this book, if the entire process of writing up a report is new to you, you might wish to start at the beginning and take each section in order.

7.1 The purpose of a report

You have now completed a state of the art, cutting edge, incisive and comprehensive study (or at least, this is your belief). However, other people can only know of the brilliance of this research by being told about it in some way, usually through a written report, which will offer details on what you've done, why it was done and what the outcomes were. For an undergraduate, a large proportion of marks is likely to be assigned to the final report, and success will depend almost entirely on the quality of the writing and presentation. It is therefore important to consider the way in which this work will be presented from the earliest stages through to the concluding comments. This is true whether the research was quantitative or qualitative and what follows will in large part be applicable to both approaches.

7.2 Writing guidelines

Ideally, a study should be written up as it progresses (it really is easier this way, rather than trying to remember what you did after the fact, which is the usual way for the majority of students). Mapping out the main points of the literature review as you do it will often serve as a guide in the formulation of hypotheses and will clarify design and methodological issues – points made right at the beginning of this book in Chapter 1 (see especially Section 1.5). Writing up the methodology section while it is still fresh in your mind will save you hours of work at a later stage, as will keeping a strict record of your references from the beginning (this goes for a bibliography as well, though note that a bibliography is quite different from a reference section; see Section 7.6). The point here is that if you are going to (or might) cite material in the body of your report, this must be properly referenced (see Box 7.15), with authors, year and journal, etc. Noting this information at an early stage will avoid frantic scrabbling through scores of journals when it comes to writing up. One of the most common mutterings overheard in university

libraries everywhere (from students and authors of textbooks alike) is, 'Where was that reference?'

Another area where it is important to keep a track of what you are doing is in the results section. Writing up your results as you conduct the analysis will identify any significant gaps while there is still sufficient time to fill them. Alternatively, this might also help you to recognise when further analysis is unnecessary – a common problem with many undergraduate reports is over-analysis of data, which creates needless work for both the student and the supervisor. However, even the most conscientious of researchers may have to make amendments to their report at the last minute, and it is only when discussions and conclusions have been written that the overall structure may be assessed (this is the reason why you should always write the abstract *last*). It is important to allow yourself the time to read your work critically before it has to be submitted, to reflect on its contents and to make any necessary changes. This is why you should make notes as you go along, and the following should serve as a guide:

1 File complete references of articles or books that you have read, with details of the main points of studies or theories.
2 Write down the arguments behind your hypotheses. It is all too easy, during the course of a lengthy project, to lose sight of what the original aims were. Being able to return to some statement of intent will serve as a reminder as to why you are doing this. This may seem an odd point to make but students often experience periods of alarm when, bogged down by scores of questionnaires, rating scales and transcripts, they feel they have lost direction.
3 Carefully record the means whereby you recruited participants, with details of the numbers agreeing or refusing to participate. This can become an important issue if you are hoping to generalise from your sample to a wider population – subject numbers and sampling procedures will be key limiting factors in how much you will be able to say here.
4 Note any changes that you may have made to questionnaires or other instruments, and the arguments behind the changes. It is important to demonstrate how your research developed and one of the elements a supervisor will be interested in concerns your choice of, for example, questionnaire items: Why ask these questions? Why in this format?
5 Record details of pilot studies, and any modifications made as a result of those studies. As with the previous point, it is important to show how your

research developed and how you ended up adopting a particular approach. Pilot studies often play a key role in determining the final structure and format of research; they should therefore be described in detail.

6 Maintain a log of the exact procedures you employed, with appropriate justification. Much of the criticism levelled at undergraduate projects revolves around procedural problems – not enough detail, no explanation of why this approach was adopted, etc.

7 Keep track of coding procedures. Not only will you be expected to give an account of this in your report but, from a practical point of view, it is easy to forget which particular numerical values you used to denote responses on a multi-item questionnaire. To change a coding frame in the middle of a study can be fatal.

8 Keep a detailed record of all analyses carried out and why you did them. Apart from the obvious necessity of being able to report this as part of your write-up, there is a risk of losing sight of what you are trying to do at this stage; wading through pages of SPSS output showing descriptive statistics, numerous t-tests and the odd analysis of variance can be confusing (what an understatement), not to mention a major contributor to the sense of panic that often strikes at the analysis stage of a research project. Faced with a tearful student wielding the results of umpteen correlations a supervisor will typically ask: 'What was it you were trying to do?'

Keeping research notes like this can take many forms, although perhaps a diary or lab-book format is the simplest; keeping up with reading, meetings with supervisors and notes needs a certain amount of self discipline, and it is surprising how often one simply cannot remember such details at a later stage. You really will be saving yourself time and trouble if you keep an accurate running record of your research activities in some organised format. Relying on memory alone, or random scraps of paper, will not be effective; your supervisor will (or should) keep a diary of your progress and it is very much in your own interests to do the same.

7.3 The structure of a research report

The basic structure of your write-up should normally follow the familiar layout of most research reports; i.e. it should consist of the four major sections:

Introduction, Method, Results, and Discussion, in that order, headed by the title and abstract and followed by the reference list and any appendices (see Box 7.1). Part of the reason for keeping to this conventional format is that the reader will know just where to find each piece of essential information about your research. You should therefore make sure that your report conforms to this layout as much as possible, and that relevant information is where it should be.

The report on a research project is obviously likely to be more substantial than the average laboratory report. A common question from undergraduates though is 'how long should the report be?' The answer, however, no matter how unsatisfactory, must be: *whatever it takes to report the research concisely, but clearly, accurately and completely*. Having said this, most student researchers will probably have some sort of length indication specified by their department or tutor (e.g. 'about 10,000 words'). This is always a rough indication, since an assessor is not actually going to count the words (big surprise, especially to those of you who like to include a word count as part of submitted work), but any such limit is worth bearing in mind and a report should always endeavour to end up somewhere within the recommended range. One of the most annoying aspects of undergraduate reports for supervisors is unnecessary length – a product of over-writing and a sense that every concept, theory or piece of previous research must be explained in great detail, especially in the introduction. In most cases this is not necessary and a general overview of established theory is sufficient, except when a particular study or issue forms the basis for the current piece of research, in which case detail is essential.

7.3.1 Title

This should be concise but informative, and should give a clear indication of what the project is about, e.g. 'Invisible barriers to women's advancement in academic institutions', or 'Regional differences in the perception of European stereotypes'. Readers should be able to tell, from the title alone, whether a report is of interest to them, or of relevance to their own research. A title that is too general may be at best uninformative and at worst misleading: for example, the title 'Gender and socialisation' gives no indication of which aspects of either gender or socialisation were investigated. If a report is likely to be placed on library access, or in other ways made available to a broader readership, it is important that the title contains the relevant keywords

---

Box 7.1   The structure of a typical project report

Title
Brief, clear, accurate; don't try to be funny or whimsical (10–12 words at most).

Abstract
Approximately 100–150 word summary. Say briefly what it's about, what was done, and what was found. Write this last!

Introduction
What was this research all about? What relevant previous work was there? What did they find? Is there a central theory, or a debate about different theories? Was the present study the same (a replication)? If not, how was it different? In either case, what were you trying to do (aims)? And what did you expect to find (the hypotheses)?

Method
Four sub-headings, setting out the structure of the study, as follows:

1   *Design*. What sort of study was it (e.g. an experiment, a survey, a case study)?
Repeated measures design, independent groups, or a mixed design?
What were the dependent variables (what was measured)?
What were the independent variables (what varied across different subjects)?
What did participants have to do?
2   *Participants*. How many? Any *relevant* description.
3   *Apparatus*. What materials or equipment did the study need?

4   *Procedure*. Briefly describe what happened. Quote the instructions given to the participants.

Results
A written presentation of summary results, not individual subjects' data. For example, give the mean and standard deviation for the dependent variable for each different condition. If any graphs or tables help to clarify the results, put them in here, but don't merely duplicate tabular data – figures are only useful if they clarify, or highlight, data in a manner not possible with tables. Report the statistics used, and say briefly whether the results supported the hypotheses or not.

Discussion
An examination of your results, comparing them with previous findings. What conclusions do they point to? How do you interpret your findings? You could also suggest improvements or variations in the design, or further hypotheses that might be tested.

References
Only list references actually cited earlier in the report. If it is important to mention other sources used, though not explicitly cited, these should be given in a separate bibliography.

Appendices
This is the location for the raw materials used in the study – stimuli, examples of questionnaire and so on. Raw data and computer print-outs are not recommended, unless there is a case for inclusion. Supervisors will normally inform you of their expectations here.

Box 7.2   Common errors in the title

Some authors try to apply snappy titles to their work, incorporating puns, innuendo or otherwise playing on words, presumably in the hopes of appealing to journal editors (or amusing supervisors enough to gain an extra few marks). For example:

New treatment in substance abuse: not to be sniffed at

or

**Freud and the unconscious?
Dream on…**

Amusing as these may be, they don't actually offer much information about the studies and would be likely to be overlooked in the early stages of a literature review for this reason. And in case anyone is wondering, editors and supervisors would not be impressed.

that any interested readers would be likely to use in their literature search (e.g. 'regional differences', 'academic institutions', or 'European stereotypes'). This is of particular importance today when, increasingly, researchers are using the Internet and other electronic databases to carry out keyword searches.

7.3.2   Abstract

The abstract is a short summary of the main information contained in the project report as a whole. It should ideally be about 100 or 150 words in length. Although the abstract is positioned at the beginning of the report, it is often the last part actually to be written. It will certainly be easier to write the summary when the report is finished than the other way around. Normally the abstract should – very briefly – identify the problem studied; the hypotheses tested;

the method employed, including the number and kinds of subjects; the results obtained; and the main conclusions drawn. Statistical details should usually be excluded, unless you have used a novel type of analysis, or have departed from the norm in any other important way (e.g. used a non-standard significance level, etc.). In short, an abstract should be like an extremely condensed version of the full report, providing key information from the introduction, method, results and discussion sections.

Writing a good abstract (one that conveys key information clearly and accurately, without exceeding the length limit) is difficult, but it is important. Like the title, the abstract may be accessed by online search systems, so it should contain enough specific information to enable a researcher to find the work in the first place, and then to decide whether to read the whole thing. This is becoming increasingly important with the advent of modern databases since the abstract (and the title) will often be the first point of contact others will have with a researcher's work. It is therefore important to get it right (see Box 7.4).

Box 7.3 Common errors in the abstract

In the search for brevity some writers reduce the information content of an abstract to the point where it becomes impossible to judge the nature of a study without reading the entire report. This is a particularly common problem among undergraduate students, but it is not exclusive to them.

A study on consumerism among a stratified sample failed to demonstrate significant differences among any of the comparison groups on any of the 15 differentiating behaviours. In all cases the null hypotheses were accepted.

An abstract of this nature is virtually useless. There is no real indication of what the study was about, which aspects of consumerism were being studied, or who the participants were. Nor is there any indication as to what kind of statistical analysis was carried out in order to test the hypotheses – whatever they happened to be. Equally unhelpful is the two-page abstract in which the writer is incapable of summarising the important elements of the study:

In a study carried out over five days between April 1st and April 5th one hundred subjects participated in a between-groups experiment on choice behaviour, with choice being determined as a preference for vegetarian versus non-vegetarian food in a canteen environment. The participants were initially drawn from a local population comprising primarily university undergraduates, all of whom lived within the campus area, except for a small group who commuted from a neighbouring district. Of these, the population was known to comprise 80% males and 20% females, with an age distribution roughly... arghh!...

This amount of detail, if extended to the rest of the study, would provide an abstract almost as long as the report itself, which is as counter-productive as the previous, minimalist example.

Box 7.4 Abstract: checklist

A good abstract should contain the following information:

1   The research issue being explored. This would comprise the research question, or the theory being investigated in the study.
2   The hypotheses being tested – the specific predictions that form the bases of the study.
3   The design of the study – the way in which it has been set up to explore the hypotheses, expressed in the language of design (e.g. repeated measures; counterbalanced).
4   The key characteristics of the participants, insofar as this information is relevant. There is little point, for example, in offering detail on age unless age influenced, or explained, the findings in some way.
5   The key characteristics of any apparatus used, again only insofar as this may be relevant – if findings can only be explained by reference to the specifics of apparatus, or if replication could not take place without this particular information.
6   The outcome of the study, in terms of whether or not hypotheses were accepted or rejected.
7   A comment on any unusual features of the study, if appropriate.

7.3.3 Contents

If the purpose of a write-up is a final report rather than an article intended for publication (which, alas, is something few undergraduates actually consider), a list of contents could be provided, based on section or chapter headings. This is particularly important if more than one experiment is being reported, or if a project moves forward through a number of successive stages. Also included here should be details of any appendices, and this is probably an appropriate point at which to remind you to number the pages – again, something often forgotten by keen (or late) students. A look at the contents section of this book provides a good example of the level of detail that is useful in highlighting what is to follow, and readers can judge for themselves how useful (or otherwise) this feature is.

7.3.4 Introduction

This is the first major section of the report. A good introduction should provide the reader with the essential background to the project, starting out with a broad description of the particular research topic that is being dealt with, and moving on through a clear and accurate account of the previous research that has led up to the project. You should be able to show that your particular study is a natural development of this previous work, and that it adds something – even if that something is only that an effect is (or is not) replicated with a different sample. It is also important to show that you are aware of current or recent work relevant to the study, and that the important theoretical issues are understood.

There is no one correct way to begin an introduction, but it is probably a good idea to start off with a brief overview of the area of study to set the scene for what is to follow. For example, if a study concerns the relationship between occupational status and spending patterns, one could begin by describing the general assumptions made about this relationship, followed by a delineation of the aspects of social class and purchasing to be considered in further detail in the report. If a study concerns ways of coping with a particular illness, you could begin by describing the aspects of the illness that may be found stressful, followed by an outline of the model of stress and coping that you intend to use as a framework for analysis. The introductory paragraphs should therefore outline, in a general way, what the study is about and which aspects of a given issue you are exploring.

The central part of an introduction should cover the relevant research that forms a background to the project. If the research is based on one major published study, describe this in some detail, including the number and type of participants used, the design of the original study, the measures taken, and the method of analysis. This amount of detail is necessary since, in your own study, you will probably be using a similar design, with similar types of people. If the aim is to refute or criticise a previous piece of research, you will still need this level of detail, if only to demonstrate how, by using a different mode of analysis from the original, for example, you generate completely different findings. Following on from this you should

comment on the study that is serving as a platform for your own work, taking into account such issues as the adequacy of the subjects, measures, design and analysis used, the extent to which the results may be generalised to other populations, and any theoretical implications of the results. You can then describe other studies in the area using this general framework, although unless they relate directly to the research issue, or provide a further foundation for what you are going to do, these should not be presented in anything like this amount of detail. In this way, the major areas of interest, related issues and matters pertaining to the particular approach you are taking, can be clarified as you proceed. Consequently, hypotheses or research questions when they are finally offered – usually in the concluding phase of the introduction – should not come as a surprise to the reader: every aspect of the hypotheses should have been mentioned at an earlier point in the introduction and should follow on naturally and logically from what has gone before. It is a common experience of supervisors to come to the aims, objectives and hypotheses section of a report and then to have to go back through the introductory discussion to try and find out where these hypotheses came from and what their rationale might happen to be. It is worth mentioning that this can be extremely irritating for a supervisor, so consider yourselves warned.

The introduction should normally lead towards an overview of what the study will actually do (but saving the details for the next section) and should conclude with a statement of the hypotheses that the study actually tested. It is often useful to state these twice: first as a general prediction of outcomes (e.g. that certain patterns of social relationship would be associated with type of schooling – denominational versus non-denominational); and then as a precise experimental hypothesis, e.g.:

It was therefore hypothesised that significant differences in the perception of traditional marriage roles would be observed between participants from a denominational school background and those from a non-denominational school background; it was further hypothesised that this effect would be moderated by gender, with male participants demonstrating fewer differences than females.

It is also useful at this stage to identify (as much for your own benefit as the reader's) the independent and dependent variables so that it is always clear what is being tested. The more precise hypotheses can be, the more straightforward will be the conduct of the study itself. (And the more likely you will be able to recover

Box 7.5   Common errors in the introduction

1   Writing an anecdotal, subjective background that is based more on personal opinion than a sound knowledge of the field.

2   Trying to cover the entire history of research in the field: be selective, and review only that which is directly relevant to your own study. This is especially important in areas that have proved popular among researchers (imagine trying to review the last 50 years of research into personality and you will get the point).

3   Explaining too much: you may assume some theoretical knowledge on the part of your reader. You should not have to define common terms – unless, of course, you are using them in a specialised way. (It is worth considering the nature of your readership here. A report for publication in a scientific journal will not have to spell out the characteristics of various measurement scales in questionnaire design. A presentation to undergraduates, on the other hand, might require that the structure of, for example, a Likert scale, be explained.)

4   Explaining too little: we are not all experts in your field, so write as if for the intelligent, interested, non-specialist. In practical terms a balance will have to be struck between this and the previous point.

5   Failing to show how your review of the relevant literature leads up to, and provides a rationale for, your particular study.

6   Failing to state just what it is that your study is seeking to accomplish. A frequent form of this error is failing to state your hypotheses at the end of the introduction.

from the sense of panic common to the middle stages of a project, when there is a danger of losing sight of what it was you were trying to do.)

Pilot studies may also be mentioned in the introduction if they have contributed to the development of hypotheses or research questions. Otherwise, the convention is that details of pilot studies are given in the method section, especially where they relate to developing questionnaire items or strategies for data gathering.

7.3.5   Method

The method section is the next major part of a research write-up, insofar as it presents all the information about how the research was actually carried out. Its purpose is to present a detailed description of the conduct of the study in such a way that the reader can follow the natu-

ral timeline, or sequence of events, that characterised the study, from general introduction through specific hypotheses to actual testing and data gathering. This is an important section since it provides the opportunity to explain what you actually did. All that has gone before is abstract, concerned with theory and hypotheses. The method section is concerned with the concrete: Who participated? How were participants assigned to groups? What was measured? What checks were made on extraneous factors? These are typical questions posed by anyone reviewing or assessing a report and the answers should be readily available in this section, simply because of the detail offered by the researcher. From a practical point of view the method section also provides an insight to a supervisor as to how careful and systematic the student has been in the conduct of their study. This is the section in which design flaws become highlighted and the limitations of the study underlined. Often, when criticising the findings of a study, a supervisor will return to the method section with comments such as, 'you cannot make this generalisation with such a small sample', or, 'by doing it this way you overlooked an important issue'. Frightening as this revelation must be to many undergraduate readers, it nonetheless makes the point that this part of a report is central to the way in which a piece of research will be evaluated. If a study is flawed it will show up here but, if the researcher understands enough about the issues and how they were tackled, the limitations outlined here will form the basis of much of the later discussion section in which the writer will attempt to justify the conclusions drawn, demonstrate that she understands why hypotheses were not supported, and be able to outline ways in which the issues might be more effectively explored.

A second reason for providing a detailed method is that there will be occasions on which a researcher will wish to replicate a particular piece of research; perhaps the study has broken new ground in its field, or perhaps its findings are unexpected, or even suspect in some way. Or perhaps a researcher wants to know if particular effects can be reproduced under different circumstances, or by using different types of participant. Whatever the case there will be occasions on which a researcher will feel that there is reason to replicate previous work, and the only way this is possible is if there exists sufficient detail on how the original research was carried out. Now realistically, this will rarely be true of most undergraduate research. As we have previously stated, studies at this level are more often carried out for demonstration and experiential purposes than to genuinely extend our understanding of the human condition. Yet, as part of this process, an ability to produce replicable methodology is an important skill for anyone intending to pursue their interest in society beyond the graduate level.

The following sections illustrate the major divisions that comprise a typical method and describe the ways in which this part of a report would be structured.

7.3.6 Design

This, the initial part of the method section, describes the formal structure of the study. It is usually brief and concise, but lacking in specific details about subjects and procedure, and it is generally couched in the technical language of a research design (between-subjects; repeated measures; counterbalanced, etc.). First, you will specify what kind of investigation has been carried out (e.g. was it an experiment, an observational study, a survey, a case study, and so on). You should then define the variables either measured or manipulated in the study, making the distinction between independent variables (or predictors) and dependent variables (or outcome measures). This ought to be a straightforward task, since these matters will have been sorted out in the early stages of a study. However, supervisors are often surprised at the confusions that appear over the description of variables present in a study, even in cases where the rest of the work is of a high standard. (If this is still a problem, a review of Chapter 2, Sections 2.4.6 and 2.4.7, will be helpful.)

This difficulty of correctly identifying variables can sometimes be aggravated in correlational studies where identification is sometimes less clear – variables are related or associated with one another but not always in an obvious cause and effect manner – but you should usually be able to distinguish between the variables that you want to find out about, and the variables that you are just using to get there (predictors). You should also specify any important extraneous variables: i.e. factors which under other circumstances might be considered independent variables in their own right, but which in this case might have to be controlled for. (Our discussion on the distinction between multiple regression and partial correlation in Chapter 5 (Section 5.6) is a useful guide to the issue of when a variable is extraneous or not.)

Another important design element is whether you have used repeated measures (within-subjects design), independent groups (between-subjects design), or a combination of the two (mixed design). (See Chapter 2, Sections 2.5.2 and 2.5.3.) This should be accurately reported, especially in experimental studies (note that

correlational designs by definition use repeated measures). The factor levels that combine to form the experimental conditions should be described if appropriate, as should the method by which the subjects were assigned to groups. Box 7.6 provides an example of the information expected in a typical design.

A common mistake made by undergraduates is to confuse design and procedural matters. It must be remembered that the design of a study is the plan of campaign, formulated before the study proper is implemented. Consequently when decisions are made it isn't possible to know how many participants will actually respond to your questionnaire, or whether your particular experimental manipulation will produce a revolt among one of your groups. This is why the design is a formal statement of intent, expressed in general terms and using the language of experimentation. If still in any doubt about this, the whole of Chapter 2, should be reviewed. Box 7.7 also illustrates this point.

Box 7.6   A typical design

In a 2×3 quasi-experimental design, male and female patients were assigned to one of three exercise conditions. The dependent variable was post-operative recovery time, measured in days to a predetermined level, and the between-groups independent variables were gender (male or female) and exercise regime (none, moderate and regular). The covariate of age was controlled for.

Box 7.7   Common errors in the design

Many people, and especially those new to the scientific report, readily confuse procedural elements with the design. By way of example, what follows is an outline of procedural matters:

Eighty subjects were used in the study; 40 males and 40 females, of varying ages and backgrounds. Both groups were treated identically, being shown a video, prior to the experimental manipulation, in which the procedural details were explained. The manipulation itself comprised a small parts assembly exercise in which a number of rivets, washers and bolts were assembled in a predetermined order and then inserted into a pegboard. On completion of the experiment each subject completed a questionnaire which rated various attitudinal factors on a 1–5 scale...

The key point about a design is that it should serve almost as a schematic map or diagram of a study in which the major elements – and only those – are illustrated.

If your project is at the more qualitative end of the spectrum, you should still try to give a formal and objective description of your project under this heading. Thus you should clarify the method (e.g. observation, or semi-structured interview), the main issues under consideration, corresponding to dependent variables (e.g. types of non-verbal behaviours, expressed sources of stress at work), other variables or factors corresponding to independent variables and covariates (e.g. gender, age, employment status), and time factors, such as the frequency of repeated observations.

The final element in this section is shown in Box 7.8, comprising a checklist of key points that you should review before you consider any other developments in your study. It is worth remembering that if you have come up with an inappropriate design, or if you are unclear about key design elements, everything that follows will be affected.

Box 7.8   Design checklist

Your design should contain the following information:

1   The nature of the study (e.g. experimental, survey, case study, etc.).
2   The structure of the design (e.g. repeated measures, independent groups, etc.).
3   The independent and dependent variables.
4   Extraneous variables and any controls used to reduce their effect.

7.3.7   Participants

Give *relevant* details of those who participated in your research, including the number of subjects who comprised your sample, their age and gender, and on what basis they were allocated to subgroups. Any participant profile characteristics that might have affected their responses or behaviour should be mentioned, and you should explain how these were dealt with (e.g. 'to allow for any possible gender effect in response, equal numbers of male and female participants were present in each of the groups'). You should also state how the participants were obtained, and give refusal rates if appropriate. You should aim to give sufficient detail to enable you and the reader to decide the extent to which your subjects were representative of the population. For example, if you recruited participants through a self-help group or

---

Box 7.9   Participants section: an example

The subjects, all members of a university subject panel, were 60 undergraduate volunteers (30 males, 30 females), who participated in the survey voluntarily. The median age was 19 years (range 17–23). Subjects were assigned to either the frog group or the newt group on a quasi-random basis, with the constraint that equal numbers of male and female subjects were included in either group. Given the nature of the task, the subjects were screened to ensure that their eyesight was normal or corrected to normal.

---

through a newsletter, you may have distributed 100 questionnaires but had only 40 returns. This should be stated, since it may imply that your results are applicable only to a subsection of the target population. While this may be a limitation of your project it is not something to be hidden, or indeed to be ashamed of. In this case, the possible limitations of your results should be considered in the discussion element of your report, as mentioned in the previous section on methodology. See Box 7.9.

7.3.8   Apparatus (or materials)

Give full details of all equipment, apparatus and materials used. Trade names and model numbers of pieces of equipment should be given. The full names of published tests should be given, with references. Details of pilot studies may be given here, if they confirmed the utility of apparatus or materials, or, alternatively, if they indicated the need for changes or alterations. If questionnaires or other test materials have been changed in any way, give full details and a rationale for the changes made. For example, you may have changed the wording on a questionnaire item originating in the USA to make it more suitable for a UK population, or you may have omitted an item because it was unethical or irrelevant within the context of your project.

If you have used a fairly lengthy questionnaire or interview schedule, you may wish to give some representative examples of items in this section, and refer the reader to an appendix where the entire list can be found. If your questionnaire incorporates a number of different sections or subscales, make it clear what these are and how they are to be calculated. If you have written a computer programme for your study, give a careful explanation of what it actually does. The programme itself can be listed in full in an appendix.

You may have devised an interview schedule for your project. In this case, describe the main areas covered in the interview and indicate the sources of any particular questions or wording. Give the interview schedule in full in an appendix.

7.3.9   Procedure

Describe exactly what was done, and include verbal instructions given to subjects. If instructions were provided in handouts or with test materials, include these in an appendix. Bear in mind that the function of this section is to give the reader sufficient detail to repeat the study. (In reality we accept that rarely will anyone wish to replicate an undergraduate study, except under exceptional circumstances. The point is that, if someone wished to do so, there is sufficient detail here to allow them the opportunity.) And of course, we mustn't forget the key role of the procedure in assessment. For many supervisors, how you carried out your research is the most important element of your report.

Indicate the circumstances under which the subjects responded (e.g. in a designated room on their own, in groups, in their own homes, in the library), the order in which test items were completed (e.g. whether the order was randomised or fixed, and if fixed, what the order was), and the approximate length of time required by subjects. You should also clarify here the extent to which participants were offered anonymity, the instructions participants were given with regard to terminating their involvement in the project, any payment offered, and de-briefing or feedback procedures. You may have given some of this information in earlier sections; however, it is important to provide a full and clear description of the procedure in this section, even at the risk of repeating yourself.

The method is the second major section of the report, but is often the first to be written. The reason for this is that most of the technical details, the structure, and the practical details of the study have to be decided in advance. The method section is also the easiest to write, since you do not have to invent anything or be creative in any way: you are simply reporting factual information about your study.

7.3.10   Results

If you have conducted a quantitative study, this section should contain all the objective outcomes of your study: the factual results, as generated from analyses and

without any attempt at discussion, inference, or speculation. This should be presented in conventional text format, as in the rest of the report (that is, say in writing what occurred, with appropriate t-values, F-ratios or whatever). The temptation to expand and speculate here is, admittedly, huge. After all, this represents the point at which you have finally learned whether or not your predictions have been justified, hypotheses upheld or theories supported. However, the discussion section is the place to argue about the implications, not the results section. (The names given to these different parts of a report, by the way, ought to be something of a give away!) At this stage, you should present first the descriptive statistics, which summarise your data in a standard form, and second, inferential statistics, which test whether your results can be distinguished from chance and hence whether your hypotheses have been upheld. It is not usually appropriate to report individual subjects' raw data unless your study requires it, e.g. in a case study, where you may only have the one subject. Similarly, any arguments as to what your findings might imply will not be made here; this section is purely for the statement of the results of your study and nothing more. Probably the easiest way to think of this is that the reader, having read through the introduction and focused on the aims and hypotheses, will now want to find out what actually happened. Moving to the results ought to show, clearly and concisely, whether or not hypotheses were accepted, theories supported or indeed whether or not the experiment (if that's what it was) worked.

Descriptive statistics should normally consist of the means and standard deviations of your main outcome variables (which may be compared with any available published norms), and this would include not only global summary measures, but also those for any appropriate subgroups or conditions. For example, you may wish to give separate means and standard deviations for males and females, or those in different age groups. The descriptive statistics can often be conveniently presented in a table, or alternatively in a figure (see Section 7.4) if the nature of tabulated data is potentially misleading, or if there is so much of it that the information to be expressed is obscured. (It is worth noting, though, that tables and figures should be used as either–or alternatives. It is not appropriate to present the same data twice, once in each format. What would be the point?)

If you are using a questionnaire or materials that other authors have used, compare your results with theirs at this stage. Thus you should be able to demonstrate that your sample has provided data that fall within an expected range (or not), and that these data are suitable for further statistical analysis. Both of these points may be raised in the discussion.

If your sample appears to be different from other samples in some important way (e.g. your participants have different profile characteristics, or they obtain markedly higher or lower measures on particular questionnaire items), you may still be able to carry out further analysis, but you should indicate the nature of the differences and show that the necessary steps (e.g. data transformation, re-coding) have been taken. The presentation of descriptive statistics is important, and forms the logical starting point of further analysis. Moreover, as experienced researchers and reviewers are aware, inspection of descriptive statistics is often sufficient, on its own, to determine the outcome of a quantitative study. When two mean scores, for instance, are close to one another it is often clear that no real difference exists between the groups, obviating the need for any further analysis. Indeed, many a supervisor will criticise a student for proceeding with a comprehensive and complex inferential analysis of data, when inspection of (and understanding of) the descriptive statistics would have clearly indicated that no effects were present. A useful thing for students to know! For this reason it is worth having a good look at the relatively straightforward statistics in Box 7.10 before moving on to the main analysis.

The results of the statistical analysis should then be presented in a clear and logical way. The most obvious approach is to deal with each hypothesis in turn, in the order given at the end of your introduction. The aim is to show clearly what your data say about each one, and then to state simply whether this evidence supports it or not. Generally speaking this requires you to report the appropriate significance test, giving the value of the statistic, the degrees of freedom, and the associated probability. You should then help the reader by translating (briefly) what the test is telling you into a straightforward verbal statement, while avoiding the temptation to expand or speculate. See Box 7.11.

Always bear in mind that you must clarify your results for the reader. It is tempting to use short-hand when describing certain variables, particularly in tables. Tables derived from computer print-out usually bear the abbreviated labels used to code variables rather than the full variable name. If you do have to use shortened names in tables, provide a key underneath the table. For example:

Variable	mean	sd
Ichygrp	7.53	0.09
Squish	16.21	0.22

Ichygrp – incidence of cholesterol in the young group

Squish – number of newts run over

Box 7.10

Example:

Mean post-operative recovery time for males = 13.75 days	$n = 12$
Mean post-operative recovery time for females = 13.44 days	$n = 13$

In this example the means are so close to one another that it would seem unlikely that the groups differed in any meaningful way. Further analysis here would be pointless, unless the sample sizes were extremely large. A difference of 13.75 to 13.44 might take on a different complexion (i.e. become significant) were it maintained across thousands of patients. But not in this case.

Box 7.11 Reporting the results of analyses

1 *Correlation*
A significant negative correlation was observed between cyclists' age and number of newts run over ($r = 0.43$; $df = 29$; $p > 0.01$).
Note: this can also be expressed as $r_{(29)} = 0.43$; $p < 0.01$. Or the exact probability can be given, as $r = 0.43$; $df = 29$; $p = 0.0005$.

2 *Independent t-test*
A non-significant difference was observed in absenteeism rates of blue and white collar samples. (t(equal variances) = 1.51; $df = 22$; $p > 0.05$).

3 *ANOVA*
A significant main effect of fishing experience was observed on the numbers of trout landed in competition ($F = 14.5$; $df = 1$; $p < 0.05$).
No main effect of lure was observed on the numbers of trout landed during competition ($F = 1.77$; $df = 1$; $p > 0.05$).
A significant experience-by-lure interaction effect was observed on the numbers of trout landed during competition ($F = 9.7$; $df = 2$; $p < 0.05$).

4 *Chi-square*
A non-significant association was observed between participants' sex and their response to a questionnaire item (Do you support an extension to the motorway system? Yes/No) (chi-square = 2.75; $df = 1$; $p > 0.05$).
Note: as in example (1), all significance values can be given as the exact probabilities computed.

When you are presenting results, describe relationships as fully as possible to avoid confusion: for example, it is clearer, if more lengthy, to say 'scores on the measure of job stress were significantly correlated with scores on the "wishful thinking" coping scale' than to say 'job stress and wishful thinking were significantly correlated'.

Although the results section often contains a large amount of numerical and statistical information, it is nevertheless part of the text of your report and should be written in English. It is not acceptable simply to present a series of tables or diagrams, unless there is also a clear accompanying text which explains in plain language what your illustrations show. Even less appropriate would be to base this section on computer print-outs which are notoriously minimalist. Moreover, unless you have gone to the trouble of labelling your data, groups and subdivisions in SPSS will be presented by their numerical code. One of the most common criticisms of the results section of a write-up is that tables and graphs are unclear.

If you have lengthy or complex results, however, clarity is often greatly helped by including appropriate illustrative tables or figures. These can be a real help to the reader in understanding the overall pattern of your results, and therefore in following the argument. Sometimes, however, they can simply be confusing and counter-productive, or irrelevant and annoying. Box 7.12 provides a results checklist, which is a useful guide to what ought to be covered in this section.

7.4   Tables and figures

Tables are easily produced by a word-processor, a spreadsheet package or even by the statistics package used for analysis, and usually consist of summary numerical data (e.g. means and standard deviations, correlation coefficients, etc.), presented within a system of rows and columns representing various categories (e.g. different samples, categories within samples or experimental conditions). See Table 7.1.

Figures usually involve a more pictorial mode of presenting the data (e.g. barcharts, histograms, scatterplots, etc.), and are either produced directly by your statistics package or indirectly by means of specialist software for diagrams and graphics. Increasingly also, many integrated word-processing/spreadsheet/drawing packages offer this facility, bringing the opportunity to create effective illustrations within everyone's grasp. Generally speaking, the data contained in tabular form are precise (actual numerical values are used) whereas figures offer a less exact though often more immediate impression. Figures 7.1 and 7.2 demonstrate the point.

All tables and figures must be numbered (e.g. *Table 1*; *Figure 1*) and should be given captions that are self-explanatory. The reader should be able to understand what a table or figure is all about without digging through the text to find out. At the same time, the information displayed in tables or figures should not be mysteriously independent of the text: it *must* be discussed, explained, or otherwise used in some relevant way. Common written comments next to tables and figures are, 'What is this?' 'What does this show?'

The whole point of using graphs, figures and tables is to report, accurately and clearly, the outcome of

---

Box 7.12   Results checklist

1   Have you presented descriptive statistics that represent the data fairly and adequately?
2   Do the results as shown deal with each hypothesis stated at the end of the introduction?
3   Are all the results of your analysis presented appropriately?
4   Are all tables and figures correctly labelled?
5   Is it possible to assess the outcome of the study by consulting the results alone, without the need to refer to other sections of the report?
6   Have you included results that are not relevant to the research issue in general or the hypotheses in particular, or to which you do not refer again?

Table 7.1   Mean number of racist terms recorded in one week in six daily newspapers (with standard deviation).

	Mean no. of racist terms	SD
Paper 1	679.73	95.42
Paper 2	588.66	76.32
Paper 3	624.29	59.45
Paper 4	696.75	64.77
Paper 5	701.61	122.50
Paper 6	828.03	101.45

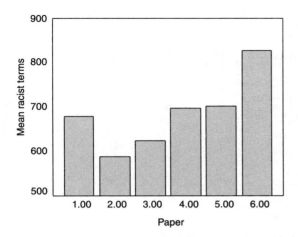

Figure 7.1 Average number of racist items recorded by six newspapers in one week.

a study. However, this section of any written report is often the main source of misleading, inaccurate and inappropriate information. Figure 7.3 shows a typical example. Here the researcher is guilty of two errors. On the one hand, there is simply too much information offered on the line graph and it becomes almost impossible to identify any trend or pattern in the data. On the other, there is no information on what each of the plotted lines is measuring: the legend for the graph is missing. Furthermore, this particular researcher seems to

have lost the ability to count, as can be observed by closer inspection of the figure in question.

In the next example, Figure 7.4 demonstrates how a sneaky researcher can manipulate the vertical and horizontal axes of a figure to maximise an effect. Presenting data in this form suggests that there are indeed huge differences between the sexes when measured on an attitudinal issue, in this instance perceptions of active discrimination against women in work.

Compare this with the final illustration in this section, Figure 7.5, in which the axes have been manipulated in a different, but equally misleading way. The data are the same as for the previous figure, but the impression created is totally different, achieved by manipulating the vertical (y) axis.

This kind of manipulation is not recommended and the sophisticated reader is likely to pick up on such attempts to deceive quite quickly. If in any doubt how best to present data fairly and objectively, most current statistical software uses a recognised format for graphs which provides an acceptable standard. If still in doubt, there is an old adage beloved of statisticians long gone now, that the vertical axis should always be 3/4 the length of the horizontal! Combine this with axes showing true zero points and extending just beyond the highest data value, and you have solved the problem, or at least attained consistency.

This section concludes with a checklist to serve as a reminder of what tables and figures are supposed to be doing. This is shown in Box 7.13.

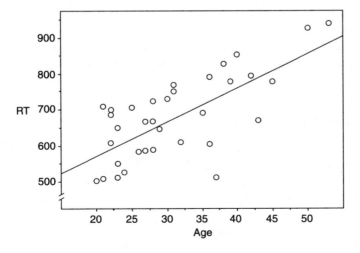

Figure 7.2 Mean response time (RT) in milliseconds to joke about frogs' legs by age.

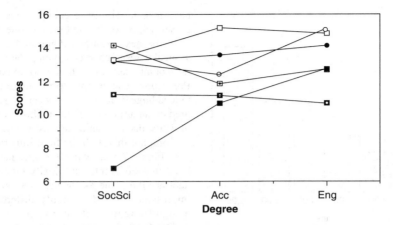

Figure 7.3   Exam performance scores in five subjects across three degrees.

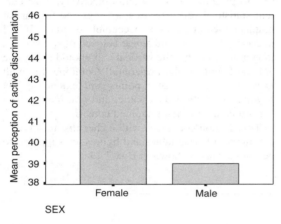

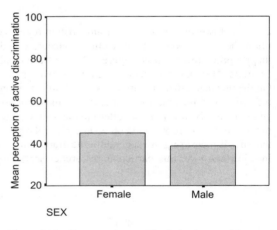

Figure 7.4   Scores on an attitude instrument for males and females. The barchart demonstrates a huge difference between the sexes.

Figure 7.5   Scores on an attitude instrument for males and females. The barchart demonstrates no real difference between the sexes.

Box 7.13   Tables and figures checklist

1   All data that are relevant to the study must be shown, either as a table or a figure.

2   All tables and figures must be clearly labelled and numbered. Axes should show the appropriate units of measurement and the variables represented on them.

3   Table and figure labels should state clearly what is being presented, in general terms. Specific information about the content of a figure or table can be presented in the form of column headings for a table, or the legend for a graph.

4   The numbering of tables and figures must be logical and sequential so they can be readily referred to in any discussion.

5   Duplication should be avoided – data should be presented in one format only. If a table offers a clear presentation of data, an additional figure on the same data is of little value.

6   Over-complexity should be avoided. If a table or figure cannot present findings in a clear and unambiguous manner, the data must be reorganised or a different mode of presentation sought.

7.5 Discussion

This is the section that probably demands the most from your creativity, where you try to make sense of it all, to relate your findings to previous research and explain what happened in your study – in particular this is where the hypotheses are reviewed in the light of the results. The best guidance would be to start off by restating, in straightforward and general terms, the main results of your study, and indicating the implications of these results for your hypotheses. Then you can draw on the main points of your introduction: for example, you can indicate whether your results are consistent or inconsistent with the findings of other researchers, or whether they support one theory rather than another.

You have to present some explanations for your results. This may be easy if your results are entirely in the expected direction and all of your hypotheses were supported. It may be less straightforward (although more interesting) if your results were not consistent with the results of other researchers. Under these circumstances, you have to review all of the potentially relevant points made earlier in the report: you may have used a different subject pool, used a slightly different procedure, changed the test materials in some way, and all of these may have affected your results. You should not attempt to hide any such discrepancies between your study and those of others; rather the effects of discrepancies and variations should be highlighted, since they tell you something very important about the strength or robustness of any predicted effects. Moreover, being honest and 'upfront' like this also indicates that you appreciate the limitations of your study, which in itself is commendable. More importantly, from an assessment point of view, if you don't do this, your supervisor certainly will. One of the most irritating characteristics of tutors everywhere is their unerring knack of finding the flaws in the research of their students.

Overall, you should ensure that you cover all of the main points raised in your introduction. Thus if you mentioned the possibility of gender differences in the introduction, you should raise this issue again in your discussion, even if you were not able to examine gender differences (for example, because of limitations within the subject pool). One of the aims of the discussion is to highlight the limitations of your project and areas worthy of further investigation. You are not expected to conduct a study that covers every option; on the other hand, you are expected to discuss the

> **Box 7.14 Discussion checklist**
>
> 1 Have you discussed all the important issues raised in your introduction?
> 2 Have ideas crept into the discussion that are not really related to the study?
> 3 Does the discussion concentrate purely on the findings, or does it consider broader issues?
> 4 Conversely: does your discussion take sufficient note of the actual findings?
> 5 Are there any findings you have not discussed?
> 6 Have you considered whether your data might support an explanation other than the one you prefer?
> 7 Does the discussion point to original thinking?
> 8 Are your conclusions clear?

strengths, weaknesses and limitations of your work in a clear and objective tone. (Remember the point made above about supervisors.) You should also consider ways in which your project might have been improved, and the direction of any future work that may be profitably undertaken in this area.

A very important point to note is that the failure to uphold your hypotheses does not mean that the study has 'failed', which is often the view of students new to research. To show that something is *not* the case can be as important as showing that it *is* the case: a null result does not mean that you have nothing to say. You should not, therefore, write your discussion of a null outcome in an apologetic way; yes, we all like to get a 'significant result', but the rejection of a hypothesis can be equally informative, and may lead to new ideas.

The discussion should end with a paragraph or two of conclusions. It may be tempting at this stage to make rather sweeping statements. Remember the limitations of your study and try not to go beyond your own results. A useful checklist that can be applied to the discussion section appears in Box 7.14.

7.6 References

The references section of a report offers an alphabetical listing (by first author's surname) of all the sources mentioned, or referred to in the main text of the report: research by others, book chapters, commentaries and quotations – any material in fact to which you have made reference in the body of a report must be cited. An important point here, and one that is a traditional source of confusion to many undergraduates, concerns the difference between a reference section and a bibliography. References, as already mentioned, relate to work actually cited. A bibliography, on the other hand, is a listing (again alphabetically, by first author) of any work which was consulted, browsed or which in some way contributed to the background, formulation and conduct of your study. For instance, in reviewing the type of research carried out in a particular area you might have read several journal articles and book reviews, none of which provided specific material to which you referred in your report. However, insofar as they did contribute to the overall foundations of your work, they are still worth mentioning. This is the function of a bibliography – an opportunity for you to provide an overview of your own research into a topic.

The format for presenting references tends to vary slightly from publication to publication, but the majority of social science journals conform to a set of formats favoured by the major journals of sociology, economics,

psychology and politics, the essence of which we have used in offering our own guidelines, as follows.

Citations in the text itself should be by author's surname and date only, which is the minimum information needed to correctly identify the full reference where it appears at the end of the report (see Box 7.15 for examples). Any other information, such as book title, journal number and so on, is redundant here and serves only to distract. In multiple citations, reference your sources in alphabetical order. In the (relatively) rare case in which more than one article has been published by a single author in the same year, and you wish to cite all, or some of this work, such publications are distinguished using the letters a, b, c etc. after the citation: e.g. Boelen, 1992a, Boelen, 1992b. The identifiers (a, b, c) are used in the order in which you cite the work in the text, and not in the order in which they were published in the particular year in question. And of course, the identifiers accompany the full reference at the end of the report. (This last point might come as

---

Box 7.15   References and citations

What follows are examples of good practice in citing the source of papers, articles and books in a research report. Editors and publishers of course will have their own preferences and many 'house styles' exist in how references should be formatted, and by and large these should be adhered to when submitting work to a professional journal or academic editor. For most purposes, though, the following will serve as a useful set of guidelines.

Journal articles
Boelen, W. A. M. (1992). Street corner society: Cornerville revisited. *Journal of Contemporary Ethnography, 21,* 11–51.
Seidel, J. V. & Clark, J. A. (1984). The Ethnograph: A computer program for the analysis of qualitative data. *Qualitative Sociology, 7,* 110–125.
Note that: (a) capital letters are not used in the titles of the articles except at the beginning of sections (or when proper names are used); (b) inverted commas are not used; (c) journal names are given in full; (d) journal names and volume numbers are italicised (or underlined, if you are not using a word-processor).

Books and chapters in books
Berkowitz, L. (1993). *Aggression: Its causes, consequences, and control.* New York: McGraw-Hill.
Williams, R. (1976). Symbolic interactionism: Fusion of theory and research. In D.C. Thorns (ed.), *New directions in sociology* (pp. 115–138). Newton Abbott: David & Charles.

Note that: (a) capitals are not used in the titles except at the beginning of sections; (b) inverted commas are not used; (c) book titles are italicised (but not chapter titles); (d) page numbers are given; (e) place of publication, then publishers, are cited last.

Citations in the text
In the text itself, sources are cited by surnames and date only. Citation can be direct or indirect:

• Direct: Archer (1991) found higher testosterone levels in the more aggressive group.
• Indirect: Higher testosterone levels were found in the more aggressive group (Archer, 1991).

Quotations are best avoided unless the full quotation given is of direct relevance to your own work. If you do quote verbatim from an author, give the page number as well, e.g. 'Comparisons…revealed higher testosterone levels in the more aggressive group' (Archer, 1991, p. 21). If there are two authors, give both surnames using 'and' for direct citation and '&' for indirect, e.g.

• Direct: Barry and Bateman (1992)…
• Indirect: (Barry & Bateman, 1992).

If there are more than two authors, give all the names in the References section (e.g. Johnson, Karmiloff-Smith & Patry, 1992). In the text, use '*et al.*' (e.g. Johnson *et al.*, 1992).

something of a surprise to some students who, in reproducing references from other sources, include the alphabetic identifiers without knowing why.)

7.7 Appendices

These should include the details of statistical calculation, and all test materials and examples of any stimuli used in the study. Note that most tutors and examiners will not welcome reams of computer output, even in an appendix, and raw data are certainly not welcomed (although there is an understanding that they could be made available for inspection should it be required). If your study is qualitative in nature, however, you may wish to include interview transcripts, etc. Again, if in doubt, you need merely consult the typical format used in a standard journal (or ask your supervisor).

7.8 Presentation and style

Remember that presentation is important. Try to ensure that your work is free from spelling and grammatical errors. Check your work for errors before you hand it in. The style of writing should be plain and relatively formal, and you should use the past tense throughout and write in the third person; many novice researchers frequently use 'I' and 'we' in their writing ('we felt repeated measures were more appropriate'), but this tends to create an impression of informality and lack of scientific rigour. And, whether accurate or not, impressions do count. It is much better to place some distance between yourself and the report, as in: 'It was found that/observed/noted' (except for a qualitative report in which the views of the author may be central).

7.9 Writing up qualitative research

Research is research and its presentation ought to follow a standard set of guidelines and procedures.

7.9.1 The background to a qualitative report

If your research conforms to the quantitative tradition then this statement will be essentially true. Many years of debate and refinement have led to a convergence of style and structure that now characterises the majority of hypothesis-based work, as most of the preceding sections illustrate. For qualitative research, however, our statement could not be further from the truth, and for a number of reasons.

First, the aims of qualitative research are not necessarily the same as those of quantitative research. We have made this point before, during our discussions on different research approaches in Chapter 3, and more fully in Chapter 6, but it is an important point and will not suffer from repetition. Most of what we call quantitative research is concerned with hypothesis and theory testing, and prediction, and while this is possibly an oversimplification (exploratory work that aims to understand and describe can still be quantitative) it generally holds true.

Qualitative research on the other hand is more likely to emphasise the descriptive and understanding elements of research (though, confusingly, it can readily be applied to the testing of hypotheses in certain situations). In grounded theory research, for instance, the researcher is unlikely to have posed any hypotheses at all until after much of the research and data collection has been completed – which is, in fact, the point of this approach. Likewise, ethnography and the anthropological tradition aim to describe cultures, groups and societies with which the researcher might be unfamiliar. It follows then that research of this type cannot be theory-driven. And finally, to emphasise the point, phenomenological research (which aims to understand the perceptions and experiences of others from their point of view) will not be valid unless the researchers can effectively put aside their own views, beliefs, experiences or theories.

A second explanation for the fact that qualitative research does not fit comfortably into the structural model of the quantitative approach is that there are various techniques and traditions. There is, of course, more than one set of techniques appropriate for quantitative studies. We know that surveys, correlational research and experimentation reflect different traditions, but they are unified in their broad goals, the modes of analysis used to treat data and the procedures for presenting findings. The different traditions in qualitative research, on the other hand, far from converging on an agreed set of procedures, have tended to develop distinct approaches to the conduct, analysis and presentation of research. To argue then that all qualitative research can be presented (let alone carried out) according to one particular set of principles would fail to do justice to the distinctiveness of the different approaches and succeed only in raising the ire of just about every researcher in the field. This is not to say that it hasn't been attempted. In a recent paper by Elliot, Fischer and Rennie (1999) a number of guidelines were proposed for the publication of qualitative research in the field of psychology.

Elliott *et al.* (1999) would be the first to admit that their guidelines comprise only a list of tentative suggestions about what would make good practice in dealing with qualitative studies. Moreover – in what could well be a pre-emptive strike against the army of critics waiting to retaliate – the authors freely accept that these guidelines cannot possibly be applied to all qualitative research, and they would certainly be unhappy at the prospect of imposing a constraining structure on what is a diverse and continually evolving field. However, we recognise the need to confront the issue of presenting the findings of qualitative research. Increasingly, qualitative method is appearing as an important component of undergraduate programmes and it is important that we, as tutors, advisors and supervisors, offer practical advice on dealing with the end product of their work – the write-up. This is where we, the authors, stick our necks out; what follows is a general set of suggestions for writing up qualitative research. We impose the same caveat as other authors, namely that our advice will not be appropriate in every situation, but at a general level it should provide a useful starting point.

7.9.2   Guidelines on writing up qualitative research

The report on a qualitative study will normally take the form of a narrative or a story, typically comprising four parts: introduction, method, results/discussion and conclusion.

Introduction

This would cover the following aspects:

*   *The background to the study*, including any theoretical issues that are to be explored. A rationale for the study must be offered since the reader will want to know what prompted the research, what it was hoped to learn and what the implications might be in terms of, for example, changes in social policy.
*   *The context of the study*. It is important to inform the reader of any and all factors that might influence the perceptions and experiences of participants, the researcher's view of events and a subsequent reader's interpretation of the stated research find-

ings. This would include – where relevant – the political climate at the time of the study, economic factors, geographic location, the nature of the participants themselves and their history, and the social and cultural forces that may have influenced events. By way of example, if we were exploring the problems experienced by refugees from the former Yugoslav republic (FYR) attempting to adapt to our own society, we would need to understand a great deal about the culture they left behind, the political structure, and their role within that society. We would have to offer details on the political system they were entering, the social structures and divisions with which they were attempting to merge, and the attitudinal and value systems with which they would be confronted. All of this would have to be made available to the reader or reviewer to facilitate a judgement on the relevance of the work.

*   *The perceptions of the researcher*. One of the salient issues in the qualitative/quantitative debate concerns the role of the researcher. Traditional positivism requires that the researcher disassociates himself from the object of research, lest his perception of reality become contaminated by his own views and experience. Other researchers, especially those in the qualitative tradition, would argue that this is impossible – we perceive the social world in terms of who we are and where we come from. Hence, insofar as our interpretation of events or our understanding of others' experiences may be coloured by our own nature, we must make clear those factors that might bias our perceptions of events, and what we did to overcome such bias. For instance, if our research concerned the experiences of black, working-class women, it would be of considerable enlightenment to our readership to learn that we were white, middle-class males with no experience of our participants. Of particular interest would be the steps we took to make it possible for us to approach such a group with any hope of understanding their lives, their hopes and their fears.

*   *The nature of the research*. There are many ways of exploring our social world, most of which are an outcome of the compromise between objectives, participants and practical considerations. If our aim is to come up with some kind of hypothesis about a particular set of beliefs or about how experiences are formed out of particular social and political policies, we might adopt a grounded theory approach; if we are trying to walk in other people's shoes our approach would be phenomenological (they are not mutually exclusive, by the way). If we

have access to only a handful of people who share a particular experience our preference might be for a case study approach, where other scenarios might lead us into participant observation, and so on.

Method

This is the major part of the report in which the researcher details what was actually done, how it was done, what changes were made and how the research evolved. It will cover the following points: what was done, how interview schedules were developed, how decisions were made on what was to be observed, how the researcher was accepted into the group, how data were collected and recorded, how the form and content of questions changed, why the issues changed, how a theory evolved, how the researcher adapted, changed viewpoints and modified her approach, what the researcher did to ensure that what seemed to be occurring was a true representation of the reality. Importantly, the issues concerning the approach taken must be considered in detail, demonstrating a clear understanding of any assumptions that were taken on board. All of this must be accompanied by substantiating and illustrative examples. It would not be enough to say, 'we felt participants were uncomfortable with the format of the original interviews and therefore modified our questioning', unless we were able to demonstrate that what we felt actually reflected our participants' real feelings. This brings us back to an issue we raised right at the beginning of this book, whereby all research can ultimately be evaluated in terms of the question, *How do you know?* How do you know your participants were uncomfortable? Do you have transcripts of conversations? Do you have journal entries? Do you have issues raised during group discussions? Have you sought the advice of colleagues? Have you confronted your participants with your view of events? Finally, have you explained what you have done in such a way that the reader can not only follow your progress but make a judgement about how well you have carried out your study? If, at the end of the day, a reviewer is obliged to say, 'I can't judge because I don't know…' then you have not written this section well enough.

Results/discussion

This is likely to be the most substantial section of your report. Generally, you will want to present your results and your interpretation of those results in tandem. The most important point to bear in mind is that your reader should be able to understand what you found and what you made of it. You might start out by saying how you went about the analysis – whether you took a chronological approach, for example, and how you developed themes. You will probably find it easier to present your results under various headings, and themes are useful here. For each section of your results, you must provide good evidence to support your interpretation – quotes, for example. Remember to include 'outliers' – participants who, for one reason or another, had a different story to tell. Above all, try to be honest and clear when you talk about your interpretation.

Conclusion

Here you review your study both in terms of its conduct and its findings, in the following terms:

- *A restatement of the aims of the study*. Why you did the study.
- *A review of the procedure*. Why you chose this method, how it evolved, what the limitations were.
- *A review of the findings* and your interpretation of the findings.
- The steps you have taken to ensure the *validity* of your interpretations.
- *How the findings relate* to the issues that prompted the research in the first place.
- What, if any, *theoretical issues* developed from your research.
- The *implications* for your research.

In all of the above the key question, *how do you know?*, is especially pertinent. How do you know your participants felt this, how do you know these are the implications, how do you know these were the problems? In fact, when it comes down to it, the best advice we can offer on writing up qualitative research is, when you make a point, interpret an event or propose a finding, always ask yourself, how do you know? Equally important, when the time comes for someone else to review your work, how will *they* know?

This ends our brief review of qualitative writing. We recognise that many researchers will take exception to what we have said but, in such a fluid environment, this has to be considered something of an occupational hazard. We are happy enough to have offered at least a number of pointers to writing up qualitative research which, while providing some structure for undergraduate research, are hopefully also general enough to allow for the diversity of tradition and method that characterises the field. At the end of the day what you, the student, ultimately write has to be based on a compromise among a number of significant elements, some philosophical, some practical and some personal. And, most important of all, we must not forget the role of the supervisor. For an undergraduate to embark on a qualitative project without the advice and support of a tutor experienced in the field is to court disaster.

7.10 Presenting a report

7.10.1 Oral presentation

There is an increasingly common expectation – if not a requirement – that undergraduates offer an oral presentation of their work to staff and fellow students at some stage during the conduct of a project. Timings vary, with some colleges and universities scheduling presentations at some point before data collection begins, while others wait until the entire project is completed. Either way, presentations are now a familiar part of undergraduate life and they serve a variety of functions. At the most obvious level they provide the student with an opportunity to show off, as it were. After all, a great deal of reading has probably gone into the development of a research project, only a fraction of which is ultimately used in the study proper. How satisfying to be able to demonstrate to your tutors that you have actually put considerable effort into your work (especially useful in those cases where presentations comprise an assessable component of a research methods module). Presentations also demonstrate the depth of your familiarity with a topic and tutors will often ask probing questions about issues which, even if they did not form a part of your study, you might be expected to know something about if your reading really was comprehensive.

If presentations occur at an intermediate stage then they serve the extremely useful function of generating constructive feedback, with an audience being given the chance to offer advice ('you need a larger sample for this type of analysis', or 'have you read...?'). And of course, finally, having to prepare and give a presentation can now be regarded as an important element of general research methods training. Anyone hoping to pursue a career in the field will find that giving conference presentations and research papers is a major method of contemporary information dissemination.

Consequently, a few guidelines on presentation techniques might come in useful.

A good starting point for looking at presentations is to consider their purpose. The aim of a presentation is to describe, in the course of a 10 minute talk (sometimes longer), the study that you have carried out. During the presentation you must identify the research issue you have explored, outline the research background to the issue and provide a rationale for what you have done. The actual study must be described in sufficient detail that an audience can follow your design and procedure, and results should be offered in a format that describes the outcome without confusion. Finally, you should be able to present your view of the implications of the study, and all in a manner that is interesting, informative and accurate. All in all, a pretty terrifying prospect!

In structure a presentation should be like a trimmed-down version of a standard research report, comprising more or less the same major sections and subdivisions. It will have a title, much like the report title, followed by a brief statement of what the study was about. This is not quite like an abstract since data and findings would not be offered at this stage, but more like an expanded explanation of the title, highlighting the general research area and stating the hypotheses that were being tested ('an observational study in the area of... and exploring the specific issue of...').

A review of the background to the research is important, and this will take the form of a summarised version of the literature review found in the written report. Naturally, key studies would have to be mentioned, with their findings, along with any research that provides a rationale for the study, ending with a statement of the hypotheses to be explored.

An outline of the procedure followed would be offered next, with illustrations provided of questionnaires or stimuli. Data should be described in descriptive terms, followed by precise details of results. While most of the other sections would tend to be presented in general terms, this results section should be full and precise. It remains only to make concluding comments about the conduct of the study, how the findings relate to the research issue in general and the hypotheses in particular.

7.10.2 Practicalities: giving a presentation

The previous section outlined the content of a typical presentation, but said little about how this material might be presented. This section attempts to offer some practical advice.

A key point to remember, when preparing for a presentation, is that an oral exposition of a piece of work differs from a text version. In the write-up you have ample opportunity to explain in detail the conduct of previous research in your field, to include the results of complex statistical analyses and to discuss your findings at length. In a presentation this is not possible to anything like the same extent. For one thing, there are time constraints in a presentation and, contrary to popular undergraduate belief, 10 minutes is not really that long; what you say has to be a much condensed version of your study, but one that nevertheless contains the essence of what you did. For another, while a reviewer or assessor can re-read the contents of a report, or follow up material in appendices, a presentation is a 'one shot' affair. You have a single opportunity to say what you want, to make your points and show that you have done a good job. So how do you do this?

The starting point is your written report. If this is completed before presentations are given (as is the norm) then you already have all the information necessary for an oral version. You actually have too much information, so the report should be read carefully and important information extracted. Box 7.16 offers a summary of what is required.

The next stage is to decide how best to present the information gleaned from the full report. Some undergraduates will simply write a summary, based on their notes, and the presentation comprises a rather tedious reading aloud of this summary. This is not a particularly effective method of giving a presentation. It tends to be dull, it doesn't allow the audience to focus on key elements and it can also be intimidating for the speaker; with no other source of stimulation the audience's entire attention is focused on the oral presentation itself.

A far better solution is to make use of some form of visual aid. Overheads, slides and computer-generated screen graphics are all ideal and most departments will happily make facilities available for students. The advantages of this approach are considerable:

1   The key points of a study can be put on an overhead or slide allowing you to emphasise to your audience what the important elements of the study were. For instance, you might display the hypotheses being tested as you explain procedural matters, making it easier for your audience to appreciate why you carried out your study *this* way, as opposed to *that* way.

2   Complex information can be presented more effectively in this format than by verbal explanation. Just imagine trying to explain the results of a multiple group comparison analysis verbally. A table or a graph projected onto a screen will describe at a glance what might take you several minutes to explain.

3   A series of overheads tends to impose its own structure on a presentation, covering, as they usually do, the logical sequence of activities that comprised the study (e.g. you will probably have, in order, overheads displaying the title of the study, examples of previous work, statement of hypotheses, procedural matters, results, etc.). They also serve as *aides-mémoire*, reminders of what you need to talk about next, or which part of your notes to consult. Relying totally on notes, without this kind of external structure, can lead to confusion and loss of place, especially if the notes are extensive.

4   Using visual displays takes pressure off the presenter, especially useful for the nervous undergraduate who can panic quite freely in a corner while everyone's attention is focused on a projected image somewhere else.

Clearly there are advantages in using presentation aids of this type, but there are certain cautions that should be made. First, the temptation to cover your slides with everything you want to say should be avoided at all costs. The purpose of these aids is to present key points and illustrations. Any more than this and it would be as easy to provide each audience member with a text version of your talk. Legibility is another issue. If you've never used overheads before it's important to find out how big writing or font sizes need to be so an audience can read them. And third, organisation is important. There is nothing guaranteed better to destroy a nervous presenter's confidence than to discover their slides are in the wrong order, or that one is missing. Take it from two lecturers who know.

Material in support of overheads has to be considered. Previously it has been suggested that a slide can act as an *aide-mémoire*, triggering recall in the mind of the presenter and reminding them what to say next. In fact, only skilled presenters and lecturers are likely to be able to do this well and, unless a talk is well rehearsed, students are advised to use notes to accompany each overhead. Even experienced lecturers are often caught out by an overhead whose existence, never mind content, comes as a complete surprise to them, recognisable when a staff member is caught staring blankly at a screen, for some time.

Box 7.16   Talking it through

The following is a suggested listing – with comments – of the major elements that should comprise an oral presentation. They appear in the typical order in which they would be introduced to an audience. They also represent the likely content of a series of slides or overheads which would be used as a basis for a presentation.

1 *A title for the presentation*, which will be based on the title of the study itself. Accompanying notes would expand on this title, identifying the research area in which your study was based, and outlining the research questions posed.
2 *An outline of key research in the area.* An overhead would display the authors of research, the date of the published work and the research findings. These might be in terms of mean scores for different groups, or a description of factors identified in the research (e.g. Cattell (1969): 16 personality factors identified, viz....). Accompanying notes would expand on the studies cited, explaining the findings in more detail and demonstrating how they formed a basis for your work.
3 *A statement of the aim of the study*, in general terms, and statements of the hypotheses being tested. Notes would expand on the aim, reminding the audience of how the stated aim has developed from previous research (or whatever), and each hypothesis would be explained in turn – what the basis for each hypothesised prediction was, and what the expected outcomes were.
4 *A description of procedural elements*, such as the sample characteristics (where relevant to the conduct and findings of the study), details of any apparatus used, including questionnaires and standardised test instruments. In the case of tests or questionnaires, examples of items, coding and scoring systems can be displayed. Full copies might also be distributed among the audience.
   Notes here would provide descriptive details of how samples were drawn, why certain characteristics were controlled for (e.g. extraneous variables) and how subjects were assigned to groups, if appropriate, and whether or not the design was within- or between-

groups. Details would also be given on questionnaires, including pilot study data if appropriate. An explanation of the development of items would be given and the role and composition of sub-scales discussed.
   (Note: a lot of information is covered in this section and this might be represented in several overheads – e.g. one might deal with subject characteristics, there might be two or more giving examples of test items and there might be an additional slide reviewing the findings of a pilot study.)
5 *A summary statement identifying independent and dependent variables and noting any extraneous factors.* Notes would briefly review the procedure, reminding how independent variables were manipulated and explaining how outcome measures were taken.
6 *Presentation of results.* Key findings would be illustrated, first in the form of summary statistics, and then in terms of analysis. These would include means, *t*-values, *F*-ratios and correlation coefficients, for example. Probability values would also be shown.
   Notes would indicate how the statistics were derived and what tests were carried out and any significant effects highlighted.
7 *More results.* If additional analysis was carried out to further explore a finding, or you wish to highlight some unusual or worthy finding, this should be presented next. Graphs of various types are useful here.
   Notes would explain why additional analysis was necessary (e.g. 'it was noted that mean scores for males in the sample were higher than previous reported norms'), and any figures would be discussed.
8 *Hypotheses would be restated* and upheld or rejected in light of the results. Notes would expand upon the relationship between the findings and the predicted outcomes. Explanation would then extend to reconsidering the entire research issue in view of the study just outlined. The presentation at this point is likely to return to the kind of general discussion of issues introduced at the very beginning.

Examples of test materials can also be made available to an audience, especially if a questionnaire has been custom-designed for a study. Even copies of standardised tests might be distributed if an audience comprises largely fellow students who might not be familiar with specialised instruments.

To conclude this section on presentations, it is worth noting that giving a presentation is a skilled activity, and therefore requires practice to develop. Few undergraduates are going to be superb at this

task but, with a bit of organisation and a lot of preparation, presentations can be made competent and interesting.

7.11   Review

Any study, no matter how elaborate and irrespective of its contribution to the fount of human knowledge,

---

Box 7.17   Some typical assessment criteria for project reports

Originality
To what extent is the choice of research area, and the general orientation of the study your own? Does the work show some originality in design or approach?

Initiative
Have you shown initiative in collecting data or in preparing test materials?

Introduction
How well have the research issues been identified and explained? Is the review of the literature relevant and thorough? Has the scope of the project been clearly presented? Are the hypotheses unambiguously stated, and is it clear how they relate to previous work?

Design
Is the design of the project appropriate for the research question? Have issues concerning sampling and control been addressed? Have independent and dependent variables been correctly identified? Has this section been expressed in the appropriate language of design?

Participants
Were the participants representative of the population? Have their relevant characteristics been described? Are recruitment strategies presented? Are response and refusal rates recorded?

Apparatus/materials
Have the details of apparatus been recorded in detail? Have the details of questionnaires, etc., been presented? Are justifications provided for the choice of materials,

and for any changes made to published materials? What data result from these measures?

Procedure
Is it possible to understand exactly what procedures were followed in collecting data? Are these procedures appropriate? Could the study be replicated on the information provided?

Results
Are the results clearly presented? Is the analysis appropriate for the level of data? Does the analysis actually address the hypotheses or research questions under test?

Discussion
Are the results discussed with reference to the issues raised in the Introduction? Are the results discussed with reference to previous findings and relevant theory? Are any problems or limitations of the study fully understood and discussed?

References
Are all references given in full? Are they presented in a standard format?

Presentation
Is the project well presented? Is it free from spelling errors? Is it well written? Are arguments clearly and carefully presented?

(Note: the sections on Initiative and Originality, while relevant for any piece of research, are likely to be particular issues for undergraduate studies.)

---

will ultimately be judged on the written exposition of the background, design, conduct and findings of the research. This is true whether the report is based on an undergraduate project, represents a submission to a periodical editor or is a published article in an international journal. In every case, a reader, tutor or reviewer is looking for the same kind of thing – evidence that the study has been well carried out, the data competently analysed and the research issue fully explored. A judgement here can only be based on the written report or article and, while your own research might not necessarily set the world of academia alight, if you have followed all the guidelines in this chapter, you will at least guarantee yourself a fair and objective hearing. Box 7.17 is the concluding illustration in this chapter and it offers a summary of the main points a reviewer or tutor will be looking for in a written report. It will be in the interests of all readers to study this summary carefully!

It only remains to offer once again the advice that, if anyone is still unclear about any element of report writing, the flowchart at the beginning of this chapter should guide them to the appropriate section. We wish you luck.

7.12   Further reading

Cresswell, J.W. (1998) *Qualitative Inquiry and Research Design: Choosing Among Five Traditions.* Thousand Oaks, CA: Sage.

Day, R.A. (1989) *How to Write and Publish a Scientific Paper*, 3rd edition. Cambridge: CUP.

Denzin, N.K. and Lincoln, Y.S. (1994) *Handbook of Qualitative Research.* Thousand Oaks, CA: Sage.

Elliot, R., Fischer, C.T. and Rennie, D.L. (1999) Evolving guidelines for publication of qualitative research studies in psychology and related fields. *British Journal of Clinical Psychology*, **38**: 215–229.

Howard, K. and Sharp. J.A. (1983) *The Management of a Student Research Project*. Aldershot: Gower.

Kantowitz, B.H., Roediger III, H.L. and Elmes, D.G. (1994) *Experimental Psychology: Understanding Psychological Research*, 5th edition. St Paul: West Publishing.

Leeds, P.D. and Ormrod, J.E. (1989) *Practical Research*, 7th edition. New Jersey: Prentice Hall.

Miles, M.B. and Huberman, A.M. (1994) *Qualitative Data Analysis*. Thousand Oaks, CA: Sage.

Index